VERNON AND IRENE CASTLE'S
RAGTIME REVOLUTION

Vernon and Irene Castle's

Ragtime Revolution

Eve Golden

THE UNIVERSITY PRESS OF KENTUCKY

Publication of this volume was made possible in part by a grant from
the National Endowment for the Humanities.

Scholarly publisher for the Commonwealth,
serving Bellarmine University, Berea College, Centre
College of Kentucky, Eastern Kentucky University,
The Filson Historical Society, Georgetown College,
Kentucky Historical Society, Kentucky State University,
Morehead State University, Murray State University,
Northern Kentucky University, Transylvania University,
University of Kentucky, University of Louisville,
and Western Kentucky University.
All rights reserved.

Editorial and Sales Offices: The University Press of Kentucky
663 South Limestone Street, Lexington, Kentucky 40508-4008
www.kentuckypress.com

11 10 09 08 07   5 4 3 2 1

Library of Congress Cataloging-in-Publication Data

Golden, Eve.
 Vernon and Irene Castle's ragtime revolution / Eve Golden.
     p. cm.
 Includes bibliographical references and index.
 ISBN 978-0-8131-2459-9 (hardcover : alk. paper)
  1. Castle, Vernon, 1887-1918. 2. Castle, Irene, 1893-1969. 3. Dancers—United States—
Biography. 4. Ballroom dancing—United States—History. 5. Ragtime music—History
and criticism. I. Title.
 GV1785.A1G55 2007
 792.8'0280922—dc22
 [B]

2007026425

This book is printed on acid-free recycled paper meeting
the requirements of the American National Standard
for Permanence in Paper for Printed Library Materials.

Manufactured in the United States of America.

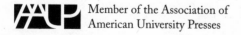 Member of the Association of
American University Presses

To Ragtime Cowboy Joe Rocco

CONTENTS

Acknowledgments   ix

Introduction: New York, December 31, 1913   1

1. Take Me Back to Dear Old Blighty   4
2. About Town   9
3. Only Forty-five Minutes from Broadway   19
4. "We would be much happier if we just relaxed and enjoyed school life"   25
5. "I could tell by looking at him that he was not my cup of tea"   30
6. Zowie, "the Monarch of Mystery"   33
7. "They liked to test out their guns"   37
8. Enfin . . . une Revue   41
9. "I saw the fat years ahead!"   45
10. Everybody's Doing It   51
11. "Two adolescent palm trees"   58
12. "Gowns are more or less a business with me"   63
13. "The best dancing music in the world"   68
14. "More like a pair of schoolchildren"   73
15. "Syncopation rules the nation"   78
16. "The Most Talked About House in New York"   86
17. "Dancing with Vernon was as easy as swimming with water wings"   95
18. "The spirit of success . . . oozes from these two young people"   102
19. "The Castles Are Coming! Hooray! Hooray!"   106
20. "We were both miserable on those vaudeville tours"   116
21. "Their enthusiastic followers never . . . go to bed at all"   124

22. "Mrs. Castle is exhausted" 130

23. "Castles in the subway, / Castles in the 'L'" 134

24. "Oh, give me a gun and let me run to fight the foreign foe" 140

25. "When I get old I shall be able to tell our children all about the Great War" 148

26. "Kiss all the pets for me, dear" 161

27. "A super motion picture of . . . epoch-making magnificence" 164

28. "He was out to see the Kaiser defeated" 176

29. "An hour's pleasant diversion" 180

30. I Love My Wife, but, Oh, You Kid! 184

31. "Never in my life have I been subjected to such humiliation" 190

32. "His plane dove straight into the ground" 194

33. "Death is nothing to me, sweetheart" 197

34. "Robert was sweet, sympathetic, and besides he did all of my bidding" 206

35. "A well-known dancing dame" 209

36. "Poor Irene Castle. She certainly isn't what she used to be" 216

37. "Jazz, jazz, jazz! . . . The paradings of savages" 223

38. "To Chicago high society, she was a chorus girl" 228

39. Orphans of the Storm 234

40. "What do you do for an encore to what they had?" 237

41. The Story of Vernon and Irene Castle 242

42. "Isn't old age awful!" 248

Appendix: Stage and Film Appearances of Vernon and Irene Castle 253

Notes 268

Bibliography 298

Index 302

Acknowledgments

My thanks to the following people and institutions for their invaluable help: Christopher Blyth; Ken Brown (Deseronto Public Library); Paul Collins; Cornell University; John Culme (footlightnotes.tripod.com); Barbara Davis (New Rochelle Public Library); Mick Davis; Steven Dhuey; William Drew; Iris Fanger; Armond Fields; Anna Gomersall; Christopher Gray (the *New York Times*); Keith Greene and William Garrapy; Terry Harbin; C.W. Hunt; Suzi Jex (Norfolk Record Office); Marek Kohn; Charlotte Kreutz; Bradley Kuiper; Howard Lee Levine; Glen Martin; Stephen O'Brien; Frank Olynyk; Michael O'Neal; Orphans of the Storm Animal Shelter; James Robert Parish; Michael Reed; the Alpha Phi Chapter of Sigma Chi, Cornell University; Charles Silver (the Museum of Modern Art); Wendy Sterry (Norwich City Council); Erik Stogo; Robert Taylor (Billy Rose Collection, New York Public Library); April Wagrel; Sonny Watson (streetswing.com); Mary White (the History Center in Tompkins County, N.Y.); Spats White; Nancy Winter.

The helpful and well-informed members of the Straight Dope Message Board and the Aerodrome Message Board.

Richard Kukan, an extraordinary editor (especially in these days of "toss it into spell-check"). He never let me get away with a clunky phrase, repeated word, or dubious fact.

Carolyn Hetherington, for sharing the story of her mother's tragic romance with Vernon Castle.

And especially Irene Castle's son, William McLaughlin, who was so helpful, friendly, and open about his remarkable mother.

NEW YORK, DECEMBER 31, 1913

It's a chilly Wednesday evening in Manhattan, just above freezing, and you're out on the town for some fun. Maybe you're a tired businessman, an out-of-town tourist, a pretty little ribbon clerk, a bored housewife on the loose. Here you are in Times Square, bundled up in your fur or overcoat, and you want to have some drinks, a bite of food. You might go to the theater and see Anna Held at the Casino, Billie Burke at the Lyceum, Bert Williams at the Palace. But if you are really in the swing of things in 1913, you'll want to go out dancing.

The newly opened Biltmore Hotel, near Grand Central Terminal, does not allow dancing, but most other hotels do. The Waldorf, Plaza, Astor, and the McAlpine have all converted restaurants or parlors into upscale dance halls and hired orchestras to play the latest in ragtime. The Vanderbilt offers an added attraction: a cotton-wool "snowball" fight at the stroke of midnight.

One of the big events that December was famed restaurateur George Rector's opening of his new eponymous establishment at Broadway and Forty-eighth Street; Nora Bayes, Florenz Ziegfeld, and Lillian Lorraine attended the event. "The new Rector's," says *Variety*, is a sure bet to put a dent in the takings of competing "New York restaurants-dancing-cabarets." It features, in addition to a number of singers and comics, a generous helping of ballroom dancers: Golden and Golden ("Whirlwind Dancers"), the Dixon Trio ("Novelty Dances"), and future *Scandals* producer George White, "who will dance afternoon and evening." Not to be outdone, the Garden, at Fiftieth and Broadway, advertises itself as "New York's Leading Cabaret" and "The Real Bohemian Rendezvous of New York." Churchill's ("Better Than the Theatre") can be found at Forty-ninth and Broadway, or by calling BRyan 5175.

A newcomer has to be careful to avoid the rougher joints. Recently, Murray's on Forty-second Street was raided and two dancers were arrested on gambling charges. *Variety* claimed that female dancers were "wont to 'steer' strangers into their rooms to gamble." Unwary visitors are warned of other dangers to one's pocketbook: "some of the places that harbor the midnight revellers are making it a condition of service at a table that champagne must be ordered."

As an added draw, some of these cabarets feature star dancers, such as Andre and Sherri, who advertise themselves, rather boldly, as the "Foremost Exponents of the Tango in America." Sadly, Maurice and Florence Walton are out of town this month, touring in San Francisco, and Mae Murray and Carlos Sebastian have been lured away from the New York Roof to a well-paid engagement in Chicago. Some cabarets feel that these star performers are overhyped and overpaid, that "people go to those places to dance and are not particularly interested in the professionals, who, however, have a certain drawing power that is not disputed."

Even the help at these cabarets are bitten by the dancing bug this New Year's Eve in 1913: according to *Variety*, "the waiters in these places . . . after the hour of closing arrives, go to a place in the Times Square section where they trot for the remainder of the night."

To make your night on the town a complete success, you *must* stop at Castle House, the newly opened East Side dancing school and club that has swiftly become *the* hot spot for high society and tourists alike. Located at Forty-sixth Street and Madison Avenue, well out of the rush of Times Square, "The Most Talked of House in New York" is a magnet for everyone who wants to go out dancing in a safe, fashionable, and socially acceptable atmosphere. If you're lucky, you may see the Castles themselves: Vernon and his wife, Irene, who dance and mingle nightly at Castle House. If you are amazingly lucky, one of the Castles might actually deign to dance with you.

Despite the many elegant couples swirling around the two ballrooms of Castle House, everyone knows when the Castles themselves appear. Vernon, impossibly tall and slim, in a new-style tailless dinner jacket, Irene in a pared-down creation by Lucile, her shockingly short hair held by a jeweled band. Lost in the music of James Reese Europe and his orchestra (another shock: black musicians in a white establishment), they swirl and swoop and twirl through the crowd. This is a couple obviously in love with each other, their fame, and the sheer joy of the dance.

The Castles seem to own New York: The two top theatrical managers of the day are fighting a very public duel over them—Vernon has nonchalantly signed contracts for himself and Irene to dance for both Charles Dillingham and William Hammerstein in the new year of 1914. They will soon appear in the smash-hit show *Watch Your Step*, which will introduce Irving Berlin to Broadway. They are already in negotiation to open Sans Souci, a Times Square basement nightclub, and soon they will cast their net even further: 1914 will see the openings of Castles by the Sea in Coney Island's Luna Park and a rathskeller and rooftop garden above and below Schubert's 44th Street Theater.

The gay and glamorous pre–World War I years are bringing to the Castles unimaginable fame, wealth, and influence; only Fred Astaire and Ginger Rogers (who portrayed the Castles in a 1939 film) will become a more famous dance team. Vernon and Irene have become the personification of ragtime, opening the way for the cabarets and nightclubs that will become permanent fixtures in New York and other big cities. Before the Castles, the only places to go out dancing were private parties and the lowest of public dance halls and beer gardens. Their sponsorship and inspiration has brought about the advent of dancing establishments where nice people can go and bring their children—and where nice people and their children may misbehave.

In the years ahead, even greater fame awaits Vernon and Irene: he as a war hero, she as a movie star and animal rights activist. Separation, tragedy, and death will befall them before the jazz age of the 1920s sweeps them into history. But now, as 1913 becomes 1914, they have the world at their feet.

CHAPTER ONE

TAKE ME BACK TO DEAR OLD BLIGHTY

William Vernon Blyth was born in Norwich, England, on May 2, 1887, into a family of hotel keepers. His paternal grandfather, William Blyth, had since 1872 been the proprietor of Norwich's Royal Hotel Branch, located not far from the city's train station. When Vernon was six the hotel was rebuilt and renamed the Great Eastern. It was a three-story building of red brick; the ground floor had a welcoming, awning-shaded veranda overlooking the River Wensum, with a whitewashed corner entrance on Prince of Wales Road.

Though at its economic height in the seventeenth and eighteenth centuries, Norwich was still a thriving town in the mid-Victorian era, when the Blyths settled there. Wandering around town in his youth, Vernon would have daily seen the city's famous Norman cathedral, with the tallest Romanesque spire in England; the fifteenth-century Dragon Hall on King Street; the gray stone Guild Hall from the 1400s; tidy brick homes dating back four hundred years; "new" Georgian houses a little farther from the town center—indeed, enough history to become jaded and bored with the treasures at his feet. If Vernon had any interest in history or architecture later in life, he gave no sign of it.

Vernon's parents, William Thomas Blyth and Jane Finley, had married in London's borough of Islington in the summer of 1879, when William was twenty-two and Jane only sixteen. Besides Vernon, they had four daughters, Caroline, Gladys, Stephanie, and Marjorie (all but Marjorie older than Vernon). Vernon's mother died in late 1891, only in her late twenties. There is no record of what caused Jane's death, though early death was not uncommon, of course, in the nineteenth century: perhaps it was a sixth pregnancy or perhaps one of the infections or influenzas that carried off so many. Vernon was only four when his mother died, but if he suffered any trauma from the loss, he never spoke of it. He was fortunate to be surrounded by his sisters, an affectionate father, and a hotel full of cousins and boarders. Nine years after his first wife's death, in the spring of 1900, William Blyth married twenty-five-year-old Norwich native Lucy Elizabeth Johnson, who gave Vernon, then fourteen, a baby half brother, Colin Blyth, in September 1901. Vernon's new stepmother was anything but wicked, and he grew quite fond of her. Having little memory of his own mother, he never resented her replacement.

Young Vernon divided his time between Norwich and London, where his father ran a pub on James Street in fashionable St. Marylebone. The 1891 census shows quite a group residing in the rooms over the pub: not only Vernon, his parents, and siblings, but also two cousins, two barmen, a barmaid, and two domestic servants. Ten years later, we find him back in Norwich at the Great Eastern, living in an even more crowded and rollicking household. His aging grandparents still ran the hotel, assisted by his father and stepmother, his Aunt Lacey and Uncle Samuel, and a bevy of chambermaids, kitchen maids, and barmen, all catering to the dozens of hotel guests who came and went.

Growing up in hotels and pubs, Vernon would have been exposed to the full range of human behavior; his parents had to be unflappable in the face of their sometimes rowdy, quarrelsome, and even criminal guests. "The customer is always right," even when it resulted in legal trouble: Vernon's grandfather was fined for "permitting drunkenness" at the Great Eastern in 1896, and his father for "selling out of hours" in 1921.

Vernon's nephew, Christopher Blyth, notes that Vernon's father and stepmother followed a pattern that would be echoed in Vernon and Irene Castle's marriage. "My grandfather was a businessman but a poor judge of character," says Blyth; "in other words, he lent a lot of money to people never to see it repaid. It was my grandmother, Lucy, who was the businesswoman and she kept the family on the straight and narrow!"

The Blyths were a close, affectionate family, much given to bear hugs. As the only son for a good part of his childhood, Vernon was spoiled, and rarely disciplined, by his father and sisters. A lifelong admiration for all things French enabled the family to trick the boy into good behavior, however: "when he wouldn't eat anything or wear something they had bought for him, they only had to tell him it 'came from France' to have it meet with approval in his eyes. If it was his dinner, it was always 'French chop' and 'French peas.'"

All through his life, Vernon was struck by sudden enthusiasms; one of his earliest was for electronic gadgets. In the late 1890s, when many houses were first being wired for electricity, Vernon somewhere acquired some wires and bells (probably pilfered from a work crew wiring a nearby home) and gamely attempted to hook up his London house. "He was immediately stamped in the family as an electrical engineer," Irene wrote in her memoirs, "though I never saw him show any knowledge of electricity in later years, and he certainly never offered to wire our house with bells. Nor did he have any suggestions for repairing them when they were out of order."

Vernon began his education at College House in Lowestoft, some twenty miles outside Norwich. At the age of thirteen he entered Norwich School, which he attended from January 1900 through the summer of 1903. In interviews and her memoirs, Irene claimed that Vernon graduated from the University of Birmingham with a degree in engineering—but the university's record keepers are "unable to find any trace" of evidence that Vernon even attended, let alone graduated.

More likely, he went to work in his family's hotel and London pub after graduating from the Norwich School. It is likely that his placatory and charming personality developed through waiting on and pleasing customers. Vernon could defuse a quarrel or smooth over any social disturbance. But he never managed a hotel: that profession requires a hardheaded business sense as well as bonhomie. Vernon never picked up this skill. Money fairly flew out of his pockets, and in later life he agreeably signed every contract placed in front of him, leading to no end of double bookings and even lawsuits.

No hint of "the show business" had ever brushed the Blyth family until one of Vernon's sisters, Caroline, changed her name to the more euphonious "Coralie Blythe," went on the stage, and married Lawrence Grossmith. The Grossmiths were an old theatrical family; the first George Grossmith was a friend of Charles Dickens and gave penny-readings from his novels. His son, also named George, Coralie's father-in-law, created the lead baritone roles in many Gilbert and Sullivan operettas: Jack Point in *The Yeomen of the Guard*, Sir Joseph Porter in *H.M.S. Pinafore*, General Stanley in *The Pirates of Penzance*, Ko-Ko in *The Mikado*, and Reginald Bunthorne in *Patience*, among others. He was also a noted author; his 1892 comic novel, *The Diary of a Nobody* (written with his brother Weedon), is a delight not to be missed. Both of his sons, George Jr. and Lawrence, became successful actors. By the time he wooed and won Coralie Blythe,

Lawrence Grossmith was well launched on what would be a nearly fifty-year career as a light comic actor, specializing in "silly-ass" roles. Beginning with a 1900 Lily Langtry tour, Grossmith ferried regularly between London's West End and Broadway.

Coralie's success never equaled that of her husband—or her brother—but she did work steadily onstage through the 1910s in both England and the United States. She had a small role in the London production *Mr. Popple of Ippleton* (1905) and appeared with her husband in *The Girl behind the Counter* in the spring of 1906—a show that, while important enough for the Grossmiths, would change Vernon's life. Coralie's *Variety* obituary also credits her with such shows as *Havana, Nobody Home, The Circus Girl,* and *The Silver Slipper,* but since the obit also says her mother was an actress, it must be regarded with some skepticism.

Vernon's own introduction to show business seems to have come not through his sister but through magic. Like many teenage boys, he was fascinated by sleight-of-hand tricks and, being both dexterous and personable, he made his way to the famed St. George's Hall, a London theater operated by the magician John Nevil Maskelyne. After many years of running "England's Home of Mystery" out of a hall in Piccadilly, Maskelyne had opened St. George's in 1904, and Vernon became a regular patron when he was in London. According to Irene, "He hung round till he learned to do many of the simpler tricks and until he solved some that were supposed to possess a dash of the mysterious. Often as a fancied onlooker from the audience he was able to go on the stage and confound the conjurer."

Rather than paying attention to the family business, Vernon earned small fees—very small fees—as an entertainer at parties and small clubs; at theatrical amateur nights, he earned nothing but the experience. Irene wrote, more than a little condescendingly, "Everybody encouraged him, but he was always eager to take up new things, like a child with a new toy. The thing or the feat that he mastered yesterday had little attraction for him to-day." He acquired an agent, Keith, Prowse, and Co., and got his first professional gig at a country house, where, said the *Dancing Times,* "he offered the guests a little singing, a little conjuring, and a little storytelling" for a fee of 15 shillings.

Exciting news came for Coralie and her husband later in 1906, when American comic and producer Lew Fields bought the rights to *The Girl behind the Counter* for a proposed 1907 production—along with much of the cast. The Grossmiths were booked to sail for America in the summer of 1906, but they would not be idle while waiting for *The Girl behind the Counter* to open; Fields planned to use some of his imports in another show, *About Town*, which would go into immediate rehearsals.

In early July 1906, Vernon and his father joined the Grossmiths on the *Teutonic*, sailing from Liverpool; they arrived in New York on July 19. Vernon was leaving the England of Edward VII and entering the boisterous United States of Teddy Roosevelt. New York in 1906 was a city bursting at the seams with new buildings, new technology: the Astor and Knickerbocker hotels brought an added glamour to Times Square during this era (Times Square was, indeed, renamed after the New York Times building opened there in 1904). The enormous Hippodrome Theater, where Vernon would one day perform, had opened the year before and, even more notable for show business folks, the trade paper *Variety* had published its first issue on December 16, 1905.

Vernon was dazzled and delighted by New York; he toured it from south to north (a lot easier after the IRT subway lines opened in 1904, running from City Hall to the Bronx). His father, though, was less impressed. No one knows if he was terrified, disgusted, or just plain homesick, but William Thomas Blyth took the first available ship back to England. Left to his own devices, Vernon took to hanging around backstage at the Herald Square Theater, where *About Town* was to open at the end of August; here he would meet Lew Fields, the man who would not only launch his theatrical career but would also become his father figure and professional mentor.

CHAPTER TWO

ABOUT TOWN

Vernon's backstage caperings while visiting his sister attracted the attention of Lew Fields, thirty-nine-year-old theatrical magnate. In the 1870s, Fields had teamed up with Joe Weber, another Jewish ghetto kid from New York's Lower East Side. Their bumptious, rude comedy had made them stars by 1890: the taller, explosive Fields and the shorter, bumbling Weber (think Abbott and Costello, but with German or Yiddish accents). At their Weber and Fields Music Hall, they produced and starred in a series of hit shows from 1896 through 1904, when the team broke up. Their specialty was burlesque, in the old sense of the word: parodies of current Broadway hits. "Weberfields," as they became known, also discovered or cultivated an impressive number of stars: Lillian Russell, David Warfield, De Wolf Hopper, Marie Dressler—all appeared in support of the team. When Weber and Fields broke up in 1904, both of them embarked on careers as independent producers.

There was plenty of musical comedy competition when the new season opened on Broadway in 1906. *The Red Mill* starred the comedy team of Montgomery and Stone; the naughty *A Parisian Model* starred Anna Held and was dazzlingly produced by her husband, Florenz Ziegfeld; over at Madison Square Garden, the light and fluffy *Mamzelle Champagne* became a scandalous must-see after architect Stanford White was murdered in the theater on opening night, June 25.

About Town was staged in the new Lew Fields Herald Square Theater on West Thirty-fifth Street, owned by theatrical impresarios Sam and Lee Shubert. To celebrate the Shuberts' new business relationship with actor/manager Fields, the theater (which was demolished in 1915) was redecorated in swags of red satin and mythological paintings.

During *About Town*'s rehearsals, Coralie's kid brother hung around backstage, fascinated by the atmosphere, making friends and entertaining people with his magic tricks and amusing banter. Far from being annoyed by the gangly, bumptious teenager, Fields was charmed and intrigued. Sensing both talent and enthusiasm, he cast Vernon in a small role in the show, as Viscomte Martino. Fields coached the acrobatic youngster and was impressed with what he saw: as Fields's biographer notes, "Even in the midst of the most foolish pratfall, [Castle] maintained an air of grace and elegance."

If Vernon still had any illusions about the glamour of show business, they were quickly put to rest. In his marvelously depressing 1910 novel *Predestined*, Stephen French Whitman describes the rehearsals for a big-budget Broadway musical: "in an old hall on Sixth Avenue, up two flights of stairs, using a loft with discolored walls, a low ceiling stained by leaks, and a bare, splintery floor. Whenever the pianist, hired for the rehearsals, stopped his exertions, one could hear the trains rumbling on the elevated railway. At the passage of expresses, violent concussions shook the building, all voices were drowned; the players closed their mouths, dropped their arms, and waited." Aside from the intrusion of the elevated, things have not changed very much in the past hundred years.

When he was cast in *About Town,* Vernon changed his name from William Blyth to Vernon Castle; his reasons for this have never been adequately explained. Either William Blyth or Vernon Blyth would have made a perfectly acceptable stage name, and his family was hardly the type to be embarrassed at him being on the stage. Perhaps he wanted to distance himself professionally from his sister, Coralie Blythe, to avoid any implication of nepotism. Irene later guessed that Vernon took his stage name from Windsor Castle, thinking it sounded high-toned. But it's equally possible, given his early love of things French, that he was familiar with the ruins of the twelfth-century Vernon Castle in France, or he may have read Jane Austen's early work *Lady Susan,* which contains the line, "I am sometimes disposed to repent that I did not let Charles buy Vernon Castle, when we were obliged to sell it" (a line that must have caused many giggles in the mid-1910s).

About Town was a slapdash comedy about a cabdriver (Fields) who impersonates a bank president. Lawrence Grossmith had a large supporting role as the Duke of Slushington; Vernon's sister, as Millie Bounder, "a society pest," got to sing several songs. Also in the cast were popular musical comedy performers Edna Wallace Hopper and the team of Louise Dresser and Jack Norworth (their imminent divorce made headlines, as did Norworth's later marriage to star Nora Bayes). Buried deep in the chorus was a teenaged dancer named Mae Murray, in what may have been her New York stage debut—she and Vernon became friends and would cross paths again. The director, Julian Mitchell, was one of Broadway's top talents, despite being stone-deaf (he also directed and choreographed many editions of the *Ziegfeld Follies* as well as the hits *The Pink Lady, Little Nellie Kelly,* and *Sunny*).

When *About Town* opened in late August, Fields had another hit on his hands: the *Chicago Chronicle* called it "a broadly humorous creation . . . laden with all sorts of comic situations, laugh-provoking dialogue and frothy music." The *New York Times* praised the "kaleidoscope of gorgeous theatrical effects" but felt the score was "musically ordinary." The show was scattered with comic routines and musical numbers that blithely ignored the plot (during one number, chorus girls ripped off each others' paper costumes). About a month into the run, Fields decided to beef up business by adding one of the Broadway parodies he and Weber had made famous: *The Great Decide,* a spoof of the Western drama *The Great Divide,* was added to the program and became as popular as *About Town* itself.

Despite generally positive reviews and the addition of the parody, business slowed down considerably by the end of 1906, and *About Town* took off on an eighteen-city tour. And there was another thing in which all could take comfort: thanks to his partnership with the Shubert brothers, Fields could breeze from one huge, well-managed Shubert theater to the next as the company moved from town to town. Nonetheless, touring was an exhausting prospect for the cast and for the crew, who had to unpack and set up backdrops, scenery, and props at every stop—and then pack up again. But it paid the bills: shows quite frequently lost money during their Broadway run, making their profit on the road. Having grown up in hotels and being accustomed to frequent travel between London and Norwich, Vernon adapted well to the road. His easy good nature and the fact that he found "roughing it" great fun made up for the torment of squeezing his long frame into skimpy hotel beds and skimpier train seats.

After an exhausting six months on trains, in hotels, and eating at greasy-spoon diners, the cast and crew staggered back to New York for a few last performances before disbanding in June 1907. By this time, Vernon was understudying his brother-in-law, which indicates just how fond Lew Fields was of this newcomer—and how much promise he showed.

Fields's next show was to be *The Girl behind the Counter*, the British production whose purchase had brought Vernon and the Grossmiths overseas in the first place. But when the show went into rehearsal in late June, it had been heavily rewritten ("Freely adapted and reconstructed," according to the program) by Edgar Smith, a playwright and lyricist whose career stretched from the 1880s through 1930. The upshot was that Coralie Blythe and Lawrence Grossmith found themselves out of work, while the neophyte Vernon was handed three roles. By the time Smith and Fields got through with it, *The Girl behind the Counter* had turned into a wild musical comedy about henpecked Henry Schniff (Fields), who comes into money and, by means of various tortuous plot devices, winds up impersonating a department store floorwalker, a soda jerk, and a store detective, while his wife and daughter frolic through high society.

Besides Vernon, the cast included Louise Dresser and tiny, sprightly musical comedy actress Lotta Faust, who had been a hit in *The Wizard of Oz* in 1903. Vernon appeared briefly but to great effect in three roles: John Blobbs ("a waiter at the Jardin de Paris"), Hon. Aubrey Battersea ("a friend of Lord Gushington"), and—most memorably—as Hawkins, yet another waiter at the Jardin de Paris. The Jardin de Paris scene was a comic high point of the show. Vernon was joined onstage by four other waiters, nonprofessionals, chosen for their bizarre appearances (a fat man, a midget, a tough, and a sourpuss). Lew Fields, as their boss, bellowed his instructions on being a perfect waiter: "Always remember, the first duty of a waiter is to look insulting. . . . In about ten minutes come around and brush the crumbs into [the customer's] lap."

After three weeks of out-of-town previews, *The Girl behind the Counter* opened at the Herald Square Theater on October 1, 1907, to a full and enthusiastic house and positive reviews. Vernon garnered his first press notice: the *New York Times* mentioned him by name as one of the cast members who "contribute to the general entertainment." Not a rave, of course, but quite impressive for a young man in his second show. "Lew Fields has never been funnier," the *Times* added. "*The Girl behind the Counter* is one of the best entertainments New York has seen, and is sure to draw the crowd for many weeks to come." This time, the show could not be accused of musical mediocrity—the German song "The Glow Worm," by Paul Lincke, with English-language lyrics by Lilla Cayley Robinson, was inserted and became a smash hit, still performed today (it was later rewritten by Johnny Mercer and murdered repeatedly on a saxophone by Lucille Ball on *I Love Lucy*).

The season between the summers of 1907 and 1908 was an amazing one for musical comedies despite a financial panic caused by the bankruptcy of several major Wall Street brokerages. The influential smash hit *The Merry Widow* opened on October 21 and ushered in a wave of Viennese operettas (as well as a fashion for sweeping, feather-bedecked "Merry Widow" hats); *Three Twins* (June 15, 1908) made a star out of Bessie McCoy; Florenz Ziegfeld produced his first *Follies* (July 8, 1907); there was also a revival of the hit *Mlle. Modiste* playing. But despite the stiff competition, *The Girl behind the Counter* brought in about $15,000 a week and played a very respectable thirty-eight weeks in New York.

While *The Girl behind the Counter* was still running, Fields began rehearsing a small-scale production in cooperation with the Shubert brothers. *The Mimic World* opened at the huge Moorish Casino Theater on Broadway and Thirty-ninth Street on July 9, 1908—a dead, hot time of year when many shows closed down. *The Mimic World* was a song-packed revue in three acts, described on its program as a "rollicking resume of matters and things theatrical." True to the Weber and Fields spirit, it incorporated jabs at *The Merry Widow* and even "Schniff," Fields's character from *The Girl behind the Counter*.

Vernon had his first meeting during this show with the hugely influential choreographer and dance director Ned Wayburn, who was at the beginning of a long, illustrious career. Wayburn would go on to choreograph six seasons of the *Ziegfeld Follies*, as well as many other productions, and would open his own dance school for professionals. If Vernon was essentially a self-taught dancer, he certainly got some background and input from Wayburn, who specialized in creating the kind of acrobatic character dances in which Vernon would soon excel.

Sadly, Vernon had little dancing to do in *The Mimic World:* he played the small role of Buddicombe, valet to Lord Dundreary (played by Roy Atwell); also in the cast were Irene Bentley (wife of playwright Harry B. Smith) as a Merry Widow, Lotta Faust as Mademoiselle Ou La La, and future musical comedy leading man Charles King as "an American college chap." It was an enjoyable, lightweight piece of fluff, which after its New York run went on tour in the fall of 1908.

The Girl behind the Counter was revived for another season, opening in Chicago in August. In parodying the then-popular (and scandalous) Salome dances, Fields found himself in an unaccustomed legal and censorship mess: Lotta Faust, performing a comic but still highly erotic Salome strip-dance, was arrested in Chicago (the judge dismissed the charge, and Fields dismissed the dance from the show). *The Girl behind the Counter* played in another twenty-nine cities through late 1908 and early 1909, when Fields began rehearsals for his next show, *The Midnight Sons*. Working overtime, Fields produced *The Midnight Sons* while also preparing the musical *The Rose of Algeria* for a September opening at the Herald Square Theater. He produced both shows solo, without backing from the Shuberts, and did not appear himself in either production (*The Rose of Algeria* proved to be a quick flop).

Vernon was handed a nice showy role in *The Midnight Sons* ("A musical moving picture in eight films," according to its program), which opened on May 22, 1909, at the Broadway Theater on Broadway and Forty-first Street. *The Midnight Sons* tells the story of a senator's four playboy sons who must go out and find jobs; the agreeably loose plot took the audience into their various places of work (a hotel, a theater, etc.) and gave cast members the opportunity to shine with various specialty acts. The cast included the effervescent (and fully dressed this time) Lotta Faust as Merri Murray, "America's leading chorus lady"; obese female impersonator George Monroe as Pansy Burns, "who won't cook for everybody"; Fields comic standby Lillian Lee as Lily Burns, "who won't cook for *anybody*"; and future stage and screen leading man Taylor Holmes as A. Case Daly, "a wine agent" (Holmes is best known today as Marilyn Monroe's potential father-in-law in *Gentlemen Prefer Blondes*).

Vernon made an impression as Souseberry Lushmore "in search of his home," the first of his acrobatic comic drunks (a type later perfected by comic Leon Errol). "I had more fun every night in that stag banquet scene than in all the twenty years I had lived in England," Vernon later claimed. He even opened the show, though that was not usually the best time at which to appear, as latecomers rattled programs and *Excuse me*'d down the aisles. As the curtain rose on the senator's farewell banquet, the guests sang him off with "High! High! High!" and Vernon entered hilariously to sing

"Call me Bill." It was his one and only song, but he reappeared through the show, and the *New York Times* gave Vernon a rave in its opening paragraph: "Two novel scenes, Blanche Ring's songs, Lotta Faust's back, and Vernon Castle's clever fooling, may carry *The Midnight Sons* . . . into summer success." The songs "Yip-de-addy" and "The Billiken Man," both performed by Blanche Ring, were popular, but nothing to compare with her rendition of the catchy "I've Got Rings on My Fingers" by R. P. Weston and F. J. Barnes, which became the show's breakout smash hit and Ring's theme song for the next three decades.

This was funny little Lotta Faust's third and last appearance with Vernon in a Fields show, singing "The Soubrette's Secret" and "Carmen the Second." Shortly after the show ended its long New York run on the first of January 1910, she entered a hospital, where she died on January 18.

The real showstopper was not Vernon nor Lotta Faust nor Blanche Ring, though; it was the breathtaking, hilarious "theater set" in act 2 created by scenic designer Arthur Voegtlin. As the curtain rose, the audience found themselves faced with a sort of mirror image: another theater audience, made up of actors and wax dummies. The cast performed their specialties to this "set piece," keeping their backs to the real audience. As the hubbub rose and fell from the astonished and delighted (real) audience, the joke sank in: the wax dummies filling the seats facing them included caricatures of famous New Yorkers—performers, society folks, and theater critics. Until the unveiling of Ralph Barton's famed "caricature curtain" at the 1922 show *Chauve Souris*, *The Midnight Sons* set proved Broadway's biggest and best inside joke.

The Midnight Sons was a hit with audiences and critics alike: newspapers overflowed with such praise as "immense," "colossal," "unequalled." It ran for nearly three hundred performances, leaving New York to hit the road on January 1, 1910. By that time, Vernon had left the show for a larger role in *Old Dutch*, a Fields/Shubert production that opened at the Herald Square on November 22, 1909.

In *Old Dutch*, Fields used a plot that was already old in 1909: Fields and his daughter (Alice Dovey), vacationing in the Tyrol, have their identities stolen by a crook and his moll (John Henshaw and Adah Lewis). The crooks' high living and the tourists' travails were played up for all the low comedy (and interpolated songs and comedy routines) that playwright Edgar Smith could contrive. The show had an impressive cast; in addition to Vernon, a bumptious tourist couple was played by veteran comedienne Eva Davenport and rotund comic John Bunny, who went on to become one of the film industry's first great stars.

Vernon portrayed another comic tourist: Algernon Clymber, "in the Tyrol for his health." Accompanied by six lovely chorus-girl "Clymber sisters," he sang "Algy" in act 1 and appeared in small walk-ons throughout the show.

Also in the cast—making her professional debut—was nine-year-old Helen Hayes, the future "First Lady of the American Theater." Watched over paternally by both Lew Fields and Vernon, little Helen found "the actors and crew were my playmates, and the backstage area was my special, magical playground." A playground with some naughty children: despite Fields's orders that everyone watch his or her behavior around Helen, she was soon the fascinated witness to a chorus-girl catfight, complete with one protagonist screaming, "Fuck you! Fuck you!" at her rival. "I thought it was all most exciting," said Hayes.

Even more exciting than cussing chorines was Hayes's violent crush on Vernon Castle, who treated her as a kid sister, carrying her piggyback up and down the backstage stairs and presenting her with affectionate notes and gifts. It may have been no more than friendliness on his part, but little Helen was smitten. "It was a real, consuming passion," Hayes remembered some eighty years later. "I was violently jealous of any lady whom Vernon so much as smiled at."

Not as big a hit as Fields's previous shows, *Old Dutch* still did good business, running for a respectable eighty-eight performances through the beginning of 1910. "It is a good show, and ought to make a hit," wrote the *New York Times* reviewer, adding another bouquet for Vernon: "Vernon Castle, in his excellent work with a very small part, which he enlarged by his own personality, deserves a special niche by himself."

Lew Fields, one of New York's busiest producers, had an impressive seven shows running on Broadway during 1910, and he was acting in two of them. Musicals, straight plays, operettas; he was working himself into a nervous collapse. One of these many shows was *The Summer Widowers*, which opened June 4, 1910, at the Broadway Theater. Helen Hayes was once again in the cast, making eyes at Vernon backstage. It was another old, old plot, most famously recycled in *The Seven Year Itch:* a boisterous femme fatale (in this case, Maud Lambert as Fritzi Fluff, "an absent minded prima donna") cavorts innocently with a group of harried husbands whose wives are all away from the city for the summer. Into the mix are thrown a lady detective (the brilliant comic actress and vaudeville favorite Irene Franklin), romantic sons, a wisecracking chorus girl, and characters bearing such names as Gertie Gherkin, Sandy Beach, Virginia Ham, and (as played by Helen Hayes) little Psyche Finnegan.

Vernon portrayed Oxford Tighe, "American agent for Eyzzzsst, the new Hungarian Cordial," which provided for plenty of spitting jokes. Once again, he got his own song, this time well enough into act 1 so the whole audience got to see it: Vernon (and a chorus of "Madcaps") sang "I Never Know How to Behave When I'm with Girls, Girls, Girls," a pretty self-explanatory number. "A sort of three-ring circus affair," said the *New York Times* reviewer, who seemed overwhelmed by the show.

Vernon professed himself to be quite pleased with his good reviews but was sufficiently stung by references to his physical appearance that he saved one clipping, which he pulled out of his pocket and read with rather a hurt air to a reporter: "Vernon Castle, the narrow-gauged comedian, was very good. Mr. Castle can best be described as a tracing of humanity. A born pin scratch, and it is safe to predict a long, narrow successful life for him. We hope to see him squeeze his way into popularity; in fact, he will, for it will take but a small crevice for him to do so." Vernon snorted, "I've been called about everything in the dictionary," but this was "the limit."

In an effort—successful, by and large—to top the theater set of *The Midnight Sons*, scenic designer Arthur Voegtlin created a breakaway apartment house, five stories of rooms visible to the audience. Every room of the "St. Vitus Apartments on Riverside Drive" had something going on: Fields's biographer describes girls sewing, a band rehearsing, a poker game, a cook and a policeman flirting—and Vernon Castle hiding under a bed while Lew Fields tries to shave looking in a mirror. In the last act, Vernon got to do an eccentric turn choreographed by Ned Wayburn, which led the way to a whole new future as a dancer.

By 1910, Vernon Castle was more than just a reliable member of Lew Fields's "family." He was now rivaling his brother-in-law, Lawrence Grossmith, as a popular comic actor. It was only a matter of time till a producer handed Vernon a stage vehicle that would carry him on to independent stardom—and Lew Fields was well known for letting his fledglings fly the nest to greater success. The three biggest male comic stars of the day (besides Fields himself) were Eddie Foy, Raymond Hitchcock, and De Wolf Hopper, all headlining in their own Broadway shows and making a fortune on tour. A new class was coming up behind them, a handful of young men who specialized in either light romantic comedy or broad slapstick: Leon Errol, Victor Moore, Harry Watson Jr., the comedian and juggler W. C. Fields, and a handsome sparkplug named Douglas Fairbanks. As the 1910s dawned, it looked as though Vernon would be joining their ranks.

Chapter Three

Only Forty-five Minutes from Broadway

"I don't think there's a childhood I would trade for mine," Irene Castle wrote late in her life. And, indeed, it seems in retrospect impossibly quaint and bucolic: a lovely hometown; upper-middle-class, eccentric parents; zany show business friends; even Irene's constant fights with her sister sound like fairly harmless sibling rivalry.

She was born Irene Foote on April 17, 1893, the second (and last) child of successful doctor Hubert Townsend Foote and his wife, the former Annie Elroy Thomas. Her home was New Rochelle, New York, a booming town "only forty-five minutes from Broadway," as George M. Cohan wrote in his backhanded 1906 tribute to the community:

> Oh! What a fine bunch of rubens,
> Oh! What a jay atmosphere;
> They have whiskers like hay,
> And imagine Broadway
> Only forty-five minutes from here.

So wrote Cohan—perhaps to kid his friend Eddie Foy, who had moved to New Rochelle in 1903—but the town was never the rube-filled Hooterville he depicted. It had been settled in the mid-1600s by Huguenots (French Protestants who had been fleeing persecution since the infamous St. Bartholomew's Day massacre of 1572). New Rochelle grew steadily but slowly until the mid-nineteenth century, when the New York and New Haven Railroad made it a virtual suburb of New York City. The population grew from 9,057 residents in 1890 to 14,720 ten years later. By the time Irene was born, the town boasted lovely homes on beautifully landscaped property, parks and a rowing club, theaters, a large shopping district—everything to make former Manhattanites want to settle down.

By mid-decade, show business folks were flocking to New Rochelle; those who didn't move there permanently became summer residents, rooming at one of the many local boardinghouses and enjoying the Rowing Club on Echo Bay.

In 1909 the moving picture industry came to New Rochelle with the opening of the Thanhouser Film Corporation. Over the next eight years, Thanhouser would produce more than one thousand films and employed such stars as Jeanne Eagels, James Cruze, Marguerite Snow, and Madeline and Marion Fairbanks ("The Thanhouser Twins"). Among Thanhouser's more noteworthy movies—many of them filmed in and around town—were Dickens adaptations, H. Rider Haggard's *She*, *Dr. Jekyll and Mr. Hyde*, *The Merchant of Venice*, *Tannhauser*, *Silas Marner*, and the hugely successful adventure serial *The Million Dollar Mystery*, starring the lovely and fearless Florence La Badie. It wasn't all Shakespeare and Dickens; among Thanhouser's more esoteric (and fascinating) titles were *Don't Pinch My Pup*, *Tillie, the Terrible Typist*, *Ferdy Fink's Flirtations*, and *That Poor Damp Cow*.

The Foote line can be traced back through Captain John Foote, who fought in the American Revolution, to Nathaniel Foote, who was born in Essex, England, in 1592. He and his wife, Elizabeth Deming, sailed to Watertown, Massachusetts, in 1633.

Irene's paternal grandfather, Edward Bliss Foote, was as famed in his day as Irene herself was to become. Born in Cleveland, Ohio, he moved east to edit the *New Britain Journal* and the *Brooklyn Morning Journal* before getting a degree at Penn Medical University in 1860 and opening a New York office at 120 Lexington Avenue, at the corner of Twenty-eighth Street. Foote wrote numerous books (including the hugely successful *Medical Common Sense*, *Plain Home Talk*, and *Science in Story*) and lectured all over the world: "His patients may be found wherever the English and German languages are spoken," wrote an early biographer. He was also a vice president of the American Secular Union, dedicated to the separation of church and state, and edited *Dr. Foote's Health Monthly*. Foote was an advocate of phrenology and other notions of the day since discredited. But Foote was well ahead of his time in many ways: he wrote in favor of equal rights for women (including in employment and pay); he advocated drinking fresh water and avoiding fast food (even unhealthier in the nineteenth century than today); he even went so far as to call for sexual freedom and to offer birth control advice.

Foote, who founded the Thomas Paine National Historical Association and ran it from his home and office at 120 Lexington Avenue in New York, has inspired Paul Collins, Paine's recent biographer, to comment, "Foote was perhaps the first American sexual reformer to hide in plain sight." He even manufactured and sold birth control devices, both effective (diaphragms) and somewhat less so ("electro-magnetic preventative machines"). Notorious postal inspector and moralistic busybody Anthony Comstock declared Foote a danger to the nation.

One hopes animal rights advocate Irene read the 1870 edition of her grandfather's *Medical Common Sense:* "The dawn of the millennium cannot light up human hands and arms red with blood of slaughtered animals." Certainly her lifelong love of pet monkeys may have been influenced by a bizarre series of children's books her grandfather wrote featuring "Sammy Tubbs, The Boy Doctor," and his companion, a mischievous Curious George prototype named Sponsie. The fifth volume, Paul Collins writes, is "a Victorian sex-ed manual. For children. Starring a monkey." Sponsie and his alter ego, Sponsie II, Collins notes with relish, end in curiously un-George-like ways: one monkey becomes a suicidal alcoholic and is shot in a duel; the other "has his rectum shot off" and is "disemboweled by the belt drive of an industrial knife sharpener." Which explains why Disney and Dream-Works are not competing for rights to the Sponsie stories.

E. B. Foote died in 1906, when Irene was thirteen. His son, Hubert Townsend Foote, born in 1859, followed his father and older brother into the medical field, perhaps as a consequence of witnessing another brother's illness and untimely death from appendicitis.

Hubert was expelled from Cornell University in upstate Ithaca, New York (a town his daughter would later call home), after he and several fellow students set off a Civil War-era cannon on campus, damaging the college's chemistry building. He transferred to New York University in Manhattan, from which he managed to graduate with no further havoc, specializing in homeopathy, a controversial "alternative" medical theory positing that the body can heal itself with the help of minute, diluted doses of "the one substance that will cause similar symptoms in a healthy person." He was riding the crest of a wave: homeopathy was wildly popular in the nineteenth century, according to *The Great American Medicine Show*. "By 1900, there were 22 homeopathic medical colleges in the United States and more than 15 thousand homeopathic practitioners, about one-sixth of the American medical profession."

Hubert married New Haven native Annie Elroy Thomas on May 29, 1884. Irene's mother was to be her best friend and role model: a highly energetic and well-educated feminist, Annie was the daughter of Connecticut-born David Stevens Thomas, press agent for the Barnum and Bailey Circus. Her childhood was a whirl of travel, show business, and adventure. In 1875, the fourteen-year-old Annie Thomas ascended in a hot-air balloon over New York's Madison Square Garden; according to Irene, her mother was the first female in the United States to make a balloon flight. (Annie and her pilot made a safe descent in New Haven.) Annie Thomas was particularly proud of her grandmothers: her mother's mother "was a Goldthwaite, of Massachusetts, the genealogy of the family going back to pilgrim days," and her father's mother "a Bond, of Boston, a woman noted in New York club circles for her brains and executive ability."

Annie Thomas, schooled in France and Germany, returned home a worldly and fearless young woman. When she married Dr. Foote at the age of twenty-three, he was already sharing a medical practice with his father at their Lexington Avenue office. The couple and their growing family moved to New Rochelle, and Dr. Foote made the famed forty-five-minute commute to New York City every day.

Dr. Hubert Foote and his wife were living on North Avenue when their daughters were born: Elroy Bertha in late 1886 and Irene in 1893. They remained in the large, rambling house on North Avenue until 1906, when Dr. Foote and several of his neighbors sold to a real estate firm, and Halcyon Park, a residential community, was put up on the site. The family moved to an even larger house, placed in the center of a larger yard, a few blocks away, on Pryer Terrace. The house was hidden from the street by a long driveway "lined with horse-chestnut trees ... and [there was] no sign of the big red barn and the many kennels that my father had erected in the back of the house."

Like most children, Irene was alternately entertained and mortified by her parents. Dr. Foote "never allowed himself to be shocked by anything my mother did," Irene recalled. On one occasion, long before it was fashionable to do so, Mrs. Foote trimmed her hair, inspired by a neighbor who had done the same: "I can remember her telling me that she rushed straight home and hid behind a screen," terrified of Dr. Foote's reaction. Foote failed to be shocked or angry, and "it was a bit of a letdown for my mother, like coming into a drawing room wearing a false nose for laughs and not getting any!"

On the other hand, Irene herself was shocked and embarrassed by one aspect of life as a doctor's daughter—"Life with father was one continual round of questions about my digestive and elimination processes," the rather prim Irene later shuddered to recall. Nor does she mention in her family reminiscences that when she was ten, her father patented the unfortunately named Foote Vaginal Syringe, a rubber douche he proudly described in his patent papers as "preventing soiling of the user's extremities or the clothing and allowing the use of the syringe in a standing position." But she admired her father, says Irene's son, "because of his strong affection for her mother. Irene absolutely adored her mother."

Thirteen-year-old Irene had the Beechmont Oval park right across the street in which to play. "I used to play with boys all the time," Irene said in a *Photoplay* interview. "I cannot remember when I could not ride and swim. I learned to dive through boys throwing me in the water. I suppose that's where all the fear was knocked out of me."

The bane of Irene's childhood was her older sister, Elroy (and, one may safely assume, the feeling was mutual). Elroy bridled at being drafted as a babysitter, and Irene proved a handful. The girls waged "a direct, straightforward honest type of warfare, in which every skirmish was an open and often bloody affair," throughout their childhoods. Irene was spoiled, headstrong, and willful from an early age, finding fiendish satisfaction in burning her sister's stamp collection and cutting up her photo album with scissors. Much to the relief of both sisters (and their parents), when Elroy entered her teens, she was sent to St. Mary's Episcopal Convent in Peekskill, New York, while Irene remained at home.

Irene had a colorful, theatrical bent from an early age, insisting that her birthday parties be epic affairs (in mid-April, they could often be held outdoors). She also showed a precocious contempt for some of the social mores of her day: "She insisted on having as guests every child that caught her fancy," Irene's mother wrote. "I remember the consternation of some of the mothers because for two successive years a little colored girl was one of the invited, and Irene's delight when the second year little Ruby won the prize in the birthday cake."

Irene's fondness for Ruby is mirrored in her relationship with the Foote family servant, Walter Ash. Ash—a short, stocky black man who had been working for the Footes since the late 1890s—was treated with a sort of affectionate paternalism. Frustratingly, he left behind no letters, no interviews, so we see his story only from Irene's perspective. "We regarded him as a member of the family," wrote Irene, adding the jaw-dropping comment, "His mother had been a slave so he was used to being a family retainer." She was obviously very fond of him, and after her marriage, he was to prove a friend in need and more resourceful than Irene and her husband. The paradox of her lifelong friendships with, and assistance for, blacks and her occasionally condescending and contemptuous statements about them perhaps has its origin in her nineteenth-century upbringing.

Chapter Four

❦

"We would be much happier if we just relaxed and enjoyed school life"

All was not idyllic in the Foote family as Irene entered her teens. Her father's homeopathy could not cure the tuberculosis that steadily weakened him and compelled the Footes to take frequent winter trips to Mexico for the dry, warm air. Mexico did not prove to be healthy for Foote's finances: he speculated on a sugar plantation and lost his inheritance. Still, Irene described the family's financial situation as "comfortable."

Irene developed an active interest in the opposite sex that was to continue unabated for her entire life. Dreamy evenings at the New Rochelle Yacht Club led to romances with local boys Ted Reynolds, who took her boating and proposed regularly, and "Brother" Whiting, whom she still remembered decades later with a sigh as "a handsome auburn-haired athlete." Irene even attended a football game with a maharajah's son who, she was chagrined to find, came only up to her shoulders (she retained her distaste for men shorter than she, and her husbands averaged around six feet).

Of all her early romances, the one with Brother Whiting (his real first name has been lost to history) proved the most serious. The Footes thoroughly disapproved of Whiting; for one thing, Irene—at fifteen or so—was too young to get that attached. And Whiting seems to have had an early version of the James Dean/Marlon Brando bad-boy appeal that is always lost on parents: Irene recalled that he could be "sullen and moody and difficult and went for days without speaking to anyone except in mumbles."

As the fall of 1908 approached, Irene was full of plans and schemes: she couldn't marry Whiting till she turned eighteen, but she hoped to escape her parents' eagle eyes and flee to New York, where she could stay with a relative—a female surgeon named Molly Bond. (Irene referred to her as "Aunt Molly," though neither of her parents had any sisters.) Aunt Molly wisely turned down the role of Irene's chaperone, and her parents, eager to keep her away from both Whiting and the many temptations of New York, decided to send her to boarding school.

National Park Seminary, in Silver Spring, Maryland, was a large scattering of thirty or so lovely buildings in a wooded retreat of thirty-two acres. It had begun as a hotel in 1890 and four years later reopened as a school for girls. Most of the structures—a chapel, dorms, gymnasium, sorority house—were built between 1894 and 1915, in an entertaining mélange of architectural styles. Irene joined about 270 other classmates, who were schooled by forty-two faculty members. She recalled the school as "lovely" and "fashionable," two traits she admired in people and institutions alike. Surrounded by upper-middle-class schoolmates, she pledged a sorority (but later claimed to have forgotten which one) and became best pals with Brooklynite Margaret Jelliffe and Chicagoan Florence Eisendrath, whom Irene nicknamed "Spider," for reasons one shudders to imagine. Margaret and Spider quickly became Irene's devoted (and cowed) slaves, making her bed, doing errands for her, and covering for her when she was late for class. "I had a mind of my own and a pretty clear view of things," Irene recalled of her overwhelming teenaged self. "I don't care how young you are, as soon as you find a devoted fan, you impose on her."

Irene found herself popular, albeit financially embarrassed, surrounded as she was by rich schoolmates who luxuriated in showing off their wealth and showering Irene with gifts that she could not reciprocate. "Dr. Foote did not believe in allowing young people to handle carelessly sums of money," her mother later wrote, "and refused flatly all appeals for an income that would permit repaying in kind the flowers, candies, and even jewelry that were heaped on Irene by her friends."

A born athlete (though also an accident-prone one), Irene joined the school's swim team as soon as she arrived. This indirectly led to scandal and the look that would be associated with her for the rest of her life. "I first cut off my hair," Irene recalled in 1921, "so that I could go swimming during a vacant forty-minute period and appear in my next class" with dry hair. But there seems to have been more to Irene's haircut than convenience—remember her remarks about the sensation her mother had secretly hoped to cause by cutting her own hair. "I became a radical," Irene proudly recalled of her first shearing, and one suspects that—lacking money—she used this shocking new look to become the center of attention and a fashion leader.

It worked: within a few days, her more adventuresome classmates began following suit and cropping each others' hair: "New bobbed heads popped up regularly each morning at breakfast, and, as the truth leaked home, irate parents wrote indignant letters to the principal, so that the joy and comfort I had found in my short hair became short-lived." This was in 1909, the end of the Gibson Girl era but still a time when women were expected to pile their long, luxuriant hair loosely atop their heads (often aided by hairpieces), secured into a chignon with multiple hairpins and combs—the convenient "bob pin" had not yet been invented.

A short history of short hair: for most of the nineteenth century, women wore their long hair pinned and tied up into elaborate constructions, often aided by false curls and chignons. Very early in the century (up till about 1820), very short, almost mannish, hair was popular in Europe, though the style never really caught on in the more conservative United States. Throughout the century, famous women would periodically make news by shearing off their hair (actress Adah Isaacas Menken and *Little Women*'s Jo, both in the 1860s). So, short hair was not altogether unheard of when Irene cut hers in 1909. Women's hairstyles circa 1910 were varied, but all were rather labor intensive (in the days before modern shampoos, conditioners, sprays, mousses, and blow-dryers). The famous Mary Pickford sausage curls were already well established, even before Pickford herself had come to fame. Older women—or those more interested in a dignified look—wrapped their hair closely about their heads, covering their ears. As the 1900s gave way to the 1910s, the huge bouffant look changed to a "smaller head," as unwieldy tea-tray and Gainsborough hats also shrank down into turbans, toques, and shakos.

As Irene and her school friends discovered, not everyone looked equally good in short hair. Irene was lucky enough to have a roundish face, high cheekbones, and delicate bone structure. Her less-blessed friends must have looked gawky and equine in their inexpertly chopped hair. Irene's was curly, as well; any friends with straight, thin hair would have been unhappily surprised at the results of their experiment.

As more and more parents complained bitterly to National Park Seminary's principal, Irene panicked: "There was only one thing left for me to do, run." Borrowing money from one of her loyal slaves, Irene hiked to the nearest streetcar, took it to Washington, then caught a train for New York. There she showed up on the doorstep of Aunt Molly, who, horrified, called National Park Seminary and had the principal cart Irene right back to school.

Irene was welcomed back, though with stern lectures and harangues about how "'we' would be much happier if 'we' just relaxed and enjoyed school life instead of looking for ways to complicate it, or escape from it." Irene promptly made plans to elope with Brother Whiting. Caught once again, this time she was expelled from National Park Seminary. About the same time, Elroy's early marriage broke up, so Dr. and Mrs. Foote, vacationing in Cuba, found themselves saddled with two unhappy daughters.

Settled back into her New Rochelle life, Irene pined for Brother Whiting (banished by his father to a lumber camp) and took frequent trips to New York City to shop and see the shows. One of the plays Irene enjoyed most was the musical comedy *The Three Twins*, which opened in June 1908. The show's breakout star was twenty-year-old Bessie McCoy, a wild, boisterous performer who stole the show and became the object of Irene's schoolgirl crush. Dressed in a baggy Pierrot costume with pointed hat and floppy gloves, McCoy sang what was to become her lifelong theme song, "The Yama-Yama Man." The lyrics warned of a comic boogeyman:

> Maybe he's hiding behind a chair
> Ready to spring out at you unaware!

But the verses were delightful nonsense, to a "Mary Had a Little Lamb" meter:

> A man sold some powder good for bugs
> But the man he must have lied.
> It wasn't good for bugs at all—
> The poor little bugs all died!

Irene wasn't the only audience member smitten with McCoy. Journalist, novelist, and all-around adventurer and self-promoter Richard Harding Davis fell madly in love with her, left his wife, and in 1912, married McCoy and took her away from the stage.

Bessie McCoy lived in New Rochelle, and Irene began imitating her—"I wanted to be just like her. It took no effort to make my husky voice sound like hers and I worked very hard to copy her steps and mannerisms."

Irene's accommodating mother sewed a Yama-Yama Man costume, and Irene began imposing her imitation on any and all handy victims: "the Ladies' Aid Society or the Garden Club or the Yacht Club or any amateur endeavor that needed free entertainment."

Irene's mother had long been resigned to her daughter's love for dancing; Irene was kicking her feet to the rhythm of music "before she could walk alone. . . . At the age of five she made her stage debut in a charity production, one of many little fairies." Her only dance teacher had been a local woman named Rosetta O'Neil, who taught local children the typical waltz, Boston, reel, and soft-shoe steps every young person was expected to know. Irene was picked to perform in a charity show, performing a "Radium Dance," inspired by the famed Loie Fuller, complete with Fuller's trademark swirling skirts, black light, and glowing, radium-painted fabrics (radium was often used for stage effects before its dangers were known).

There's no telling how good or how bad she was as an ersatz Bessie McCoy, but McCoy's mother, who saw one of her performances at a New Rochelle party, was kind enough to tell the girl her imitation was "very good." That was all the encouragement Irene needed: she pestered her mother about a distant cousin who worked for theatrical producers Klaw and Erlanger. Irene and Mrs. Foote visited his office, where something small, "perhaps in the chorus," was hinted at. Her cousin was not biting. He sensibly told the girl that the show business was tough, and that even chorus jobs were contended for viciously. "I had the determination, but received no encouragement," she sighed in frustration. Irene returned home to her garden parties and ladies' clubs.

Mrs. Foote was by now aware of one aspect of Irene's character that would later annoy Irene's husbands to no end: her perfectionism was accompanied by a shockingly unprofessional laziness. "As Irene hated real work," her mother noted, "I would stand with a hot head and cold feet in the wings, fearful of a mis-step, knowing she had shirked many hours of preparation; but the mis-step rarely came, and if it did it was so cleverly covered by some interpolation that it did not detract from the beauty of the whole."

Dr. Foote looked on Irene's dancing with fond bemusement and willingly paid for both lessons and costumes. His only concern was whether Irene could earn any money at her art: he was a firm believer in women having careers but felt that Irene was neither talented nor hardworking enough to survive in the competitive and risky theatrical world.

CHAPTER FIVE

"I COULD TELL BY LOOKING AT HIM THAT HE WAS NOT MY CUP OF TEA"

In the summer of 1910, Vernon took rooms at a New Rochelle theatrical boardinghouse that someone had recommended to him: the famed forty-five-minute ride got him out of the city and to a quaint town with a quiet, small-town atmosphere, congenial friends, and much cleaner air than Manhattan. It was there—at the Rowing Club—that he met seventeen-year-old Irene Foote. They were introduced by their mutual friend Gladwyn MacDougal, a middle-aged Canadian who was friendly with Dr. and Mrs. Foote (MacDougal had been treated to many a rendition of Irene's "Yama-Yama Man"), and who knew Vernon from his work as a theatrical manager.

Irene was swimming in Echo Bay, adjacent to the club. "[I] pulled myself up on the float to sit in the sun, when a tall, very thin young man pulled himself onto the opposite side of the float." It was not love at first sight: "I could tell by looking at him that he was not my cup of tea," Irene later wrote. She was still recovering from the broken heart given to her by the brawny, athletic Brother Whiting. Vernon showed no interest, either, and the two of them sat side by side for some time, sunbathing and ignoring each other.

Then fate, in the form of Gladwyn MacDougal, took a hand. Seeing his two friends on the float, he swam over and introduced them: once Irene found out that Vernon was an actor ("the first actor I had met"), he suddenly became a lot more attractive. She bluntly admitted in later years that at first she was interested in this young man as a rung up the ladder, not as a potential boyfriend. "My heart skipped a beat. My mind immediately began to make plans and weave schemes. . . . I turned loose every ounce of charm I could muster to hold his attention." Vernon, within a few minutes, remembered he had a friend waiting for him and ran like hell.

That evening, she encountered Vernon again; he was with Kathleen

Clifford, an actress, who sparked Irene's jealousy. Forty years later, Irene could still recite with disgust Clifford's vulgar getup: "a lavender wool suit with a little toque of violets on her head, and in her hand, to my utter amazement, she held a large gold-mesh bag with a huge K.C. spelled out in diamonds. Around the neck of her suit coat was lopped a gold chain that sneaked across her bosom and disappeared into her belt. I had no idea what was on the end of it. But it had a good-sized diamond every three inches, as far as I could see."

Somehow, Irene managed to wrench Vernon from the spectacle that was Kathleen Clifford, and within a couple of weeks, the two genuinely began to like each other. Young, athletic, good-humored, Vernon and Irene were able to put aside (for the time being) Irene's theatrical ambitions and just have a good time in each other's company. The Footes welcomed him into their home, and Vernon luxuriated in the first family he'd been with since leaving his own. Every Sunday, Mrs. Foote cooked him dinner and packed him box lunches to take back to the city. Dr. Foote took Vernon out on his boat, the *Hully G.* (a variant of the expression *golly gee*).

We'll never know what specifically attracted Vernon to Irene (although her good looks and brains must have been a start), but Irene managed to overcome her physical indifference to Vernon. "I liked his manners. He had a lovely, gentle voice and a calm disposition, which came in handy when our boat was becalmed and my father was leaning over the prow, shouting." By the end of the summer, the two found they were a couple. "It was not long before my feelings for Vernon began to change," wrote Irene, and she worried that he saw her only as a starstruck, ambitious kid (which, of course, she was). One night on the Footes' front porch, Vernon kissed Irene for the first time, "and I realized he was as much in love with me as I was with him."

Vernon proposed to Irene on Christmas Day, 1910. If Irene had any doubts or second thoughts, she never expressed them. Irene's father was charmed by Vernon but, quite sensibly, did not see him as son-in-law material. "He contended that actors never had any money" and further felt that this would be a "mixed marriage" culturally. "He was opposed to people of different nationalities, even though they spoke the same language, marrying," said Irene. "That was the only argument he was able to stick to."

Vernon was making a very respectable salary of $75 a week in *The Summer Widowers*—but when that show ended, he'd be without work for goodness knows how long, and performers were not paid for the rehearsal period in the 1910s. Irene didn't seem worried over this prospect, but the Footes were. Vernon, for the first (and last) time in his life, set to and actually saved money, $400, "and he was terribly proud of himself."

No one ever got anywhere by standing in Irene's way, and her parents knew her well enough to step back and, with some misgivings, give the couple their blessings.

CHAPTER SIX

ZOWIE, "THE MONARCH OF MYSTERY"

By the late summer of 1910, Irene's campaign had begun: she was fond of Vernon and found him an agreeable, amusing companion, but at this stage he was mostly a step up the show business ladder. "He was very nice about it, but, as I remember, he showed no particular enthusiasm," she admitted.

In the fall of 1910, Vernon returned to his duties in *The Midnight Sons* and had less time to spend with Irene in New Rochelle. Dr. and Mrs. Foote vacationed in Mexico, still hoping the warm, dry air would be good for the doctor's tubercular lungs. Sister Elroy was studying at Pratt Institute in Brooklyn, living in a small flat on Columbus Avenue in Manhattan. Despite her longtime problems with Elroy, Irene moved in with her to be closer to her new beau.

Nagged insistently by Irene, Vernon in turn insistently nagged Lew Fields till an audition was arranged. On the stage of the empty, cavernous Broadway Theater, a nervous Irene asked for more light and went into her act. "I had come in from New Rochelle with a pianist, who feebly accompanied me in the huge dark theater. I danced with castanets a sort of Spanish tarantella." Even Irene confessed that she sounded "like a very tired horse crossing a wooden bridge." Lew Fields sighed heavily and offered her a small part in a touring company of *The Midnight Sons*, which Irene turned down, not wanting to endure a road tour for such a minuscule role.

Fields wanted nothing more than to send this amateur out on tour and get her away from Vernon. In his thirty-some years as an actor and producer, Fields had seen his share of ambitious girls (and boys) doing what they could to get into the show business. This Irene Foote was nothing special that he could see: just another spoiled debutante who thought she could act, or sing, or dance. Pretty, but too young and skinny and untrained. The fact that she could put one over on his adored Vernon Castle was disappointing.

The Summer Widowers took off on tour in October 1910, after 140 performances on Broadway. When it arrived at Brooklyn's Majestic Theater in mid-November, Irene joined the cast, in her professional stage debut. She was given a tiny walk-on role, as "Mrs. Lamb," and a dressing room to share with little Helen Hayes—the jealousy flared violently. When Hayes found there was indeed something going on between Irene and Vernon, "the drums of doom started to beat in my heart.... I'm afraid I made backstage life pretty unpleasant for Irene." *The Summer Widowers* closed at the end of 1910, and Irene had her first New York credit under her belt, even if it was Brooklyn and not Broadway.

The next Lew Fields extravaganza, *The Hen-Pecks,* opened on February 4, 1911, at the Broadway Theater. This show contained a star-making role for Vernon and would prove to be Fields's most successful production in several years. It starred Fields as rural farmer Henry Peck, whose daughter Henoria (Gertrude Quinlan) runs off to the big city, bedazzled by the glamour of Zowie, "the Monarch of Mystery, the third and last attraction of the season at the Cove's Temple of Amusement, Melodeon Hall." Zowie was played, with great panache and a red wig, by Vernon.

The surprise hit of the show occurred when twenty-year-old Blossom Seeley, as Henella Peck, climbed on a table, sang "Toddling the Todalo," and danced a wild, syncopated Texas Tommy (the dance was first popularized by a black dance team, Johnny Peter and Ethel Williams, in San Francisco, around 1909). Vernon also got a nice specialty number, "It's Not the Trick Itself but It's the Tricky Way It's Done," in which he utilized not only his comic talents but his old magic routines, polished at St. George's Hall back in London.

Another high point occurred in act 2, with a scene that hearkened back to the glory days of Weber and Fields—but this time it was Vernon who partnered Lew Fields. The routine was set in a barbershop, where Henry Peck, hiding from his wife and daughters, has disguised himself as an Italian barber; in comes his archnemesis, the home-wrecking magician Zowie. For the next ten or fifteen minutes, chaos reigned, as the gleeful Fields put Zowie through the most slapstick of tortures: strangled, scalded, slapped around, choked on shaving cream, jounced up and down in the barber's chair, hosed down, and finally set afire (Vernon wore a safely combustible wig). The audience howled, and critics hailed a great new comedy team, the hot-tempered Fields and his lanky stooge, Castle. "Any man who can succeed at making his fellow man laugh as did Lew Fields at the Broadway Theater last night need not feel that he has lived in vain," wrote the *New York Times*, adding that Vernon, "no longer forced to depend solely upon a freakish personality for his humor, is genuinely amusing, as well as clever."

Vernon celebrated a major change for the better in his private life, too. He and Irene were married on Sunday, May 28, 1911, Hubert and Annie Foote's twenty-seventh wedding anniversary. The wedding took place at the Foote home in New Rochelle, with family friend Rev. Benjamin T. Marshall presiding. The Footes went all out, despite their reservations: bridesmaids, a crepe de chine wedding gown from B. Altman's, bowers of dogwood and smilax bedecking the house—but, as in any comedy, there was no groom. He'd gone canoeing at the Rowing Club and had lost track of the time. To Irene's relief and the Footes' possible disappointment, he showed up by 5:00—just in time for the ceremony—charmingly unable to fathom the concern he'd caused. The couple spent their wedding night in New York, at the Knickerbocker Hotel in Times Square (the building still exists, one of the belle epoque ghosts of the Midtown area).

After *The Hen-Pecks* closed in June 1911, Fields and his family went on vacation to Europe; the Castles took the opportunity for their honeymoon. They sailed on the S.S. *Minnehaha* on June 11; it was Irene's first trip to England. On their honeymoon cruise they won thirteen out of fourteen shipboard events, including the three-legged race, and Vernon befriended a small boy who was under the impression that the "Castles" were the king and queen of England.

For a starry-eyed bride, Irene was in a snit. On her arrival in England, she found the women "dowdily dressed" and her new in-laws rather common and overly effusive. She patronizingly thought Vernon's beloved father was Dickensian and dwelled on her mother-in-law's unruly hair. The Blyth home was "awkwardly laid out"; the ginger ale was warm. Not surprisingly, Vernon and Irene began to quarrel. "I found everything in London inferior to New York. I complained bitterly at this, that and the other thing not being just as it was at home, all of which must have been unbearable to Vernon."

Irene was pretty unbearable to Norwich, too: for the first and last time in her life, the future fashion icon made the mistake of overdressing. In this midsized provincial town, Irene paraded around in a navy blue coat with a black satin hood, and the locals followed her and pointed as if the circus had come to town. Years later she was able to laugh at herself; a fast learner, Irene soon made other women look vulgar and pretentious by wearing pared-down, elegant clothing.

The breaking point was bananas. Small, speckled bananas. When these horrors appeared on the Blyth dining table, Irene was unable to hide her contempt. That night, she (figuratively) held the bananas up to her husband as a joke, and he unexpectedly exploded: "It was rude of you to pass up the bananas. She was proud of them." Irene's disappointment and frustration and embarrassment came to a head, and their first (though not last) real fight boiled over. The Castles returned from their honeymoon in late summer, wondering what they'd gotten themselves into.

When Lew Fields returned from his own vacation in August, *The Hen-Pecks* went back into rehearsal—with Irene replacing actress Nan Brennan in the tiny role (three lines) of Mrs. Murgatoyd. Brennan was a minor but rising star in Fields's company, and to make up for bumping her from *The Hen-Pecks*, Fields cast her in two later shows. In 1914 Brennan married well (the New York City tax commissioner) and left show business. *The Hen-Pecks*, and the newlywed Castles, moved to Philadelphia and Pittsburgh in the fall, and opened in Chicago in late October—a disastrous performance. The company and the sets arrived late, and the actors, tired and cranky, gave an "*awful*" show, as Fields put it.

The situation got worse when Lew Fields's father died and the show closed for a week in November 1911. A devoted family man, Fields ignored the "show must go on" tradition without a second thought, and the company idled until he returned to pick up their tour through the Midwest. The Castles landed back in New York at the end of 1911, exhausted, exhilarated, and with their pockets full of hard-earned salary.

But not for long: for their first Christmas together, their tiff now forgiven and forgotten, Vernon bought Irene a diamond ring "that must have cost nearly five hundred dollars." Irene began strap-hanging on the subway gloveless to show it off (and was lucky indeed to have held onto it for more than a week). The $500 diamond ring was not an aberration: Irene learned very quickly that her new husband loved nothing more than throwing his money around. "To the waiter who served him he gave an amount equal to the check, contending that it was not extravagant, since the waiter worked harder than he did."

CHAPTER SEVEN

"THEY LIKED TO TEST OUT THEIR GUNS"

Actress Elsie Janis wrote bluntly of the Castles in her memoirs: "Vernon was the most tactful person I ever knew! Irene the least! The result was that women, unless they knew her well, were not terribly enthusiastic about her. To know her well was about as easy as getting chummy with the Sphinx!" Janis eventually did become friends with Irene, but only after the two were no longer theatrical rivals and both had heartbreaks to nurse.

We have no surviving accounts to tell us Vernon's opinions of his wife's overwhelming personality, but Irene had ample opportunity to write about Vernon. She once claimed, "I have never heard of anyone who disliked him, and I don't believe he really disliked anyone, either, but he could get most delightfully bored; things had to keep up a pretty lively tempo to hold his interest, and even those he loved bored him at times." His public image was one of unflappability: always calm, serene, brushing over the hurt feelings sometimes left in Irene's wake. But he was also a bundle of energy and could be childish as well as childlike in his moods. "There was no one who could keep up with him," said Irene. "He rode and swam harder than anyone else and could outsit anyone at a party, requiring very little sleep, and despising, more than anything, an idle moment. He seemed absolutely tireless and more alive than anyone I have ever known."

Irene, as the keeper of the Castles' flame in later years, reminisced fondly of their years together as blissful, joyous, free of strife. But the Castles, as many of their contemporaries recalled, loved a good fight: if not with managers or rivals, then with each other. Vernon's spending, his boyish insouciance, Irene's distaste for rehearsal and her star complex—all were good reasons for verbal battles. These were, after all, two young people who barely knew each other, and who found themselves thrust into a very strange world of constant hard work (involving close physical contact and cooperation), as poverty and unimaginable wealth equally dangled before them. "They liked to test out their guns," said their manager, Elisabeth Marbury, adding, however, that "these recurrent scenes invariably ended in sunshine, and in renewed turtle-doving." Their fights seemed staged for the sheer fun and effect, compared by Marbury to a rich little boy who puts on rags and begs in the snow for "the attention of onlookers" and "sympathetic comment." The term *drama queen* had not yet been coined, but it seems to perfectly suit the Castles at the dawn of their fame.

There were also snide, unpleasant insinuations in the newspapers that Vernon was gay, though in the 1910s no one could actually come out and say such a thing. But he was referred to as "lisping," "drawling," "sashaying," "flighty"—all the stereotypes associated with gay men. There were several reasons for this: to some Americans, "British" and "effeminate" went hand in hand. Vernon was an actor and a dancer, both putting him under suspicion. He was slim, graceful, natty, and well dressed, and wore wristwatches, which were considered pretty effeminate before World War I. When he spoke of enlisting in the war, there was a lot of rude disbelief in the press. The rumors continued after his death, as no publicity was given to love affairs with other women (Irene made quite sure of that).

Were the Castles genuinely a couple, or was theirs a marriage of convenience? A little of both, probably. Irene's son, William McLaughlin, feels the marriage was indeed a love—or at least affection—match and insists his mother never would have submitted to a sexless union, even in her teens. "Whether they were in love or whether they were in 'excitement' of an adventure together might be a little hard to tell," says McLaughlin. "I'm not sure there really is a dividing line: somewhere along the line you melt friendship, convenience, accommodation and so forth into something that might be called 'romance.' I think they were romantically inclined."

While Vernon was in *The Hen-Pecks,* he got an offer from a French producer, Jacques Charles, to appear in a Parisian revue in an extended version of the barbershop sketch. Lew Fields had sold Charles the rights and reluctantly agreed to let his star comic strike out on his own. Now that Irene had gotten her hooks into him, Fields felt, Vernon was of little future use anyway. Both Castles were eager to see Paris, and Charles even agreed to write a part for Irene in the show. Just as 1911 became 1912, the Castles sailed for Europe, accompanied by the Foote family servant, Walter Ash (he traveled second class, the Castles first, of course).

"As I look back, our going to Paris seems to me to have been one of the most courageous of long chances," said Irene. They were certainly taking a chance, and as it would turn out, this trip would hasten the end of Vernon's promising career as a comic. But he felt he'd gone as far as he could with Lew Fields, and both Castles still felt a bit stung by his response to Irene's audition. They didn't know what awaited them in Paris, but they were young and full of optimism.

They disembarked in Antwerp, "where we were fascinated by the cathedral and narrow, winding streets." Irene was "particularly interested in the milk carts drawn by dogs. We found them very serious-minded dogs, that were trained early in life to attend to business alone." Then off to Brussels, "which we found a baby Paris." It was in Brussels that Irene saw and fell in love with a lace Dutch cap, which Vernon duly sprung for; the hat soon became Irene's trademark and was copied all over the world.

Arriving in Paris, their party was stopped at customs, where Irene tried to smuggle in five hundred cigarettes and Vernon was held for his matches and playing cards: the couple was finally allowed into France, less 600 francs in fines. Along with Walter, they had brought an English bulldog given to them by Irene's father: they named her Zowie, after Vernon's breakthrough role.

The Castles settled into the hotel room Jacques Charles had reserved for them (at their expense—and remember, no one was paid for rehearsal time back then). All but broke from their encounter with customs, Vernon, Irene, and Walter Ash went shopping for less expensive quarters and found something straight out of *La Bohème:* a two-bedroom attic apartment at 44 rue Saint-Georges, "halfway up the hill to Montmartre." Vernon and Irene had one tiny bedroom, Walter Ash the other, and the remaining room served as their dining room and general parlor. It even had a private bath, quite a luxury. But it had its drawbacks: the ceiling was so low and tilted that Vernon could barely stand upright, and the rent—though minimal—still had to be paid.

Jacques Charles informed the couple that his revue was undergoing a bit of trouble and the opening would have to be put off for six weeks; he kindly advanced Vernon 200 francs, but that did not last long, with food and rent for three people and a dog. The weather was cold and rainy, and the trio had to walk everywhere to save on transportation costs; their clothes and shoes quickly became bedraggled and disreputable looking. Things got so bad that Irene pawned a gold watch given to her by Aunt Molly—which she claimed was ugly anyway.

More trauma struck when one of Irene's perfume bottles broke and the contents splashed into Zowie's eyes. The poor dog was in agony, and the last of their money went to the veterinarian, who sold them an eyewash. "I felt entirely to blame," said Irene, "and was picturing myself driving [Zowie] around through the parks day after day (because she loved driving) to make up for the loss of her sight." Zowie, happily, recovered.

With the weather so awful, the Castles and Walter were stuck inside, playing cards. On the few nice nights the threesome strolled around Paris, peeking (for free) into the doorways and windows of nightclubs and cabarets.

According to Irene, they were rescued from starvation and eviction by Walter Ash. But her version of "artful colored servant saves grateful white folks" reads too theatrically and is too condescending to be viewed without skepticism—and unfortunately we do not have Ash's version of events. According to Irene, Ash disappeared every night, to return covered in mystery and toting food, champagne, flowers, and cash. Quizzed by the Castles, he admitted to winning the prizes from Albert, a neighboring *valet de chambre*, by shooting craps.

Irene told this story endlessly in years to come, even weaving it into a series of radio shows she did in the 1930s: a sharp, dice-throwing Ash (sounding on radio a lot like Eddie Anderson as Rochester) slyly and comically saving the day. It *might* have happened, but it's just as likely that the Castles and Walter Ash simply scrimped and saved and went without till Jacques Charles put them on his payroll.

When they did happen into money, they spent it faster than it came in, rushing with Walter to the best restaurants, where the three of them ordered champagne with their meals and a steak to take home to Zowie. "There was so little left for the rent that it never seemed worth saving," reasoned Irene, "and the glass of wine washed our cares away and kept our misfortunes from swamping us."

CHAPTER EIGHT

ENFIN . . . UNE REVUE

Enfin . . . une Revue (which means, appropriately enough, *Finally . . . a Revue*) was a hodgepodge in two very long acts, divided into seven tableaux. Vernon's barbershop sketch, performed in act 1, did not go over well at all with French audiences (of course, his new partner may not have had the comic timing and skills of a Lew Fields). It was a "complete and abysmal failure," recalled Irene. In act 2, tableau 4, came the Castles' big moment, a dance that Irene always felt was their very best, based on Hans Christian Andersen's tragic tale of doomed love, "The Brave Tin Soldier." With Vernon in a silver lamé uniform and Irene in white taffeta, they enacted the story: "The tin soldier falls in love with the paper doll and pursues her madly around the stage, his legs held stiff. . . . Finally, frustrated, he throws himself into the fire and melts down, squiggly-like, enveloped in chiffon flames. And the heartbroken doll frantically runs back to the oversized fireplace and jumps in after him."

If the audience was impressed with the Castles' take on Andersen (and there is no indication that viewers were as impressed with it as Irene herself was), it exploded with glee over their act 2, tableau 6, appearance as M. and Mme. Flirt. Backed by the eight *Flirteuses*, the Castles finally "found themselves," breaking out in a wildly energetic and very American dance routine to the tune of "Alexander's Ragtime Band." The dance itself was a hastily improvised combination of the Texas Tommy and the grizzly bear, both of which were new to Paris. Although it was based loosely on the tabletop performance Blossom Seeley had given in *The Hen-Pecks*, Irene recalled the dance as "even rougher, full of so many acrobatic variations that I was in the air much more often than I was on the ground." The Parisians went mad for it, and Jacques Charles happily kept them on, the failed barbershop routine forgotten and forgiven.

They were somewhat surprised to find themselves a hit as dancers; "in the days before we were married, though we went to many of the same parties, I am sure that we never danced together," said Irene. "Necessity made us dancers."

Vernon and Irene stayed in *Enfin . . . une Revue* for two weeks—long enough to pay off their advance salaries to Charles, and long enough for their ecstatic press clippings to reach New York (carefully sent on by Irene to be disseminated through the Broadway community, then as now a very small world). They handed in their notice: as Irene said, "the stench backstage was just too strong for me." Still fairly broke, if a little more famous, Vernon, Irene, and Walter Ash spent the early spring of 1912 wandering around in the improving Paris weather, nonchalantly looking for work.

The Castles' good press had reached Louis Barraya (affectionately known as "Papa Louis"), proprietor of the Café de Paris—not to be confused with the popular club of the same name in London. The Café de Paris had, as Irene nostalgically recalled, "an air of true graciousness . . . an elegant gaiety. . . . It was not a place, it was a social convention." The Castles wisely asked if they could "case the joint" before attempting to dance there. All dance floors are different, and even beginners like the Castles knew that the size and shape of the room would affect their routines. Papa Louis arranged for them to sit at a small table (and eat a free dinner) as they listened to the orchestra and gave the dance floor a professional once-over.

By now, Irene was down to her last good gown, which had also been her wedding dress a year earlier—simple white crepe de chine, slim-lined, topped with one of her precious lace Dutch caps. Irene wore no jewelry, most of it having been pawned. She remembered 1912 as a particularly over-the-top, vulgar season for Parisian fashions; most of the café customers were decked out in their biggest jewels, immense feather-laden Merry Widow hats, tightly "straight-lined" corseted dresses dripping with lace, bows, and flowers. Irene, on the other hand, was the very picture of the chic, understated "American Girl" look, later to be associated with Grace Kelly and Jacqueline Kennedy: spare, understated hair and makeup, little or no jewelry (and that very good and very small), clothing of the best cut and fabric and of the simplest lines. It helps to be tiny, small-boned, and to have perfect facial features, which describes Irene pretty well. If she *felt* underdressed, she outshone every well-padded, overdone dowager in the house.

By midnight, the Castles had eaten, looked around, and mentally plotted out some dance routines—when Papa Louis approached. One of their customers, a "Russian gentleman," had seen the Castles dancing in

Enfin . . . une Revue and wished to see them dance again. *Now.* He was one of the café's best customers, and Papa Louis made it known that this request was not to be denied. The Castles all but panicked. They had not yet rehearsed with the orchestra or on the dance floor; Irene's simple dress had a train, which she hastily pinned up; they had just eaten a heavy meal; and neither of them was "keyed-up" enough, as she put it, to put on a good performance.

"Both of us were quivering with nervous excitement," and they were a hit—especially with the Russian gentleman, who gave Papa Louis 300 francs to give to the Castles. Vernon somehow got it into his head that the tip was an insult to a professional and ordered Louis to return it—Irene kicked him, hard, and pocketed the money. "Tips amounted to more than our salary," as she recalled of the next few weeks at the Café de Paris. Customers would approach the Castles at their table, at the door, even in the toilet, and hand them bills of various denominations and currencies. They also asked Vernon and Irene to dance for them privately, at parties, and the two happily accepted, becoming the new pets of Paris society. They even went to London to dance at a party, sharing the bill with Ballets Russes star Vaslav Nijinsky.

Their café act was something new and fresh in Parisian nightlife: they went on at midnight, starting their dance from their ringside table; this was the first time, Irene claimed, that performers did not enter from the wings or backstage. Their dance was rougher in style than those for which they later became famous: more comic and acrobatic, "rough and tumble," as Irene recalled. As the money poured in (their Café de Paris salary was 100 francs a night), Irene was smart enough to maintain her quiet chic: simple white dresses, no jewelry. She made every other woman in the room look like an overdressed frump.

For all that she suddenly represented the latest in fashion and the new wave of dance, Irene was still a very sheltered teenager. This became clear when a "handsome, statuesque woman" in black velvet began following the Castles from club to club, her eyes clearly set on Irene. In an effort to be friendly to her public, Irene sat down at the woman's table and tried out her high school French. "She surrounded one of my hands with two of hers and plunged into what I think was a compliment on my dancing ability," Irene recalled. She invited Irene to tea at her house and seemed somewhat put out when Irene replied that she *and her husband* would be glad to come.

Later that night, at l'Abbaye (another popular French club), Irene's admirer appeared again and cut in during a dance, sweeping Irene away from her partner, "and started doing a sort of hootchy-kootchy dance with me pressed very close to her." The sophisticated Parisians raised not an eyebrow, but little Irene was stunned and baffled. Vernon and their companions were hugely amused by this turn of events and gave Irene no help at all.

That night, back at the hotel, Vernon had a facts-of-life talk with his wife about how some ladies prefer ladies and some gentlemen prefer gentlemen. "I was not shocked but I was surprised," Irene said of her introduction to this new world. It's not known exactly what Vernon said (Irene's memoirs, published in 1958, are understandably coy on the subject). But he must have given her a sympathetic and straightforward explanation, as both Castles enjoyed personal friendships and professional relationships with gay men and women for the rest of their lives. Certainly, their most important supporter was an openly gay woman, and Irene's son notes that in later years she spent many a vacation on Fire Island in New York with gay friends. Paris in 1912 turned out to be an important growing experience personally as well as professionally for the young couple.

CHAPTER NINE

"I SAW THE FAT YEARS AHEAD!"

By mid-April 1912, Vernon and Irene had accomplished as much in Paris as they felt they were going to. Irene was homesick for America, and Vernon wanted to get back to New York to pick up the shreds of his old career and see if he could incorporate this new dancing business into it. That May, Irene received a cable from her mother: Hubert Townsend Foote had finally died from the tuberculosis that had been weakening him for years. Irene booked the first passage she could, and Vernon made plans for another visit to his family in England before joining his bereaved wife in America (not the most sympathetic of husbandly reactions, it must be noted).

Irene sailed for the United States, clutching Zowie to herself, camped out on a deck chair, looking for icebergs. It had been less than a month since the sinking of the *Titanic*, and Irene was taking no chances that she and Zowie would miss out on a lifeboat. "In the confusion of abandoning ship, they would think I was carrying a baby," she hoped. "A very ugly baby."

She arrived safely, as did Vernon soon after, and the Castles took up the problem of finding work. They politely avoided Lew Fields, who had just reunited with Joe Weber in *Hokey-Pokey* and was preparing another show, *Hanky-Panky*, for a summer run. Taking a letter of recommendation they'd gotten from Jacques Charles, the Castles approached Louis Martin, manager of the Times Square restaurant the Café de l'Opera. Irene requested $300 a week, and it took Martin several days to swallow his shock and agree to their demands. He must have heard some promising word of mouth, as he also agreed to give them a suite of rooms in the Café's building.

Martin placed cards on each table announcing that "Mr. and Mrs. Vernon Castle will appear at twelve o'clock," and their new career was off. Each midnight, the small orchestra started up some ragtime dance number, and the spotlight caught the slim, unobtrusive, and tastefully dressed couple at ringside. Then up they sprang, twirling onto the small dance floor and taking away the breath of the diners: forks paused in midair, champagne went warm and flat, as the Castles ushered in a new way of dancing.

As untrained dancers, the Castles invented their technique as they went along, and Vernon proved to be a natural choreographer and partner. "All we did was to write on paper about what we thought we would do," Irene recalled. "This custom of writing out our dances first was almost always adhered to in later days. The first dances we wrote we never even rehearsed, though we might have had the stage at any time."

Vernon was the mastermind, the choreographer; but Irene's talent—and it was not a small one—was an ability to follow, to instantly change course, change tempo, read Vernon's mind. "By keeping my eyes firmly fixed on the stud button of his dress shirt, I could anticipate every move he was going to make and we made it together, floating around the floor like two persons sharing the same mind."

They also had *fun* while they danced, and that came across and added to their appeal. They were not smoldering and overtly sexual; they laughed as they danced; their "great sense of bubbling joy" transmitted itself to their audience. Neither Vernon nor Irene were as effective as solo dancers or with other partners—they were as much playmates as husband and wife, and in their brief career, the fun never had a chance to get old.

Their first famous dance was created off-the-cuff. At a late-night party for actress Elsie Janis (who would soon have a professional run-in with Irene), the exhausted Castles "clowned around like taxi drivers taking a joy ride." "Instead of coming *down* on the beat like everyone else did, we went up. The result was a step almost like a skip, peculiar-looking I'm sure, but exhilarating and fun to do." Dubbed the Castle walk, the dance became a sensation in dance-crazed New York, and the Castles' private lesson bookings increased tenfold (as did their fees). The Castle walk was easier to learn than the now-waning bunny hug and grizzly bear, and was a more polite (though still undignified and somewhat hilarious) step.

Vernon himself admitted that he stole the basic idea for the Castle walk from acrobatic comic Leon Errol, who specialized in the same sort of drunk dances that Vernon had done onstage. By 1915, when self-proclaimed originators of the fox trot and the Apache dance were quarreling with each other in the press, Vernon sent a letter to a show business trade paper: "My dear Mr. Errol: I read where it is said that you were the first to introduce the step that is known as the Castle Walk. In case it is any satisfaction to you, it is quite correct. I got the steps from you about four years ago, when you were doing a very wonderful dance called the Grizzly Bear at a burlesque theater in Pittsburgh. With best wishes and many congratulations to you on your art, I am a sincere admirer, Vernon Castle."

Vernon and Irene were an instant hit. But for all their talent, good looks, and ambition, the Castles never would have become "the Castles" without the help of two geniuses of the show business world: their agent, Elisabeth Marbury, and their arranger and accompanist, James Reese Europe.

Elisabeth Marbury and her longtime companion, Elsie de Wolfe, were two of the most remarkable women of their time. Plump, sociable, and well educated, Marbury had her first success as a literary agent and theatrical producer in 1888, acting as Frances Hodgson Burnett's agent in producing her book *Little Lord Fauntleroy* on Broadway. By the turn of the century, Marbury had virtually invented the profession of literary and theatrical agent: among her clients were Oscar Wilde, George Bernard Shaw, Edith Wharton, W. Somerset Maugham, Eugene O'Neill, Daniel and Charles Frohman. Shortly after discovering the Castles, Marbury revitalized the musical comedy by initiating the small-scale, intimate "Princess Shows" produced at the tiny Princess Theater on West Thirty-ninth Street. *Nobody Home* (which featured a dancing teacher named "Vernon Popple," played by Lawrence Grossmith) and *Very Good Eddie* (both 1915), *Oh, Boy* (1917), *Oh, Lady! Lady!* and *Oh, My Dear!* (both 1918) drew on the talents of Marbury's clients Jerome Kern, Guy Bolton, and P. G. Wodehouse. She discovered Cole Porter in 1915 and began pushing his songs to the Shuberts and Charles Dillingham, ushering in one of the great songwriting careers of midcentury.

Tiny, plain Elsie de Wolfe was a failed actress, having appeared to no great effect in a handful of shows between 1895 and 1904 (and she got those roles only because of Marbury's influence). While not a brilliant actress or a great beauty, de Wolfe had an enormous amount of style and flair, with the push and energy to back it up. Her groundbreaking career as a decorator began in 1908, when she designed the interior for McKim, Mead, and White's Colony Club, New York's first exclusive club for ladies (the building, at 120 Madison Avenue, is now the American Academy of Dramatic Arts). De Wolfe's interior design was a revelation: swept away were the dark woodwork, ferns, and overstuffed furnishings popular at the time.

New York's elite saw her pale, uncluttered walls, eighteenth-century French furniture (painted cream or white), light, breezy curtains, and colorful throw pillows, and a New Look was born. "I opened the doors and windows of America, and let in the air and sunshine," she justifiably bragged. By the time her 1913 book *The House in Good Taste* was published, Elsie de Wolfe was a leader in taste and style, and America's foremost interior designer.

Elisabeth Marbury and Elsie de Wolfe lived much of the year at their red brick house on Irving Place in New York; summers were spent at the Villa Trianon, on the grounds of the Palace of Versailles in France. Both homes were showplaces and salons: the cream of society and the literary, theatrical, and artistic worlds flocked to "the bachelorettes'" parties. Marbury and de Wolfe were the Gertrude Stein and Alice B. Toklas of prewar New York, their "Boston marriage" an acknowledged part of their legend. New York historian Lloyd Morris wrote that the women ushered in "a new society in which wit, intelligence, style, creative achievement, and a lively interest in the arts took precedence over wealth and family." Marbury's biographer, Alfred Allan Lewis, painted a charming picture of their at-homes: "The scene was one of amiable disarray with not enough chairs to go around and people filling the Turkish corner, sitting on the floor and up the stairway in a daring new spirit of platonic intimacy."

One glimpse of the Castles performing at a Paris party convinced Elisabeth Marbury that here were performers who could be marketed to great advantage. "I had sensed the approach of the dancing madness," she wrote in her memoirs. "I saw the fat years ahead!" In 1912, Marbury signed the Castles, acting as their agent and as their entrée into the very important world of high society.

Irene, ordinarily money conscious, hired her old friend Gladwyn MacDougal, who had first introduced the Castles to each other, as their "personal manager." MacDougal "had a lovely sense of humor. We enjoyed having him around," which seems a minor talent to justify earning 10 percent of what would soon become a small fortune. It's uncertain how much MacDougal actually accomplished, or how he worked with the powerhouse Marbury, but the Castles kept both agent and manager on their payroll throughout the peak years of their career.

Elisabeth Marbury made sure that no opportunity for publicity, no chance for a quick buck, was passed up in the mad whirl of the early 1910s. "I obtained private engagements for them everywhere at fabulous prices," she said, not hesitating to recommend the entertainers to her friends and *their* friends. "I can recall two bookings in Washington, afternoon and evening, for which they received twenty-five hundred dollars" (and for which Marbury, as all agents, collected her percentage).

The Castles—unlike many professional dancers of the time—held the aura of social acceptability. "We were clean-cut; we were married and when we danced there was nothing suggestive about it," wrote Irene. "We made dancing look like the fun it was and so gradually we became a middle ground both sides could accept."

Mrs. Stuyvesant Fish was among the first society figures to endorse the Castles and hire them for her parties. Unlike the many of New York and Newport's "400," Mrs. Fish was a scampish woman with a great sense of humor and adventure. She once hosted a party for a mysterious prince, who turned out to be a small monkey in formal wear. (Mrs. Fish, a woman after Irene's heart, also hosted a dogs' dinner—Mrs. Fish's own dog wore a $15,000 diamond collar.) At one of Mrs. Fish's parties, Irene recalled, the hostess informed the startled Castles that she had promised her guests that a brand-new step would be introduced by them that night. "We went out and did all of our old routines down to the last step," said Irene. No one noticed, and the next day the papers proclaimed the "new dances" a hit.

High society loved the new dance steps, but not all of its members were graceful or adept. The only society figure who was a brilliant dancer and terrific partner, according to Irene, was the bulky but light-on-his-feet William Randolph Hearst. The Castles met the newspaper magnate and political hopeful in the early 1910s, before he'd met the love of his life, chorine Marion Davies. Irene became lifelong friends with Hearst and his wife, Millicent (and, in a rare triple play, with Marion Davies as well). "If I showed him a step *once*, he remembered it," said Irene of Hearst. "He also had the spring in his knees that is vital to a good dancer."

Things did not go as well at the Chatfield-Smiths' in Long Island ("Chatfield-Smith" seems to have been a pseudonym Irene used out of politeness or fear of a lawsuit). The Castles were able to get their usual fee of $100 a night (which was soon to skyrocket) and took a taxi from Manhattan to Long Island. The Chatfield-Smiths' butler greeted them at the door—and ushered them into a clothes closet, where they were to wait like strippers in a cake till the guests had finished their dinner and were ready to be entertained. "I was mad as a snake," Irene recalled. To make matters worse, the Castles were expected to fawn over their hosts and ask them to dance. The man of the house, said Irene, "stepped all over my satin slippers, puffing his Roquefort-cheese breath in my face."

The Castles were discovering that dancing, unlike acting onstage, was as much a "service industry" as Vernon's work in his family's hotel. They soon raised their prices to $300 an evening, which was willingly paid.

CHAPTER TEN

EVERYBODY'S DOING IT

To understand why the Castles became such a phenomenon, it's important to see that they came along at exactly the right time: in the early 1910s, in New York, just as ragtime music was catching its second wind and ragtime dancing was spreading like wildfire. Had they met and married five years earlier or five years later, they would have had very different lives. Had they not been so slim and attractive, had they not won the attention of society doyenne Elisabeth Marbury . . . But Vernon and Irene lucked out, and they had the talent and the ambition and energy to grab their opportunity and run with it.

The great difficulty in writing about ragtime is that there is little agreement about exactly what ragtime was. One musicologist defines it as "an instrumental composition . . . in duple meter, with a syncopated melody against a regular, oom-pah style . . . usually sixteen measures each." Another calls ragtime "a syncopated composition for the piano, written in duple time, made of three or four melodic sections of 16 or 32 measures each." Which meant nothing to the hordes of people who loved, hated, bought, danced to, and even composed "ragtime" during its heyday (roughly 1900–20). Composer and bandleader James Reese Europe wrote that "there never was any such music as 'ragtime.' 'Ragtime' is simply a nickname, or rather a fun name given to Negro rhythm by our Caucasian brother." Even Irving Berlin, composer of the most popular of "secondwave" rags, admitted, "You know, I never did find out what ragtime was."

To most people, any tune or song that was peppy, danceable, modern was a "rag," a situation not helped by record companies that willy-nilly labeled their releases rags, one-steps, tangos—whatever would help them to sell. As early as 1898, ragtime had become a national craze. In the *Witmark Monthly*, the journal of the song publishers M. Witmark & Sons, it was observed: "It's 'ragtime' here and 'ragtime' there, and it is getting to be that all 'ragtime' sounds alike to me." Historian Rudi Blesh described the heart-pounding effervescence of this new music: "Ragtime was far and away the gayest, most exciting, most infectiously lilting music ever heard . . . as healthily extrovert, as brimful of energy, as the barefoot American boy."

Vaudeville performers brought ragtime to the public. Sophie Tucker was known in her early years as "The Mary Garden of Ragtime," and Ben Harney (a singer and author of such songs as "You've Been a Good Old Wagon but You Done Broke Down") was singing rags in theaters as early as 1896. At Tony Pastor's, he was dubiously billed as "The Inventor of Ragtime."

The spread of this new music for a new century was helped partly because of new technology: older forms of music had been disseminated through sheet music, local composers and musicians, and band concerts, but with the invention of the Gramophone and the Victrola, music came directly into the home with no effort (and in a more professional, unadulterated form).

The reaction to ragtime presaged the rock 'n' roll revolution of forty years later. Classical musician Edward B. Perry compared rag to "a dog with rabies. . . . Whether it is simply a passing phase of our decadent culture or an infectious disease which has come to stay, like la grippe and leprosy, time alone can show." The magazine *Musical America* editorialized in 1913, "It exalts noise, rush and street vulgarity. It suggests repulsive dance-halls and restaurants." Another critic: "Like a criminal novel, it is full of bangs and explosions, devised in order to shake up the overworked mind."

Almost the exact same cavils would be heard against jazz, rock, rap, hip-hop. But not all old establishment figures disliked ragtime. "I can't help feeling that a person who doesn't open his heart to ragtime somehow isn't human," wrote Hiram Moderwell in the *New Republic* in 1915. "You simply can't resist it." In 1914 the *Harvard Musical Review* brushed off many objections as snobbery: "Most people seem to have a peculiar, highly sensitized faculty of closing their ears to what they are unwilling to recognize as music."

Although ragtime is said to have been "born" in 1896, the first rumblings were heard in the 1870s and '80s. The creation of black musicians in New Orleans, Chicago, and St. Louis, it all began to come together with the World's Columbia Exposition of 1893 in Chicago; amateur and professional musicians from all over the United States gathered to play, inspire, and steal from one another, and for the first time the public at large got to hear this new brand of music.

Although developed by American blacks (some of whom were African born and bred), ragtime was diverse from the first, and its earliest composers and musicians were both black and white, male and female. Most composers were young, in their late teens and twenties when bitten by the ragtime bug.

Ragtime's first acknowledged master was Scott Joplin. He was born in 1868; his father was a former slave (who had taken the name Joplin from a family that had owned him), his mother a free woman from Kentucky. Both parents were musical, and Scott Joplin's own talent showed quickly: in his boyhood home of Texarkana, Texas, he was given piano lessons by local teachers. The Joplins even spent their hard-earned and scarce cash on a piano for their son.

By the mid-1890s, Scott Joplin was adapting church music, pop tunes, marches, and classical compositions into his own peculiar style. "He did not have to play anyone else's music," an acquaintance later recalled. "He made up his own, and it was beautiful; he just got his music out of the air." He moved to St. Louis, Missouri, and refined his style, performing most often at the Silver Dollar Saloon. Joplin was not, however, the first person to publish a "ragtime song"—twenty-three rags were published in 1897; Scott Joplin's first published piece was "Maple Leaf Rag" in 1899; after a slow start, it became a hit and established his reputation.

By 1901, Joplin was billed on his sheet music as "The King of Ragtime," and few (except perhaps Ben Harney) disputed his title, although literally hundreds of composers all over the United States were churning out rags and faux rags at the time. A series of classics emerged from Joplin over the next few years: "The Easy Winners" (1901); "Elite Syncopations" and his most famous work, "The Entertainer" (both 1902); "The Cascades" and "The Chrysanthemum" (both 1904); "Bethena" (a lovely 1906 waltz); "Heliotrope Bouquet" (written with Louis Chauvin, 1907); his only tango, "Solace," and "Euphonic Sounds" (both 1909); "Magnetic Rag" (1914). But Joplin was a composer, an artist, and a man with a mission—not a hardheaded businessman. His aim was to make ragtime—"Negro music"—respectable. He spent years writing an opera, *Treemonisha*, which was not performed until decades after his death—while other composers were churning out marketable tunes and raking in (admittedly small) royalties.

Out of his sixty-some published pieces of music, forty-one were the classic piano rags for which Joplin is remembered. Heard today, his works seem closer in spirit to Chopin and Bach than to Irving Berlin—Joplin's rags are smooth, melodic, intricate, and almost stately at times. Many of them were marked "not fast" on the original sheet music. Joplin wrote *The School of Ragtime* in 1908, in which he scolded "publications masquerading under the name of ragtime." Determined to defend the reputation of his music, he continued, "Syncopations are no indication of light or trashy music, and to shy bricks at 'hateful ragtime' no longer passes for musical culture." But, sadly for Joplin, "light and trashy music" was what sold, and the deluge was about to break.

Joplin's early work was typical of first-wave ragtime, which peaked and began to decline by 1909. The second wave of ragtime hit in 1911, propelled by a different kind of composer: white, often eastern European Jews populating New York's songwriting district, Tin Pan Alley (West Twenty-eighth Street). Twenty-three-year-old Irving Berlin became the nation's most popular—or at least most heard—songwriter. The epoch-making song of 1911 was Berlin's huge success, "Alexander's Ragtime Band." It's not clear why this one tune, still sung today, has become the signature of its era—it's far from Berlin's best work, and it's not even easy to dance to (the contemporaneous "King Chanticleer," "Too Much Mustard," and "Everybody Two-Step," on the other hand, still yank you out of your seat and onto the dance floor). But "Alexander's Ragtime Band" reigned supreme and established Irving Berlin in the public's mind as the new King of Ragtime. Historian Mark Sullivan expressed the views of the upper classes when he wrote, "With 'Alexander's Ragtime Band,' Berlin lifted ragtime from the depths of sordid dives to the apotheosis of fashionable vogue."

Berlin was born Israel Baline in Russia; his family emigrated to the United States in 1893, when he was five years old. Growing up on New York's Lower East Side, "Izzy" left school to help support his family: by the time he was in his midteens, he was a singing waiter, eagerly picking out his own tunes after hours on the restaurant's piano. His first song, "Marie from Sunny Italy," was published in 1908. Berlin was a businessman as much as a composer and lyricist: he wrote what sold, be it nostalgic ("I Want to Go Back to Michigan"), sentimental ("When I Lost You"), humorous ("How Do You Do It, Mabel, on Twenty Dollars a Week?"), flirtatious ("Kiss Me My Honey, Kiss Me"). He wrote dialect songs of every sort ("Sweet Marie, Make-a Rag-a-time Dance Wid Me," "Colored Romeo," "Abie Sings an Irish Song," "Yiddisha Nightingale"). And, of course, rags: by 1913 his entries included "Yiddle, on Your Fiddle, Play Some Ragtime," "Draggy Rag," "That Opera Rag," "Oh, That Beautiful Rag," "The Ragtime Jockey Man," "That Mysterious Rag." His catchy "Everybody's Doing It Now" (1911) became a battle cry of the times:

> Everybody's doing it (doing it, doing it)
> Everybody's doing it (doing it, doing it)
> See that ragtime couple over there—
> Watch them throw their shoulders in the air
> Snap their fingers, honey I declare
> It's a bear, it's a bear, it's a bear!

And yes, "Everybody's doing it" was a double entendre in 1911 as much as today. The song promptly spawned parodies and tributes, such as "I Can't Stop Doing It" and "I Love to Do It."

Some of the second-wave ragtime tunes have become standards: "The Grizzly Bear" (with Irving Berlin's lyrics, it was a 1910 hit for Sophie Tucker), "Hitchy-Koo" (1912), "Waiting for the Robert E. Lee" (1912), "Ballin' the Jack" (1913), "That International Rag" (Berlin again, 1913). The lyrics of that last song were quite accurate:

> London dropped its dignity
> So has France and Germany
> All hands are dancing to a raggedy melody
> Full of originality
> The folks who live in sunny Spain
> Dance to a strain
> That they call the Spanish Tango
> Dukes and Lords and Russian Czars
> Men who own their motor cars
> Throw up their shoulders to that raggedy melody
> Full of originality
> Italian opera singers have learned to snap their fingers
> The world goes 'round to the sound of the International Rag!

The *Daily Express* said much the same thing, less musically, in 1913: "In every London restaurant, park and theatre you hear [Berlin's] strains; Paris dances to it; Vienna has forsaken the waltz; Madrid has flung away her castanets, and Venice has forgotten her barcarolles. Ragtime has swept like a whirlwind over the earth." In 1912 *Collier's* editor Norman Hapgood complained that between showings of movies at a theater, the audience was subjected to sing-alongs of "The Oceana Roll," "Alexander's Ragtime Band," and "That Raggy Rag."

This new surge of ragtime owed much to eastern European klezmer music, probably because many of the younger composers and musicians grew up listening to it. Klezmer—still popular today—developed in the seventeenth century, deriving its name from the klezmorim, traveling musicians who played at everything from weddings to funerals. When the klezmorim began coming to the United States in the late nineteenth century, their music came with them: the sprightly dance tunes (*bulgarisch, freylehk, serba,* and the still-familiar *hora*) seeped into American popular music. Indeed, James Reese Europe's 1914 recording of "Castle House Rag" sounds like perfect klezmer.

The year 1913 was one of cultural, artistic jolts: on February 17, the Armory Show opened in New York, giving Americans their first disquieting glimpse of Cézanne, Picasso, Gauguin, Edward Hopper, and Marcel Duchamp's infamous *Nude Descending a Staircase.* "Modernistic" and "cubistic" became synonyms for everything new and dissonant. London's *Daily Sketch* openly compared the "Ragtime Craze" to "the cult of the ugly as perpetrated by M. Matisse and M. Cézanne." (Oddly, the year's most scandalous painting was the old-fashioned, classical nude *September Morn,* which became a cause célèbre when professional do-gooder Anthony Comstock ordered it removed from an art dealer's window.) That summer, Stravinsky's *Le sacre du printemps* premiered in Paris, causing a riot in the audience. The sixty-story Woolworth "skyscraper" opened in Manhattan. Everywhere, it seemed, there was change and growth in 1913: New York's spanking-new vaudeville house, the Palace, opened; many typically twentieth-century products made their debuts in 1913: zippers, Lifesavers candy, Brillo pads, Henry Ford's assembly line.

With the onslaught of the new, of course, the old got swept aside, and that included the classic old-style rag, along with its proponents. By the mid-1910s, Scott Joplin and his wife, Lottie, were living in Harlem, just keeping their heads above water. While in midtown Manhattan, the newer, more commercial ragtime was being published, Joplin continued to deride what had become of "his" music while working on his unmarketable symphonies and operas. He died at the age of forty-nine in 1917. By that time, even Irving Berlin's style of ragtime was being supplanted by a newer form of pop music just rising out of the South and Midwest: jazz.

CHAPTER ELEVEN

"TWO ADOLESCENT PALM TREES"

In the autumn of 1912, an opportunity arose for the Castles to gain some public notice. In September, producer Charles Dillingham signed Vernon to appear in *The Lady of the Slipper*, a musical comedy retelling of Cinderella. Twenty-three-year-old rising star Elsie Janis was cast in the leading role, with the comedy team of Montgomery and Stone backing her up. Janis, who described herself as "an ambitious puppy, striving to please but with one eye on the thickness of my part," was accompanied everywhere, including auditions and rehearsals, by her notorious stage mother.

Vernon was handed a nice little role, not too demanding, with a lot of dancing. Irene, on the other hand, was not happy. Dillingham had written her into the show on Vernon's insistence (and also because Irene's star was beginning to rise). But it could hardly be called a role. Aside from one second-act dance with Vernon, she was to introduce acts and scenes, dressed as a harlequin. Enter one side, prettily display a title card, then off. It "could have been played by a robot," she complained.

Worse still, their combined salaries hardly paid enough for rent and clothes, let alone making up for what they'd lose by staying with *The Lady of the Slipper;* the Castles would have to give up their highly paid private parties and lessons; only the midnight gig at the Café de l'Opera would still be a possibility.

Vernon, who never cared much about money and was happy to be back onstage, didn't mind. But Irene was determined to get out of the show—how to do so, though, without breaking her Dillingham contract and risking a lawsuit? Irene's solution was typical of her daring and single-mindedness. She simply got herself fired.

Elsie Janis recalled the bombshell arrival and departure of the Castles, who "looked like two adolescent palm trees." At a dress rehearsal in Philadelphia, Janis recalled, Irene entered in a modern Paris hobble-skirted gown and "suddenly pulled up her skirts like a naughty little girl, showing her 'complete understanding.' . . . Mother's gasp of dismay must have been heard in Trenton!" Irene shamelessly recalled herself "skipping all over the stage with my bare legs showing, then I dropped the train and modestly wiggled off."

Elsie Janis and her mother, Charles Dillingham, Victor Herbert (the show's composer), the director, and the authors all descended on Irene, as Vernon casually leaned back and kept out of the way. They raged, they pleaded, they tried to reason: but Irene, as a "dance specialty," had contracted approval of her costume and insisted that adding chiffon or panels would ruin the line and ruin her dance. So the dance, and Irene, were removed from the show, with no financial penalty. "The joke was decidedly on us," said the show-businesswise Janis.

The Lady of the Slipper opened at the Globe Theater (now the Lunt-Fontanne) at Forty-sixth and Broadway on October 28, 1912, with Vernon and without Irene. Vernon stayed with the show till shortly after the New York opening, commuting from Philadelphia (about two hours,) then hurrying from the Globe to the Café de l'Opera in time for their midnight performance.

Meanwhile, Charles Frohman was producing a musical called *The Sunshine Girl* at the Knickerbocker Theater on Broadway and Thirty-eighth Street. Frohman (who would become, in 1915, one of the more famous casualties of the *Lusitania* sinking) was one of the few really well-liked theatrical producers in New York. A froglike man of great humor and goodwill, he was known as a star maker, ushering Maude Adams, Billie Burke, Ethel Barrymore, and others to the top of the heap. Elisabeth Marbury convinced him to cast Vernon in a sizeable supporting role, as "Lord Bicester, known as Bingo, a young stockbroker." The show starred the peaches-and-cream blonde Julia Sanderson, already a minor star (she would become a major star the next year in *The Girl from Utah*). Vernon scored first billing on the program, as his was the first character onstage; he performed five numbers in this show. In act 1, Vernon sang "Josephine" with a passel of chorus girls and a duet with the star, Sanderson, called "Ladies." In act 2, he sang (and, of course, danced) to "Little Girl, Mind How You Go," "Who's the Boss?" and "In Your Defense."

At the insistence of Elisabeth Marbury and both Castles, Irene was given a slender spot in the show, billed simply as "Mrs. Vernon Castle." She appeared in the middle of act 2, after Vernon's "Little Girl" number, and danced with her husband for the first time before a large audience. Irene's beauty and her flowing, chic gowns were a big draw, helping to get the Castle name and image before the public while Marbury slowly built the couple's "brand."

The Sunshine Girl opened on February 3, 1913, and ran for a very respectable 181 performances, closing in September. The *New York Times* liked the show, Julia Sanderson, and this non-Fieldsian Vernon, "now happily allowed to appear something near human, and accompanied in his fascinating dancing by the lovely Mrs. Castle." The *Washington Star* also singled out the Castles' "wonderful performance," and the *New York Evening Sun* wrote that Vernon "ran away with the lion's share of the honors . . . original, unique, delightful" and was able to carry off musical numbers "without one shred of voice" (agent Marbury herself admitted that both Castles' singing was "somewhat painful"). This *Sun* review was one to clip and save: Vernon and Irene's dance duet was "easily the one sensation of the night. . . . Vernon Castle was the name on everyone's lips as the audience left the theater." Marbury and Frohman's gamble was a huge success: the early spring of 1913 saw the rise of the Castles as a team—but, sadly, the end of Vernon's fame and success as a comic actor.

During the run of the show, he sat for one of his first interviews, for *Metropolitan* magazine. The reporter found him between scenes in his dressing room, surrounded by costumes hanging on pegs and a small icebox full of "magnums of grape juice, *un*fermented." When asked about the social propriety of dancing the tango, Vernon snapped, "Vulgar people will make any dance vulgar. Even the waltz is not nice when vulgar people dance it."

He went on to show he was already dissecting and analyzing dance steps from a teacher's perspective, stating that "people rarely have the patience to learn to do it [the tango] well." The tango was harder to learn than the waltz, said Vernon, because "you have to dance against time—to let a note go by while you're doing no step at all. You must keep a little bit behind the music rather than all on a note as in the turkey trot or waltz."

Around the same time, the first in what would become a flood of newsmen came sniffing around Irene, too. She modestly told a *Cosmopolitan* reporter, "My husband is a professional, and I am glad to be a helpful amateur." *Cosmopolitan* went on to be the first to comment on her "dark eyes, languishing smile, and the lissome grace of a Persian odalisque." It wouldn't be long before Irene's charms would become more interesting to the press than Vernon's views of the dance.

Green Book reporter Ada Patterson cornered Irene in her dressing room for a chat, finding her surrounded by cut flowers and balancing Wallop, "a tiny, shaggy brown terrier," on her knee. Unlike Vernon, Irene did not claim to be an expert on dance—either as a performer or historian—and told Patterson her real ambition was "to leave off dancing when she is twenty-five. To have a permanent home at New Rochelle. To have a good-sized family."

While performing in *The Sunshine Girl,* the Castles moonlighted one night in April to appear at a fund-raising benefit for women's suffrage, showing both their advanced political views and their burgeoning popularity. They were joined at the Belasco Theater by such luminaries as Jane Cowl, Margaret Wycherly, and artist James Montgomery Flagg. Actors gave readings, artists drew portraits, the Castles danced, and Vernon auctioned off a Flagg portrait of his wife for $31.

As the weather heated up in the early summer of 1913, Irene wilted; she left *The Sunshine Girl* rather precipitously and boarded a ship for Europe. She begged Vernon to accompany her, but as Irene's mother put it, "Vernon was far too conscientious for that, and remained two weeks longer, patiently drilling a man to take his place." The separate sailings raised the first rumors in the press that the Castles might be on the verge of a split.

In the summer of 1913, Vernon and Irene were engaged for another round of performances at the Café de Paris, and the Casino de Deauville in Normandy. They hobnobbed with vacationing American socialites, now their acquaintances, if not friends, and Irene began a flirtation that may have become a decade-long affair.

In her memoirs, Irene reproduces a photo of herself and the breathtakingly handsome Grand Duke Dmitri, taken in the 1920s. Dmitri Pavlovich Romanov, Grand Duke of Russia, was two years older than Irene, making him just twenty-two when they met in 1913. A nephew of Czar Alexander III and first cousin of the then-current czar, Nicholas II, Dmitri would, in three years, be involved in the torturous assassination of Rasputin. But in 1913, he was better known as a flighty playboy. "When we danced he swooped me around the floor with long steps, leading firmly but carelessly," said Irene, still breathless over him years later.

Dmitri trailed the Castles around Paris and kidnapped the more than willing Irene for trips to nightclubs, long drives in the country, 4:00 A.M. breakfasts at Maxim's, and goodness knows what else. While the unsuspecting (or very good-natured) Vernon visited his family in England, Dmitri agreed to keep Irene "from being lonely." He showered her with orchids and jewels from Cartier's, took her to the opera, and, one night, lunged for her in his motorcar. Irene claimed to have shed a few tears of pretty distress and rushed to her husband's side in England.

Considering Irene's very healthy sexual appetite, Dmitri's dashing good looks, Vernon's laissez-faire attitude, and the fact that she was still seeing Dmitri a decade later, the possibility certainly exists that Irene, two years into her marriage, was willing to have her head turned.

CHAPTER TWELVE

"Gowns are more or less a business with me"

Not having succeeded in turning Elsie de Wolfe into a star, Elisabeth Marbury set her sights on Irene Castle: twenty years old, slim as a reed, with perfect "camera bones" and a sense of self-entitlement worthy of an opera diva, Irene was material ready for the molding. Marbury was well aware of the popularity of publicity photos and their ability to create and sustain stardom. Actresses such as Adah Isaacs Mencken and Lily Langtry became as well known for their publicity photos as for their performances. By 1910, the art of the publicist was at its early peak. People who would never see Irene Castle dance could still marvel at her beauty and innovative fashion sense in newspapers and magazines.

Through Elsie de Wolfe's connections, Irene had found a clothing designer who was perfectly in tune with her chic, pared-down style. "Lucile" (also known as Lady Duff-Gordon after her 1900 marriage) had been in the fashion business since the late 1890s. The younger sister of wildly over-the-top authoress Elinor Glyn, Lucile had conquered London, Paris, and New York by the early 1910s. Her designs were noted for their long, sleek look, low necklines, and slit skirts—tailor-made (literally) for Irene Castle. She wrote fashion advice columns for William Randolph Hearst. "I would create tea gowns and ball dresses, dainty little frocks for debutantes and sophisticated models that looked the last word in wickedness," Lucile reminisced. "It is a lesser form of art, I know, but to me it meant a great deal, my life's work and I was tremendously in earnest over every dress I created."

Irene had Lucile send her three or four gowns a week, at a huge cost. Irene was clearheaded about what styles suited her as a woman and as a dancer. "Gowns are more or less a business with me," she said; "they're part of my stock in trade. Anything fussy detracts from my dancing. I must wear only young-looking things and I won't wear clothes that fly up and hit you in the face." Legend has it that Irene Castle "abolished the corset," but this was not the case: "The well-fitting corset is a support, especially for the spine," she said in 1915. "I should be sorry to see it go." But she hoped that "they will become less cumbersome; they will be so made that they will be an aid to a woman, not a handicap."

She sensibly added, "My idea of dress is to wear what is individually becoming to you regardless of whether it is supposed to be stylish or not," advice that still holds true today. The future animal rights activist added, "Of furs I cannot have too many. . . . The pelts of all the gray and white foxes in the world would not satiate me."

Despite her talent, Lucile was a dangerous choice as a designer in 1913—her reputation had been tarnished by the questionable conduct of the Duff-Gordons aboard the *Titanic* in 1912. When the ship foundered on April 14, the Duff-Gordons and their maid wound up in lifeboat 1 with only nine other people, though it was equipped to carry forty. Lucile was grilled at the *Titanic* hearings as to why her boat was so empty, and why it did not go back to rescue others. A chatty and heartless newspaper article about her experiences on (and off) the *Titanic* under her name also caused her grief: Lucile denied writing it and claimed that a *London Daily News* reporter had made the whole thing up. "Lucile" was not a name to be associated with in 1913, and it was brave of the Castles to take her up.

Irene loyally continued to patronize Lucile well into the 1920s, after she'd become passé. Lucile declared bankruptcy in 1923, by which time Irene was creating her own clothes. The designer, who is today better known as a *Titanic* survivor than for her life's work, died, broke, in 1935.

Irene's fame rose just on the crest of a huge change in women's fashions. The so-called flapper look of the 1920s is associated with shorter skirts, bobbed hair, long, lean lines—all of which were popularized by Irene Castle before World War I.

Up till 1908, the Gibson Girl look was still the reigning mode: the bustle was long gone, but chic women still looked like hourglasses in their corsets and wore acres of petticoats, loosely piled mounds of hair, elaborate hats. The great change began with Paul Poiret's 1908 collection and the costumes of the Ballets Russes, designed by Leon Bakst. What began as a fashion aberration became a rush to couturiers all over the world, and fashions changed as radically as they ever would in the twentieth century. Gone was the wasp-waisted corset. Hair was worn closer to the head, and tea-tray hats were replaced by turbans and wraps. The waistline rose upward into an Empire look; skirts became shorter and leaner (brief, bizarre experiments in the early 1910s such as hobble and lampshade skirts never caught on but survive in fashion prints of the day). The fauvist paintings of Matisse, Dufy, Rouault, and Utrillo contributed bright, violent colors and sharp angles to fashion designs.

A typical fashion photo or drawing of 1913, when placed next to one of 1907, looks as if it came from a different century, more as if they depicted a grandmother and granddaughter. So the world was more than ready for an Irene Castle to model and embody the new look: she was beautiful, slim, and moved like a dream, and women imagined that they, too, could look like Irene in short hair, a lightly corseted figure, and flowing chiffon. Reality was not always so kind; matronly women looked better in the Gibson Girl fashions. The 1910s were not a good time to be middle-aged or zaftig.

It was also not a good time for women who look ghastly in short hair (and they are legion). By 1914, the Castle Bob was becoming a fad in many circles, to the horror of husbands and fathers. "All the smart hairdressers are kept busy snipping with their gleaming shears at all the pretty little budding debutantes' heads, and not a few full-blown ones, besides," noted a December 1914 newspaper piece. "Bob pins" (later called bobby pins) became a necessity for keeping short, flyaway hair in order.

And once it was off, growing it back was a problem: "I want to let my hair grow," said Irene herself, "but I lack the courage to face that dreadful in-between stage. I have started many times, but always weakened when my hair looked too long and straggly to wear down and was not long enough to put up." She also confessed to nervousness about the future, asking if one can "grow old and gray, still with short hair? Will it not seem a bit kittenish and not quite dignified?"

Huge hats and big hair, Irene declared, were "out." "A top-heavy or uncomfortable head dress is as difficult to dance with as shoes that are painful . . . if [a woman's] hair is in danger of sliding down, or she is wearing a heavy hat that will not stay in place, she is sure to hold her head stiffly and ungracefully."

Newspapers ran complimentary articles about Irene's style and horrified articles about the growing fad of women cutting their long, flowing hair. "They saw Mrs. V. Castle's bobbed hair and the handwriting on the wall at the same time," wrote a *Cleveland Leader* reporter. "Every woman in her heart knew intuitively that a new style in hair had been set. . . . Sooner or later their lovely long tresses would have to go." The article interviewed two recent converts, one of whom cried all night after having twenty years' growth chopped off and made into a switch; another woman "tossed her head defiantly and said she was glad she had done it." The "flapper style" of the 1920s had been born—in the early 1910s.

One of Irene's early fans was teenaged Cecil Beaton, who went on to become a world-renowned photographer, costume designer, diarist, gadabout, and insufferable snob. Beaton felt that Irene Castle and French music hall star Gaby Deslys were the two most influential fashion figures of their day (Deslys was known for her bizarre, surrealistic hats). "When Mrs. Vernon Castle suddenly appeared," said Beaton in his book *The Glass of Fashion*, "she was greeted with the shock of recognition that people always reserve for those who—as Wordsworth once said—create the taste by which they are to be appreciated. . . . It is no coincidence that Stravinsky's early music and Picasso's cubist period coincided with the success of a woman who was to be one of the most remarkable fashion figures the world has known. Mrs. Castle was as important an embodiment of the 'modern' in the social and fashion sense as these artists were in the world of art."

Quite a burden for a woman barely out of her teens to shoulder, but Irene was up to it in terms of energy, imagination, and unflappable self-confidence. If the fashions of the day did not suit her, she adapted them: "I could not dance in a hobble skirt, therefore I wore simple flowing gowns, that would leave my legs free. When we danced in Paris I could not afford jewelry to compete with the patrons so I went to the other extreme and wore none at all." Another innovation was the Castle Band, worn across the forehead to keep her short hair in place. Irene had very fine, flyaway hair, and early in her career she improvised a headband made from a pearl necklace: by the next week newspapers were advertising Castle Bands to keep your Castle Bob in place.

Irene's influence can be compared to Jackie Kennedy's fifty years later. Indeed, their styles were much the same: simple, elegant, expensive, well suited to their fine-boned features. As Beaton noted, "There was something terrifically healthy and clean about her. . . . Mrs. Castle put the backbone to femininity, showing its vertebrae instead of its dimples, and was thus an important reflection of the social attitude of her period, an embodiment of woman's declared emancipation."

Vernon never really became a style icon, but he was also very fashion-forward (he wore wristwatches before World War I made them popular). By 1915, he had made the tailless evening coat acceptable. It was also a necessity: while dancing in cramped restaurants and crowded parties, he found that his tails were sweeping glasses off tables and into laps or slapping people in the face. Off came the tails, and a new fashion was born, "an effect similar to the jaunty cut of an Eton jacket."

All this fame, Irene found, had its downside. She hated interviews and had very little patience with reporters who either asked stupid questions or expected her to carry the conversation. Mostly, though, she became acquainted with false friends, the bane of the celebrity. "People will be very nice to us," she said to a *Green Book* reporter, "and we'll like them ever so well—and then they'll ask us to dance for them. Then a fellow's heart takes a flop. Sometimes I get the horrid feeling that everybody is nice to me not because they like me, but because they think they can get something out of me. That's a terrible feeling, isn't it? Because everybody likes to be just liked."

Chapter Thirteen

"The best dancing music in the world"

If Elisabeth Marbury invented and promoted the Castles' look and public profile, James Reese Europe was largely responsible for their sound. The composer, musician, and bandleader was an imposing figure: tall, solidly built, with a stern, serious gaze. He was born in 1880 in Mobile, Alabama, to a former slave (his father, who later went to law school at Howard University) and a freeborn mother. Highly educated and ambitious, the Europes and their children moved to Washington, D.C., in 1889. Musical talent ran in the family, and young James learned the piano from his mother.

Europe entered show business as musical director for the all-black show *A Trip to Africa* (1904) and went on to fill the same duties with *The Shoo-Fly Regiment* and *The Black Politician* before composing and conducting began to attract his interest. Forceful, intelligent, and dedicated to the cause of black musicians, in 1910 Europe helped to found the Clef Club, a combination booking agency, unofficial union, and social club (and was elected its first president). In 1911, while the Castles were still finding their feet, James Reese Europe was a star in New York musical circles, giving band concerts, filling his Clef Club duties, and playing at dances (often at white society people's homes). In May 1912 came true stardom when the Clef Club Orchestra played "A Symphony of Negro Music" at Carnegie Hall; it was so popular that the event was repeated in 1913 and 1914. His orchestra played at dances for President Wilson's daughter and for the governor of Virginia, at Boston's Copley Hall and at the Manhattan Casino.

Europe's Society Orchestra signed with Victor Records in 1913, the first-known black orchestra to obtain a U.S. recording contract. In late 1913 and early 1914, the orchestra was in Victor's New York recording studio, cutting a series of brilliant, trend-setting discs. (Thanks to modern technology, many of these are available on CD or on the Internet and are well worth searching for.) Europe's recordings are still exciting to listen to: ragtime, but with a little John Philip Sousa and a little klezmer and a little early jazz. The strong percussion and strings blended with the clarinet and brass into a distinctive voice, and the energy and athleticism of the music still comes through after more than ninety years. His "Castle House Rag" (recorded on February 10, 1914) in particular is bouncy and infectious—instead of using the then-popular woodblocks or a drumbeat to accent the breaks, Europe chose a bell-like chime, giving the strong, raggy tune exactly the lighter-than-air feeling the Castles epitomized; and the band members, on "Too Much Mustard," shouted out in (carefully planned) "spontaneous" glee. Europe's "Too Much Mustard" is one of the loosest and most delightful covers of that terrific song.

The Castles probably met James Reese Europe on August 22, 1913, at a Newport, Rhode Island, party given by Mrs. Stuyvesant Fish, but they did not get the opportunity to dance to his music till that autumn. At a private party—the identity of the host has been lost to history—Vernon and Irene were accompanied by Europe's Society Orchestra, and a whole new world opened to them. Too many dance bands of the day were still adjusting to ragtime and had a lead-footed "oompah" sound to them. Vernon was always quick to remind audiences that Europe's was "the best dancing music in the world," and Europe was delighted to find such famous and good-natured stars to accompany. Vernon and Europe became fast friends; Europe called Vernon "one white absolutely without prejudice."

Vernon also befriended Europe's wildly talented drummer, Buddie Gilmore, to Irene's dismay. Suddenly, Vernon was seized by one of his periodic ambitions: he wanted to become a drummer. Gilmore was more than happy to tutor Vernon, who bought a complete set of drums and invited Gilmore over for lessons. Vernon incorporated comedy into his drumming, tossing his sticks about and making faces, so his enthusiasm and personality made up for whatever finesse and training he may have lacked.

Vernon did not lack much in the way of practice, according to his long-suffering wife: "Drumming is all very well in a restaurant . . . but in a house, beginning almost before breakfast and ending some time after midnight, it becomes a little trying," said Irene. "I can remember often imploring him to take up something quieter." On some weekends, Europe and composer, pianist, and bandleader Ford Dabney would show up, and piano music as well as drums would ring out over the neighborhood for hours on end.

In April 1914, the Castles were invited by Europe as guests to his National Negro Orchestra benefit at the Manhattan Casino—some twenty-five hundred paying attendees saw the Castles dance to Europe's music. The Castles' friendship with Europe and his band also gave them entrée to the burgeoning community of Harlem, in northern Manhattan. With the opening of the subway in the early 1900s and the influx of blacks streaming in from the South (New York's black population increased by 66 percent in the 1910s), the fabled Harlem Renaissance was just dawning. Europe took the Castles to the newest uptown nightclubs and dance halls, long before the age of the Cotton Club. At some establishments, they were the only whites allowed in, and only if they were accompanied by a black "sponsor." Listening to black musicians and watching black dancers kept the Castles' repertoire fresh and varied.

James Reese Europe signed with Joseph W. Stern & Company, one of the biggest publishers of sheet music. In the spring of 1914, Stern issued fifteen compositions by Europe (some of them cowritten by his frequent associate Ford Dabney). Ten of these were related to the Castles (of course, they might have been previously composed numbers, ready to have a marketable "Castle" label slapped on them). The most popular were the "Castle House Rag" and the "Castle Walk" (both labeled "trot and one step"). Also released by Europe's orchestra that season were "Castles in Europe" ("Innovation Trot"), "Castles' Half and Half," "Castle Maxixe," "Castle Innovation Tango," "Castle Combination Waltz," "Castle Perfect Trot," and two versions of "Castles' Lame Duck Waltz." A year later, in March 1915, came "The Castle Doggy Fox Trot." It must be stressed that these were only a small portion of the music composed by James Reese Europe between 1908 and 1919.

The 1910s were a particularly touchy time for a white dance team and a black orchestra to be associating publicly and spreading good racial cheer. On the one hand, a young generation of black Americans, born after the end of slavery, was moving north for better jobs and more social freedom; the NAACP was founded in 1909 and the National Urban League in 1911. But on the other hand, a huge, sometimes violent backlash was also taking place. In 1912, black heavyweight champion Jack Johnson caused public outrage by marrying a white woman; in 1913, President Woodrow Wilson officially introduced segregation into the federal government; in 1915, D. W. Griffith's brilliant but racist *The Birth of a Nation* resulted in riots and protests; an estimated fifty to sixty blacks were lynched annually through the 1910s.

James Reese Europe may have been a public hero to some, but he also had to fight resistance from black civic leaders, some of whom decried dancing and ragtime as much as their white counterparts. Adam Clayton Powell preached that "the Negro race is dancing itself to death," and in some circles Europe was seen as a race traitor rather than a pioneer. Europe angrily answered, "I have found that dancing keeps husbands and wives together and eliminates much drinking, as no one can dance and drink to excess." That the casual racism of the times went both ways can be seen in Europe's statement: "The Negro plays ragtime as if it was a second nature to him—as it is. . . . Our symphony orchestra never tries to play white folks' music. We should be foolish to attempt such a thing. We are no more fitted for that than a white orchestra is fitted to play our music." In 1915, Europe claimed that blacks possessed "a superior sense of rhythm."

This brings us inevitably and uncomfortably to the word "coon," which both Vernon and Irene used freely. While not as pejorative as "nigger," it was a certainly not a nice word, even in the 1910s. But it was widely used in show business circles: "coon songs," "coon shouters" (blackface singers), "coon bands" were terms used by white and black artists alike. The main reason the word was so beloved by songwriters was laziness; it rhymed with nearly everything: spoon, moon, June, tune. Language historians cite "coon" as meaning a frontier rustic in the early 1800s; by the 1860s, however, coon had come to mean a black person—and the popularity of coon songs continued well through the 1910s. Titles that did not raise an eyebrow at the time included "If the Man in the Moon Were a Coon," "Mammy's Little Pumpkin-Colored Coons," "The Coon with the Yaller Streak." Music publisher Isadore Witmark noted that "All Coons Look Alike to Me," written and composed by black musician Ernest Hogan, "became so popular . . . that his own people took offense; his tune became for him a source of unending misery, and he died regretting that he had written it."

And of course there was a casual racism in songs even without the "coon" label. "May Irwin's Bully Song" is unlistenable to today, and any number of now-horrifying titles were published and happily sung less than one hundred years ago: "Dar'll Be a Nigger Missing," "My Little Zulu Babe," "Pickaninny Nig." Some coon songs remain popular today: "Darktown Strutter's Ball," "Waiting for the Robert E. Lee," "Bill Bailey" (ponder a moment on the line about the "fine-toothed comb").

Though blacks got far more than their fair share of abuse, it was not an era of delicate feelings, and popular songs poked lethal fun at Asians ("Down in Winky, Blinky, Chinky Chinatown"), Italians ("I'll Take You Back to Italy," in which the singer at one point tells her husband, "We'll have a leedle wop"), Irish ("O'Brien is Tryin' to Learn to Talk Hawaiian," "The Mick Who Threw the Brick"), Jews ("Sadie Salome, Go Home," "Since Henry Ford Apologized to Me"); there were songs making fun of stutterers, fat people, country rubes, lazy men, and gold-digging women ... No one was safe, and anyone who complained was brushed off for being a poor sport.

CHAPTER FOURTEEN

"MORE LIKE A PAIR OF SCHOOLCHILDREN"

A good many dance teams came and went without leaving a permanent mark on history. Who today remembers Frances Demarest and Joseph C. Smith, Jack Jarrott and Louise Alexander, or the Marvelous Millers? Still, many soon-to-be-famous personalities made their debuts as imitation Castles. The teenaged brother-sister team Fred and Adele Astaire studied and copied the Castles carefully. French music hall star Mistinguett discovered and tutored (in more ways than one) her young partner, Maurice Chevalier; their style was more acrobatic and sexier then the Castles' (some feel they popularized, if not invented, the Apache dance). Vernon's *About Town* pal Mae Murray successfully teamed with future stage and film star Clifton Webb. Both Bonnie Glass (in 1915) and Joan Sawyer (in 1916) partnered an elegant youth billed as Signor Rodolpho—he soon changed his name to Rudolph Valentino and became the biggest film star of the 1920s. Evelyn Nesbit, the infamous "Girl in the Red Velvet Swing" from the 1906 Stanford White murder case, entered the fray as a dancer (partnered by Jack Clifford).

Even teenaged George Burns, in his pre–Gracie Allen days, got into the act. "The tango was the dance of the day, and I went in for it in a big way," he later deadpanned. "My sideburns were the talk of Second Avenue." Burns earned spare cash through the dance contests that proliferated at this time: "I was one up on the other contestant because I had two steady partners. Big Rose Cohen and Little Rose Cohen. Big Rose Cohen was a wonderful tango dancer, and Little Rose Cohen did a terrific Peabody. I was pretty well fixed to win a contest with either one or the other of them."

Dance historian Julie Malnig notes in *Dancing Till Dawn* that many of these dance teams were managed by the female partner: even dizzy little Mae Murray had a financial interest in the Folies Marigny and acted as her own agent. Joan Sawyer ran the Persian Garden Room in Times Square and did all the hiring and firing; Bonnie Glass managed the Café Montmartre and ran through a series of male partners.

The Castles' chief competitor was the sleek, handsome Maurice Mouvet (always billed just as "Maurice"), a handsome man of great ego and mysterious background. He was born in 1888, in New York, Paris, or Belgium, depending on which source one believes, and was a star by 1907, when he performed the tango and the wildly violent Apache dance in Paris. Maurice, who claimed he learned the dance "from one of the original Gunmen of Paris," performed it at the Café de Paris with his first partner, Leonara Hughes (who died in 1910). Julian Street called Maurice, in 1912, "the king-pin of the cabaret, high priest of the decadent dance. . . . There was a rumor that, in the violence of a dance, he had once (and once is enough) broken his woman partner's neck. . . . Almost every cabaret in New York has its Maurice."

Maurice had been a hardworking dancer and a star before Vernon ever met Irene; he saw the Castles as amateurs and upstarts, and this dislike was heartily reciprocated. Irene reiterated the rumor that he killed his first wife in an Apache dance and sniffed that he and his second wife, Florence Walton, copied from the Castles: "I have heard that imitation is the greatest form of flattery. If so, Florence was flattering me to pieces."

In the introduction to his 1914 book, *The Tango and the New Dances for Ballroom and Home,* Maurice is modestly described as "without question one of the most wonderful dancers of modern times. . . . He is the most popular dancing instructor society ever engaged. Most of the four hundred who took up the latest dances took private instructions from him." So much for the Castles.

Despite his glamour and air of mystery and menace, he was a good ambassador for the dance. The sinuous tango, Maurice wrote, "is no more suggestive nor immoral from any viewpoint than the most dainty old fashioned waltz. Indeed, if the dancer wished to dance in a suggestive manner, the old fashioned waltz presents just as available a medium as the modern tango. To condemn the dance for the fault of the dancer is manifestly unfair, and yet that is precisely what has been done in the case of the Tango."

To the critics of the dance, Maurice parried, "the older order of the dances is passing away. . . . It is the old tale of new times, new people, new customs. The new music crept in and caught the popular ear, the new dance steps had to follow. Ballroom dancing was dead practically. The onslaught of the syncopated rhythms gave it life. The newest steps are practically kindergarten steps. Any child can do them. . . . I maintain, and this heartily, that the new dances with their bracing, crisp measures, their insistent action and their whirlwind rate of speed are the nearest approach to childhood games that have ever penetrated adult ballrooms in the guise of amusement."

By now, the Castles had moved into the family home at 120 Lexington Avenue (it's not known if Irene paid rent to her sister, the co-owner; one hopes so). It was not then, and is not now, a fashionable neighborhood, but it was clean, respectable, and convenient—the Lexington Avenue subway had been completed in 1904, and there was a convenient stop at Twenty-ninth Street and what is now called Park Avenue South.

New York in the early 1910s was perhaps at its loveliest: the marble confections of Grand Central Terminal and Pennsylvania Station; the New York Times building on Times Square, not yet stripped down and uglified; the stately New York Public Library on Fifth Avenue; the Flat-iron Building; the late, lamented Madison Square Garden; and the breathtaking, gaudy mansions lining Fifth Avenue. There were, it's true, the dark, clattering els up and down Second, Third, Sixth, and Ninth avenues, but New York at the dawn of the Castles' fame was easily as beautiful and elegant as London, Paris, or Berlin.

The Castles' typical daily routine in the year 1913 saw Vernon rise at 9:00 A.M., after maybe six hours' sleep, tops; he and Irene breakfasted at 9:30 (if the publicity photos are to be believed—in reality, Irene may still have been snuggled in bed). Then uptown to a rented studio, where Vernon's time was divided into half hours from 10:00 A.M. till 1:00 P.M.—he gave dancing lessons to New York's elite and their children. A dollar a minute was his fee: twenty minutes' instruction time, five minutes on either end to greet one customer, bid good-bye to another, and perhaps vanish for a bathroom or cigarette break. Not all of his customers were women; Vernon always had a female dancer on hand so he could teach men as well. He would demonstrate a step, let the lady take over, and lightly, amusingly, chirp dos and don'ts to his male stand-in.

From 1:30 to 2:00, Vernon had lunch, then back to the grind: more classes from 2:00 to 6:00. Irene met him for dinner at 6:45; she was never much of a cook, so they either ate at a restaurant or trusted their cook to serve them at home. At 7:30 P.M., the Castles arrived at the Knickerbocker Theater to put on their costumes and makeup for that evening's performance of *The Sunshine Girl;* after the curtain fell at 11:00 or thereabouts, their day was not over. Far from it: they washed off their stage makeup and dashed up the street to the Café de l'Opera, where they danced several sets from 11:45 till 2:30 A.M., when the sidewalks rolled up in Times Square. One of the thrills of seeing *The Sunshine Girl* was following the stars up the street, patting them on the back, and asking for a dance (Vernon frequently said yes; Irene almost always said no).

By 3:00 A.M., the tired couple took a taxicab home—one hopes Louis Martin had one waiting for them at the door, though cabs cannot have been hard to come by at closing time in Midtown (then, as now, a cabdriver would balk at taking them the unprofitable few blocks back to their home).

Add to this schedule the Wednesday and Saturday matinees of *The Sunshine Girl.* And while Vernon was teaching, Irene was performing her own professional duties: posing for photos, shopping for dancing dresses, giving endless interviews and frequently losing her temper with reporters.

By the fall of 1913 their schedules were more than full, they were hugely overbooked. In one week of November, just after *The Sunshine Girl* closed, they gave dance exhibitions in Chicago at the Athletic Club, the Hamilton Club, the Colonial Club, the Germania Club, the Automobile Club, and Rector's Chicago branch. "The call of the west has got into our blood," said Vernon, explaining their first professional trip west of New York. The call also got into Maurice Mouvet's blood: he and Florence Walton were engaged at Chicago's Sherman House that same week, to the fury of Vernon and Irene.

The Castles stayed in Chicago for three weeks—very cold and snowy weeks, making travel hazardous and time consuming. They expressed their delight with Chicago, and vice versa: the utterly charmed reporter from the *Examiner* found them to be "more like a pair of schoolchildren out on a frolic than a staid man and wife.... Their grace is so deliciously childish and wholehearted that the lure of their dancing draws you in spite of yourself."

Despite having both Elisabeth Marbury and Gladwyn MacDougal as agents, Vernon still managed to create a considerable professional faux pas late in 1913. In August he had signed a contract to dance at William Hammerstein's rooftop club at the Victoria Theater in the coming year. Then, in

October, he signed with Martin Beck and Charles Dillingham to dance at the Palace. As January 1914 approached, the Castles discovered that the biggest and most intractable producers in New York were expecting them to appear exclusively at their respective theaters.

The trade papers had a field day with Vernon's naive goof. "Let Willie Hammerstein do his durndest!" said Dillingham. Hammerstein did his durndest, sending a process server to threaten the Castles with jail or a hefty fine if they appeared for anyone but him. Amazingly, the quarrel was settled out of court: it was ruled that Vernon and Irene were to dance twice daily at both theaters beginning the week of January 12, for an engagement of about six weeks, depending on the box office. The Castles (with Europe's orchestra backing them up) brought the carriage trade out to Hammer-stein's and the Palace, in addition to the usual blue-collar and middle-class crowds, a phenomenon "noticeable chiefly by the increased number of silk hats and lorgnettes." The only downside (except for Vernon and Irene's exhaustion from the four shows a day) was an objection filed by the Musi-cian's Union against the Castles for having James Reese Europe's "colored orchestra" onstage with them at Hammerstein's.

The Castles also encountered a bit of backlash and bad press at about this time; not everyone was thrilled by their act or charmed by their looks and personality. A Connecticut paper sniped, "There is no passion in their dancing, it is as if two feathers floated downward and up." The *Dramatic Mirror* kidded Vernon for looking "very Fifth Avenue, or should I say Pic-cadilly," with his "jeweled waistcoat buttons . . . small waist and hollow chest most ultra" and Irene's "hair in a bizarre side-swipe." That same paper delivered the nastiest blow: "The dancing of the Castles is of a peculiar angular style. It is distinctive. . . . Yet we prefer the graceful dancing of Maurice and Florence Walton."

CHAPTER FIFTEEN

"SYNCOPATION RULES THE NATION"

As the Castles' triumphant year of 1914 dawned, they took temporary leave of New York for a trip up to Boston, where they danced at Copley Hall, the Hotel Somerset, and half a dozen private parties. Irene showed off a brilliant new emerald green and black gown, and both Castles showed off their maxixe step, which garnered "screams of 'brava.'"

There were already many dancers onstage, in nightclubs and cabarets. It was possible to make a decent living for a brief period of time, till one's vogue passed, at that profession, but Elisabeth Marbury and the Castles had their eyes on bigger venues: high-toned dancing establishments and schools. These institutions were ripe for expansion in the early 1910s, as the ragtime craze escalated in New York and other large cities and, gradually, in small towns as well.

In the early 1910s, there was no place—in small towns or in large cities—for "nice young people" to go dancing when the urge struck. If a respectable shopgirl, clerk, socialite, or young banker on the loose felt like going out for an evening of innocent flirting, socializing, and ragtime dancing, they had very little choice: there were private parties; there were low-class beer gardens and dance halls; some restaurants and hotels were giving daytime "tango teas" or "thés dansants," hiring bands and removing tables for a tiny dance floor. But all of these options were socially suspect—and, not a small matter, they were tiny and crowded, with poor music and open to "just anyone." Being spotted at a tango tea or one-stepping with strangers at a restaurant amounted to social disaster. Girls were sent to boarding schools for less.

As long as people have danced, others have objected to it. In newspapers and books, and church pulpits, public dance halls and private parties alike have been painted as the doorways to hell and an invitation to illicit sex. Warnings abound in contemporary books about the waltz, the quadrille, the polka, the German.

In 1912, publisher Edward Bok fired fifteen female employees of the Curtis Publishing Company in Philadelphia for dancing the turkey trot during their lunch break. A young lady of Millwood, New York, was hauled into court by a justice of the peace whose own peace was disturbed by her strolling by his house singing "Everybody's Doing It" and dancing an improvised turkey trot on the sidewalk. Not only was she found not guilty after telling the jury that "she sang the song because she liked it, and danced because she could not help it when she heard the catchy tune," but the newspapers reported that the trial ended with the defense attorney singing the song for the jury, who "called for an encore." It seemed everybody was indeed doing it.

In the censorious book *Immorality of Modern Dances* (1904), it was stated outright that "the Christian Religion forbids modern dances"; the book invoked "the awful fate of Sodom and Gomorrah [as] examples of the awful hatred God feels towards those who indulge in impurity." The author writes in hushed tones of "seeing men and women whirling each other about furiously in the mazes of the seductive dance," further asking, "Would a lady with a spark of self-respect . . . place her head upon the shoulder of a man, place her breast against his, and allow him to encircle her waist with his arms, place his foot between her feet, and clasp her hands in his?" *Goodness, yes,* at least a portion of the audience must have inwardly thought. The *Immorality* author goes on: "Hour after hour it [the music] whirls its giddy kaleidoscope around, bringing hearts so near that they almost beat against each other, mixing the warm mutual breaths, darting the fiery personal electricity across between the commingled fingers, flushing the face and lighting the eye with a quick language."

A 1917 study of dance halls in Chicago turned up the kind of low-class trash that Elisabeth Marbury wanted to distance herself from: "Saloonkeepers and prostitutes are in many cases the only chaperones. . . . Men and women become intoxicated and dance indecently such dances as Walkin' the Dog, On the Puppy's Tail, Shaking the Shimmy, The Dip, The Stationary Wiggle, etc. In some instances, little children—of whom there are often large numbers present—are given liquor and become intoxicated, much to the amusement of their elders. Many of them are forgotten by their parents in the excitement of the dance, and play upon the filthy floor, witnesses of all kinds of degradation." Again, the description of these halls and their goings-on read like advertisements for soft-core porn: "Couples stand very close together, the girl with her hands around the man's neck, the man with both his arms around the girl or on her hips; their cheeks are pressed close together, their bodies touch each other; the liquor which has been consumed is like setting a match to a flame; they throw aside all restraint and give themselves to unbridled license and indecency."

Mordecai Franklin Ham's 1916 screed against *The Modern Dance* is fascinating for his exhaustive list of the dances being performed in Texas: "turkey trot, grizzly bear, bunny hug, honey bug, Gaby glide, pollywog wiggle, hippohop, ostrich stretch, kangaroo canter, dizzy drag, hoochie coochie, Salome dance, necktie waltz, Bacchanalian waltz, hesitation waltz, love dance, shadow dance, wiggle-de-wiggle, pickaninny dandle, fuzzy-wuzzy, terripan toddle, Texas Tommy, Boston Dip, kitchen sink, cartel waltz, boll weevil wiggle, Arizona anguish, Argentine ardor, lame duck, chicken flip, grizzly glide, maxixe, shiver shake, cabbage clutch, puppy snuggle, fado foxtrot, syncopated canter, lemon squeeze, hug-me-tight, tango, etc., etc." One gets the feeling the inventors of the Arizona anguish and the kitchen sink were having some fun with Mr. Ham.

As late as 1916, Ham was casting doubt on the morals of women like the ostensibly lily-pure Irene: "No woman who dances virtuously can be a good dancer," he wrote. "The most accomplished dancers are found among fallen women. . . . In order to be a good dancer, a woman must reciprocate the feelings of her partner, and few do this to the extent the abandoned women do."

Melvin Drumm, in *The Modern Dance and What Shall Take Its Place* (1921), listed Seven Reasons for Not Dancing, many of which must have seemed pretty dubious even in the early 1920s: "crowded ball-rooms and late hours, which would be injurious to my health," "freedom with the sex of which I would be ashamed," "ministers and good people in general are against the dance," "the dance has a bad name," "it is usually accompanied with drinking," "the dance is a temptation for the young man," and "the dance would be an insult to God, and I don't propose to do anything that would insult God."

Reformed dancing teacher Thomas A. Faulkner, author of the 1894 *From the Ball Room to Hell,* updated his admonitions in 1916 in *The Lure of the Dance* for the ragtime crowd, seeing as how "the dance craze has developed with such incredible rapidity during the last few years into one of the most irresistible and dangerous attractions in the form of amusements." All those who failed to heed Faulkner met with a swift and sure doom, to his ill-disguised glee: "A minister in San Francisco refused to endorse my first book. He said his son indulged in parlor dances occasionally. . . . I made it a point to look into the young man's life and found out that he . . . was spending his evenings in a dance-house sending his and many other souls to Hell. A short time afterwards he was killed in a bawdy-house on the Barbary Coast. Just imagine, if you can, the anguish of his parents when they learned the truth." And imagine, if you can, the "sympathy call" from Thomas A. Faulkner.

"Ragtime madness" was taken quite literally by some. In 1915, Dr. S. Grover Burnett, former president of the medical school of the University of Missouri, stated flat out that "many of the cases of insanity developed in the United States within the last few years may be traced to modern eccentric dances as a causal source. . . . One-tenth of the insane of this country have lost their minds on account of troubles which may commonly be traced to modern dances."

The height of double messages was reached in a disapproving 1915 account of what sounds like the best party *ever*, sighted by an early morning train passenger near Narragansett Pier, Rhode Island:

Myriads of roysterers, in fantastic and strange garb, in ôutré costumes and next to nothing costumes, dancing the turkey trot in the sands and in the water. . . . There were slim painted girls in the diaphanous gaubes of Pierettes, butterflies, fairies and snow queens, their thin silks hanging wetly to their supple limbs, their white arms twined round the necks of chosen youths garbed as devils, cavaliers, clowns, Arabs and mountebanks and what not. All were madly dancing in the foam of the incoming surf. And the booming surf mingled with the shrill, ecstatic and abandoned cries of the dancers, creating a sound that the sun had never heard before. Far out into the water some were dancing. They moved to the lay of a wild violinist who, garbed as a satyr, stood neck deep in the water and holding his instrument safely above the waves played amorous tango music for those who danced about him. Occasionally a girl, exhausted by her dance, would sink into the water in her silks and paint and be lifted forth by her partner and carried to the beach. There on the sands were hundreds of less hardy folk who had not braved the water. These danced the tango and the Castle walk back and forth over the seaweed and the conch shells, their costumes flying in the morning wind, their voices lifted in careless joy of life.

One longs for a time machine and a ticket to Rhode Island.

Along with the anti-dance books came reams of articles and books praising the modern dance as clean, wholesome exercise and giving (mostly unfollowable) instructions. Troy Kinney, in his *Social Dancing of To-Day* (1914) noted carefully of his collaborator, John Murray Anderson, "His reputation has been attained not chiefly on the stage or in restaurants, but in the homes of leaders of good taste." Social dance, protested Kinney, was not an evil but "a well-spring of good spirits and a fountain of youth for millions of men and women. Every one benefits by it." Even the suspiciously sexy and Latin tango, he claimed, is "a beautiful and irreproachable dance—assuming, of course, its performance in the clean spirit usually found in good society. Any dance can be made suggestive or offensive. So can walking."

"The new dances are not improper dances," agreed Caroline Walker in her 1914 book, *The Modern Dances: How to Dance Them.* "On the contrary, they are just as proper and graceful as the time-honored waltz and two-step, and far more interesting, both to young and old, than their predecessors ever were." One of the dances she recommended was the Castle walk, "so simple that it is difficult to describe. . . . To the on-looker the Castle walk appears very foolish—and it is—but it is great fun for those doing it." Music critic H. E. Krehbiel was less tolerant, writing that "in this year of pretended refinement, which is the year of our Lord 1913, the [ragtime dances] are threatening to force grace, decorum, and decency out of the ball-rooms of America."

A fascinating glimpse of New York at the dawn of the nightclub age is given in the guidebook *Welcome to Our City,* by the delightfully crotchety Julian Street, who seems to dislike everything about Manhattan. Published in 1910 and updated in 1912, the book turns a particularly harsh light on the spread of cabarets and ragtime dancing at the beginning of the Castles' career, just before their influence began to be felt: "From Louis Martin's— where there is now a ballroom, in addition to the cabaret, Maurice has moved up town, to Reisenweber's, which is, at this moment, perhaps, our principal temple of Terpsichore. Three floors, at Reisenweber's, are given over to the one-step, the tango, the turkey-trot and their variants. People even go there to dance at tea-time, in the afternoon."

Street gives us colorful entrée into some of New York's night spots of the early 1910s: "They even have lights under the tables, at Murray's, so that a pink glow comes up through the cloth . . . dining there is like dining on a stage set for the second act of a musical comedy . . . the Café de l'Opera suggests a big spectacular effect at the opera. . . . The color scheme is blue and gold, with black marble columns surmounted by golden capitals representing bulls' heads—or are they calves of gold?"

The cabarets went on and on, much to Street's disgust. "From Little Hungary in Houston Street to Pabst's vast armory-like restaurant in 125th, you will find them everywhere: rag-time, turkey-trotting spots up in the city map; gay cabarets, jay cabarets; cabarets with stages and spot-lights, cabarets without; cabarets on ground floors, in cellars, and on roofs; cabarets where 'folks act gen'l'mumly,' cabarets where the wild time grows. . . . You can't escape it! The town is cabaridden! Cabarotten!" As a very catchy 1913 song lamented,

> Syncopation rules the nation
> You can't get away from it—get away from it
> It causes agitation
> You can't get away from it—get away from it
> Lawyers and physicians
> Men of high positions
> Great big politicians
> Pal around with the rag musicians!
> You try it, can't deny it
> You can't get away from it—get away from it
> On Sunday, just like Monday
> You can't get away from it—get away from it
> Even small-town preachers
> Are engaging tango teachers
> You can't get away from it—get away from it
> You can't get away from it at all!

Restaurateur George Rector installed a tiny dance floor in his popular Times Square establishment in 1910 and found that "all they wanted to do was dance, and we accommodated them with a dance floor that measured thirty feet by twenty. The entire 1,500 all tried to dance on this postage stamp at the same time."

Humorist George Jean Nathan complained of "The Deadly Cabaret" taking over from respectable restaurants and theaters in a 1912 issue of *Theatre* magazine: "No restaurant so humble that oysters may not be swallowed to the tune of 'Snap Your Fingers and Away You Go'; no café so meager that Pilsner may not be gulped to the giddy whirl of the 'Fandango Flip-Flop.'" Nathan decried the quality of the shows and performers at these nightspots. "The very best of these New York cabaret shows . . . has a bill that is made up of two women singers, a banjo player, a male vocalist, a team of dancers and a young girl performer who jigs an accompaniment to her tunes. . . . Where the cabaret shows are not patently vulgar, they are plainly stupid."

To make matters more difficult, the municipal government was getting concerned. In 1910 the awkwardly (but descriptively) named New York Commission on Amusements and Vacation Resources for Working Girls was formed, and it ruled that "reckless and uncontrolled" dancing was taking place, leading to debauchery. By 1912, New York's Mayor Gaynor was being pressured to censor "racy" music, though how the mayor was to accomplish this was somewhat unclear. Harassed by social reformers (and understandably cranky after having been shot through the throat in 1910), Gaynor attempted to crack down on nightlife by ordering Police Commissioner Waldo to enforce a 1:00 A.M. curfew on all establishments serving alcohol. In the first wave of this anti-vice campaign, the cabarets and restaurants of Times Square were raided, customers tossed out or arrested, and the owners and employees hauled into court.

"This all-night guzzling and vulgarity is at an end in New York forever, I hope," the mayor rather laughably predicted. He was up against it: at one club, the police ordered customers out and they flatly refused to go. The police (in a rather horrifying flouting of fire laws) locked the patrons in for the night, and they proceeded to have a grand old time till 6:00 A.M. (except for those who climbed out the back windows and fled). Judges and district attorneys failed to bring in the convictions Gaynor expected, and he soon began to get discouraged. His campaign was lampooned by comic Nat Wills in the song "New York, What's the Matter with You?" in the *Ziegfeld Follies of 1913:*

Goodbye, my tango, farewell, you cabaret life!
Now I've got to go home when the curfew rings
And do the Grizzly with my wife!

Gaynor's attempt to silence ragtime was derided as useless by humorist George Fitch, who wrote, "The winter of 1913–14 will live in history because of the dances, which spared neither young nor old."

꧁꧂

Chapter Sixteen

"The Most Talked About House in New York"

The Castles had fame, cachet, lots of work coming in—but they needed a "command post," a focal point to serve as a gathering place and magnet for their growing cult of followers (and a place to attract the all-important press, as well). That's how the idea of Castle House, a combination club and dancing school, was born.

But setting up a moderately famous dance team in an East Side hall was not enough: Elisabeth Marbury knew that she had to "sell" the Castles, she had to remake them in the most marketable of images. "Time was essential, as the craze might die out," she wisely realized. "I conducted the publicity myself." The best way to make Castle House into a paying success was to market it—and the Castles and ragtime dancing—to the upper and middle classes, who had thus far been wary of ragtime. Marbury presented the Castles as a clean-cut, wholesome married couple—which indeed they were. Beautiful, elegant, but safely sexless. The Castles had already moved away from the wild, stomping frottage of the turkey trot and the bunny hug and were exemplars of a smoother, simpler dance style. All Marbury had to do was make them into celebrities worth coming to see—and at the same time, promote them as the only teachers and performers of ragtime safe for your sons and daughters.

Sometime in the fall of 1913, Elisabeth Marbury had a brainstorm and realized how she might be able to promote the Castles to their—and her—advantage. Lunching at the Ritz-Carlton, she glanced across the street toward 26 East Forty-sixth Street, a two-story brick house that had until recently been the home of Madame Osborn, couturiere. "The thought of making it into a smart dancing-centre flashed across my mind," Marbury later recalled. "I visualised the trade-mark, 'Castle House.'" The interior was perfectly suited for the purpose: the entryway was a lovely marble foyer with a fountain, and elegant stairways led up either side to two large second-floor rooms. Elsie de Wolfe, of course, redecorated the interior in her characteristic light, airy style. It was safely away from the hubbub of Times Square, on the corner of Madison Avenue. (Castle House is long gone; on the site today is the rear entrance of the elegant 1923 Roosevelt Hotel.)

Castle House was to be different—it had to be, if it were to succeed and break through the clutter of dance halls and restaurants and hotels offering tea dances. Elisabeth Marbury, as was her habit and talent, took over all arrangements and brooked no argument; the Castles, being new at the business, *gave* her no argument. "I selected able assistants and instructors, for the morning hours were to be given over to classes," Marbury wrote. "I arranged with Jim Europe . . . so that I had him furnish the music." Marbury recognized that time was of the essence if the dance craze was to be exploited at its peak: "The cream had to be quickly skimmed from the pail." Although she herself had arranged for James Europe to play, Marbury was too smart not to know that many of New York's elite would balk at dancing to a black orchestra; another pianist hired for Castle House was the white musician Henry Lodge (he was the composer of a number of popular rags, including "Temptation Rag," "Red Pepper," "Oh! You Turkey," and "Demi-Tasse").

Marbury, familiar with New York society schedules, made sure that Castle House opened late in 1913—in time for debutantes to experience their first taste before the end-of-the-year balls were held. Morning lessons for the eager young elite were overseen by the Castles but actually given by carefully chosen teachers, selected for their proper looks and demeanor as much as their talent. No ragtime cabaret stars in Castle House!

The Castles, of course, gave dancing exhibitions for their students and the avid mothers, and Vernon (for increasingly large fees) gave lessons. But the establishment's name was really made during its famous afternoon teas, served by the more modern (but still socially elect) of Marbury's acquaintances. The always-agreeable Mrs. Fish, Mrs. William Rockefeller, Mrs. Oakley Rhinelander, Mrs. Anthony Drexel, and others took time from their charities, luncheons, and social rounds to pour tea and dispense sandwiches to their daughters and the daughters of their friends. It was great fun; they got to mix with the young people and even with the Castles—Vernon and Irene's glamour drew old and young alike.

From 4:00 till 6:30 P.M. general dancing prevailed, with the Castles themselves making appearances from time to time. "Let's go down to the

Castles' castle" became a smart-set quip within a week or two of Castle House's opening in mid-December 1913. Upon entering the marble foyer—with a fountain burbling prettily—the guest paid $2 to the front desk cashier ($3 on Friday or Saturday), and "Cupid in green knickers smiles, draws back and the red satin barricade is lifted," as *Theatre* magazine described the impressive entryway. Then up one winding stairway or the other, to Europe's hot black band or Lodge's sweet white one. Cakes, tea, sandwiches, and lemonade were handed out—included in the admission price—by society grand dames and their offspring.

The Castles inadvertently trained one of their chief competitors: Arthur Murray took lessons from Vernon and Irene as a teenager (he'd been teaching dance since 1912 but leaned the newest, hottest steps from the Castles). He even briefly taught *for* the Castles, as a stand-in for Vernon. By the 1920s, the Arthur Murray Dance Studio was the nation's most successful chain, one that continues today, more than a decade after Murray's death in 1991.

Early in 1914, *Vanity Fair* sent its "Non-Tangoing" correspondent to check out New York's latest hot spot. He wrote in "The Most Talked About House in New York" that what struck him was how happy and lighthearted the crowd was, with little of the usual showing off and social one-upmanship; dancers seemed not to care if they made fools of themselves, as long as they were having a good time. "All were genuinely interested and genuinely enjoying themselves," he wrote. "The music ceased in the outer room and immediately began in the inner, without an instant's pause. Everyone was on his feet or on his partner's, dancing to a happy-hearted, spirited tempo. The waitresses, who had been passing tea and cakes and chocolate and coffee éclairs, beat a hasty and dodging retreat. A sense of disappointment came over me: I felt I had been grossly deceived by the newspapers, by my own minister, by the Roman Catholic clergy, and by our Neighborhood League for the Promotion of Purity and Moral Order."

Vernon and Irene, tipped off to the presence of a reporter, breezed by to welcome him. "They were absolutely innocuous in every way," he wrote, to Marbury's delight: this was exactly the nonthreatening image she was aiming for. "They were not demonstrators of dancing; they were merely dancing for the cheerful fun of the thing. . . . Their youthful eyes were shining. They loved it." The "Non-Tangoer" continued with what might have been a Marbury-penned press release: "I felt my pulpit and newspaper-founded beliefs slipping away and deserting me. . . . Where was the shock I had looked for? Not here, certainly, for these dances were so simple, so musical and so irrefragably innocuous. 'And the Grizzly Bear, the Bunny Hug, the Turkey Trot?' 'Dead, all dead,' was the answer [from Vernon]. 'They were all ugly dances, and no dance can be ugly and live. They died the victims of complicated gracelessness.'"

"From the first day we opened our doors people poured in by the hundreds," Irene recalled. "They had their choice of two orchestras, a chance to be served tea by a real society woman, an opportunity to see the Castles, and a slim chance of dancing with one of them, if their luck held. We did a thundering business."

There was more than a suggestion of social elitism and exclusion implicit in Castle House (described by Irene as "a place where their children could go to learn the dance without being exposed to the discredited elements"). *Smart Styles* reported in February 1914 that Castle House was already established as a veritable country club in the city, patronized by "some of the most prominent members of society . . . women of serious purpose and high social standing bring their daughters and their sons, their husbands and their fathers to dance. . . . During every holiday, two afternoons are reserved for the juniors, and on these occasions, the younger people of society who are at home from school or college flock to Castle House."

The most blatant admission of this "Not Our Kind, Dear" policy was spelled out in *Theatre* magazine, in March 1914. The $2 (or $3) entrance fee was "a gentle but decisive cold shouldering of all save the elect and the friends of the elect." When asked, "How do you separate the sheep and the goats without offense?" the Castles were shockingly forthright and blunt in their answers: "I don't dance with the latter class," Vernon admitted, "with a slightly weary air." Irene added, "Nor I . . . I have a list of brilliant excuses. They don't meet their friends here. They are not comfortable and don't come again." A bit of nastiness crept into one interview, which referred to Irene as looking "less like a dancing genius than a keened-eyed little business woman when she whispered, laughing, 'They pay the most ridiculous prices.'"

One might think the Castles would have made more money in the long run by getting $1 from thousands of customers, rather than $2 from hundreds. But they were more than Castle House alone, they were a franchise: a high-toned, upper-middle-class franchise. Marbury had big plans for them, and it was worth sacrificing "the goats" in order to establish themselves as the great white hopes of the social dance.

Castle House, as Irene noted, was a success from the day of its opening; part of the thrill was the chance of seeing (or even dancing with) an actual Castle. Vernon and Irene had become huge stars in the past year, and there weren't many venues where one could actually rub shoulders with celebrities. The excited reporter from *Theatre* magazine observed as the Castles breezed into their establishment one evening and the crowds parted like the Red Sea: "A slim, girlish figure, straight and reedlike, mounts the stairs. A fresh-faced girl, seemingly from one of the Fifth Avenue girls' schools, crosses the floor, weightlessly, without any noticeable motion. She is remindful of the heroines of novels who float, or glide, but never do anything so vulgar as merely walk . . . an unusually thin young man of fair hair and boyish, beardless face. These are the Castles, Vernon and his wife. . . . New York society has adopted them as its own, because into what had seemed hopelessly vulgar they have injected their own essential refinement."

Upstairs at Castle House, Vernon presided over his office, in which he pretended to pay bills and read over dancing contracts, though he was noticeably lax about actually *doing* either of those. A reporter found him "surrounded with all the efficient devices which usually strike a chill to the marrow of an artistic temperament—typewriters, correspondence files, card indexes, and so on." Vernon chatted amiably about dancing, noting in a very gentlemanly way that "I much prefer to dance with an old woman or with a homely woman who is a fine dancer than with the prettiest woman you can show me who is at the same time a poor dancer."

As an American resident of eight years' standing (and a businessman of very shaky skill), he noted the difference between the two countries. "Over in England no one seems to have the moral courage to give you a direct 'no' if he doesn't wish to do business with you. You are first put off with one excuse and then with another, and that wastes such a frightful amount of time. Here I find that a business man makes up his mind quickly and definitely, and when he decides not to do business with you he does the next best thing by telling you so directly and leaving you free to take the matter up with somebody else."

For all their catering to the upper classes, the Castles and Elisabeth Marbury also reached out—though in a rather patronizing way—to the blue-collar and middle-class crowds, who also had money to spend. Socialite Anne Morgan, Marbury's friend, instituted a series of dances and dance classes on West Thirty-ninth Street for "working girls" in which Irene took a particular interest. "Working girls have just the same desire to dance as any other girls," said Morgan in January 1914. "If they get the right sort of help they will dance as gracefully as anyone else. If the boys and girls meet in this house and dance they won't have to meet on the street corner. . . . These girls want to be good and decent, to dance and have a good time."

The imposingly battleshiplike Marbury was a visible presence at these dances. One reporter jotted down her mode of attack: "Miss Marbury noted some little crudenesses in the dancing steps and when she called the girls aside and suggested that shoulders wiggle less and bodies sway more gently, she met with this response: 'But, Miss Marbury, you see we've never been taught how to dance the new movements. We're just making them up the best we can.'"

To be fair, Irene's interest in the less fortunate was something she invested time and money in for the rest of her life. In 1914, she and Vernon held a benefit for the Beth-El Sisterhood and Settlement at the Waldorf-Astoria, raising funds for the 350 orphans in the establishment. Irene visited Beth-El, taking along one of her dogs to entertain the children. They danced at a March 1914 Carnegie Hall recital given especially for children, and the *New York Herald* noted "the largest audience that Carnegie Hall has held in many a day."

They were also persuaded to give a "Democratic Dancing Night" at Castle House, where the hefty $2 and $3 admission fee was generating some ill will. On April 20, the price was lowered to $1 for those over twenty-one and 50¢ for the younger patrons. Elisabeth Marbury assured all comers that "we will have the same atmosphere, the same supper and the same Castles" as at their more exclusive evenings.

No hot new club lasts forever. Castle House continued to rake in money and customers well into 1915, though the Castles themselves lost interest early on. In May 1915 Irene told the pseudonymous movie magazine writer "Mae Tinee," "At first we were there all the time. Now we have fifty teachers and Vernon only shows up once in a while to hand out diplomas and things." Not surprisingly, Castle House began to fall out of favor, and by 1916 it had given way to its many competitors.

Even before Castle House opened, Vernon fell prey to a suggestion from Jules Ensaldi, a headwaiter for Louis Martin at the Café de l'Opera:

why not open a club in Times Square? Ensaldi, said Irene, "combined all the talents of a social dictator with the acquisitive habits of a business tycoon," and he easily convinced Vernon they could double their money with very little trouble. He already had the site picked out: a cellar club in the Heidelberg Building, at Forty-second and Broadway, that had been closed by the police as a clip joint.

Times Square in 1914 was New York's epicenter of show business and fashion, but it was not a place where Castle House's usual clientele would linger after the theater. The lovely Times Tower stood in its center, surrounded by the hotels Astor and Knickerbocker, the newest and biggest theaters, and various restaurants, cafés, and many less savory businesses.

Edward Shaw was hired by Ensaldi to supply $47,251 worth of "chattel" for the establishment: tables, chairs, restaurant equipment. Irene hired Elsie de Wolfe to make the dank cellar over. It was "an ugly room with great square columns supporting it and a paper-thin wall separating it from the subway." De Wolfe painted it rose and gray and installed lights "until it almost glowed through the sidewalk." James Reese Europe's band was booked, and the January 1914 opening was promising, with Castle friends Cornelius Vanderbilt, George J. Gould, Mrs. William Astor Chandler, Mrs. Herbert Harriman, William Rhinelander Stewart, and Diamond Jim Brady attending. (Irene had no great admiration for Brady, whom she found insufferably vulgar: "He glistened with very chunky yellow diamonds, which surrounded his watch and sparkled from his cuffs and glared from his shirt front like headlamps.")

The Castles received two-thirds of the profits and were largely absentee landlords. Irene hated the underground space, and Vernon was too busy in early 1914 to spend much time at Sans Souci, as the club was named—an unhappy choice, as it turned out. Almost from the first, there was an air of failure about the place.

Both Vernon and Irene later claimed to be totally innocent of the way the club was run: for one thing, waiters would plop "tempting little dishes of tomatoes, sardines, radishes and cucumbers and a package of cigarettes" on the table in front of customers, who assumed these were free for the taking—when their bill arrived, they found differently (cigarettes went for an expensive 60¢ a pack). One newspaper reported: "When protest was made to the waiters they answered with unassailable logic that the things were eaten or smoked and therefore should be paid for."

The Castles may have claimed innocence regarding their waiters' grafting ways, but they were front and center for another clip joint tactic. On the rare occasions they showed up at Sans Souci, the Castles agreeably danced with the thrilled customers—who were presented a whopping $20 bill "for one lesson." As one paper noted, "Very few of those who had this expensive experience ever returned to the resort." A reporter in early 1914 claimed to have overheard a conversation between two young men about town:

> It seems that one of the young men had recently attended a dance place, presided over by Mr. and Mrs. Vernon Castle. He had danced once with Mrs. Castle, then there followed a little supper, consisting of one bottle of wine with squabs as the main course: and it did not give the speaker the slightest uneasiness until the bill met his eye. What was his astonishment to discover that it amounted to sixty-five dollars. The bottle of wine was rated at twelve dollars, the rest of the menu was in proportion, and the dance with Mrs. Castle, in which she had so graciously offered to show him a new step, was down for twenty-five dollars. The sixty-five added up properly. "What could I do? I paid it, of course! But I've been saving money for my friends ever since by telling them my experience."

Irene defended herself and Vernon in her memoirs, claiming that restaurants did not have cover charges in those days, so in order to make a profit, "we put a card on the tables stating that when the entertainment started, only champagne would be served. Every drink other than champagne was a dollar a drink. This was not well received." When one customer objected to paying a dollar for a glass of ginger ale that would have cost him a nickel a bottle elsewhere, "Vernon reached down, picked up the check and tore it into very small pieces. 'Just remember before you come the next time that this is our rule.'" One doubts that customer came back the next time.

Not surprisingly, Sans Souci did not last as long as the more respectable Castle House. By May 1914, only four months into its run, it was shuttered by the New York Fire Department, which refused to issue a new license, as "there are not sufficient means of quick egress from the Sans Souci in case of fire or panic." The Castles, who had other problems and occupations by then, gave it up as a bad job and let the club stay closed and ready to be leased to another sucker.

Sans Souci was gone, but the lawsuits lingered on: Edward Shaw sued the Castles and Jules Ensaldi for unpaid bills and was awarded $25,279. He charged that the Castles "corruptly and fraudulently had dealings as officers and directors contrary to their duty and in violation of the law, and by these corrupt dealings the defendants appropriated to their own use large amounts of money belonging to the defendant corporation and its creditors, of whom the plaintiff is one." Ensaldi fled to Paris and was never heard from again.

꧁꧂

CHAPTER SEVENTEEN

"DANCING WITH VERNON WAS AS EASY AS SWIMMING WITH WATER WINGS"

Eager to take advantage of the Castles' wave of popularity, Elisabeth Marbury instituted what would today be called a multimedia blitz. In the spring of 1914, movie cameras were set up at Castle House before a small audience of invited friends, and Vernon and Irene went through half a dozen or so steps. The short film was released with the imaginative title *Mr. and Mrs. Castle before the Camera* and was a big success, bringing $35,000 a week to vaudeville managers. "The picture is life-size," marveled one reviewer, "and it is remarkable how fascinating the tango dancing is really holding the entire audience until the very finish when Mr. and Mrs. Castle are brought to the front with a gracious little bow."

Following up on this success, the Kalem Film Company released a series of shorts, featuring Joan Sawyer and Wallace McCutcheon, called *Motion Picture Dancing Lessons*. Rosie Dolly of the Dolly Sisters also made a dance instruction film, in 1915, with Martin Brown.

Shortly thereafter, while *Mr. and Mrs. Castle before the Camera* was still playing in movie houses, Harper & Brothers came out with *Modern Dancing*, a hardcover, 176-page instruction manual fully illustrated with photos: of the Castles posed, frame enlargements from *Mr. and Mrs. Castle before the Camera,* and a few fashion portraits of Irene. In her introduction, Marbury put forth in very clear terms her faith in her clients and her reasons for promoting them: "Mr. and Mrs. Castle stand pre-eminent to-day as the best exponents of modern dancing." But in her eagerness to sell them as socially acceptable, Marbury did her best to squeeze every bit of sex, spontaneity, and fun out of the dance, and out of Vernon and Irene. While protesting that dancing is "one of the supreme human expressions of happiness and exultation," she stressed over and over that "the One Step as taught at Castle House eliminates all hoppings, all contortions of the body . . . all fantastic dips. . . . The Castle Tango is courtly and artistic. . . .

The Hesitation Waltz is a charming and stately glide, measured and modest." In other words, dancing that your Sunday school teacher or your most easily shocked auntie would approve of.

This was, of course, an effort to offset the protests of the religious and social reformers who cried that all dancing was evil and all dance halls and schools must be shut down. Marbury overstated her case in several ways, insisting that "moral dancing" was "a healthful exercise and a fitting recreation," and noting there was more harm in "a sensational moving-picture show . . . suggestive sex-problem dramas . . . the latest erotic novel." She stressed that the poor tenement dweller and the middle-class shopgirl would benefit from uplifting, moral dance instruction as well: "I have talked to hundreds of girls about their dancing, and they have put into my hand the golden key to the situation by saying with a puzzled smile and questioning eye: 'We're dancing wrong? Well, maybe; but we don't know any other way to dance. Do you?' We do, and we can teach them . . . dances can be made graceful, artistic, charming, and above all, refined."

Vernon himself, in the text of *Modern Dancing,* came off as less of a scold and a schoolmarm than Marbury. "Almost any girl who does not dance is either an invalid or the piano-player," he joked on the very first page, and went on to deny the vulgarity of modern dance. "It is possible to make anything immoral and vulgar; all depends on how it is done. A vulgar man or woman betrays lack of breeding even in walking across the room."

Dancing, argued Vernon, was good exercise "and keeps one absolutely fit . . . a valuable health and youth preserver." He elaborated on this: "The man and woman who sit briefly at a café partaking of a salad and perhaps a cocktail and then arise and dance are the man and woman who will live longer and healthier and happier than they who . . . sit feeding and drinking through the evening. . . . the sale of alcoholic drinks has actually decreased and the sale of soft drinks increased in the city restaurants and cafés where dancing is permitted."

Vernon's sense of humor came through in his *Modern Dancing* instructions. "One last word about the Lame Duck," he advised. "If you exaggerate you lose all the Duck and it is simply Lame." He was also honest in admitting that not everyone was going to be able to learn every dance but shrugged philosophically, "If you don't learn the dance, you get a little exercise and a lot of experience." He added encouragingly, "If, when mistakes happen, you keep on dancing, in nine cases out of ten no one will know about it but yourself. On the other hand, no one can miss your mistake if you get confused and stop."

On dancing "grace and etiquette" in general, Vernon wrote, "Both good dancing and good manners require a man to stand far enough from his partner to allow freedom of movement; he should not hug or clutch her during the dance. . . . Flouncing elbows, pumping arms, fantastic dips, and whirlwind turns all detract not only from the grace of the dance, but from the charm of the dancer."

Irene was asked to contribute a chapter on fashion, which certainly helped sales of the book. Her advice was typically sensible and in good taste. "While fashion decrees the narrow skirt, the really enthusiastic dancer will adopt the plaited one," she advised, also deriding the "long, stiff corsets decreed by fashion. . . . Personally I use and recommend a special corset made almost entirely of elastic, very flexible and conforming absolutely to the figure, which at the same time it supports." Indeed, Irene credited the dancing craze for abolishing fussy, torturous styles: "Simple coiffures have become the fashion because they do not become untidy when dancing. . . . The long, awkward, and often soiled train that used to drag behind women in the afternoons and evenings is no longer seen. The fashions of 1914 have done away with it because you could not dance in a train!"

Modern Dancing was one of countless dance manuals that were published in the ragtime rush of 1908–18. By the 1910s, dance schools had been earning their keep for a century by teaching resentful children the waltz, quadrille, minuet, Virginia reel, perhaps a sedate polka. Now they were being besieged by adults demanding to learn to turkey trot, bunny hug, and tango. The instructors themselves were, to put it mildly, at a loss.

To make matters more difficult, dancing is a skill that must be learned by doing. The shelves full of dance instruction manuals published in the early 1910s were less than helpful. J. S. Hopkins's *The Tango and Other Up-to-Date Dances* (1914) was typical of the genre. His instructions on how to dance the one-step must have left many readers in tears of frustration, tossing their gramophone records out the window:

Step One: Four steps—back—a quarter turn—four steps forward.

Step Two: A complete turn to the right on four counts. (Note that this step is not completed at this point.) The object of the turn, the hardest part of the dance to master, is keeping the feet as close together as is possible and on the floor.

Step Three: The drag step—so called because the right foot is brought to the left in a close position. This step counted 1, 2, 3, 4, 5, 6, 7, 8, the 2, 4, 6, 8 being closed positions.

Step Four: The Grapevine, sometimes called the Serpentine Step. Counted 1, 2, 3, 4, 5, 6, 7, 8. Positions: Gentleman's left foot to side—1; right back—2; left side—3; right forward—4; left side—5; right back—6; left side—7; right forward—8. Counterpart for lady. This step can be made very effective by putting a slight dip on 2, 4, 6, 8, and is then called the Grapevine Dip. After Step No. Four we complete Step No. Two, a complete turn on four counts, which completes the dance.

In *Modern Dancing,* Vernon tried to make his instructions as simple and user-friendly as possible. To dance the one-step, he wrote,

The dancers stand directly in front of each other, the lady's right hand in the gentleman's left. The elbows should be slightly bent, not held out stiffly, like the bowsprit of a boat, as this not only looks awkward, but is uncomfortable and often dangerous to the other dancers. The gentleman's right hand should be a little above the lady's waist-line, more or less under her left shoulder-blade; but this, of course, depends upon the size of the lady. All I would say is: Don't stand too close together or too far apart; be comfortable, and you stand a good chance of looking graceful. The lady's left hand should rest lightly on the gentleman's right shoulder. She should not curl her arm tightly around his. The gentleman usually starts forward and the lady backward—the reason being that the lady is generally more graceful and can go backward with greater ease, and a man can also see where he is going and thus prevent a collision with other couples. Now to begin with the dance: the gentleman starts forward with his left foot, and the lady steps backward with her right, walking in time to the music. Bear in mind this one important point: When I say walk, that is all it is. Do not shuffle, do not bob up and down or trot. Simply walk as softly and smoothly as possible, taking a step to every count of the music.

His instructions for his own Castle walk were even more to the point:

First of all, walk as I have already explained in the One Step. Now, raise yourself up slightly on your toes at each step, with the legs a trifle stiff, and breeze along happily and easily, and you know all there is to know about the Castle Walk. To turn a corner you do not turn your partner round, but keep walking her backward in the same direction, leaning over slightly—just enough to make a graceful turn and keep the balance well—a little like a bicycle rounding a corner. If you like, instead of walking along in a straight line, after you have rounded your corner, you can continue in the same slanting position, which will naturally cause you to go round in a circle. Now continue, and get your circle smaller and smaller until you are walking around almost in one spot, and then straighten up and start off down the room again. It sounds silly and is silly. That is the explanation of its popularity!

In each chapter of *Modern Dancing*, Vernon offered a little background on the step under discussion (the dances taught included the one-step, tango, hesitation waltz, Castle walk, maxixe, and variations of all of these) with notes on each dance's spins, turns, step-outs, and particular difficulties. As an example of his chatty, informal teaching style: "I advise you to cease counting and try to do the hesitation when the music seems to 'ask for it'—if you know what I mean." And, somehow, you *do* know what he means.

Still, it is all but impossible to learn to dance from a book. Dance instruction records were also made, including one overseen by George Hepburn Wilson, editor of *Modern Dance* magazine. E-nun-ci-ating care-fully in a stilted voice, a narrator recorded one-step instructions: "Use it in con-nection with print-ed instruct-ions, which we furn-ish," he advised. It's all hugely unhelpful.

The real reason that the Castles managed to rise above the rest of the ballroom dance teams was not so much their talent, their clean, fresh looks, or even their social éclat: it was Vernon's genius as a dancing teacher. He was a self-trained dancer, which may have worked to his advantage. Having started from scratch himself, he was able to sympathize with the two-left-footed students who felt helpless and self-conscious. Vernon did not come on as an "expert"; he was a good-natured fellow who joshed and cajoled and teased his students into having fun learning to dance. Irene recalled him dancing with apparently brilliant, graceful students, "when really he often confided to me afterward that the woman couldn't dance at all, and that he had dragged her around."

Another of Vernon's greatest talents was as a partner. "Dancing with Vernon was as easy as swimming with water wings," said Irene. Mae Murray, who later partnered onstage with Vernon at short notice, said that "he guides one perfectly, seeming not to guide at all. So many male dancers cause their partners to worry about the next step, that one gets the sense of the girl overworking and worrying. But I don't think there's another adept partner in the world like Vernon Castle . . . when we started on a dance, he would say, 'Don't worry, I'll take you through,' and yet one was not really conscious of his presence. Dancing with Vernon Castle was really like dancing alone."

Of course, the Castles and their cohorts were also responsible for a great many bruised shins and inferiority complexes. Even in a day when all middle- and upper-class children were sent to dancing lessons, not everyone was comfortable or talented on the dance floor. The charm—and the danger—of these new ragtime dances was that you could squeeze your partner tight (without "leaving space between you for the Holy Ghost") and totter laughingly around the room. A ragtime party is seen in the background of the 1913 Keystone comedy *A Strong Revenge,* and all the performers do is grab one another and energetically hop around to the music (actors—even Mack Sennett's—might be expected to be more talented dancers than the public at large).

Irene, however, was a flop as a teacher, and after a few unhappy weeks, she gave it up. She even tried to avoid dancing with paying customers at Castle House, a major source of tips and goodwill: "Somehow, little men eighty-five years old and far too short for me were always asking me to dance. . . . I lacked the necessary patience. . . . I was never anxious or amenable to dancing with the customers." A bit unwisely for business, she even told one reporter, "Nobody needs to take lessons. The real way to learn is to go to a dance and watch people who know how, then practice."

Many of the dances taught by the Castles were variations of the all-popular one-step and two-step. The one-step (basically what it sounds like: a brisk walking dance) had been around since the mid-nineteenth century and probably originated in country folk dances; the two-step seems to have evolved in the 1890s. In the years 1905–10, the bouncy, disreputable dances associated with ragtime began sweeping the country: the fox trot, bunny hug, turkey trot, and the like.

Vernon took Elisabeth Marbury's advice to tone down the wilder dances to appeal to the "better class." Dancer Ethel Williams recalled the boisterous dances of the early 1910s, such as the Texas Tommy, which Blossom Seeley had popularized: "A kick and a hop three times on each foot, and then add whatever you want, turning, pulling, sliding. . . . Your partner had to keep you from falling—I've slid into the orchestra pit more than once." The turkey trot, the bunny hug, and the grizzly bear were undignified, jouncing steps involving a shocking amount of partner hugging, arm pumping, kicks, and general bouncing up and down. All three dances came from San Francisco, which in itself was enough to stamp them socially suspect.

Probably the most popular of the new dances—lasting for decades—was the fox trot. Vernon Castle was briefly given credit for inventing this step, which he rightly laughed off. Vaudeville dancer Harry Fox also claimed credit for this syncopated version of the two-step, but it can be traced back to at least 1905, before Fox's fame. The maxixe can be traced by dance historians back to mid-nineteenth-century Brazil; by the 1910s, it evolved into a combination of two-step and polite tango. Maurice Mouvet danced a sensuous version of the maxixe; the Castles did a smoother, sambalike variation, more suited to their polite clientele.

Most frowned-upon of all was the sensuous tango, which dated back to mid-nineteenth-century Argentina. Although the Castles danced a sanitized version, it was most closely associated with the heavy-breathing variations popularized by Maurice Mouvet and Rudolph Valentino. Just as sexy, but also quite violent, was the French Apache dance, patterned after a fight between a low-class Parisian pimp and a prostitute. It was popularized by Maurice Chevalier in France and brought to the United States around 1907 by Maurice Mouvet. The Castles did *not* dance the Apache: no dance could have been less suited to them.

꙰

Chapter Eighteen

"The spirit of success ... oozes from these two young people"

The money went out as fast as it came in. In the spring of 1914, Vernon bought the Ely estate on Manhasset Bay, near Long Island Sound. An upscale area rich in fishing, boating, and horseback riding, Manhasset Bay was a lovely spot for weekend relaxation, convenient enough to the city for quick getaways. Although the area had been served by the Long Island Railroad since 1895, Vernon preferred hopping in his roadster and driving back and forth, to the enrichment of the town's coffers (he was regularly pinched for speeding).

Vernon paid $70,000 for their estate, to the amusement of locals, who reported that it was worth $40,000, tops. As if that expense weren't already out of their league, they added a houseboat/dressing room, and all of their friends and acquaintances came out to spend weekends (with the Castles footing the food and servants' bills). Vernon took up polo, playing proudly with Broadway stars Will Rogers and Fred Stone. "That dancer didn't scare worth a darn," said an admiring Rogers. "We all had many a tilt with him and he never flinched."

Vernon thoroughly enjoyed being a man of property and "was always galloping around somewhere, playing polo or tennis," said Irene. The front door had a glass upper pane, and when the doorbell rang, Vernon would get on his hands and knees and crawl up to it, trying to identify the caller by peeking through the keyhole before deciding whether to answer or not.

One of the main advantages of the Long Island estate was as a boardinghouse for their ever-increasing collection of pets. The star of the assembly was Tell von Flugerad ("Tell" for short), a German shepherd Vernon purchased in Europe in the summer of 1914 for $1,000. Soon, Vernon had twelve police dogs, "most of which I have bred myself ... we have cows and horses as well as the kennel of dogs." While in Coney Island, scouting locations for a summer dance palace, Vernon and Irene drove past a donkey farm and sped in for a look around. They spotted a donkey foal, and Irene fell in love. "The owner insisted upon giving it to her," Vernon said, "so we took it home in the back seat of the car. It's surprising how difficult it is to make a donkey sit down in the back of an automobile."

In addition to the German shepherds and Zowie the French bulldog, the Castles always kept at least one tiny yipping lapdog, which one reporter nearly sat on as it curled up under a comforter. Irene, obviously not a cat person, laughed, "We call her Kitty and Pussy and talk to her just like she is a cat. She wags her tail and never knows how she is being insulted." The Castles bragged shamelessly of smuggling "Kitty" into England past quarantine in bags or wrapped in blankets: "She's so used to it that if she has a pillow thrown on her or is sat upon suddenly she never whimpers."

Irene's son notes that Vernon and Irene "got famous so quickly, I would liken them to professional athletes: one day they're in college and the next they're getting $10 million salaries—money goes to their heads." But the Castles got such *fun* out of their overpriced new home: togged out in riding clothes, tearing around on horseback, buying dogs, dogs, and more dogs to fill the house and the yard, having weekend house parties, putting in new tennis courts. They certainly didn't inspire Fitzgerald's *The Great Gatsby*, but the Castles were a precursor to that new money, relaxation-at-any-cost Long Island lifestyle.

While Irene laughed at Vernon being "charmingly irresponsible," she was no financial genius herself. Elisabeth Marbury recalled being handed a $1,500 bill by a collector for a horse Irene had bought while on tour. "Their day was never complete unless they had bought something," Marbury sighed. "Motor-cars were purchased with a joyous carelessness I have never seen equaled. Fur wraps fell upon Irene's lovely shoulders like manna from heaven."

Irene lamented Vernon as "a soft touch . . . a benevolent Bank of England." He overtipped and overspent. Attending a car show in Manhattan, he drove home in a $5,000 Minerva, a high-end Belgian model known as "The Car of Kings and Queens"—then he hired Elsie de Wolfe to redecorate the interior.

Vernon, said Irene, "was fond of persons who had a sense of humor, and he had a very keen one himself. . . . He loved the comic strips and cartoons of the evening papers." "Darling, I love the Krazy Kat you sent me," Vernon was to thank Irene during wartime. "I think they are awfully funny.

... That mouse is an awfully ungrateful little animal. He doesn't appreciate the Kat's love. I guess he's like I used to be." As for his work, the theater was another playroom to Vernon: "he went no matter how ill he was. He never got over the beginner's love of the theater's backstage. The people he met there all amused him and worshipped him."

As for herself, Irene loved being queen of her new mansion but was careful never to lift a finger around the house, hiring multitudes of servants, all overseen by Walter Ash. "I never touch the house," Irene bragged in 1915. "Since we've had money enough, I've never even ordered a meal. I won't even talk about the affairs of the house."

It's tempting to stereotype the Castles by their publicity and by Irene's own writing—Vernon as a childlike will-o'-the-wisp, flitting from one bright, shiny object to the next, shallow and empty-headed as a comic strip character; Irene as a hardheaded, humorless dynamo, barreling through life, leaving a trail of injured in her wake. This is unfair to both of them. Vernon's writings, and his friends, show an intelligent, tirelessly energetic, and forward-thinking man; Irene could be disarmingly lazy, unsure of herself, dizzy about money, and fiercely loyal to her friends.

Part of their charm was their youthful animal spirits. In photos, Vernon and Irene look stately and adult to our modern eyes—but remember, Vernon had his twenty-seventh birthday in May 1914, and Irene had turned twenty-one the previous month. To see this healthy, energetic young couple swooping and swirling and kicking around the floor made audiences' hearts race. Younger people wanted to emulate them, and older people felt their ennui fall away.

And their social éclat also paved their way to success. Working-class girls idolized Irene as the last word in chic and looked to Vernon as a prince in white tie (though, admittedly, their blue-collar boyfriends sneered at this British butterfly). Upper-class society folk were charmed by the Castles' manners, ease, and low-key good taste (carefully coached, of course, by Elisabeth Marbury and Elsie de Wolf). And the teeming middle class recognized them as fellow social and economic strivers.

What's not obvious from still photos, what can be sensed only by contemporary writing and from watching them on film, is how *sexy* the Castles were on the dance floor. The couple, entwined around each other, wrapped in each other, as they sinuously whirled around—no wonder they had to play down sex appeal in their carefully posed photos and moral writings about how dance is good for the soul and the body. The opportunity to dance at Castle House with Vernon or Irene must have seemed close to adultery.

And—while Vernon was really the greater talent of the duo—Irene was both innovative and graceful in her style as well. Cecil Beaton recalled, "Previously dancers had made softer use of gesture, but Irene Castle moved her hands sharply, with a masculine boldness, the wrists arched, the fingers straight as bread sticks. . . . She invented a whole balance of movement, with the pelvis thrust forward and the body leaning backward, giving her torso the admirable lines and flat look of a Cretan sculpture. . . . The 'trademark' of the raised shoulder became a sort of fetish that many women were to copy. . . . Yet Irene Castle's boyish impression was counterbalanced by an extreme femininity, an equally strong suggestion of allure, despite the fact that she employed none of the usual feminine attributes."

One reporter in 1915 viewed them critically, wondering, "Just what is it that makes the Castles' performances so fascinating, why they 'get away with it' in such brilliant style. . . . Other dancers, perhaps technically better dancers than the Castles, work themselves to death and get one-tenth of the applause." It wasn't so much technical ability that spurred their stardom, he resolved, but "it is the spirit of success that almost oozes from these two young people that makes everyone split new kid gloves in admiration."

∾ᬒᬊᬒᬊᬊᬊ

"The Castles Are Coming! Hooray! Hooray!"

As the Castles' profile rose in early 1914, Elisabeth Marbury came up with a new scheme, one that would earn them more money and publicity than a regular vaudeville tour: the Castles would dance from city to city, from coast to coast. In the 1939 biopic *The Story of Vernon and Irene Castle,* their 1914 Whirlwind Tour was cleverly depicted by director H. C. Potter, cinematographer Robert de Grasse, and choreographer Hermes Pan. Fred Astaire and Ginger Rogers were shot on an outdoor set, dancing atop a huge map of the United States, one-stepping happily and smoothly from one coast to the other.

The real tour was quite another story. For one thing, a cross-country tour turned out to be impossible, so they never got further than the Midwest. Each show was to be half dancing exhibition and—to drum up local excitement—half dance contest, judged by the Castles. Irene did not like this idea: mingling with the public at large had never been her favorite pastime, and she felt that "a stage is a conspicuous place . . . most people would think twice about climbing up on a stage." She was wrong about peoples' willingness to participate, but the competition did, predictably, result in some hard feelings.

The evening with the Castles began with a snappy overture by James Reese Europe's orchestra, followed by Vernon and Irene doing a one-step. Castle House dancers Jean Ott and Holton Herr did the hesitation waltz while Irene changed frocks; she and Vernon then danced a tango. Another costume change while Europe played "The Dance Furore," then the Castles demonstrated the maxixe, half and half, and gavotte.

Europe's band played during the intermission, and at most stops, Vernon came out from backstage to take the drums over from Buddie Gilmore. According to the *Boston Transcript,* he "produced such a hellish noise as no Tartar band ever could equal, drowning even the music of the orchestra, to the great delight of the audience."

After the intermission, Vernon gave a talk on the dos and don'ts of dancing, which he delivered with a breezy, offhand comic touch. "Mr. Castle is a comedian," noted a Toronto paper admiringly. "He gave a very funny little talk on dances and dancing, and when the other members of the company from Castle House [Margaret Geraty, Sterling Pile, Dorothy Taylor, and Raymond Kirwan] were giving exhibitions, he made remarks which kept the audience on a broad grin. They showed how dances should and should not be danced, and the should nots closely resembled some fantastic dances which have been noticed during the past winter in nice, proper Toronto. Mr. Castle said, 'You notice, we are not wrestling with our partners this season. It is not necessary to sink down on one knee to be a good waltzer.' It was very entertaining, but one hopes that youthful Toronto will take to heart Mr. Castle's remarks that certain of the dances are not meant for the ballroom."

The big finale, the Castle Trophy Tournament, was a minefield for local pride and hurt feelings. Often, several talented couples would be in the running, so, Irene recalled, "we had to depend on Jim Europe's ability to change the tempo of the piece he was playing without an apparent pause. Without changing the tune he would jump from one-step to waltz time and in this way we were able to weed out the couple or couples who did not at once perceive the change and swing easily into the new time."

The tour was to open in Boston and wind up back in New York twenty-four days and thirty-five cities later, culminating in a final exhibition at a "Carnival of Dancing" to celebrate the opening of a new dance palace, Danseland, atop Madison Square Garden. It was widely promoted and advertised with the slogan "The Castles Are Coming! Hooray! Hooray!" The company would bring along the thirty-five Castle Champion Cup-winning couples, for one last grand dance-off.

It was a happy little band that took off from Grand Central Terminal, and Vernon was determined to keep it happy. The Whirlwind Tour train consisted of three cars: one for the Castles, one for Europe and his eighteen musicians, and one baggage car/diner. Banjo player William Elkins recalled the group as "one of the most perfectly disciplined organizations and one in which everyone enjoyed themselves."

One way of maintaining discipline as well as comradeship on the long, arduous trip was the regular "mock trials" held for major and minor infractions of the peace. No one was absolved, from the Castles to the lowliest stagehand. Lateness, flubs onstage, chewing gum onstage, wearing brown shoes with evening clothes, drinking, breaking theater taboos (such as hats on the bed, whistling) were all causes for trial. Unless they themselves were the defendants, James Europe played attorney for the prosecution, and Gladwyn MacDougal attorney for the defense (the jury changed from trial to trial). If found guilty, the prisoner was either spanked or had to buy sandwiches and beer for the company at the next stop (the Castles themselves, when charged with lateness, escaped the spanking and bought champagne, not beer, as penance).

Infractions were not always so innocent: William Elkins recalled the trial of one of the dancers, who had been overheard using the word "nigger" backstage (not directly addressing one of the company but chatting with a local stagehand). The word was already so loaded by 1914 that the Castles insisted on a trial as soon as they were informed of the incident. The prisoner pled guilty, and Vernon fined him $50, a huge amount of money at the time, or he was encouraged to buy "champagne, sandwiches, and refreshments for the whole troupe which cost him at least fifty dollars." When the offender objected, Vernon—looking as threatening as was possible for him—suggested that the all-black jury "might be a little rough." The refreshments were bought, and, Elkins recalled, the word "nigger" was never again heard on the tour. Shortly after the tour ended, an appreciative James Reese Europe was quoted as saying the Castles were "the best friends of the colored professional. . . . Race, color, creed nor religion mark their lives."

The tour started off with a bang in Boston: "Castles Score Tango Triumph," read the headlines. "Both Mr. And Mrs. Castle are artists who are familiar with their profession. And the one-step and waltz were turned into movements of irresistible artistic beauty through their interpretation. Not even the art of a [Geraldine] Farrar or a [Lina] Cavalieri could have drawn more enthusiastic gatherings." The same paper noted the excited throngs crowding to get in to the Boston Opera House. One would have thought "there was a premiere at the opera or that Melba, Farrar or Caruso were singing. Every car that passed the door brought its gay assembly which then packed the vast auditorium."

Not everyone, it must be added, was charmed by Vernon: a Detroit reporter had a terrible time deciphering his British accent and wasn't quite sure if he was kidding when he said, "Frankly, I must say that I have not seen bettah dawnsing in any city than heah in—what town is this? Detroit?—Detroit."

"The whole performance," noted the *Rochester Times*, "was conducted with an agreeable informality. . . . Mr. Castle is a diverting comedian and his various interpolated remarks never failed to provoke amusement." The Castles' dancing was "full of an incomparably graceful animation and strangely fascinating," and Vernon again came to the rescue when the locals took to the floor for the dance-off: "Mr. Castle . . . contrived to make the youthful contestants perfectly at ease."

They closed out April with stops in Washington, D.C., Pittsburgh, and Baltimore. At that last venue, Vernon paused long enough to chat with a reporter about his views of dance and dancers. "There has been such a tremendous amount of misunderstanding about the modern dances that we just decided to make this trip for the purpose of demonstrating what ballroom dances really are," he told the *Baltimore News*. "There is a great deal of very beautiful dancing that is perfectly alright in itself, but which has no place except on the stage. The first consideration in all good dancing . . . is selflessness. There are steps, no matter how artistic they may be, that . . . take up space on the floor and crowd other dancers. You know how all the skaters who wish to do fancy figures are sent into the midst of the rink while everyone else skates around on the outside? Now, in a ballroom, the same thing should be the case. Except for the fact that there is never any room in the center of a ballroom for fancy dances."

They toured the Northeast at the beginning of May: Erie, Pennsylvania; Philadelphia; Hartford, Connecticut; Rochester, New York. In Buffalo, New York, on May 2, the *Times* called the Castles the "greatest living tango exponents" and mistakenly touted "Europe's most famous tango orchestra."

Dancing from one town to another might be like leaping from a rose garden into quicksand. An unnamed vaudeville performer in a 1925 *Saturday Evening Post* article recalled how wildly audiences could vary from city to city: "Steel-ribbed Pittsburgh could not be expected to enjoy the same things in similar fashion with rose-grown Portland, Oregon—the personality of the house manager and staff, these and fifty other elements contribute to determine the quality of an audience. . . . Detroit is soft for comedy acts, either classy or hokum, but tough for highbrow musical turns. Youngstown—try to make 'em laugh there, that's all! A comedian playing Baltimore will sometimes insert a suggestion of the risqué when he would not think of pulling the line in Minneapolis." Vernon and Irene were getting to know the country city by city, and which ones to avoid in the future.

Audiences varied from night to night and according to how long the show was to play in that city. As actor Bennet Musson wrote in 1910, you soon learn that "the small city variety does not warm up quite so soon; that it does not wish to be taken off its guard, or to be considered unsophisticated, so it is a bit offish at first. That the proportion of cultivated, well-read persons . . . is probably greater [in a one-night show]. So you play to that night-stand audience earnestly and heartily."

Many audiences in 1914 had never seen a black orchestra perform before; Buddie Gilmore was the only performer other than the Castles to be onstage, so the audience could see and enjoy his acrobatic and entertaining form of drumming. Stage managers were informed beforehand that this was to be an integrated troupe, so anyone who had a problem with that simply did not book the show. There was no trouble finding unsegregated hotel or restaurant accommodations (still a problem as late as the 1950s and '60s with traveling musicians), as the members of the Whirlwind Tour troupe slept in their train and ate on the run: "take-out" food was brought to them in the theater or on board the train. With their breakneck schedule, there was no time to sit down in restaurants.

The *Philadelphia Telegraph* reporter noted what many eager dancers must have found to be their experience: the Castles danced with a grace that "makes the hardest dance look like the simplest, teases the watcher into the belief that it is an accomplishment of ease until practice hours later at home bring disappointment and the knowledge that the dancing of the twentieth century is an art acquired by hard practice only." And not *only* hard practice: the sad truth is, some people never could accomplish even the simplest steps with a fraction of the grace that the Castles exhibited.

Seeing the Castles in person for the first time, many audience members were struck with how thin they were: in the early 1910s, the well-fed Edwardian silhouette still held sway, and the ultra-chic slim lines of dress designers Poiret and Lucile had not yet hit the smaller towns. Over and over, the press coverage stressed how *little* there was to the Castles: "Mr. Castle is about six feet tall and weighs 84 pounds," read a typical article, from the *Detroit News*. "His lower limbs extend from the ground up in the customary manner—like a gas pipe. Mrs. Castle is very comely—and very thin ... everything said about Vernon goes for Irene. Except that she weighs 68. When the Castles appeared everybody gasped, most because they were in the presence of The Castles; others because the Castles are so thin."

In early May, the Castles arrived in St. Joseph, Missouri, where reviews of the orchestra were decidedly mixed, one paper lauding "the African band," another writing, "The highly praised Negro orchestra headed by one widely grinning Mr. Europe is rather below the average of such organizations. Its chief attraction was a particularly black and particularly busy drummer, whose feats of contortion ... so excited the jealousy of Mr. Castle that ... he took charge of the drums himself and demonstrated that while the colored man whom he had displaced could perform upon only eight instruments at one and the same time, Mr. Castle could manage nine or ten without difficulty."

The troupe moved through Hutchinson, Kansas, and St. Paul, Minnesota. Irene tried to be pleasant to reporters in Minneapolis but came off as just a tad condescending, telling them "what lovely cities Minneapolis and St. Paul are! I had no idea they were so close together or so—shall I say—*metropolitan*. New Yorkers have such a *peculiar* idea of the rest of the country. The St. Paul audience was *adorable* last night. I had no *idea* there were so many nice-looking people outside New York."

Things started to go a bit sour in Minneapolis, where bad scheduling and exhaustion were catching up with the company. The Castles were scheduled to appear after their regular performance at dances at the Radisson and at Le Trianon on Sixth Street but never showed, "although there were many, many people anxious to see them and dance with them." One paper huffed angrily that "Mr. and Mrs. Castle balked last night at mingling with Minneapolis dancers. Not one single Minneapolis man danced with Mrs. Castle, not one single Minneapolis maiden had the proud privilege of gliding with Mrs. Castle's husband. . . . Mr. and Mrs. Castle left Minneapolis on a midnight train."

The further west they got, the more mixed their reception was. Not that there weren't always plenty of people eager to see the Castles and enjoy a night of competitive dancing. But there was a tinge of resentment, as well, at these New Yorkers come to town to show the hicks what they were doing wrong. Irene made things worse in Omaha, where she let slip a few terse words to a reporter: "Speaking of Western dancing, Mrs. Castle was far from complimentary. 'The farther we come from New York, the more exaggerated seems to be the dancing. The dip, bend and kick went out a year ago. What we teach is simple, graceful dancing.'" Omaha was not amused, and Irene was advised to watch her tongue.

Through mid-May, the Castles and their band worked their way through Milwaukee, Cincinnati, Columbus, and Youngstown, Ohio. Things got really ugly in Akron, Ohio, where local dancing instructor W. D. Lynch and Vernon "almost came to blows Saturday night following the dance tournament." After the Castle Cup was awarded to Akron's winning couple, Professor Lynch proceeded to give a talk to the audience. Vernon asked him to hurry things along, as the company had a train to catch: "'Oh, you'll catch the train soon enough, when I get through with you,' was Lynch's rejoinder," said a local paper. "Mr. Castle made a movement like a pugilist who intends to feint out his opponent. 'Get off the stage, this is our show,' said Mrs. Castle. 'Well, it's a mighty poor show at that,' said Lynch."

There were other problems with the tour as well, caused by Vernon's impetuously signing contracts with Charles Dillingham to appear in the revue *Stop! Look! Listen!* and with the Shuberts to appear in *The Belle of Bond Street.* In Philadelphia the Shuberts served them with injunctions stating that if they danced for anyone else they'd be held in contempt and "liable to a heavy fine and imprisonment." When the process server approached them at the stage door, Vernon managed to slip inside, leaving his wife to face the music. Irene took the papers, read them, and threw them back in the process server's face. In the end, the Shuberts hired Gaby Deslys and Harry Pilcer to replace the Castles in *The Belle of Bond Street;* Dillingham took the hint and also hired Deslys and Pilcer for *Stop! Look! Listen!* which was produced in 1915.

It was off next to New York State (Albany, Syracuse, Utica); New Haven, Connecticut; and Providence, Rhode Island. The Whirlwind Tour company finally staggered back into New York for its grand finale on May 23. By the time the tour members reentered New York, noted the *Evening Mail,* that city had "five rooftop dances, and practically every restaurant in town has cleared a space for tangoing."

Depending on which newspaper you read, the climactic Madison Square Garden show was either the grandest exhibit of the year or a huge crashing flop. The *New York American* fell into the former camp: "A worthy culmination, for this grand dance event was the greatest of its kind that has ever taken place anywhere.... The Garden never looked so pretty. The sight that met the eye at night, when several thousand dancers were on the floor was charming in the extreme, but perhaps the gay costumes of the pretty women who congregated in the afternoon was even more effective. Nothing like it exactly has ever been seen in New York, or anywhere else, for that matter." The huge audience was a "well-dressed and well-mannered throng . . . a happy crowd, for each member of it was delighted to dance and see others who were the most proficient in modern steps probably in the whole world."

Another reporter disagreed, even down to the decor: "The 'gorgeous decorations' consisted of strips of blue cotton cloths sparsely strung around the enormous hall, and workmen began tearing these down before the last patrons were out of the Garden . . . the dancing contests were so devoid of interest that the Garden was empty before 11:00, at which hour it was intended that the public dancing should begin. The Great Dancing Carnival for the Castle Cup was the biggest fizzle New York has seen in years, despite the tremendous advertisement given it in advance."

When the money was added up, the Castle's total gross was $85,000 for the four-week tour, the weekly expenses of the trip running between $9,000 and $10,000. They brought in an average of $5,800 a day ($1,700 at the matinees, and $4,100 at night, with box seats going for $5). The most profitable cities had been Boston ($7,500), Philadelphia ($6,400), and Chicago ($5,000), and the poorest receipts were in Milwaukee ($1,900) and Columbus ($1,800). The Whirlwind Tour was estimated to have made $15,000 for its promoters.

Irene claimed that after the dust had settled from the Whirlwind Tour, she and Vernon received a dance-off challenge from their old bête noire, Maurice, who offered to dance against them in Madison Square Garden before a panel of judges (prechosen by Maurice). "We laughed and . . . never even bothered to answer the challenge," said Irene.

Right after the tour ended, Irene was rushed to the hospital, where her doctor, Bolling Lee, performed an appendectomy—a very serious and dangerous procedure in those pre-antibiotic days. "Mrs. Castle will not be out of peril before a week at the earliest," Lee told reporters on May 27. When asked if "over-dancing" had caused Irene's illness, he scoffed, "Dancing has nothing to do with it. She is subject to appendicitis, having had previous attacks—a very severe one, as a matter of fact, in Paris last year" (where, the reporter might have responded, she'd been *dancing*).

In May, while Irene was recovering from her appendectomy, plans were already well under way for yet another Castles endeavor. Despite the failure of Sans Souci, Vernon and Irene were persuaded to back another dancing club, this one at Coney Island's Luna Park, to be called Castles by the Sea. (A popular dancer named Adelaide and her partner, J. J. Hughes, jumped on the bandwagon and opened a Brooklyn dancing school they wittily named "Bensonhurst-by-the-Sea.")

Luna Park had opened, to great success, in 1903, and managed to reinvent itself every season. One entered through the light-bedecked Court of Honor to be greeted with a re-creation of Venice, complete with Grand Canal and gondoliers. Other features included the Trip to the Moon, 20,000 Leagues under the Sea, and War of the Worlds exhibits, a Shoot-the-Chutes ride, a double Ferris wheel, a Helter-Skelter ride, elephant rides, and a monkey park (the latter of which must have attracted the Castles). At night the park was illuminated by more than a million lightbulbs, its spires and minarets visible for miles.

Castles by the Sea was erected near Luna Park's entrance, with a forty-by-fifty-foot dance floor on a dock overlooking the shore. It opened at the beginning of June 1914, just in time for the summer influx, and was "the one biggest and newest thing at Luna this year," according to the *Columbus Evening Dispatch*, "attracting the feet of the social crowds of Manhattan and Brooklyn." Visitors entered through the Court of Honor and Castles by the Sea's "broad staircase, bordered by growing plants, lead[ing] to the pagoda and electric fountains. Behind the trellis, festooned with vines, is the ballroom. In it are French mirrors and costly draperies. Casement windows lead to the pagoda overlooking the lagoon." Socialite Mrs. John Corbin was in charge of the establishment, aided by a corps of dance teachers and, when they could find the spare time, Vernon and Irene. One paper also noted the romantic, summery touch of "a broad porch, overlooking the lagoon extending from the dance floor, offering an excellent spot to witness the open-air circus performers." One of the attractions at Castles by the Sea was drummer Buddie Gilmore, dispatched by James Reese Europe to entertain the crowds. Anyone "with dancing blood in his system has got to dance when he hears this music," Gilmore enthused to a reporter.

On Castles by the Sea's first summer weekend, theatrical producer

William Brady and his actress daughter, Alice, were among the attendees, as were Irene's friend William Randolph Hearst and his wife, Ethel Barrymore and her husband, and Broadway star Laurette Taylor. On July 11, Irene shakily made her first post-appendectomy appearance at a one-step contest Vernon was judging at Castles by the Sea; she motored down with him from their Long Island home. After the contest, she danced a tango with Vernon, who told the appreciative crowd that "this was his wife's first public appearance since her recent illness, and that she was still very delicate."

Castles by the Sea was a huge success that summer, though it was not continued the following year, by which time Vernon and Irene had other commitments. Luna Park itself is long gone today, having burned to the ground in 1944.

Chapter Twenty

᭑᭜᭜᭜᭑

"We were both miserable on those Vaudeville tours"

Vernon and Irene were hoping to spend the summer of 1914 recovering from their Whirlwind Tour while spending some of their profits in Europe. Paris, Deauville, perhaps a night or two of dancing to pay for their passage. They sailed on July 18, aboard the *Imperator*, despite rumblings in the newspapers about "the situation" in Europe. On landing, they renewed ties with "Papa" Louis at the Café de Paris.

After the war, Irene claimed that she and Vernon had noted "a current of unrest . . . something unusual" in France and England that summer of 1914, but that would have made them pretty remarkable. Everyone who read the papers knew of the assassination of Archduke Ferdinand in Sarajevo and the angry responses from Austria-Hungary and Serbia. Few paid much attention, and it's doubtful that the Castles did, either. Governments were always rattling their sabers.

They played their date in Paris, where Irene's mother was staying, and took the train for their August engagement in Deauville on July 31, their big and small dogs wedged into their compartment with them. By the time they showed up for work on August 1, all hell had broken loose, and panicked holidaymakers were fleeing back to their homes. During those first few days of August, Germany declared war on Russia and France and marched into Belgium (thus drawing even Irene's Brussels griffon, Kiki, into the fray), France and Britain declared war on the aggressors, and within a week everyone seemed to be mobilizing against everyone else. The Casino had few guests left to enjoy the Castles' act, and even the staff members were trying to contact their families.

Where to go, how to get there? Trains were packed with refugees and soldiers; private cars were being requisitioned by the government. Vernon was already worried about his family in England. The Castles' contract had been cancelled by an "act of God," and the only way to England seemed to be by Channel boat—they cashed in their travelers' checks for Belgian francs ("worth about as much as a busted lamp shade by then") and paid thousands to be crammed onto a small boat plying from Trouville to Le Havre. At Le Havre, Vernon and Irene fought their way through crowds— their dogs beginning to panic as well, their luggage hampering their every move—and Vernon managed to obtain two refugee tickets for England. But they would have to leave Tell behind.

Irene could, and would, easily smuggle little Kiki to England in a coat or muff, but even she couldn't stuff a German shepherd down the front of her blouse. They could not give up their tickets; no one knew if or when another boat would be leaving for England. In the panic of war, getting Tell proper quarantine papers was impossible; Vernon and Irene rushed from one end of Le Havre to the other looking for a vet who would board the dog.

After rejecting one disreputable-looking establishment after another, Vernon left poor Tell in a straw-filled cage and told the kennel owner a huge reward would be his if he treated Tell "as though he were his only child." Vernon kissed Tell on the nose and pointed to the cage; Tell obediently went in, curled up, and looked pathetic. "Vernon's eyes were wet as we walked out of the veterinarian's. Nobody spoke all the way to the boat."

The Castles (and the half-suffocated Kiki) arrived in England, took a train for London, and finally landed on the doorstep of Vernon's sister Coralie Grossmith at her St. John's Wood home. While the country held its breath, men enlisted, and refugees poured in and out of London, Vernon traveled against the tide back to France and spent all of his time and energy rescuing Tell from Le Havre.

Through judicious bribery (their friend Elsie Janis loaned them some gold coins), he managed to get Board of Agriculture papers allowing Tell into British quarantine from France. The only way back to Le Havre at this point was via Paris. "Paris was like a crowded theater in which some one had shouted 'fire!,'" said Irene. Mrs. Foote was still in Paris, planning to stay there as long as was practical. Vernon tried to look up his mother-in-law, but in his upset state managed to get lost and was escorted back to his own hotel by an officious young soldier.

He hitched a ride on a troop train to Le Havre, and he and Tell were reunited. The confusion of war, and Elsie Janis's gold coins, sped Vernon and Tell's way back to England. They slipped past the quarantine board and hopped a taxi for the Grossmiths': "Evidently the British government had more serious things to consider at the time" than an unregistered dog, said Irene.

Through influential friends, the Castles managed to book passage from Liverpool to New York for themselves, Irene's mother, and both dogs. They sailed aboard the *Olympic*, and on August 27 had sufficiently recovered from their ordeal to stage a dance aboard ship, in a faux Parisian café. When the Castles stepped off the ship in New York, they looked awfully natty for war refugees. Vernon wore a light-colored pinstriped suit and a straw boater and was decked out in spats and a chic little walking stick. Irene wore a dark suit with a bolero jacket and turned-up collar. Her hat was fashionably bizarre, and her earrings dangled halfway down her neck. Irene happily clutched Kiki to her bosom, and Vernon held Tell on a metal leash.

The Castles signed for a six-week vaudeville tour with the Keith-Albee Corporation, run by cutthroat impresarios B. F. Keith and E. F. Albee who, in effect, "owned" vaudeville on the East Coast (the West Coast was largely handled at the time by Martin Beck's Orpheum circuit).

Vaudeville—or, to use a more accurate description, "variety"—was a time-honored way for theater stars to pick up extra money. From the 1880s through the 1930s, vaudeville theaters flourished all over the United States, in small towns and big cities. A performer with luck, energy, and the right talents could make a living by touring for decades with the same act. Most never really became stars, and many acts rarely strayed from vaudeville— the hugely successful Sophie Tucker and Nora Bayes spent most of their careers there, as did now-forgotten but once-popular variety mainstays like Blossom Seeley, Eva Tanguay, the Duncan sisters, Willie and Eugene Howard, Joe Laurie Jr., and Pat Rooney.

Some vaudeville performers, such as Eddie Cantor, W. C. Fields, Burns and Allen, and Ina Claire, went on to great fame on Broadway, in the movies, or on radio. It worked the other way around, too, as stars like the Castles, Ethel Barrymore, and Sarah Bernhardt used their downtime to "slum it" on the well-paying vaudeville circuits.

It was quite a coup to sign with Keith-Albee. The two had teamed in 1885, and by the 1910s had formed what was known as "the Sunday School circuit," for their insistence on squeaky-clean family fare at their theaters. This was, of course, no problem for the Castles. But other acts (comedians and singers in particular) often ran afoul of the Keith-Albee rule book: "If you are guilty of uttering anything sacrilegious or even suggestive you will be immediately closed and will never again be allowed in a theater where Mr. Keith is in authority." A famous list of forbidden cuss words was posted backstage: "slob," "hully-gee," "son-of-a-gun," among others.

The rough-and-tumble world of vaudeville may not have come as much of a shock to Vernon, raised in hotels and pubs. But it was quite a school for the sheltered Irene. As pseudonymous vaudeville historian Trav S. D. puts it, "Blacks, whites, men, women, straights, gays, old, young, Jews, gentiles, people from dozens of different nations worked together, shared dressing rooms, traveled together, ate and drank together, cooked for one another, slept together, socialized, gambled together, watched one another's performances, swapped pointers and new material, baby-sat one another's kids, loaned one another money, stuck up for one another—and, sometimes, as people do, insulted and fought with one another."

Actor Bennet Musson complained in a 1910 article, "In a week of one-night stands you will get at least one bad, old theatre. . . . Dressing room number four proves to be small, dirty, ill-ventilated and ill-lighted. It is next to the boiler room, and the heat is intolerable. Or it is near a door that opens on an alley, and the cold is unbearable. It contains a small tin pitcher and bowl, and there is no place to throw the water. There are a few hooks and nails, on which the actors preceding you have hung pieces of paper, to protect their clothes from the dirty walls." It was a long way from New Rochelle.

The vaudeville tour started off well, opening in Cincinnati at the beginning of September: "They seemed to fairly excel all their former efforts in the easy grace and artistic distinction of their dancing," wrote a local reviewer, and Vernon's amusing talks went over well, too. They danced the polka, maxixe, fox trot, Argentine tango, and one-step; Vernon was occasionally partnered by a stand-in while Irene rushed backstage to change gowns. They played to standing room only at the Cleveland Hippodrome, where a reviewer commented that "they provide one of the classiest headliners ever offered here in vaudeville. . . . They are beautiful dancers, this pair, splendid exponents of a beautiful art, and while it is modern and somewhat unconventional, there is grace in it that perhaps heretofore we have expected only from ballet dancers."

Vernon found time in Cleveland to give dance lessons—at $30 an

hour—at the Statler Hotel, telling reporter Archie Bell, "Women are naturally graceful, perhaps they are less self-conscious than men. . . . Excellent
men dancers are rare birds. There are plenty of first-class professional
women dancers who cannot find a partner that suits." He modestly claimed
he was baffled by their success in vaudeville, guessing that "people come to
the theater . . . not because they want to see us, but because they think
they'll learn about dancing." He also admitted to regrets about the falling-
off of his acting career since his Lew Fields days. "I want to be an actor. I
always did want to be one, and now I am determined that I shall be." To
that end, he and Irene were negotiating for a Broadway show to open at
the end of 1914.

The tour continued in Boston in early October, where it hit a snag—
this time, one entirely the Castles' fault. Claiming exhaustion and overwork, Vernon and Irene told the Keith-Albee representative that their salary of $1,600 a week was simply not enough and demanded an increase to
$2,500 "to tango through the week." Their act was already advertised in lo-
cal papers and at the theater, and sales were brisk: they had Keith-Albee
over a barrel, and they were forced to meet their demands.

The show business world was horrified: "Castles' Hold-Up" was the
headline in *Variety;* "Vaudeville Likely to Be Closed to Them in the Future,"
read another. It's unlikely that this move was sanctioned by either Elisabeth
Marbury or Gladwyn MacDougal, as it really was the depth of unprofes-
sionalism. The Shuberts were already unhappy with the Castles; now they
had made enemies of the very important B. F. Keith and E. F. Albee and
shown themselves to be untrustworthy to the show business community at
large. The managers, noted one paper, "will have something to say the next
time the Castles want to make a little easy money in vaudeville."

Irene hated vaudeville but loved that "easy money." The worst part—
for both Vernon and Irene—was the animal acts. Every bill had at least two;
sometimes one opened the show as a "dumb" (silent) act; another, more famous, would be featured later in the program. Everywhere the Castles
turned, they were on the bill with dogs, cats, bears, horses, doves, monkeys,
dressed up in clothing and going through amusing or acrobatic antics. Humane societies would investigate every so often, but wily trainers could get
around them (just as some acts tricked the Society for the Prevention of
Cruelty to Children by passing off underage performers as midgets).

Just a few of the more successful animal acts mentioned by vaudeville historian Douglas Gilbert were Fink's mules, Barnold's dogs, Cliff Berzac's trick mule, Jules Carr's performing bear, Cecil and Van's "wire and dog act," Mlle. Eichbrette's monkey troupe, Mlle. Fogardus's educated cockatoos and dogs, J. W. Hampton's educated dogs and geese, Lockhart's elephants, Mlle. Lucille and Cockie, the trained cockatoo, lion tamer George Marck, Nelson's boxing cats, Harry M. Parker's dog and cat circus, and Strassel's wonder seal. Professor Welton's Boxing Cats can be seen today in an 1894 film on the Library of Congress's American Memory Web site, more than a century after their brief fame.

Dog trainer Rennie Renfro (who was responsible for the performers in MGM's bizarre *Dogville* film shorts of 1929–31) insisted that his animals were treated with loving kindness. "People have been brutal to dogs in training," he admitted, "but the wise trainer wouldn't use such methods. Even if the humanitarian angle didn't enter in, it's not good business. A dog that has been beaten into tricks can't be depended upon. His spirit will break at the most critical time. He is apt to lay down in his biggest scenes and nothing on earth can bring him back to efficiency again."

Irene argued that "it is not natural for a bear to roller-skate, a horse or dog to leap any great distance into water, a monkey to ride a bicycle." She knew that show business was rife with brutal trainers and expressed her distaste with audiences who "gurgle with glee when they see a dog dressed up in some hideous circus suit, balancing a lamp on his nose, or when he climbs laboriously up a great, high ladder until he is nearly out of sight and then, hesitating as long as he is allowed to do so, leaps 30 feet into a pool below. Little do they realize that it was an electric shock through the mount on the metal platform switched on by his master in the wings below made him seem so willing to jump."

The Castles were heartbroken to see animals "shocked with electricity, stuck with needles, and starved except for the few tid-bits of reward which made them do the things they were afraid to do." It was their reaction to this horror that brought Vernon and Irene even closer together. While their dancing, their acting, and their sheer joy in each other's company provided a springboard into their marriage, it was animals that kept them united. "Thank God that I found you, who are so good to little dumb creatures," Vernon wrote to Irene a few years later. They never had children to dote on, but after acquiring Zowie in 1912, there was a never-ending Noah's Ark of birds and beasts flowing into their home.

While touring in vaudeville, both Castles made friends with the animals they encountered, with predictable results. Irene recalled, "We were both miserable on those vaudeville tours because each week brought us in contact with one more sad group of neglected animals living with only hatred in their little hearts for the man who owned them and lived by their daily efforts. Their misery seemed to fascinate me, and, try as I might, I could not leave the theater after my own work was completed. Each day I hoped I could save one who had failed to do his part well a beating."

One little dog in particular broke Irene's heart. It was part of an act comprising sixteen dogs and two monkeys, populating a tiny city, with cars and a street scene. The trainer, crouching in the wings, blew pellets at the animals to make them go through their paces. "One little dog missed his cue one night and failed to get into the patrol wagon driven by a monkey when it stopped to take him in," said Irene. "He was so terrified when the curtain fell and he found himself in the middle of the stage that he didn't know which way to turn. Before he could escape, his owner grabbed him and whipped him thoroughly for his error. The next night, through nervous fear . . . he missed the wagon again. He whimpered and cried in anticipation of what was coming to him, and again he was punished. When he missed the cue the third time, he rushed panic-stricken into my dressing room and we shut the door after him, you may be sure."

Besides dogs, the Castles also purchased a performing bear from its keeper while in Chicago and donated it to the Lincoln Park Zoo (Irene said she and Vernon escorted the trained bear to the zoo in a taxi; one hopes they overtipped the driver). Finally, they inserted a clause in their contract that they would not perform on any bill that had an animal act. It was getting too expensive, financially and emotionally.

The Castles were back in New York on October 13, when they danced for a meeting of James Reese Europe's Tempo Club at the Casino; they also filled a one-night stand at the Park Casino in Hartford, Connecticut, on November 9, which was most notable for having been arranged by Vernon "over long-distance telephone."

In the fall of 1914, Elisabeth Marbury scored what she hoped would be a great coup: placing the Castles in the *Ladies' Home Journal,* the best-selling bible of the middle-class housewife. Its publisher, Edward Bok, you'll recall, had already banned his employees from dancing the turkey trot, so this was no small feat. The October, November, and December issues of *LHJ* featured two-page spreads of the Castles, dancing the Castle fox trot, the Castle polka, and the Castle gavotte. Each article was illustrated by specially posed dance steps and a few paragraphs by Vernon describing the dance, its history and intricacies.

No sooner had the October issue hit the newsstands than Bok began getting furious letters from his readers: the Castles may have attracted New York society types to Castle House, but to most respectable Americans, they were in the same class as Little Egypt and her hootchy-kootchy. Bok ran all three articles as planned, but according to his biographer, he "could not rid the pages of the savor of the cabaret . . . he realized he had made a mistake, and was as much disgusted as were his readers." As had been discovered during the Whirlwind Tour, not all of America was ready for the dance craze, not even when exemplified by a famously respectable married couple.

Still more backlash came when the Castles were taken to task by the Sabbath Committee ladies of the Bible House, who found that the couple were giving a dance at the Astor Hotel on a Sunday: they called their ire down upon the hotel's manager and threatened to summon the authorities. They *did* call the newspapers, which reported that the Astor dance was put off till the following Wednesday.

CHAPTER TWENTY-ONE

"THEIR ENTHUSIASTIC FOLLOWERS NEVER ...GO TO BED AT ALL"

Vernon and Irene had plenty to occupy themselves with and take their minds off the recent debacles in vaudeville and in print. In November 1914 they found themselves in Syracuse, trying out the Broadway-bound musical comedy *Watch Your Step*, the first nonrevue show with songs by Irving Berlin.

The show's book was written by the prolific Harry B. Smith, who had been in the theater since 1879 and had written lyrics or book for such hits as *A Parisian Model, Miss Innocence*, and several editions of the *Ziegfeld Follies*. He recalled in his memoirs that "Mr. Charles Dillingham gave me an old play to convert into a new musical entertainment." Smith was impressed right off the bat with his musical collaborator: "Mr. Berlin . . . is ingenious in inventing unexpected rhymes. Most bards would think it hopeless to attempt to find a rhyme for 'Wednesday'; but Mr. Berlin found one. In one of the songs in this piece, a matinee idol describes his persecution by women and alludes to the elderly worshippers who attend the afternoon performances: 'There's a matinee on Wednesday, / I call it my old hen's day.'"

Irene later said in her memoirs that "everybody connected with the show" knew it was going to be a hit even before it opened, but Smith did not agree: "At rehearsals the material did not seem promising. In the cast was a character woman [Elizabeth Murray] whose specialty was singing Irish comic songs. At the dress rehearsal on a Sunday night, she remarked, 'I went to church this morning and burned candles for the success of this piece; but, personally, I think it will be a blank-blanked failure.'"

The plot, as finally worked out, involved two young lovers (played by Elizabeth Brice and Charles King) who can inherit $2 million only if they do not marry. But the plot was only a wobbly hanger on which to drape Berlin songs and amusing characters: blackface comic Frank Tinney, comedians Harry Kelly and Sam Burbank, the pessimistic Elizabeth Murray doing her Irish-dialect turn, lovely Justine Johnstone as "a hesitating typewriter." When the show tried out in Syracuse, W. C. Fields was in the cast, doing his already-famous poolroom sketch, but he was dropped from the show before it hit New York. Among the chorus girls were Marion Davies's sisters Ethel and Rose.

Vernon played, appropriately enough, a dancing teacher: "Joseph Lilyburn, who invented the steps you watch," while Irene was simply billed as "Mrs. Vernon Castle." The show was all ragtime, both in music and in jokes. Vernon sang "The Dancing Teacher" in act 1; Irene sang "Show Us How to Do the Fox Trot" later in the same act. She and Vernon danced the polka (act 2) and the one-step (act 3). The Castles had hoped James Reese Europe would accompany them in the show, and Charles Dillingham seems to have agreed at first—but to their disappointment, a standard Broadway orchestra was cobbled together instead, with musical director DeWitt Coolman trying his best to keep the stars happy.

During the pre-Broadway run in Detroit, a reporter from the *Detroit News* interviewed Vernon and Irene in their Hotel Ponchartrain room, where he was rather overwhelmed by the presence of Kiki and, especially, Tell, who was "an awful lot" of dog. "Was he named after William Tell?" the reporter asked, at which Vernon produced the old joke, "Yes, Mr. Tell was named years before the dog." Irene expressed relief at being asked about their dogs rather than their dancing: "They want to know how long the craze is going to last. Of course we don't know." "But we hope forever," Vernon added.

Irene was blithely self-confident as the Broadway opening approached, while everyone else in the cast fretted and Vernon lost sleep from worry and overrehearsal. "I couldn't imagine what everybody was so nervous about," she said, stamping herself as an amateur. "This was something I had wanted to do all my life, star in a Broadway show, and here I was getting the chance. Far from being nervous or shy, I was mad for myself in those lovely Lucile gowns."

The show opened on December 8, 1914, at the New Amsterdam Theater on Forty-second Street. Still one of the jewels of Times Square, the New Amsterdam housed the *Ziegfeld Follies* from 1913 through the 1920s, as well as such hits as *Forty-Five Minutes from Broadway, Brewster's Millions, The Merry Widow, Madame X, The Pink Lady, Sally, Whoopee!* and, more recently, *The Lion King*. *Watch Your Step* turned out to be one of the biggest hits of the 1914–15 season, which also included the popular musicals *The Girl from Utah, Chin Chin, Hello, Broadway! The Passing Show of 1915* (with Marilyn Miller), and the current *Ziegfeld Follies* (with Ann Pennington singing and dancing a "Tango-Palace" number).

The *New York Times* fell all over itself raving: "as gay, extravagant and festive an offering as this city could possibly hope to see . . . no end of fun." Irving Berlin was dubbed "the young master of syncopation," his music "born to be caught up and whistled at every street corner." The cast as a whole was praised to the skies, with Vernon "cheerfully personal" and Irene "a delight." The *Evening Sun* also loved it: "The history of twentieth-century America will be written in ragtime. . . . Don't miss it!" The *Dramatic Mirror* placed the Castles above even Irving Berlin: "it is the exquisite charm of the Castles' dancing that lifts *Watch Your Step* out of the ordinary class of entertainment. . . . Without the Castles, *Watch Your Step* seems like a small (and dressed) version of a Winter Garden show."

The out-of-town reviewers were also unanimous in their praise. A Wisconsin reporter wrote, "The dancing of the Castles has lost none of its whirlwind grace, and Vernon is doing some acrobatic stunts, including a hard fall, that makes one think some of his fragile bones will surely crack." The *Detroit News* called *Watch Your Step* "one of the first-class entertainments of the year," adding perceptively that if Vernon "hadn't had the misfortune to make piles of money hopping about, he might have been a very popular comedian." That same paper wrote of Irene that she "danced as charmingly as ever and looked very sweet and dainty. However, she better not sing. That error should be remedied."

Irene's voice earned more than one wisecrack from reviewers. This was the first show in which she had to sing, and, as Elisabeth Marbury reported, "the effect was rather painful." Even Irene admitted that it "laid them in the aisles" when she opened her pretty little mouth to sing and her rather deep contralto notes came out. A popgun with the roar of a cannon, she said, "all the booming quality of a foghorn at sea." Fortunately, Irene had little singing to do (though it was the key song "Show Us How to Do the Fox Trot"), and her graceful dancing and competent, light acting style won over audiences. Not everyone disliked her voice; reviewer May McKenzie wrote that "Mrs. Castle is a physical pastel—a little reed with pipe-stem legs and the serious face of a child. All she needed to disclose was the tough little voice to make her completely individual." Their *Watch Your Step* costar Frank Tinney got his licks in: one night during the show, he called Vernon over and asked, "Vernon, you're a good judge of music, aren't you? Well, now tell all these people what you think of Mrs. Castle's voice." According to a reviewer who was there that night, "Castle was too overcome to answer, whereat Tinney apologized for him. 'Castle's in the air,' he said."

Vernon, of course, breezed jauntily through the show, singing, dancing, clowning, drumming. He was so comfortable in his role as a dancing teacher that Frank Tinney accidentally referred to him as "Vern" several times on opening night. "Vernon Castle is genuinely artistic," wrote one reviewer, while another added that "Mr. Castle seems delighted to be back on the boards again, and works like a Trojan."

With the success of *Watch Your Step*, business at Castle House rose to a frenzy: patrons had the rare opportunity to actually meet and dance with Broadway stars. Exhausted and a little bored, Vernon began hiding out in Long Island, and Irene (who never could be bothered giving dance lessons herself) had to push him out the door to the studio, where love-struck ladies were "stacked up like cordwood" to pay $100 an hour for a dance with Vernon Castle.

While Vernon was teaching, Irene was posing: her fame skyrocketed with *Watch Your Step*, and her status as a fashion leader was further cemented. *Town and Country* featured full-page photos of Irene in the Lucile gowns she wore in the show: the same photo sitting, at Ira L. Hill's New York studio, resulted in fashion shots sent to papers around the country. *Harper's Bazaar* and *Vogue* ran lengthy articles on Irene, beautifully illustrated.

Regardless of their very public marriage, both Castles were trailed by suitors. Debutantes with their curls swept up for the first time and imposing dowagers happily paid to clasp Vernon to their bosoms and spin around the dance floor. Irene later claimed that future stage and screen star Olive Thomas was one of Vernon's conquests, but the chronology is somewhat unlikely (Thomas appeared in her first *Follies* about the time Vernon was leaving for war). Irene was pursued by socialite William Rhinelander Stewart, the scion of one of New York's most prestigious families. She dined alone with several of her beaux and admitted she and Vernon both enjoyed "outside infatuations," but if these went any farther, it never became public or caused a rift in their marriage.

As 1914 drew to a close, the Castles did not stop to catch their breath.

They were starring in Broadway's biggest hit, overseeing New York's hottest club, appearing at private parties and in vaudeville, but they still had one or two tricks up their sleeve that December.

At 216 West Forty-fourth Street stood the Forty-fourth Street Theater, which Lee and J. J. Shubert had built in 1912 as the Weber & Fields Music Hall. "The ornate cornices and capitals of the brick façade gave the building a classical appearance," writes theater historian Nicholas van Hoogstraten, "but the overall effect was diminished by the bulky enclosure of the roof theatre." Weber and Fields opened there in late 1912 in *Roly Poly* and *Without the Law* (a parody of the current melodrama *Within the Law*). By late 1914, the renamed theater was hosting a now-forgotten musical called *The Lilac Domino,* and Robert B. Mantell was booked to star in a series of Shakespeare revivals in the new year. In December 1914, the Castles signed a contract to open not one but two clubs in the building: one in the cellar and one in the rooftop café.

These clubs—Castles in the Air (above) and the Castle Club (below)—opened on December 28, 1914, while Vernon and Irene were appearing in *Watch Your Step* at the New Amsterdam two blocks away. They had nothing to do with the running or management, though they appeared there as often as possible to draw in customers; a twenty-piece orchestra was furnished by James Reese Europe. No expense was spared: the electric sign atop the building "requires a total of 1,242 bulbs. Three colors will be employed in a myriad of brilliant flashes: green, amber and deep crimson," wrote one newspaper.

"Castles in the Air has been elaborately decorated with warm-colored draperies and other furnishings, and the dance floor remodeled and enlarged," wrote another paper. "A cuisine par excellence through the personal supervision of Monsieur Pierre and Monsieur Louis, two Parisian chefs whose names are famous at the Ritz-Carlton and the Knickerbocker Hotels, is offered." The rooftop café was open from 11:00 P.M. until 2:00 A.M., at which point those patrons still able to do so scurried down to the Castle Club rathskeller, where dancing continued "until the sun rises in the heavens." With raised eyebrows, it was noted that "the Forty-Fourth Street Theater will, therefore, be the only place of amusement in New York at which some parts of it will be open throughout the twenty-four hours of the night and day."

Business went very well in late 1914 and early 1915: society friends ("Mr. and Mrs. Vincent Astor, Prince and Princess Trubetskoy, Mr. James Lawrence Breese, Mrs. James B. Eustace, the lithe Mr. Philip Lydig, Mr. and Mrs. Wm. Potter . . .") and theatergoers alike crowded in.

Vanity Fair featured full-page sketches by Ethel Plummer of Castles in the Air, "New York's Roof Garden Cabaret," noting that the club shamelessly violated the new mayor's curfews: "Just as Mayor Mitchell has arranged that everybody should go to bed at one o'clock, along comes the Vernon Castles and rearrange it so that no one can go to bed before two or three. New York is pretty well divided on this great issue, but up to the time of going to press, the Castles have it by a safe majority. In fact, victory rests so decisively that they are just launching a private club which will allow their enthusiastic followers never to go to bed at all."

But—like Sans Souci—Castles in the Air and the Castle Club proved to be a losing proposition for Vernon and Irene. Their contract guaranteed them $1,500 a week, but out of that they had to supply the band, the waiters, the food, the licenses. Operating costs exceeded $1,500, and by February 1915, they were scrambling to get out. (Their total income at this time was said to be $3,600 a week, but a loss is a loss.) Castles in the Air was reconverted into a theater in 1917, as Lew Fields's Forty-Fourth Street Roof Garden; a year later it became the Nora Bayes Theater, "unusually small and uncomfortable," according to one contemporary account. The Castle Club rathskeller went on to great popularity as a speakeasy, the Little Club, during Prohibition and as the famed Stage Door Canteen during World War II. The building was demolished in 1945 to accommodate expansion of the adjoining *New York Times* building.

CHAPTER TWENTY-TWO

"Mrs. Castle is exhausted"

All was not well with Irene, and in late January 1915, she vanished from the cast of *Watch Your Step* at the height of its early popularity. Was she sick? Was she in a snit? Were she and Vernon on the verge of a split? Newspapers put forth all of these theories, as Vernon stated that she was "resting" at St. Elizabeth's Hospital in New York, "not seriously ill," but suffering complications from her appendectomy a few months previous. Her doctor "advised that she go into the hospital and forbade her from dancing for the present."

Vernon showed a rare flash of temper to one reporter bold enough to question him on marital strife. "It is scandalous rubbish, this talk of a separation. . . . There is no sense in any suggestion of a break. Mrs. Castle is exhausted, that's what the matter is. When she is strong again she will come back to the cast of *Watch Your Step*."

What *of* the cast of *Watch Your Step?* Fortunately, Vernon recalled a dancer he'd worked with in his first show, *About Town:* tiny blonde Mae Murray, now about twenty-five years old, was still kicking about New York. She'd appeared in several shows, including Ziegfeld's 1908 *Follies,* and was gaining a name as a dancer in the wake of the Castles' success. Her most frequent partner at this time was tall, elegant Clifton Webb who, like Murray herself, would go on to Hollywood fame.

In her deliciously surrealistic memoirs, Murray recalled that Vernon and Irene "were visible proof that a man and wife could dance through life." As a fan, she was thrilled when, according to her version of the story, Irving Berlin approached her at the club where she was performing and raced her through the cold streets to the New Amsterdam, where Vernon was waiting. "This is little Mae Murray," he told the assembled cast. "She's going to see we're not dark tonight." Lucile's fitters arrived to make some emergency costume alterations while Murray rehearsed her few lines of dialogue and song.

All accounts agree that Murray was a last-minute stand-in. A contemporary article stated that she was contacted at 4:30 P.M. on the day in question and went onstage at 8:00, after meeting with Vernon for only one hour's rehearsal. "It was the proudest moment of my life," said Murray a week or two later. "Mrs. Castle is the premiere dancer in the country; to be chosen as her substitute was an honor that made me very happy." Vernon, she said, "is an ideal partner, he doesn't seem to touch the floor, he seems rather to fly through the air than to dance." The partnership of tall, elegant Vernon Castle and tiny, doll-like Mae Murray (barely five feet tall) must have been a sight to behold.

Newspaper releases insisted that Mae Murray and Irene Castle sent each other sweet little notes and flowers and thanks and compliments. "She kept sending messages to me from the hospital," said Murray, "and I kept sending messages back to her. Foolish, feminine messages like, 'what do you do when you strain a tendon?' and 'do you prefer adhesive plaster to pumice stone for calluses?'"

Reviews stated that Murray "made a decided hit and received round after round of applause." Her fame was a tonic for the Sans Souci (not the Castles' shuttered club of that name, but another night spot where she was performing). After the *Watch Your Step* curtain fell, half the audience followed her in cabs to watch her dance and congratulate her.

Irene Castle returned to *Watch Your Step* within a week. The Castles whipped up a little added interest upon her return by debuting a new dance, the pigeon walk (which, unfortunately, failed to gain much of a following).

Vernon and Irene kept busy as she recovered from whatever her illness may or may not have entailed. In the last few days of January, they performed at benefits for the Actors' Fund (alongside Montgomery and Stone, Ethel Barrymore, George M. Cohan, Frank Tinney, and Lillian Russell) and the Newsboys' Benefit (with Al Jolson, Fanny Brice, Frank Tinney, Nance O'Neil, Valeska Surratt, and Singer's Midgets).

The Castles ventured into Brooklyn in April 1915, agreeing to dance at the Claremont Avenue Rink, and got totally lost on the way over. "We came over the Williamsburg Bridge and we had to stop every half block and ask the way," complained Irene, in a cry still familiar today. That spring, in addition to their regular work, the Castles also played a week's vaudeville engagement at the Palace Theater, judged a dog show, and held a benefit for the Bide-a-Wee home for friendless animals; Irene was thrown from her horse-drawn cart (no injuries) and Vernon was fined $5 for speeding (forty miles an hour).

They also found time to sit with a reporter and ponder the past and future of dancing: "Every hundred years there's a great dancing revival," pontificated Vernon. "About a hundred years ago people stopped dancing the Minuet and took hold of their partners in the Waltz." When asked about the dances of 2015, Vernon sensibly replied, "Heaven only knows."

As the summer approached, Charles Dillingham tied the Castles down for the fall revival of *Watch Your Step*, doubling their weekly salary from $1,000 to $2,000. It was planned that the show would go on hiatus in June and reopen, probably in Philadelphia, in September. But even as he signed that contract, Vernon was planning to renege: he was looking into flight schools and had chosen the Aero Club of America in Newport News, Virginia. "Until the great war broke out," he later said, "I almost imagined that I was an American. I had been here nearly ten years and all my friends, all my interests, were American." Irene knew better than to try to talk him out of his plans, but she privately hoped—as did many—that the war would be over by Christmas.

On April 22, 1915, the Castles danced again to the music of James Reese Europe, at the Tempo Club, one of Harlem's first black musical showcases—the Castles were among the rare white entertainers invited to perform there. On that memorable night, Vernon and Buddie Gilmore traded drum solos; the Castles handed out a loving cup to the winners of a dance contest and then favored the audience with an impromptu whirl around the floor to Europe's music.

Europe would follow Vernon Castle's lead and enlist in the army well before the United States entered the war. In late 1916, he joined New York's Fifteenth Infantry regiment; although his main duties were to form the regimental band, Europe eventually saw combat. His regiment—the first black American regiment to reach France—arrived on January 1, 1918, and, according to his biographer, Lieutenant Europe was the first black officer "to lead troops into combat in the Great War. He was also very likely the first to cross no-man's land and participate in a raid on the German lines." His men—now reclassified as the 369th Infantry regiment—earned the nickname the Hellfighters for their seemingly fearless exploits. The Hellfighters served 191 days in combat, and when on leave in Paris, introduced the locals to their brand of ragtime, which was now melding into a new form of music, called "jass." James Reese Europe arrived back in New York in February 1919 a hero; he and his regiment marched up Fifth Avenue from Twenty-fifth Street to Harlem, crowds (black and white alike) cheering wildly.

CHAPTER TWENTY-THREE

"CASTLES IN THE SUBWAY, / CASTLES IN THE 'L'"

The summer of 1915 was to have been a leisurely one, with Vernon and Irene peacefully enjoying their Long Island home, being interviewed and photographed, attending horse shows and dog shows and automobile shows. But Vernon got a big idea, put into his head by first-time film producers John and Edward Cort. Egged on by Gladwyn MacDougal, Vernon decided to write a film about, and starring, himself and Irene. As usual, Vernon "plunged into it with all the zeal of an explorer setting foot on an uncharted continent," said Irene. The script, she claimed, was finished in three hours. It was all very "Let's put on a show" as she recalled it decades later: "We had one cameraman with a big boxy contraption run with a hand crank, portable and fairly easy to set up."

Despite Irene's recollections of the film as an off-the-cuff amateur production, it was reported that she and Vernon were paid $22,500 by the Cort Film Company for their participation. (The only other film the corporation seems to have completed was *The Melting Pot*, that same year.) Oliver Bailey was hired to direct: new to films, he was a playwright who went on to become a minor Broadway producer, writer, and director. The real professional in the crew was Catherine Carr, who cowrote the script with Vernon; she had about a dozen movies to her credit.

Irene recalled the cast as having been recruited exclusively from family and friends, but there were a few professionals hired. Broadway actor William Carlton played Irene's father, film veteran Kate Blancke was Mrs. Foote, and musical comedy actor Arthur Stanford was the villain, John Crosby (actress Ruth Gordon reportedly made her film debut as an extra but is not identifiable in current prints). But many of the roles were indeed filled by locals: Vernon and Irene, of course, played themselves; Walter Ash and drummer Buddie Gilmore are glimpsed, as well as other, unnamed, servants and friends; and coproducer Edward Cort played one of John

Crosby's evil henchmen. Vernon's precious Tell had a sizeable role, and at least one of Irene's monkeys made an appearance. Locations were similarly grabbed off-the-cuff: the Castles' Long Island home, the nearby Plandome Yacht Club, the back roads, woods, and beaches of Long Island.

Vernon and Carr were inventive screenwriters and made several last-minute plot changes to accommodate schedules and to address mistakes. The Castles had shot one scene of themselves escaping the villains by horseback, then another of themselves emerging, exhausted, from the ocean into the arms of their friends—later, Vernon realized they had never shot a scene explaining how they got from the horses and into the water. By that time, he and Irene were back with *Watch Your Step*, on tour in Chicago. He rented two horses, painted them to look like the originals, and he and Irene rode them into Lake Michigan to complete the scene.

The film is a fast-moving combination of elements from the Castles' real lives with a classic action/adventure plot: It begins with Vernon and Irene by their fireside, reminiscing about their first meeting and first dance; these are enacted for us in flashback. The villain in the piece is Irene's fiancé, stockbroker John Crosby, played with moustache-twirling enthusiasm by Arthur Stanford. After the Castles' marriage and success, they plan to open Castles by the Sea on the same night that a Broadway show financed by Crosby is to open—to foil their opening, Crosby's thugs kidnap Irene and drive her, kicking and screaming, to a remote shack. She's rescued by Vernon and Tell, the Castles hightail it to Castles by the Sea, and Crosby and his henchman (played by Edward Cort with more gusto than skill) meet a ghastly end.

A print of *The Whirl of Life*, happily, exists at the New York Public Library. It's a delightful film, one that has aged well. With its fast-paced action, self-deprecating comedy, and impressive dance routines, it's a silent movie that can be enjoyed by those usually intimidated or bored by films of the 1910s.

It's illuminating to see Vernon and Irene in action. Irene is lovely, especially in full or three-quarter face; but her profile does not register as well, with its small, rounded nose and receding chin. Vernon, on the other hand, looks downright homely in still photos, but seeing him in the movies one can tell why he became a popular Broadway actor: his blond hair flops boyishly into his face, his animated features make his nose appear smaller, his acting style is charming and casual.

Vernon never for a moment takes himself or the movie too seriously: his first title card describes him as "An actor. A good actor? A matter of opinion." The melodrama is accomplished with a light touch; when Vernon discovers where Irene is being held hostage, he tells her, "Courage, dear—I'll save myself at any cost, and get you later!" He does, however, note immodestly in a title card that their dancing "swept the entire country," showing vignettes of old and young, black and white, rich and poor, dancing up a storm.

It's when Vernon and Irene take to the dance floor, of course, that the film comes to life. Theaters were provided with music cues and songs—if the orchestra or lone piano didn't get the music selection and timing right, the dance sequences were ruined. The Castles are first seen taking a quick turn in a beach house, then on a small, crowded Café de Paris set—all this is an enjoyable lead-up to the grand finale at Castles by the Sea. With Vernon in white tie and black evening suit and Irene in a flowing white chiffon frock (cut well above the ankles to show off her footwork), they execute three numbers, shot from various angles and distances. They spin, dip, kick, swirl, looking light and slim and nearly weightless. They make it look so easy and enjoyable that it's no wonder people flocked to their schools and nightclubs.

The Whirl of Life opened sporadically around the country in October and November 1915, to positive reviews. The *Detroit News* noted that the writers "thoughtfully injected enough melodrama into it to keep the yarn from becoming commonplace," adding pointedly that "everybody laughs heartily at the melodrama." The *Chicago Evening Post* called *The Whirl of Life* "fresh and new—a nice picture written for the purpose of featuring the Castles, which it does in a thoroly [sic] agreeable way." The *New York Mail* reviewer had been afraid that the Castles would bring "nothing into this film but their name and their dancing" but was pleasantly surprised: "As actors, they bring a very definite art and charm."

Variety's reviewer "Jolo" loved it: "The highest class of picture . . . there is so much 'class' to the offering and yards and yards of excruciatingly funny burlesque situations." Although the reviewer took the producers to task for some obviously cheap effects and sets, he summed up *The Whirl of Life* as "a whopping big film success—of the scarcest sort, i.e., a high grade comedy."

It did good business: the Majestic in Detroit was "literally stormed by eager folk of all classes and ages" when the film opened. But *The Whirl of Life* was somewhat hampered by the lack of a major studio behind it to promote and distribute the film. Fans of action/adventure films in 1915 had plenty of other choices: Pearl White in *The Exploits of Elaine,* Ruth Roland in *Who Pays?* Grace Cunard in *The Broken Coin,* Anita Stewart in *The Goddess,* Helen Holmes in *The Hazards of Helen,* Mary Pickford's sister Lottie in *The Diamond from the Sky.* But the fact that *The Whirl of Life* combined dance numbers and a good deal of self-deprecating comedy made it stand out from the crowd. It served to reach a new audience and to cement the Castles' fame as dancers *and* as actors.

By the end of 1915, Vernon and Irene had been world famous for nearly three years, and—at least in America—the public was beginning to think they'd heard just about enough about them. Their photos were in the newspapers, on posters, on magazine covers. They had licensed their names to be used on Castles shoes (men's and women's), Castles hats, Castles corsets, Castles cigars (and cigarettes), Castles stockings, Castles jewelry. There were a dozen Castles dance records on the market, with their corresponding sheet music in the stores.

And they had begun to pop up in popular songs. In the Italian-dialect "I'll Take You Back to Sunny Italy," the singers debate: "What'll we do with the monk', he'll never-a pass? / We'll give-a de monk' to Mrs. Vernon Cast'!" The singer of the comic "I Can Dance with Everybody but My Wife" laments, "I can dance as good as Castle / But with her it's just a wrassle." Similarly, the hero of "Johnny, Get a Girl" is advised: "You can learn to wrassle / Just like Vernon Castle." And the magazine *Vanity Fair* groused,

Males buy boots like Vernon's;
Females ape Irene
Whether they be sixty,
Six, or sweet sixteen.
Irene Castle bonnets,
Bracelets, belts and coats,
Cram the streets, the buses,
The cars, the ferryboats.
Castles in the subway,
Castles in the "L,"

How I wish the Castles
Were both of them in Spain!

The new guns in town found it irresistible to bait the Castles. The dance team of Sayma and Albert sent Vernon and Irene a rude glove-slap to the face via their agent, William Morris, in 1915: "I hereby challenge you and your partner to dance for a purse of $5,000. . . . I am quite sure there is no dancing team known to any manager to-day who can dance as well as Sayma and Albert, and I will put up $5,000 to cover their title of 'best dancers in America' against the Castles." Vernon and Irene declined any reply.

More aggravation came by way of Maurice and Florence Walton, who were featured in the 1915 Shubert revue *Hands Up*. The job was obtained for them by their new representative—Elisabeth Marbury. Business was business, and the Castles remained friends with Marbury and Elsie de Wolfe, but they drifted apart professionally at about this time.

Vernon and Irene managed to have a good time despite their heavy workload in 1915. They frequented dog shows, horse races, and even a boxing match: "I enjoy a good bout as much as any man," said Irene. "I was practically the only woman among several thousand men, and they stared at me as if I were some sort of a curiosity." She was also stared at as if she were some sort of a curiosity at Belmont Park when she showed up clutching a monkey and wearing what looked like one of President Lincoln's old stovepipe hats. As for Vernon, he mused publicly about starting a horse stable of his own, although he knew privately that his plans would be taking him to war. "The sport is a splendid one," he said while at Belmont Park, "but it's frightfully expensive and I don't think I can afford an elaborate stable."

Irene had the first of what would be many serious riding accidents, injuring her leg in early March (there were some rather unfeeling cracks in the newspapers about her dancing "The Pony Limp"). It didn't discourage her from riding, though, and she caused a minor scandal by wearing a tailored men's riding outfit in Central Park. She rode astride, not sidesaddle, and photos show her in a very becoming trouser suit with long jacket.

They also added another soon-to-be-famous furry face to their zoo in 1915: Rastus (an unfortunate minstrel name), a small, dark brown monkey—capuchin, by the looks of him—who had a pert, attractive round face and who accompanied Irene everywhere. It was the first of many monkeys for Irene, who had grown up under the shadow of her grandfather's bizarre Sponsie books. Vernon was soon hooked, too, and Rastus eventually had such troublemaking brothers as Ephaim, Jeffrey, and Hallad. A reporter noted with glee that when Irene wrote letters in her dressing room, Rastus demanded pen and paper to imitate her, and when she applied her stage makeup, "Rastus takes up the eye pencil, and marks his brows, uses the rabbit's foot brush for the cheeks, and even daubs himself with lip rouge."

CHAPTER TWENTY-FOUR

"OH, GIVE ME A GUN AND LET ME RUN TO FIGHT THE FOREIGN FOE"

Ever since the Castles had returned from Europe in August 1914, the war had been preying on Vernon's mind. In December 1914, he and Irene had danced in aid of Belgian relief, and when they reopened Castle House for the season that month, first-day receipts went to the same cause. In the spring of 1915, a dance was held for the Blue Cross at Castles in the Air, "for the comfort of horses wounded in the war."

Irene noticed the change in Vernon: he was quieter, more thoughtful, even a bit embarrassed to be dancing for a living. "There must be something about the rattling of a drum that stirs up a man's emotions and makes him want to go to war," she wrote. "I don't think he cared one way or the other about the show."

Some friends felt that Vernon had to "prove himself," having been teased for being an effeminate dancer all these years. "That may have been one of the things that drove him into the Flying Corps, which was the epitome of hazard and danger," muses Irene's son. "He had never been a man's man in the public's eye," said Irene. "That may have been part of his motive for wanting to go to war in the first place, to silence the very critics who might blame him for not going."

Show business writer Amy Leslie recalled shortly after Vernon's death that "he became identified with a strange abnormal kind of girlish man which later developed into the afternoon tea party horror known as the 'tango lizard'—altogether," Leslie was quick to note, "exactly the thing Mr. Castle certainly was not and could not countenance. He was a manly chap, devoted to shooting big game, riding wild horses, taking daredevil chances with gun, rod, boat and forest." This was a time when one could not come right out and suggest that even noted female impersonators Julian Eltinge or Bert Savoy actually liked to have sex with other men, so the snide shots taken at Vernon's heterosexual bona fides were made through innuendo and inference.

Additionally, Vernon was tired and bored: he'd been in *Watch Your Step* for only half a year, but doing the same part over and over could become tedious. He and Irene had already lost interest in Castle House, and both of them hated vaudeville. He needed something new to challenge him. And certainly the lyrics of a current song must have hit home with him:

Oh, give me a gun and let me run to fight the foreign foe,
A flight up in an aeroplane would charm me.
For since I'm married I declare, I've always been up in the air,
And I'd feel at home if they'd let me join the Army!

Cincinnati Star writer Oscar A. Doob ran into Vernon outside a stage door around the time Vernon was talking about enlisting: "Delicately the young man picked his way through the muddy alley; even daintily he made his way." Consenting to be interviewed by Doob, Vernon later found himself ambushed in print, called "dainty" and "light on his feet . . . which would make him a good aviator." Vernon, Doob admitted, "seemed sorry that one did not take seriously his announced intention to enlist as an aviator."

New York newsman Herbert Duckworth stood up publicly for Vernon and against those who felt that "this side of the Atlantic would be far more wholesome without his presence." Duckworth noted that Vernon possessed the steady nerves and alertness required of pilots: "If Vernon Castle's brains are scattered, as his detractors say, providence must have scattered them most judiciously."

Through the summer of 1915, reports leaked to the press about whether Vernon had enlisted, if he was going to flight school or would be staying in *Watch Your Step* through the fall. "Vernon Castle, who has a plan to join the British Aviation Corps and help fight the Germans, doesn't seem to be making much progress war-ward," wrote one paper. "Can it be that he is to give the allies one more chance to settle the struggle before he takes hold?" Some of the coverage was downright vicious, including a paragraph in the *Toledo Blade* about the "valiant hero's" love for the "almighty dollar." "The call of Charles Dillingham . . . has hushed the call to arms for the dancer's native and late-beloved land, to a mere whisper too low for Mr. Castle even to distinguish" read the piece. "Wonder what raise in salary Vernon negotiated."

The *New York Telegraph* similarly laughed off the idea of the wispy, delicate Vernon as a war hero. "Almost nightly, his eyes blazing with feverish excitement, he has set forth to put a crimp in the Germans, and something has always happened to hold him at the Hippodrome, the Domino Room, the Beaux Arts or similar places that are strictly neutral. . . . It may be, of course, that he has changed his plan of campaign and instead of attacking the Germans by airship will serve as a drummer boy with the British forces." If Vernon had any fears or second thoughts about enlisting, these articles ensured that he had no choice: if he backed out now, he'd be laughed out of the United States. Letters from his father telling how Zeppelin raids had made Norwich "quite uncomfortable" were an added impetus.

Vernon and Irene filled a week's vaudeville work at the Palace Theater in June, after which *Watch Your Step* reopened for the 1915–16 season in Chicago. Charles Collins, reviewing the show for the *Chicago Evening Post*, saw Vernon and Irene as surrealistic cartoons: "These Castles have a bizarre fascination," he wrote. "Even in their appearances, angular and wraithlike, they seem symbols of that rhythmic madness called syncopation. . . . In their debonair leanness they give the impression of being goblins of the cafés, conjured up at midnight out of a salad bowl by a magical headwaiter."

By the time the show had finished its Boston run and was packing up for Chicago, Vernon had made his decision and told Irene and producer Charles Dillingham that as soon as a replacement could be found and rehearsed, he was off to flight school in Newport News, Virginia. He felt he'd be lost in the mob if, unprepared and untrained, he just showed up in England and enlisted; Vernon wanted to fly and knew that his age and his height worked against him. Most World War I pilots were in their early twenties and were as compact as jockeys: at twenty-eight and over six feet tall, Vernon was more suited to infantry duties. Another reason for taking his lessons in the United States was that the few Canadian schools were hopelessly understaffed and underequipped, with a waiting list of young men and not enough planes and instructors for them.

It wasn't surprising that Vernon elected to join the flying corps rather than the navy or army. The danger, the supposed glamour, the machinery all appealed to him. As World War I historian S. F. Wise wrote, "In those early days powered flight had an irresistible glamour for the bold and the imaginative. Looking down from their open cockpits at the panoramic world spread out below, it must have seemed that they were the heralds of a new and tremendous dawn."

The Royal Naval Air Service had begun an advertising blitz in April 1915, which is probably when Vernon got the idea. They asked for British subjects of "pure European descent," preferably between nineteen and twenty-three, to begin training. Another ad for the Imperial Royal Flying Corps showed a brave hero machine-gunning from a plane, with the headline, "The Young Man's Element—the Air." This ad called for "young men of fair education, alert men 18 to 30 years old," who would receive $1.10 per day while training in Canada.

Vernon enlisted in the Eighty-fourth Royal Canadian Flying Corps Squadron and began flying lessons—at his own expense—in December 1915. He would pass his flying test on February 5, 1916, and be issued his pilot's certificate on February 9. Vernon trained on Curtiss planes—Glenn Curtiss had been manufacturing planes since 1907, and his product was to play an important role in the war. Curtiss "Jennys," the JN series of military training aircraft, are still synonymous with World War I and the barnstorming stunt flyers of the 1920s. Vernon was to become a master of the Jenny, a two-seater biplane that, though not used in combat, was the primary pilot-training vehicle during World War I.

According to John Walker Harrington in the *New York City Sun*, Vernon was a natural-born pilot. "He understood as if by instinct principles and details which others found it hard to grasp. His friends first learned of his determination to go to the front as an airman when they received pictures of him on the shores of Lake Michigan taken just after alighting from a long trip over the water in a Farnham plane."

Vernon's instructor, Vic Carlstrom, recalled that Vernon "took his flying very seriously" but also enjoyed being recognized both as a star and as a glamorous pilot. He lived at the Chamberline Hotel at Old Point Comfort and would go swanning around the dining room "with his goggles hanging down around his neck, so that everyone could see he was an aviator."

Irene did her level best to take an interest in Vernon's new endeavor, even going up in a plane with one of his instructors (Vernon, as a student, was not allowed to take her aloft). "The air made me feel that I was in a new world, so confident," Irene told a reporter. "I'd like to have you up in one of the big machines," Vernon said hopefully, adding some insight on his own flying experiences: "You feel absolutely safe and so strong in yourself, when that wonderful engine responds to your every impulse."

By this time, the press had spread the word about Vernon's enlistment, and even the formerly nasty *Toledo Blade* was patting him on the back: "So many English actors of military age are remaining in America safe from danger while their country is still calling for volunteers to meet the national crisis. Mr. Castle's example should be generally emulated."

The Castles were, as always, if not broke then pretty well strapped for funds. Vernon didn't help matters by giving away two of his polo ponies and buying Irene a $1,000 string of pearls as an early Christmas present. They put their beloved Long Island estate on the market (the Castles had poured $90,000 into it in only two years). They were able to get only $49,500 for it, a figure Irene still had burned into her memory decades afterward: "Two years later, it sold for a quarter of a million dollars!"

Twenty-nine-year-old singer and dancer Bernard Granville was hired to replace Vernon in *Watch Your Step;* a star of such revues as the *Ziegfeld Follies* and the *Passing Show,* he would also become the father of 1930s child actress Bonita Granville. He was, however, no Vernon Castle, and Irene had to corral chorus boys William Holbrook and Rocky Johnson to partner her in some of the trickier numbers.

The reviews of this new touring company of *Watch Your Step* were still overwhelmingly raves. "Perhaps the only thing not modern about this big musical show," said the *Louisville Times,* "is that it is clean. There is not a song, dance, joke or costume that calls for the censor to get busy." Bernard Granville did well by himself; as a dancer he couldn't compare with Vernon, of course, but it was admitted that "few would care to make comparisons of comedy with names of the two players reversed." The *Cleveland Plain Dealer* noted that "Mrs. Castle is very entertaining as a dancer, she dances just enough, and sings a few notes, which are just a few notes too much." Indeed, even with months of singing lessons under her belt, Irene had to face another season of wisecracks about her voice. "Mrs. Castle's voice is nasal and not at all pleasing," wrote the *Toledo Blade* in March 1916, "but she displays unusual judgment in that she uses it sparingly and only within its restricted scope." Less kindly, vaudeville performer Odiva's singing seals were described by the *Columbus Dispatch* as "an imitation of Mrs. Castle."

Perhaps due to cracks like that last, Irene continued what would become a lifelong love/hate relationship with interviewers. She was terse and rude to the man from the *Grand Rapids Press* who showed up in her dressing room, giving him "a fifty-word interview" while puffing furiously on "violet-scented cigarettes." "Interviews are detestable, you know," Irene said to the interviewer. "I'm constantly pestered by reporters and the questions they ask bore me to distraction." Venturing a question about fashion, the reporter got out of Irene, "It is because I am individual that the world copies my clothes. It is because I disregard styles that I set them. It is because I am slender that it has become fashionable to be slender." She paused to light another cigarette and reiterated: "Interviews bore me dreadfully, you know."

A reporter for the *Wisconsin State Journal* had slightly better luck, though Irene sighed that "I can't see you very long" and spent much of the interview playing with—and talking about—Rastus, who boasted a wardrobe trunk to rival Irene's. Mrs. Foote had sewed her "grandchild" a sweater, tam, overalls, shirts, "even a little stiff white collar and neckties." As Rastus gamboled all over her hotel room, Irene did speak briefly of her light diet, her need for sleep, her opinion that "business women and women of property should have a chance to vote if they want to," and fame ("It's hard to tell when one's famous, except by the money one makes").

By December 1915 *Watch Your Step* was in Indianapolis, and Vernon was hard at work training, hoping to leave for Europe early the next year. He managed to get to Indiana to attend the show, hidden away in a box seat, but was soon discovered by his friends onstage and persuaded to clamber down to be greeted by his fans. "The audience began to shout for us to dance," said Irene. "Vernon quietly took me in his arms and we went into one of the routines that had been so successful in New York."

Spotting a good thing, Charles Dillingham—determined to get all the publicity out of Vernon while the getting was good—rented the enormous Hippodrome in New York for one night in late January and ordered the Castles to take a train east for a sentimental farewell performance. The Hippodrome seated five thousand people, and Irene recalled that not only was it packed, but six hundred eager patrons were seated onstage, making the dance floor a bit crowded. So many people had to be turned away that two "farewells" were given. Accompanying the Castles was John Philip Sousa's band—undeniably talented, but hardly a dance band. "He ignored our frantic signals to pick up the tempo," fumed Irene, "and his uniformed arms flailed away with the precise beat of a man conducting a military march.

...I was boiling mad, I could have kicked him." Vernon and Irene also traveled uptown to the Lafayette Theater in Harlem, where they danced—for the last time, as it turned out—to James Reese Europe's music.

Crowds of fans and friends accompanied the Castles from the Hippodrome on Sixth Avenue to Grand Central Terminal on Park Avenue to see Irene off on her return to Indianapolis. Cartons of flowers were heaped on them, and Vernon had to kiss her good-bye very publicly before she climbed onto her private *Watch Your Step* car. Vernon prepared to leave flight school and go to Canada for his final orders.

Irene reasoned, as did many other wives, "I was proud, naturally, to have him go and glad that he wanted to go. I wouldn't have had him different." Elsie Janis dropped in to sympathize: Janis's great love, actor Basil Hallam, was also departing for war. "Vernon was no more of a natural fighter than Basil was," said Janis. "Strange how the peaceful ones managed to go while the more truculent ones were still getting ready!" Janis, who became known as "The Sweetheart of the AEF" for her touring of the front lines, would lose Hallam in the summer of 1916. She was left with her redoubtable mother and a photo of Hallam inscribed, "If we still love those we lose, can we ever quite lose those we love?"

Irene had plenty of company to take her mind off Vernon as *Watch Your Step* continued its tour through the spring of 1916: one reporter counted in her dressing room Rastus the monkey, Tell and Zowie, two other dogs, and five guinea pigs. Female members of the company, either caught up in the animal love fest or hoping to curry favor with Irene, began buying pets till the train became downright dangerous, as well as aromatic. Leading lady Elizabeth Brice carried with her two cockatoos, a guinea pig, and six white mice; Edna Bates bought a dozen trained white rats from an animal act; Gertrude Rutland received a large Brazilian chimpanzee from a sailor admirer. It took half a dozen stagehands to rescue poor Rastus from the Brazilian chimp, who was then confined to the baggage car by a furious Irene.

The *Pittsburgh Post* tallied the animal population of the *Watch Your Step* touring company, though it's impossible to tell at this late date how seriously to take it: parrots (owned by Mary Ellison), a raccoon "who drinks beer and likes it" (Myrtle Ross), two small Florida alligators (Esther Ice), two angora cats (Jessie Holbrook), a gray squirrel (Libbian Diamond), and a fox "who is getting too big and thieving to carry much longer" (Edna

Stillwell). "When a young admirer says to a *Watch Your Step* girl, 'May I send you some flowers?' she replies, 'Oh, please don't. Send me an animal. I want to make the other girls jealous.'"

Before leaving the United States and show business, Vernon passed the torch. In March 1916, he saw a touring production of the musical *Nobody Home,* which starred his brother-in-law, Lawrence Grossmith, and was coproduced by Elisabeth Marbury. He went backstage to congratulate the dance team Seibel Layman and Sybil Chaulsae, calling them "the greatest dancers in America." When the team looked a bit stunned, Vernon added, "Yes, and that includes Mrs. Castle and myself, too."

Chapter Twenty-five

ॐ॑ॐॐ॑

"When I get old I shall be able to tell our children all about the Great War"

W hile Vernon was finishing up his *Watch Your Step* contract and taking flying lessons, the war was grinding on. Often called the "first twentieth-century war," it combined the fresh enthusiastic patriotism of the nineteenth century with the horrible new weapons of the twentieth (Vernon's beloved planes among them). In 1915, German U-boats blockaded Britain; more than half a million Armenians died in a genocide still being argued about today; the Allies suffered horrendous casualties on the Gallipoli Peninsula in Turkey; the first use of poison gas was recorded; the new "tommy gun," a lightweight machine gun, debuted.

The Canadian Air Force Vernon was pinning his hopes on barely existed. Due mostly to government disinterest, Canada did not have an air corps when World War I began: despite the efforts of the country's aviation pioneers, no money or research was put into flying. In mid-1914, when war broke out, the country had to race to catch up. The tiny, understaffed Canadian Aviation Corps was founded, but Vernon decided to join the British Royal Flying Corps, which, with the Royal Naval Air Service, was recruiting and training both Canadians and Americans in Canada.

Even when Vernon, pilot's license in hand, sailed off to war on the *Adriatic* in mid-February 1916, the newspapers kept needling him in ever-nastier ways. "Gosh, we bet the British army is growing impatient," wrote the *Toledo Blade*, waiting for Vernon to "come a-flying over the trenches in his trusty aeroplane and scare the Germans half out of their wits" (which, it might be added, is exactly what he would shortly do). But Vernon was as yet absent from the front lines, "forever missing trains, or having to stop to get manicured, or having to turn back and fetch some toilet article he had omitted from his service kit."

Vernon landed in England around 3:00 A.M. on February 26, 1916, and got off to a bad start by puzzling customs and immigration: his passport read "Castle," his military enlistment papers "Blyth." "There are a thousand reasons why I couldn't go back to my old name," he wrote to Irene, "but I had a great deal of hard work trying to explain it to the officer in charge. He said I should change my name legally by 'letters patent,' whatever that means."

Once in London, Vernon registered at the Savoy and raced off to the Gaiety Theatre, where his brother-in-law was performing; Grossmith, well connected, promised to put Vernon in touch socially with whatever high-ranking military officers he knew. "I'm quite excited about it, as believe me one feels an awful mutt in this place without a uniform," wrote Vernon. "I feel like a bad actor trying to see Shubert for a job." He was surprised to find London rather lively in this second year of the war, though of course it was a far different town than he'd left back in 1906: "the show business is better than it's been in years, the place is simply packed with soldiers, who look splendid."

Till his military connections came through, Vernon socialized, and he looked down his nose at the dancing styles, "five years behind the times. There are no chic women to speak of, but the men are awfully smart, and it makes one feel very proud to see how they take this war, it makes you feel awfully patriotic and sure of winning." Absence from Irene (and boredom) made his heart grow fonder: "I could cry I'm so lonely sometimes," he wrote the same week he'd arrived, "and everything reminds me of the time when we were here together." He was further dismayed by a trip to his hometown, where he found that "all my old school friends have gone, and some of them unfortunately have been killed."

Vernon finally got his commission not through Lawrence Grossmith but through a luncheon at the Royal Navy Yacht Club, where he encountered an actor/aviator friend, Robert Loraine, who took him off to the War Office. A major in charge told Loraine, "Well, if he can fly, and if you vouch for him, he can go right in," and *voilà!* on March 15, 1916, Vernon found himself a second lieutenant, Royal Flying Corps, on probation. "The rank is not so high," he said, "but it is remarkable considering the fact that I have been here only a week, and they usually have to wait months before getting anything at all, and commissions are not as easy to get now as at the beginning of the war."

He went off shopping for his kit, bragged to friends about his commission, and tried to keep his head down: "One thing I have to be careful about, and that is not to get my name in the papers, over here; it is considered the height of bad form to go in for any kind of publicity or advertising." Vernon did have his photo taken when he got his new uniform in March; "I look just like Rastus in it," he joked. "I wear one of those little monkey caps on the side of the head."

Late March found Vernon in Middlesex, recovering from a bad reaction to his typhoid inoculation and settling into training camp. Vernon's first duties included making sure the bonfires on the field stayed lit overnight, to lure zeppelins away from London. As Vernon's flight skills improved, he was promoted from bonfires to mail carrying, ferrying dispatches from Dover or Falmouth over the British Channel to the rear of the French lines.

He sent Irene his daily schedule:

6:00 A.M. Early morning flying
7:30 A.M. Breakfast
9:00 A.M. Flying and mechanics
11:30 A.M. Glass of milk and cake!
11:45 A.M. Attend lecture
1:00 P.M. Lunch
2:00 P.M. Drill and parade
2:30 P.M. Flying, etc.
4:30 P.M. Tea
5:30 P.M. Lecture
6:30 P.M. Wireless telegraphy and signaling
7:30 P.M. Dinner

"It all seems so strange and different to what I am used to that sometimes I think I am dreaming," he wrote. On his Sunday off, Vernon took the train to Norwich to show off his uniform and his new moustache; his father wept with pride and "got a lot of fun walking with me to Grannie's house because all non-commissioned soldiers have to salute me, which is of course very thrilling!"

Fellow airman John Walker Harrington stated that at first Vernon was quite clumsy in flight, but "he soon became expert at dropping bombs, in making spiral descents, in feigning to drop disabled and then making sudden recoveries. His feats soon attracted the attention of his superiors." Harrington noted that Vernon's grace carried over into his flying: "There

(Left) William Vernon Blyth, age ten (courtesy William McLaughlin).

(Right) Vernon Castle, age nineteen, at the beginning of his stage career (courtesy William McLaughlin).

Vernon's sister, actress Coralie Blythe Grossmith (courtesy Plymouth Library Services).

Irene Foote, right, with her sister, Elroy, and mother, late 1890s (courtesy William McLaughlin).

Bessie McCoy singing "The Yama-Yama Man," 1909 (author's collection).

Irene Foote imitating Bessie McCoy singing "The Yama-Yama Man," 1909 (author's collection).

Ginger Rogers imitating Irene Foote imitating Bessie McCoy singing "The Yama-Yama Man," 1939 (author's collection).

Vernon as Zowie, the Monarch of Mystery, in *The Hen-Pecks*, 1911 (author's collection).

(Left) Vernon's theatrical father figure, Lew Fields, with Lillian Lee in *The Hen-Pecks*, 1911 (author's collection). (Below) The newlyweds winning the three-legged race on their honeymoon cruise, June 1911 (author's collection).

(Above) Irene Castle and Zowie in Paris, 1912 (courtesy William McLaughlin). (Right) The "Castle Band" was one of Irene's fashion innovations (courtesy William McLaughlin).

Irene's famous Dutch cap, bought on her 1911 honeymoon (courtesy Wisconsin Center for Film & Theater Research).

The Castles in 1913 (courtesy Wisconsin Center for Film & Theater Research).

The Castles' manager, Elisabeth Marbury (left), and her companion, Elsie de Wolfe (author's collection).

The Castles' arranger and accompanist, James Reese Europe, with his Society Orchestra, c. 1914 (courtesy Photographs and Prints Division, Schomburg Center for Research in Black Culture, The New York Public Library, Astor, Lenox and Tilden Foundations).

The Castles' chief competition, Maurice Mouvet and Florence Walton, 1912 (courtesy © National Portrait Gallery, London).

The Castles at the height of their fame, 1915 (courtesy Wisconsin Center for Film & Theater Research).

Irene Castle, c. 1915 (courtesy Wisconsin Center for Film & Theater Research).

Vernon Castle, c. 1915 (courtesy Wisconsin Center for Film & Theater Research).

The Castles in their New
York townhouse (courtesy
Wisconsin Center for
Film & Theater Research).

The Castles on horseback in Long Island (courtesy Wisconsin Center for Film
& Theater Research).

Dancing the maxixe, from *Mr. and Mrs. Castle before the Camera* (courtesy William McLaughlin).

How to "take a corner" doing the Castle walk (courtesy William McLaughlin).

The eight-step, from *Mr. and Mrs. Castle before the Camera* (courtesy William McLaughlin).

The cortez step from the innovation, from *Mr. and Mrs. Castle before the Camera* (courtesy William McLaughlin).

The Castles rehearsing for the camera, 1914 (courtesy Getty Images).

Irene found Vernon's drumming—"beginning almost before breakfast and ending some time after midnight"— "a little trying" (courtesy William McLaughlin).

(Above) The Castles with Tell (left) and Kiki (held by Irene) on their Long Island estate (courtesy William McLaughlin).

(Right) Vernon and Irene (with Kiki and Tell), after fleeing Europe at the start of World War I, arrive home on the *Olympic,* August 29, 1914 (courtesy Bettmann/Corbis).

Vernon attends to his paperwork, an infrequent occurrence (author's collection).

The Castles as seen in a contemporary caricature (author's collection).

Mr. and Mrs. Vernon Castle

Vernon in full evening
dress (including monkey
Rastus), 1915 (courtesy
William McLaughlin).

The Castles reminisce in *The Whirl of Life*, 1915 (author's collection).

(Left) A newspaper sketch of the Castles at the time of their Whirlwind Tour, 1914—at bottom right is drummer Buddie Gilmore (author's collection). (Below) The cast of *Watch Your Step* as seen in a newspaper cartoon (author's collection).

"WATCH YOUR STEP" AND WATCH A LOT OF OTHER STEPS, TOO, IF YOU LIKE

Dancer and future film star Mae Murray, who briefly replaced
Irene in *Watch Your Step*, 1915 (courtesy Wisconsin Center for
Film & Theater Research).

Three sheet music covers showing
the ragtime craze of the 1910s
(courtesy Duke University).

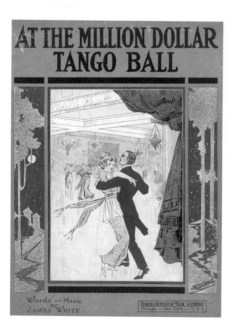

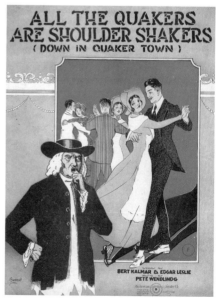

Milton Sills and Irene in *Patria*, 1916–17 (courtesy William McLaughlin).

Sheet music for *Patria*
(courtesy Eric Stogo,
Metaluna).

Irene, 1917, in her feminine version of Vernon's uniform, including a Royal Flying Corps insignia he sent her (courtesy Wisconsin Center for Film & Theater Research).

A sketch of Vernon's plane, sent to Irene along with one of his letters from the front (courtesy William McLaughlin).

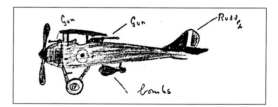

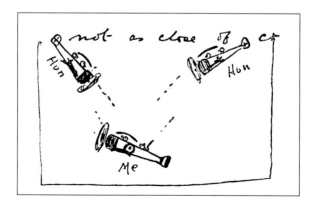

A dogfight, sketched by Vernon (courtesy William McLaughlin).

The Castles in London during Irene's weeklong visit before Vernon left for the front, May 1916 (courtesy William McLaughlin).

The returning war hero visits Irene on the set of *Sylvia of the Secret Service* (Tell sits between them), August 21, 1917 (courtesy Wisconsin Center for Film & Theater Research).

A contemporary sketch of Irene's dance in *Miss 1917* (author's collection).

Gwen Wilmot, who might have become the second Mrs. Vernon Castle (courtesy William Hunt).

The other two Muske-
teers: Vernon's wartime
pals (right) Johnny Coats
and (below) Eardley
Wilmot (holding Jeffrey)
(courtesy William Hunt).

Vernon in a newsreel frame, about a week before his death on a Texas flying field, February 1918 (courtesy Wisconsin Center for Film & Theater Research).

The wreckage of Vernon's fatal plane crash (courtesy William McLaughlin).

Vernon's Fort Worth funeral procession (courtesy Michael O'Neal).

Actress Billie Carleton, whose 1918 death propelled Irene into an international drug scandal (courtesy © National Portrait Gallery, London).

Irene and David Powell in *The Firing Line*, 1919 (courtesy Eric Stogo, Metaluna).

Irene with her second husband, Robert Treman, about to fly from England to France, June 1922 (courtesy Wisconsin Center for Film & Theater Research).

Irene on tour with Billy Reardon, 1922–23 (courtesy William McLaughlin).

An alarmingly thin Irene with her third husband, Frederic McLaughlin, at the polo matches, 1933 (courtesy William McLaughlin).

Irene around the time of *The Story of Vernon and Irene Castle*, 1939—note the art moderne bracelets (courtesy Wisconsin Center for Film & Theater Research).

Ginger Rogers and Fred Astaire in *The Story of Vernon and Irene Castle*, 1939
(courtesy The Everett Collection).

Irene and her fourth husband, George Enzinger, 1946 (courtesy The Everett Collection).

Irene, at seventy, with her dog Tippy in Bermuda, 1963 (courtesy The Everett Collection).

The Castles' graves, Woodlawn Cemetery (photo by the author).

was something so distinctive in his flight: the long, graceful lines and curves in which he sent his machine that his coming could be noted for many a mile."

"I'm improving my flying faster than anyone here," Vernon boyishly bragged, "and now I'm flying the big machines they use for fighting. They are perfectly wonderful and much easier to fly than the small powered machines, just as a big car is better than a small one."

Pilots were being sent into battle with less training than Vernon, who at least had paid for his own lessons. As pilot deaths increased, replacements were needed, and quantity was thought more important than skill. Through the spring of 1917, historian Neil Hanson writes, "large numbers of raw and barely trained novice pilots were still being sent to almost inevitable death at the Front, and it was widely believed that fatal crashes in training were averaging one hundred a month."

The airplanes being used by the Allies were undergoing hasty, emergency redesigning at about this time. Pilot deaths were increasing at a rate alarming even compared to ground troop fatalities, partly due to poor aircraft design. Guns could not be fired near or through the plane's propeller, only above, below, from the side, or (in two-man planes) from the back. In spring 1916, an "interrupter gear" was introduced, making it possible for pilots to shoot forward, the bullets passing between the propeller blades, like skipping rope.

According to Irene, the adjustment to military life was tougher than Vernon made it sound in his cheerful letters: "He was not a soldier of adventure or any other kind. He hated discipline and the restrictions attached to a life in the barracks. He loved . . . the theater, restaurants, cafés and other places of amusement." Homesickness nagged at him quite often as the months dragged on; a gramophone in camp playing selections from *Watch Your Step* made him want to cry. By July 1916, he was telling Irene, "O! I want to get back to you so badly. I shouldn't care if we didn't have a penny. . . . I often think of how wonderful it will be when it is all over."

In May 1916, Irene got leave from *Watch Your Step* to spend a week with Vernon in England before he was due to be in France. She sailed on the *St. Louis* and brought Rastus along to greet his daddy. One little girl on board took a great interest in Rastus and wanted to know if he resembled Vernon. "I told her he was sort of between the two. . . . When I pointed [Vernon] out to her she didn't seem disappointed." When the *St. Louis* arrived at the shores of England, she found Vernon on a tender, waving up frantically at the huge ship: "It was my first glimpse of him as a soldier. . . . When the gangplank between the two boats was lowered, he tore across it and into my arms."

Vernon and Irene managed to spend three days enjoying London, away from war and their career, dancing only for and with each other, "knowing full well the months would be long and weary before we could know such happiness again." The day before Irene had to leave, they took a train to the small town where Vernon was to be issued his orders and dined at an old tavern with a log fire, a "painful, silent" meal.

They were driving along when Vernon pulled over on the country dirt road, picked up a large turtle that was crossing, carried it fifty yards to a pond, and sent it on its way. "When he came back he explained to me that the natives always took them home and carved out their shells for parlor ornaments with no thought of even killing them first," said Irene.

Before leaving him, Irene wrote a prayer for Vernon, which he wore, "tied around his neck with a dirty little string":

Almighty God, if Thou art there,
Listen to my humble prayer
And keep him safe.
Keep him in your care alway,
Watch o'er him through this weary day
And keep him safe.
Make him feel my love and sorrow
Bring him back some near to-morrow
And keep him safe.

Irene returned to New York just in time to attend a performance of Lew Fields's new musical *Step This Way*—much to her consternation, Maurice Mouvet and Florence Walton were also present. Newspapers jumped on this, one describing Irene as "a curiously unsmiling person" and her rival Florence as "effusive in her applause, as she always is," though noting the couple "took themselves with tremendous seriousness."

"How sad it is to have you leave me so soon," Vernon wrote on May 13. "I can't realize it yet. It seems as though I have had a very beautiful dream and that you haven't really been here at all." He consoled himself with his "very comfortable quarters," a squash court, and the Morane and Bleriot monoplanes in which he was training.

He had a nasty scare later that week: a valve in his engine broke, and Vernon made an emergency landing "in the middle of Salisbury Plain, in the rain and miles from the nearest village, and I had to stay there for fourteen hours, before help arrived." He added a sitcom-husband note wishing Irene a happy wedding anniversary: "I forget if we were married on the 28th or 29th, but I am taking a chance on the 28th" (he was right, by the way).

On June 7, 1916, Vernon left to join his squadron in France. It was at this time he learned of the death of Lord Kitchener, the secretary of state for war, on June 5, when the HMS *Hampshire* was sunk by a German mine. "It has sort of depressed everybody," Vernon understated. He was not allowed to tell Irene exactly where he was: "somewhere in France" was the phrase of the day. He was quartered not in a camp but "in a funny little cottage, kept by an old French woman. I have to walk over a manure pile to get to my room." He hung five of Irene's photos in his room to bring a little glamour to the atmosphere.

The reason Vernon was moved to France was to provide aerial advance for the deadly, disastrous battle of the Somme in late June 1916. He was vague about it, of course, in his letters: "We are expecting a big drive all along the front, in which we hope to gain a lot of ground," he wrote on June 13. "All leave has been stopped so there isn't much chance of my being in England for some time." As the horror approached, he griped about such things as the "terrible" village, the food ("isn't a bit nice"), and the fact that "I can only get a bath twice a week, but that's considered very often here in France."

"Things are going to be very busy soon," he added. "The General was here to-day [June 16] and told all the Pilots to learn all the positions of the various places along the Front." As the battle drew near, the German pilots continued to raid France. One German flier was captured after ditching his plane, and "the squadron . . . entertained him at supper before sending him to a detention camp. We have the machine here with us. It's a 'peach,' and there are a lot of things about it which we would do well to copy if only they will." The German planes, Vernon, explained, were more comfortable: roomy and upholstered. "You can sit in them for hours and not get tired, while ours are small and make your back ache after half an hour's flight."

Flying *was* an uncomfortable business: Vernon wore a leather coat with a raccoon coat over it against the cold, "and we have to put ointment on our feet now to prevent frost-bite."

On June 22, Vernon was assigned to No. 1 Squadron in Bailleul, near the Belgian border, about ten miles from the front. He wrote to Irene that "this is the 'crack' Squadron of the Flying Corps, and I am proud to be in it." A general duties squadron, No. 1 was responsible for bombing raids, artillery spotting, and patrols. "He did especially well because he was cool under fire at all times," said John Walker Harrington. Photos had to be taken from only two hundred or three hundred feet in the air; the camera was placed in the plane so it could be worked with the foot, but it still took a good eye and a steady hand (and leg). Photographing enemy positions, Vernon thought, was one of the hardest jobs he undertook. One had to fly very low and aim one's concentration on the subject, thereby ignoring ground fire and other planes. "I had my plane hit three times with pieces of shell," he wrote on July 1, 1916, "and the concussion you get makes you think the machine is blown in half. I don't mind telling you, darling, that I was half sick with fright and jolly glad to get back home."

Vernon's first combat-area assignment was to fly low over German lines and snap photos of their positions. Shells burst all around him, but Vernon nervously zoomed up and down, shooting photos. He turned them in proudly and was soon called to see his commander, Major Prettyman. The photos were useless, out of focus, Vernon was told: they were torn up and thrown out in front of him. Vernon felt he'd been slapped in the face: like a child who hopes he'll be missed after he dies, he strode back to his plane and took off in a huff of self-pity. He flew in, stayed low, and got twenty-five perfect photos.

One of his fellow fliers recalled that Vernon's "greatest aerial exploits took place during the battle of the Somme." This unnamed pilot's recollections were recorded in late 1916; his viewpoint was much more positive than today's historians'. The attack began with a thirty-hour "strafe from the big guns, during which the German trenches were practically obliterated," he said. Then, on June 24, came Vernon's role: squadrons of planes "from fifty to a hundred darted over the lines flying very low, not more than 300 feet up. Each of these machines was equipped with machine guns and bombs. They poured a hail of lead into the German trenches and bombed them, so that the effect was very damaging to the morale of the

Germans. No sooner had the aeroplanes started than the British infantry went over their trenches with bayonets and bombs. In the meantime, the 'curtain fire' was going on, in many cases the shells going over the aeroplanes. It was the combination of artillery fire, aeroplanes and infantry rushes that brought us the gains made in the battle of the Somme."

Ninety years on, it's hard to find a historian who uses the term "gain." The battle was a morass of uselessness from its inception late in June 1916 (when 60 percent of officers involved were killed) through its dragged-out finale in mid-November of that year. Numbers vary wildly, but the BBC estimates that the "Allies advanced only 8km [five miles]. The British suffered around 420,000 casualties, the French 195,000 and the Germans around 650,000."

So many things went wrong, General Haig's refusal to rethink his battle plans being only one of them. For one thing, the bombs dropped by Vernon and his compatriots failed to do more to the Germans' barbed wire than make it even more bristly and impassible to the ground troops. German machine-gunners cut down an estimated 58,000 British troops on the first day of battle alone.

Vernon might not have felt like he was accomplishing much, but the view from the ground was decidedly different. As quoted in Neil Hanson's book *Unknown Soldiers*, Paul Hub, a German in the trenches of the Somme, wrote home, "we were targeted by aircraft and two bombs were dropped on us. I have more respect for bombs than anything else." After destroying the German trenches, "the aircraft was still circling above us, not very high up at all; but how powerless we are—we see death circling above us and can't do the least thing to avoid it."

Vernon continued climbing up the ranks at a great pace: he was taught wireless signaling and machine-gunning; on July 1, 1916, he was appointed flying officer, effective, backdated, June 10. By mid-July, Vernon was flying alongside the gunners, signaling to them by wireless where to shoot and what they'd hit. "I had never been near the big guns before and so it was awfully interesting," he told Irene. "It was a lot of fun, and quite a change for me."

As his part in the battle went on, Vernon managed to continue his correspondence, though gingerly: after being sent to a small village, he wrote Irene, "I was going to tell you why I went there, but I guess it would be indiscreet in the eyes of the Censor . . . when I get old I shall be able to tell our children all about the Great War, and bore them to tears." He voiced optimism, ill founded as it may have been in the summer of 1916. "The war is looking a little more promising now. We are winning on all points. Just around here the fighting has been terribly fierce, and the country around the firing line is just one mass of holes and rubbish. From the air it looks like a very old piece of Stilton cheese."

Being shot at from the ground and from the air made one "feel a wreck," and Vernon had brushes with death every day, but he admitted, "it's better than being in the trenches." He performed at several benefit concerts to raise money for blankets, socks, and other comforts for the boys in the trenches: "My God, how I pity them in this weather!" Vernon wrote later that year, when the frosts had set in. The "glamorous" life of the pilots was actually more dangerous, but it was also cleaner, freer, with more autonomy, and the bursts of terror came in three-hour stretches rather than day and night. He tried to calm Irene's fears: "I don't stand half the chance of being killed out here as most of the yaps do at home crossing the street," he wrote.

Even with the battle of the Somme raging on through much of 1916, a form of normal life managed to exist at and near the front. Vernon was assigned additional duties as mess president, and he had to find sleeping arrangements for new officers—his talents for arranging rowdy parties for the men and high-toned affairs for important visitors was also utilized. One night Vernon had to pull together a dinner for forty visiting officers: "I managed to get a block of ice from a hospital in a town near here," he said. "We'd never had ice here before, and I made cocktails and champagne cup." Not all the parties were so refined; a farewell dinner for some pilots "ended with their breaking up most of the furniture and drinking all the drinks in the place," wrote Vernon. "One of our guests got his face walked on by a hob-nailed boot, and it was altogether a jolly evening."

Lieutenant Colonel J. T. Bloomfield, British Royal Flying Corps, called Vernon "the life of the squadron. It was customary when his squadron had made a good bag, brought down two or three Huns, to give a dinner. At these dinners he always was a tremendous hit with his drums. He used to play four at one time, two with his feet and two with his hands, and threw the sticks up in the air and caught them. He used to start off softly and wind up with a noise and racket that was glorious."

Vernon even participated in some boxing matches: "I hadn't boxed since I was sixteen, but I didn't do so badly. I got one punch in the jaw that feels a little stiff this morning—but that's all." One of the horrors of camp, he joked, was "the frightful singing of the officers." A group was attempting the two-part harmony of "A Simple Melody," with stunning lack of success. "They didn't know how the rag part went," wrote Vernon. "I showed them, and now I realize I've made one of the biggest mistakes of the War!"

As mess president, Vernon supervised building a bathroom with three baths and a shower—and a furnace: "Before we could only get sponge baths and unless you got there early you had to have cold water," he explained. "The bathroom is one of our pet exhibits when we have guests."

He reassured Irene about the French mademoiselles, sending her a caricature of one, adding, "The best looking girl I've seen here looks like this, and had her last bath several epochs before the war." Vernon's innate snobbery peeked through in some of his letters, stranded as he was far from both Broadway and Park Avenue. There were no "nice" people in the French villages near his camp, he complained, "only peasants. . . . Do you ever remember looking over the rail of a ship and seeing steerage passengers? Well, they would be first class passengers compared to the people around here."

The nearby hospital was a source of upset to Vernon. "There's one poor chap, who has the whole of his jaws, top and bottom, blown away," wrote Vernon. "Nothing from his nose down, and he's going to live while another man who hasn't a scratch on his body, but is suffering from 'shell shock,' will die."

In August 1916, Vernon learned that Elsie Janis's Basil Hallam had been killed. "I always thought of him as having a safe job," Vernon lamented: Hallam was surveying in a balloon "when the rope broke, and as the wind was blowing toward the Hun lines he and another officer had to jump out with parachutes, and Basil's parachute didn't open." Vernon had recently seen Hallam in London, "and he said he was awfully 'fed up' with the war."

As was Vernon: "The only thing I miss is music and theaters and suppers, and well-dressed women and horses and cars and dogs, etc., etc.," he weakly kidded in the summer of 1916. "We have everything here in the way of dust, guns and aeroplanes." The following month, he wrote of a dream he'd had about his leaving the United States for the war, "and when I started to wake up I thought to myself, 'It's only a dream—I'm in bed and haven't gone to the war at all,' and just then a gun woke me up thoroughly, and here I was in my hut."

Vernon was, of course, frequently the target of antiaircraft fire. In late 1916, he was making a trip over enemy lines, "gliding his plane along as unconcernedly as though he were making a long sweep in some favorite waltz," as Harrington put it. Suddenly his plane jolted violently; Vernon said "it felt as though somebody was trying to push me out of my seat; funny sensation, just like a swift shove." A newspaper reported that "the propeller and part of the rotating motor were shot away while the machine was at a low altitude." When he landed, he unwrapped the two heavy mufflers around his neck and found a bullet lodged in them.

That same winter, Vernon got into an aerial dogfight, and part of his engine was shot off. He managed to glide his plane from three thousand feet down behind Allied lines and alighted without a scratch or a bruise. And he never seemed to resent the fellow who'd tried to kill him. "His attitude was always that of the sportsman," said Harrington. "He was not concerned about his own safety, but spoke of the fact that his adversary was a wonderful pilot, and what a fine shot the German was who had finally disabled him." When Vernon shot down a German plane and the pilot was captured with only slight injuries, he befriended his enemy, made sure he got good medical attention, and requested that he be admitted to the officers' mess (the request was denied). The grateful pilot presented Vernon with his Iron Cross, which made its way to one of Vernon's sisters and eventually to Irene.

On the other hand, propaganda had its effect even on the mild-tempered Vernon; it's startling that he wrote in August 1916, "Gee, how I hate the Germans! The terrible things they do! I really didn't believe them when I was in America, but they are most perfectly true. The dragging away of all the young French girls from 15 to 20 and making them work and be servants [a euphemism, one wonders?] to the German officers is simply frightful."

Censorship of mailed material grew stricter as the war continued; by August 1916, Vernon was no longer allowed to send any photos, magazines, or newspaper clippings to Irene, in a "neutral country." "They have even stopped the embroidered post cards that the soldiers were so fond of sending," he complained.

Still, he kept in touch with friends, letters being the only contact.

Producer Charles Dillingham heard from him: "It's not at all bad here, except we have to fly over the German lines every day and get shot at. . . . Someday they may not know who I am and accidentally hit me." He added that he was giving the officers dancing classes, so "if you want a perfectly good male chorus, we've got one ready for you." Less jokingly and a little more feelingly, he told Dillingham that he was "awfully homesick. If you can fix it so the war will be over and I can come back to a Spring production I shall be very happy."

By September, his third month at the front, Vernon was assigned to accompany bombers on their runs. He disliked dropping bombs himself: "It isn't a very pleasant sensation, as you can hear the bomb whistling through the air for about twenty seconds, and you have no idea when it's going to drop. In fact, I feel sorry when I drop them myself." He added that his job as escort was a dull one, as the Germans "keep a long distance behind you . . . in case something goes wrong with your engine, and then of course they would be on you like a pack of wolves."

Being a fighter pilot was new not only to war, but also to the human race: with the airplane so recent an invention, flying during peacetime was still a bizarre and untested occupation. Flying while shooting, and being shot at, often in terrible weather, was something no one had ever done before. A British researcher wrote during World War I that "war flying exposes the human organism to a greater strain than it has probably ever been exposed to before." Neil Hanson writes of many cases of "fainting, falling asleep in the air and hallucinations. Some pilots became ill with ulcers, insomnia and mental problems, others responded to the stresses with cynicism or black humour, or found solace in heavy drinking." Even so happy-go-lucky and calm a man as Vernon could stand only so much constant terror, excitement, and nerve-wrenching work.

Just as he began to fade, Vernon was given a week's leave, in October 1916. He took off for London: "Gee, it looks good to be in a real town." He loaded up with some food to take back to his fellow soldiers: two hundred oysters, a salmon and a haddock, a cake, and other edibles—the oysters went bad long before he got back to the front. When he returned to his job, he found—as do most vacationers—work piled up waiting for him, as well as the bad news that four of his friends had been killed. "It's darned hard luck," he wrote, "and they were four of the nicest boys in the Squadron."

Too many trained pilots were being lost, so leaves were cancelled and the men of the squadron were told they'd remain "somewhere in France" for a total of nine months, "unless of course one's nerves won't stand it. . . . My nerves seem to be quite all right so I guess I'm here for another four months." Vernon's flying skill was so admired that, in October 1916, he was put at the head of twenty-seven planes for a sortie over German lines, with Vernon at the apex of the mission's giant triangle. "It was a wonderful aerial feat of arms, which resulted in much damage to the enemy," said Harrington, "and yet the Escadrille returned without the loss of a single plane."

Vernon was reassigned yet again, in November 1916. He was given a "smaller and faster" airplane and was put on offensive patrols and air fights: much more dangerous than his previous work but also more exciting and challenging. He hated the smaller planes ("very cold in the winter") but had no say over his fate. "If you are told to go anywhere, you go, and that's all there is to it." One of his squadron mates was sent off to East Africa on one day's notice. "It happened he was very pleased," wrote Vernon, "but if that had happened to me, I should have gone mad."

Vernon did suffer an injury severe enough to require hospitalization: he burned himself on hot coffee. Trying to unscrew the top of the company's percolator, "the pressure of the steam was so great that it burst. The machine and most of the boiling water went up my sleeve." In those pre-antibiotic days, Vernon was sent to the hospital, salved with Vaseline, and bandaged up.

By late November, his exploits become more heroic and a little less embarrassing; Vernon shot down his first German plane. He'd most likely had "kills" before, having been dropping bombs on German trenches, but this was the first official notch on his gun. On November 27, 1916, flying over Vlamertinghe, western Flanders, in a Nieuport 20, Vernon shot down his first "Hun," in a large two-seater biplane. "I was invited to Headquarters to have dinner with the General," he wrote to Irene. "He congratulated me on bringing down the German machine, and we had a darn good dinner."

With a new squadron commander in December (Major Dombasle, a name that surely garnered a few behind-the-back wisecracks from his troops), Vernon had a new job. Dombasle wanted to equip the squadron with Nieuport Scout planes, and Vernon was one of the men assigned to ferry planes back and forth from a depot in Villacoublay, temptingly close to Paris.

Chapter Twenty-six

"Kiss all the pets for me, dear"

When he wasn't complaining about missing his "mate" or passing along (nonsensitive) war news, Vernon wrote about his animals. A lot. Mostly his German shepherd, Tell, and his monkey, Rastus, both of whom he seemed to miss as much as he did Irene: "Kiss all the pets for me, dear, and tell Rastus his Daddy loves him."

In addition to presents sent to Irene, he mailed Rastus "a card-board mandolin, full of sweets" and a jack-in-the-box, the latter a rather sadistic present for a monkey ("I wish I could see him open it, bless his little heart"). Disaster hit the home front in July 1916, when Tell killed one of Irene's puppies, Poudie. "I guess you had better get rid of Tell," Vernon reluctantly wrote. "I'd much rather my boy were killed, than your Poudie." But Irene kept Vernon's best-beloved dog, and no more incidents were reported. In fact, Irene was soon renting out Tell for stud, at a fee of $25.

Vernon seemed to write more about animals than about war, perhaps to cheer Irene and perhaps because he knew war news would be censored. In May 1916, he had to land a plane on a farm, whose owner let Vernon use his telephone to call for assistance. "He has the cutest farm, darling, I have ever seen," Vernon wrote. "Six dogs of different sizes and breeds; little ducks in a pond, and ever so many cows in a dairy; little colts and everything in the world that goes with a farm. . . . He must have thought I was a fool. I was so tickled with his dogs, and little ducks, only a day old, swimming about, not caring a darn about their chicken mother."

In June 1916, Vernon rescued a black and tan puppy he named Lizzie, who soon became a favorite of the company, despite her thieving ways: "Since I've been writing this letter Lizzie has brought me 3 slippers from different tents," he told Irene on July 8. "She's just gone out again. I hope she brings me a *pair* this time." Lizzie met a grisly death in August, under the wheels of a truck. "Fortunately she was killed instantly . . . it was nobody's fault."

Vernon's dancing skills were put to use when he traded fox trot lessons for a pregnant mutt named Quinnelle, who gave birth to five puppies whom Vernon tried to keep warm with a small oil stove, which "gives off more smell than heat." By October 1916, the pups were learning to drink out of a saucer: "They were very cute, they kept dipping their faces too far in the dish, and getting milk up their noses." By late that month, the puppies were crawling under the sheds, and Vernon had to "wallow in the mud" to fetch them safely out. Quinnelle, on the other hand, was no Tell: "when I talk seriously to her she doesn't understand," wrote Vernon, "she just looks up and wags her tail, and thinks I've got a piece of meat for her."

He enviously noted that the No. 3 company had "two little raggy dogs" named Push and Pull: "The only way you can tell which is which is to blow in their faces. If he puts his tongue out at you it's 'Push.' If he doesn't, it's 'Pull'—isn't that cute?"

The monkey population increased on both sides of the Atlantic: in September 1916, Irene bought Ephraim (another minstrel name), a baby brother for Rastus. ("He must be awful cute," wrote Vernon, "but I don't think there is a monkey in the world that could beat that boy Rastus.") Irene sent Vernon snapshots of the monkeys, and Vernon boyishly enthused, "Sweetie, I am just crazy about . . . Rastus and his baby brother. Gee, I'd go mad if I saw them." When Irene sent him photos of herself proudly posing in her tailored "soldier suit," Vernon pleaded with her to get a matching one made for Rastus, so he would look just like his "parents," a suggestion Irene did *not* follow up on.

In early December 1916, Vernon was in Paris to pick up and deliver a new plane and found a small Japanese monkey named Hallad (as in "Hallad be thy name") for sale—he snapped it up instantly for 200 francs and wrote that week, "he is sitting on my shoulder now trying to find a flea in my ear. . . . I was three hours last night making friends, and with the aid of a banana we have formed a relationship which I hope will turn into love, without a banana." Hallad was flown back to the front lines, bundled up, with Vernon flying low, worried about the effect of air pressure on the monkey's ears. "He will have the monkey's long distance flight record, and he may even become a Corporal." Vernon tried putting Hallad to sleep in a basket with a hot water bottle, but he soon chewed through the rubber and flooded his little bed, so he slept with Vernon in his cot.

Hallad turned out to be quite a handful. Vernon's tent mate made the mistake of leaving the monkey on its own for a day. By that evening, Vernon's quarters "looked as though a cage of monkeys had lived in it for years. There wasn't a glass ornament that hadn't been deliberately broken. He had taken a package of safety razor blades and bitten them, one by one, into small pieces [!], spilled the ink, turned on the bath water, and picked the stuffings out of the quilt and a hundred other things. To-morrow I shall put a chain on him."

Chapter Twenty-seven

"A super motion picture of . . . epoch-making magnificence"

On March 31, Irene hosted a Mrs. Castle Cabaret affair for the 110th Battalion, which was shipping out the next day. She auctioned off a dance with herself, and proceeds from the evening went to buy camp equipment. She was also feted by the American Legion and by Burton's Bantams, a regiment of men under five feet tall. In May 1916, *Watch Your Step* ventured north of the border, playing in Toronto. As the wife of a Royal Air Force hero, Irene was given a terrific greeting, and the opportunity to raise some money. One reporter noted that "Toronto girls are even now wearing what they term 'Mrs. Castle Flight Hats.'"

As the *Watch Your Step* tour wound down in the summer of 1916, Irene found herself at a career crossroads. She knew, after several years onstage, that she was not a strong enough singer or comedienne to compete with the likes of Broadway and vaudeville stars Gaby Deslys, Charlotte Greenwood, Blanche Ring, or Nora Bayes. And "Irene Castle" was not as marketable as "Vernon and Irene Castle." She knew her best bet for a career lay with motion pictures. *The Whirl of Life* had shown her to be photogenic and a competent film actress. It had been hard work, but it had also been a relatively amateurish production. With professionals in charge, surely, things would go more smoothly. Irene turned her eyes away from the cabarets and toward the movies.

By 1916, the American movie industry was no longer the ramshackle mom-and-pop business it had been five or ten years earlier. It was a huge, thriving, cutthroat behemoth, already shifting from the East Coast, where it had begun, to the Los Angeles area. One could no longer wander in off the street into the studio and hope to be discovered: one fan magazine in the mid-1910s sent an undercover reporter out to the studios, and she couldn't get even a glimpse of a casting director.

Though two-reelers (about twenty minutes long) were still being made, the real money was in features and serials. In 1916, D. W. Griffith's towering multistory *Intolerance* was released, as well as Theda Bara's *Romeo and Juliet*, Alla Nazimova's *War Brides*, and Dorothy Donnelly in what would be the first of eight (so far) versions of *Madame X*. Irene's *Watch Your Step* doppelgänger was haunting her: Mae Murray signed with Jesse Lasky in 1916 and began her own impressive film career.

Irene Castle was a smart woman and knew her strengths and weaknesses as a performer. She was lovely, with good "camera bones," and her public appeal was as a wholesome, active, all-American girl. She could not compete with such dramatic movie stars as Lillian Gish, Norma Talmadge, or Mae Marsh; the split-second comic timing of Constance Talmadge, Mabel Normand, and Dorothy Gish was also beyond her range. And no one could match the versatile skills of the Queen of the Movies, Mary Pickford. But the mid-1910s were the golden age of the action/adventure serial queens.

The most famous, today, is still Pearl White, who skyrocketed to fame with *The Perils of Pauline* (1914). A low-key, natural actress (and a smart, funny woman), White went on to star in such serials as *The Exploits of Elaine*, *The Fatal Ring*, *Pearl of the Army*, and many others. But Pearl White was hardly the only actress specializing in rousing, athletic serials—she wasn't even the first. In 1912, Mary Fuller starred in the twelve-part *What Happened to Mary?* and the following year saw Kathlyn Williams in the thirteen-part *The Adventures of Kathlyn*.

The genre proved a huge hit. While boys emulated their Western and action heroes Douglas Fairbanks, Wallace Reid, and Tom Mix, girls who didn't want to be vamps, showgirls, or simpering baby dolls could idolize such serial queens as Florence La Badie, Juanita Hansen, Grace Cunard, Ruth Roland, and Marie Walcamp. It was widely publicized that these women did all their own stunts, which was sheer nonsense (as was proven in 1922, when Pearl White's stuntman, John Stevenson, was killed while filming *Plunder*). But still, these actresses dove, swam, rode horseback, flew airplanes, engaged in fight scenes, and leaped in and out of windows. Pearl White herself was seriously injured in a fall while being carried up a flight of stairs in *The Perils of Pauline* (she suffered back injuries that plagued her for the rest of her life).

Lovely, blonde Florence La Badie embodied the ethos of the action star: "If [I] were to go up in an aeroplane and Mr. Hansell [her director] said he wanted me to fly upside down and drop within four feet of the earth and then right the machine, I'd feel that I had to do it. . . . Anything with an element of danger in it appeals to me." Director Hansell conceded, "If I were to say to her, 'Miss La Badie, go and jump out of that window, there'll be someone down below to catch you,' she'd do it without even going to the window to look. . . . She's pure steel." (La Badie, who called herself an "Indifferentist," died as she had lived, in an auto accident in 1917, at the age of twenty-nine.)

Irene knew her best bet to break into the movies was in an action/adventure serial. Fortunately, her friend and dancing student William Randolph Hearst was in need of a star for his proposed "Preparedness Serial," *Patria*, to be produced by the Wharton Studios. Hearst had been interested in films since at least 1898, when he sent a film crew to cover (some say to start) the Spanish-American War. He entered the film business as a producer in 1915 with a series of animated shorts. He was already a big name as an ambitious politician and the influential publisher of the *New York Morning Journal*, the *Los Angeles Examiner*, and other papers in Boston and Chicago. But up till late 1916, none of Hearst's films amounted to much.

Hearst's interest in show business was quite natural: in 1915, he had met and fallen in love with rising young showgirl Marion Davies, who was appearing in such revues as *Stop! Look! Listen!* (1915) and Ziegfeld's 1916 *Follies*. While Hearst and Irene were collaborating in mid-1916, his affair with the twenty-year-old china-doll beauty Davies was in its first flush of romance. A fearsome megalomaniac, Hearst was also a romantic—and as giddy as a schoolboy when the true love of his life began to return his affections. It's a testament to Irene's great tact and social skills that she was able to maintain lifelong friendships not only with Hearst and Marion Davies but with Hearst's wife, Millicent.

The wheels got rolling when, as novelist and screenwriter Louis Joseph Vance recalled, a representative of Hearst's International Film Service called to say that "Mr. Hearst wants to star Mrs. Vernon Castle in a serial having for its main theme the need of national preparedness for war. We're not in any hurry, but we'd like to have the first six or seven episodes in detailed continuity by to-morrow morning at the very latest."

The plot, as ordered by Hearst and hammered out by Vance, followed the adventures of munitions heiress Patria Channing and her efforts to channel her family fortune into national defense. She is aided by heroic secret service agent Donald Parr and menaced by a coalition of Japanese and Mexican villains intent on invading the United States.

Here is where *Patria* veers into the bizarre, and where it ran into trouble. Hearst had long had a bee in his bonnet about Japan and Mexico, and his insistence on making those countries the film's villains (in 1916, when everyone else was busily vilifying Germany) made *Patria* controversial from the start.

For her leading man, Irene was blessed with probably the most intelligent and well-read actor in the film industry: handsome thirty-four-year-old Milton Sills, a veteran of Broadway, though a relative newcomer to films. Before becoming an actor, Sills had been a professor of psychology and philosophy at the University of Chicago; he spoke Italian, Russian, French, and German, and coauthored the book *Values: A Philosophy of Human Needs*. *Patria* would be a breakthrough film for Sills, who went on to become a reliable star through the 1920s until his death of a heart attack at the dawn of the talkie era, in 1930. Milton Sills, for his part, was glad when the whole *Patria* ordeal was over. "For my many sins," he later said, "I did penance for nine months of my life in *Patria*." Irene, he was quick to note, "is delightful, droll, original, a splendid vis-à-vis on the screen. But the play itself! *Brr!* To me it was uncongenial."

The villain, the putatively Japanese Baron Huroki, was played by Swedish-born character actor Warner Oland, who later went on to fame as Charlie Chan and Dr. Fu Manchu (oddly, Oland did not look particularly Asian). Louis Joseph Vance recalled that one major casting hurdle was finding Japanese actors, with "real Japanese actors refusing to play in a story whose plot indicated Japan as a possible ill-wisher of the United States." This commendable attitude on the part of those actors resulted in villains whose makeup renders them sort of Japanese, sort of Mexican, and altogether confusing from a plot standpoint.

The first ten episodes of *Patria* were filmed on the East Coast: mostly in Ithaca, and also in Buffalo and Fort Lee. Some of the film still exists, and Ithacans delight in pointing out the buildings and bridges that still stand. Irene would become much more familiar with Ithaca in the 1920s. For now, though, it was just a place to work (it was too far to commute from Manhattan, though, so she had to stay there while filming). A lovely upstate New York town best known as the home of Cornell University—

from which Irene's father had been expelled—Ithaca was also home to brothers Leopold and Theodore Wharton, producers and directors who opened the Wharton Studios in 1914. Among the many films made in Ithaca by the Whartons before they closed down in 1920 were three *Elaine* adventure serials starring Pearl White and Grace Darling's popular *Beatrice Fairfax* serial as well as Irene's *Patria*.

Irene was signed on for a twenty-week shoot on *Patria*, at $1,500 a week—more than enough to keep her well supplied with luxuries while away from her New York home. She rented a house on Cayuga Heights and arrived in town in grand style in mid-July, accompanied by Rastus, three dogs, two servants, twenty trunks, and fifteen hatboxes, with two cars and two horses soon to join her. Irene wasn't the only star in town that summer: Pearl White and Ziegfeld Girl Olive Thomas were also filming for the Whartons.

The film was written by Vance in collaboration with J. B. Clymer (a newcomer to films) and Charles W. Goddard (a veteran of such serials as *The Perils of Pauline* and *The Exploits of Elaine*). Vance offered to tailor the stunts to Irene's capabilities. She took this as a slap in the face. "It made me *furious!* I told them I'd show them." Vance complied by providing as many stunts as he could cram in, reasoning that "she asked for it . . . she grew deeply versed in the lore of liniments and bandages and surgeons' plaster. But never once did she complain or shirk any of the hazardous risks which the scenario called upon her to chance."

Despite being somewhat of a film center, Ithaca broke out in a tizzy of excitement when Irene hit town: "I was so close I could have touched her!" squealed a fan to a reporter as crowds lined up to see Irene shoot a scene. "Many went without their midday meal" so as not to miss Irene, and when she disembarked from a ship on which she was filming, "her escorts had to make an opening in the crowd in order that she might get through."

In mid-August, the Whartons rented the naval militia gunboat *Sandoval* for a day's filming on Lake Ontario. Irene, in a white blouse and black bloomers, had to dive into the water from the ship with Milton Sills. One newspaper reported, straight-faced, "An attempt will be made tomorrow afternoon to drown Mrs. Vernon Castle." Several takes were necessary, by which time the dye from her bloomers had begun to run, and Irene was trailed everywhere by pools of black liquid. Irene prided herself on doing her own diving and swimming: "The audience feels, and rightly so, that it has been cheated, robbed of the sympathy and affection perhaps for a heroine who fails to make good 'in the pinches,' and 'fake' is a mild word which they use to express their disgust." Will Rogers, impressed with Irene's derring-do, commented, "We used to be worried about you, Vernon, out there at the front, but when we saw Irene in *Patria*, we decided she was in still greater danger. If she does another serial, she's got you beaten."

Irene did have two nasty experiences filming in the ice-cold Cayuga Lake. Agreeing to dive off the deck of another ship, she passed out from the cold upon hitting the water (despite a shot of Southern Comfort beforehand to gird her loins) and had to be fished out. During another scene, she and Milton Sills found themselves threatened by a runaway "prop" fire while atop a ship's mast. According to accounts (which may, of course, have been exaggerated by the studio's press department), the stars were dumped into the lake when the mast broke in half.

Filming ran into all the usual troubles that still plague productions. The fourth episode (in which Irene played both Patria and her evil double, the nightclub dancer Elaine) was shot in the Montmartre nightclub in Times Square, but "the scenes turned out badly," according to Vance (he did not specify if this was a technical or acting hitch). Florenz Ziegfeld threw open his *Midnight Frolics*, on the New Amsterdam Roof, to the company, and "the entire *Midnight Frolics* company was written into the story for this episode only." This scene, happily, survives, giving us a tantalizing glimpse of the New Amsterdam Theater's legendary rooftop nightclub.

The most spectacular scene was filmed in late September, when the Whartons purchased and torched a mansion at Meadow and State streets in Ithaca, with several fire companies standing by. Another fire, the following week, represented a village torched by strikers, and 250 locals took part. By the time the Whartons blew up a boxcar on the railroad tracks in mid-October, Ithacans were probably looking forward to the company's departure. Certainly the Beckers were: local papers carried the story of Selma Becker, whose brief marriage to Joseph Becker was annulled after she "took part in two scenes of *Patria* against her husband's wishes."

Irene somehow managed to ship Vernon prints of *Patria* while he was in Europe, and his criticisms show his clear-eyed professionalism. In one supposedly high-class party sequence, he complained, "most of the movie actors wear soft pleated shirts and pumps and the women wear such 'chorus' clothes. All this can only be fixed with money enough to get the very best." One scene in which Irene shot a dynamite fuse with a pistol he thought was "carrying it a bit too far. Of course I'm probably wrong, but it struck me as being a little too 'Deadwood Dickey.'"

He also fretted terribly about a scene in which she had to fall off a horse, begging her to use a double, and a flying scene, asking how much experience her pilot had had: "For God's sake don't go up with some dub who has only just taken his pilot's license. Insist please, darling, on having an experienced pilot who has done at least one hundred hours in the air. You know, sweet, if anything happened to you through any one's carelessness I'd come home to shoot him dead."

When the *Patria* company moved to the West Coast in late November 1916 to shoot the remaining episodes, they were not accompanied by the New York writers, director, or crew. Not only did a new company have to be set up, but a fifteen-hundred-acre ranch in the San Fernando Valley had to be converted into a temporary city, complete with dressing rooms, dining facilities, "a young army of extra people, stables for troops of horses and armories for military equipment."

Irene took the train west in late November, stopping off in Chicago "to bathe." She told the local papers that she looked forward to visiting Vernon overseas and that "I'd like to dance again, but I never shall unless he dances with me. I can dance with no one but him."

Irene was not pleased with the new director, Jacques Jaccard, a New Yorker who had about thirty films under his belt by late 1916 (he would work through 1936, mostly on Westerns and adventure films). She thought he gave far too much screen time to his protégé, Marie Walcamp, a blonde action star who'd already appeared in more than fifty movies. Irene complained that her own appearances in the later reels were confined to "big close-ups at the end of each episode where, smiling wistfully at the audience, I told them good night. We must have made a hundred of these." With only bits of *Patria* remaining, it's hard to tell how accurate Irene's recollections were, but she was right not to have been happy with Jaccard's work: the California scenes are awkwardly shot and lack the snap and suspense of the East Coast footage (Irene would be delighted to know that none of Marie Walcamp's scenes survive).

Work went slowly in California: the company was housed far from the shooting set and had to start out at the crack of dawn to get there by

9:00 A.M.; still, according to one paper, they "seldom start to shoot before noon." Twenty-two-year-old dancer and neophyte actor Rudolph Valentino is rumored to have appeared as an extra in a West Coast episode of *Patria*, but at this date, it's impossible to confirm or deny this.

When cornered by a reporter during the West Coast shoot, all Irene would talk about was Vernon. "That he has done well is attested to by the fact that he has been promoted several times for his daring work and bravery," she bragged. "I am very proud of him." When the journalist asked her for some comments on dancing, she brushed him off with, "Oh yes . . . You see . . . Oh, maybe you'd better wait until Vernon gets back." West Coast shooting wrapped up the first week of January 1917, with only a few "pick-up" scenes to be shot on the East Coast.

Surviving letters, telegrams, and memos from the production of *Patria* show that retakes were necessary not only because of "defective negatives," but to address such problems as making "boy messengers . . . look like Japs instead of negroes," a corpse changing position between scenes, Irene needing "a little more expression" in one close-up, and a suggestion from Hearst that there should be a scene in which Irene retires from the fray to try on clothes. "There is no excitement in this incident," admitted screenwriter Charles Goddard, "it is merely a reason for showing [Irene] dolled up and giving a little relief for the swift and thrilling stuff that goes before and after. I have been unable to devise anything exciting where Patria can be dolled up which will not involve retaking of scenes in Ithaca sets or of gumming up the plot."

In January 1917, the first three episodes of *Patria* were shown to newspaper reporters, theater-chain owners, and exhibitors across the country, and Irene, as per her contract, accompanied the reels to each preview. At the Los Angeles showing in the Hotel Alexandria, between four hundred and five hundred people crowded into the ballroom: reporters, society and show business figures, Irene and her mother (Hearst himself was absent, due to his own mother's illness). The Palace Theater in New York showed *Patria* (and Irene) off to five hundred employees of the B. F. Keith and United Booking Office circuits of theaters; the Marie Antoinette Ballroom of Spokane's new Davenport Hotel was packed when *Patria* was shown to northwestern film distributors that same month. Another gala was given at the old Ritz-Carlton in New York (not the current hotel of that name, but one on Madison Avenue and Forty-sixth Street, near the former Castle

House). This showing was accompanied by a symphony orchestra, and Irene's first appearance onscreen was greeted with an ovation lasting "several minutes."

Hearst serialized the film in his newspapers, increasing both paper circulation and movie attendance. It was heavily promoted in the trade papers to distributors and owners of both vaudeville and movie theaters; one ad had the hugely infelicitous tagline, "An attraction that will bring money into the box office in a golden stream."

Irene knew that *Patria* was not great cinematic art and deprecated her own performance in it. "I was not called on for any acting except to look terrified occasionally, and on those occasions I didn't need to act. I was," she later wrote. As exhausting and physically dangerous as filming was, Irene told one reporter, "It's elegant leisure beside appearing in a play and dancing before at [Castle House] and afterward at a roof garden." Action serials were no place for actresses who wanted to perfect their art. Pearl White, the Queen of the Serials, spoke amusingly about the frustrations of acting in them. "There *is* no acting in a serial," she told *Motion Picture Classic* in 1919. "You simply race through the reels. Your dear old mother dies in a [feature-length] photoplay, and she takes 120 feet to do it. In a serial she gets 20 feet, and has to step lively at that. I want to emote. Who doesn't?"

The Hearst papers, of course, gave the film raves to the point of hysteria and tears. Otheman Stevens of the *Los Angeles Examiner* was typical: "These three episodes leave the spectator hungry for the rest. . . . Rarely if ever has such a competent cast been seen. . . . Mrs. Castle proved not only a beautiful young woman, an actress of high intelligence, but a daring young spirit facing all manner of physical perils." That same paper's Florence Bosard Lawrence agreed: "No film displayed in recent years contains more appealing elements than the first episode of *Patria*. . . . It plays on the emotions as on a harp and the swift-moving chain of tense situations keeps one in a perpetual state of thrilling suspense." Another *Los Angeles Examiner* writer called *Patria* "a super motion picture of unrivaled artistic beauty and epoch-making magnificence."

Of course, the big surprise would have been a Hearst paper panning the film. But reviews across the board were either respectful or positive; not *everyone* could have been trying to appease Hearst. Noted reviewer John De Koven was impressed: "To see as good a serial as *Patria* . . . is a heartening experience. . . . Mrs. Castle plays a role that is a combination of Pearl White and Douglas Fairbanks with Billie Burke trimmings . . . it is not only crowded [with] the kind of hairbreath [sic] thrills that increase one's blood pressure and toy with one's heart action, but it is a fashion show, too." Reviews from papers large and small were uniformly good for both the film and its star: "Mrs. Vernon Castle . . . proves herself equal to any star of the screen in charm, pluck, and real talent"; she "lends more than her well-known name to the screen"; "Mrs. Castle shows no little ability as a screen actor." Episodes of *Patria* were frequently shown as part of a vaudeville bill—an unusual tactic—as was the case when the *Columbus Journal* reviewed it, calling it "the most absorbing act on the bill . . . a genuine thriller." The independent *Variety*'s reviewer "Jolo" (who had so loved *The Whirl of Life*) also gave a thumbs-up to *Patria*. "An ingenious melodrama . . . occasionally inconsistent but nevertheless thrilling. The suspensive interest is always interestingly depicted, in modern fashion. . . . *Patria* is a certain hit."

Not everyone took the film as seriously as Hearst may have wanted. The *Detroit News Tribune*'s Edward Speyer was hugely amused by the plot, which he described as Irene being "harassed by enemies of the United States. Japs, it seems, or Germans, or Parthians or Idumenians or something of that sort. They shoot at her, kill people, burn her home, throw her in the drink to drown, dance with her and kick her shins probably, and even steal her $100,000,000 defense fund. In the end she baffles, defeats and overthrows them and saves the United States, which is awfully kind of her."

Patria survives in a partial print: about an hour of footage. It's impossible to fairly critique the whole film from what exists now. But the earlier, East Coast scenes do move quickly and contain the proper amount of thrills, suspense, and loony plot twists for a good serial. Irene is not required to do much more than register fear, determination, and courage, but she does this very prettily.

Along with film stardom came the responsibilities of a film star: more photos, more interviews—and Irene was getting increasingly impatient with both. A *Motion Picture Classic* article of February 1917 noted that she was becoming a bit of a diva, "a bundle of nerves in a slim, fragile body," and that her photo sessions tended to end in "hysterics and nervous excitement that prevented her from working for a day or so." She'd been appearing for years in newspapers and fashion magazines; now Irene's face adorned the covers of movie magazines as well. And her coverage in *Vogue*, *Town & Country*, and the like increased with her film fame: a multipage glamour spread in a 1917 issue of *Vanity Fair* ran with the sarcastic caption, "As every reader of *Vanity Fair* knows, or should know, we have a contract to publish a picture of Mrs. Castle in every issue. Now and then, we slip up, or forget, or get careless, or misplace the picture, and the number goes to press quite incomplete. Mrs. Castle has threatened to cancel her subscription if this happens again; so, to be on the safe side, we now print seven pictures of her."

As always, one subject Irene was happy to discuss was clothing. She gave a long interview, cropped into several syndicated articles, that shows Irene's usual good common sense when it came to fashion and gives an interesting backstage glimpse of filmmaking. She recommended having copies made of costumes, especially if one did as much stunt work as she did: "It is always my ill fortune to have to dive or be thrown into the water with all my clothes on. . . . I had one little dress of cotton that shrank almost to my knees." She noted that long furs, like fox and sable, photographed better than close-lying ones, and that reds and greens photographed as black. "As all your dresses are going to be gray and white by the time they are seen on the screen," she suggested that movie costumes simply be made in those colors at the start.

Patria was not long into release before trouble erupted from a predictable source: Japan (Mexico was already mad at the United States). Japanese ambassador Hanrihara complained about the film to President Wilson, who in turn sent a strongly worded letter to Hearst, c/o the International Film Service: *Patria*, he said, "is extremely unfair to the Japanese and I fear that it is calculated to stir up a great deal of hostility which will be far from beneficial to the country. . . . I take the liberty, therefore, of asking whether the Company would not be willing to withdraw it if it is still being exhibited."

It was indeed still being exhibited, and Hearst reluctantly brought copies back to the studio for editing: Japanese flags were cut out and titles referring to nationality rewritten. "Baron Huroki" became "Senor Manuel Morales, confidential adviser of Senor De Lima, of Mexico," though Oland was still attended by kimono-clad henchmen in a Japanese-style house.

The hapless Wharton brothers lived to regret teaming up with the relentless Hearst. He reneged on $37,000 he owed the Whartons for expenses on *Patria* and two other films. They won a 1919 lawsuit against him—Hearst paid up, but he managed to torpedo the Whartons by getting their distributor, Pathé, to blackball them. The Whartons were out of business by 1920, pretty much crippling Ithaca's film industry.

CHAPTER TWENTY-EIGHT

"HE WAS OUT TO SEE THE KAISER DEFEATED"

In late February 1917, Irene sailed again for England to see Vernon, who was able to get a week's leave in London. It was a terrible, stormy crossing, rife with fears of submarines, and no Vernon to greet her at the pier. Fearing him dead or injured, she fretfully took the train to London, where she found his leave had been postponed at the last minute. Late in the afternoon of Irene's arrival, he managed to fly across the Channel in his biplane.

They reserved a suite at the Savoy; Vernon brought Hallad with him and a diamond-studded wing pin for Irene, to match his insignia. "Our reunion was a joyous one," she wrote, enabling the couple to "lie in each other's arms, shutting the world out." Not so joyous for Hallad, who met his doom that week: Vernon put Hallad in a box as he and Irene were about to go out for the evening, tossing his coat over it to keep the monkey warm in the underheated room. When they got home, Hallad had suffocated. Irene tried in vain to convince her sobbing husband that Hallad had died of a heart attack, but weeks later he wrote to her that "I don't seem to be able to get over his death. . . . It does seem a shame, and I miss him terribly."

Hallad was eventually replaced by another monkey, Jeffrey, who proved to be more trainable. Photos show him to be not as cute as Rastus, but Jeffrey was to be with Vernon to the end. "Vernon always called him 'my boy,'" Irene explained, "because 'he thinks he's a boy and you mustn't hurt his feelings.'"

It was during this leave that Vernon was notified he'd been awarded the French Croix de Guerre, which had been instituted by the government in 1915 to recognize acts of bravery in the face of the enemy. The medal itself—a cross surmounted by crossed swords, centered on a profile of Marianne, symbol of the French Republic—was waiting for Vernon in France, but he was happily able to buy the accompanying red- and green-striped ribbon to sew on his uniforms, with Irene in attendance.

Irene found London surprisingly dance-mad, despite (or because of) the war. "They are dressing in somber shades, but not in black," she noticed. The town was full of men: "Lonely men. Men on leave, with all the seriousness of war just back of them and only a few days ahead. I danced with a lot of men who only had one arm. But they didn't seem to care just so they had two good legs to get them around."

The Castles spent much of the week catching up with friends in London (a party at Ciro's, for twenty, grew to eighty guests) and playing benefit performances, including one for Queen Alexandra—with no rehearsal, on a banked stage. "There's a trick to these English stages," Vernon told his nervous wife. "You have to work with the slope. It actually helps sometimes." Irene found dancing on a slant terrifying: "I felt as though I had just flown fifty missions over German lines." As for Alexandra, "I found her to be just a charming, most gracious, sweet woman." Shortly thereafter, Irene sailed back to the United States to continue her stage and screen career; Vernon flew back, sans Hallad, to the front lines.

Despite Vernon's well-publicized heroics and life-threatening missions, his reputation as a clownish figure and effeminate "lounge lizard" (as he was described in March 1917) lived on. That same 1917 article claimed that Irene was looking for a dancing partner to replace Vernon and that an appropriate applicant must be "tall and emaciated. He should have round shoulders and a concave stomach, syncopated eyes. . . . But the prime requisite is a tango figure—a drooping, languid, willowy form." Pretty nasty stuff to fling at a decorated war hero, and it must have discouraged Vernon to no end.

Nevertheless, Vernon was also getting a lot more good press once his war record became known. His *Watch Your Step* costar Frank Tinney was quoted as saying, "Vernon Castle loved England. He despised a slacker and one of his motives for going to war was to show up the Englishmen over here. Incidentally, let me tell you that the type of Vernon Castle in England are fighting on the battlefields for their country. The monocle guys of England were the first to go. The thugs and tough guys are still hanging back." One of his students, Charles Crawford, recalled with great fondness: "In his flying classes Castle was not a teacher, but a pal." Vernon was, Crawford added, "a real man. He was out to see the Kaiser defeated and was working 24 hours a day to help do it."

If there was an occasional bad word to be said about Vernon—as a pilot, instructor, or comrade—it certainly never came from his fellow soldiers. W. O. Mullin, a mechanic in the Royal Flying Corps, stated that Vernon "was one of the most popular men on the field. Not only was he considered one of the most successful aviation instructors, but he used his talents as an entertainer to make life pleasant for the boys in camp during the evenings." Besides his drumming, he made up parodies of popular songs, many of which were not fit to be repeated to Irene. "Vernon Castle was a mighty good man," said Lieutenant Colonel J. T. Bloomfield, British Royal Flying Corps. "I knew him quite well at the front. . . . He excelled in teamwork, and always did his work as should be done."

Vernon managed to enjoy himself on what time off he could manage, and he still found flying to be great fun. John F. Ryan recalled one time in France when Vernon dropped in on a party of picnickers: "An aeroplane sailed over the inner field and presently alighted. The aviator hopped out of the aeroplane, tripped over to where the little group of picnickers were gathered, and, gallantly raising his cap, greeted them. Then he asked if he might join them at luncheon. His request, of course, was granted. The dancer then gave the picnickers an exhibition of fancy flying, and went on his journey."

On March 11, 1917, Vernon shot down his second (and, as it turned out, last) German plane, an Albatros, at Poezelhoek, Belgium, while he was flying a Nieuport 17 (a single-seater, with no observer). Vernon wrote home, "At first I was delighted that another German was gone. Now I am sorry, for he was a brave man." He didn't really want to take credit, telling Irene, "I saw four of their machines flying in diamond formation and as I was above them, I dived down on the tail of the last one and shot him down and flew away before the others had time to realize what had happened."

The very next day, Vernon's own luck nearly ran out. He was over German lines, flying at about one thousand feet when, "Bang! And I got a direct hit on my machine by a Hun Archie. It hit the engine and tore about half of it away." Vernon's training and his finesse with a plane kept him from panicking, and he managed to glide it down "just behind our second line trenches. . . . There is hardly anything left of the machine," he wrote to Irene. "As it came down it hit some barbed wire, turned upside down and landed on its back." Vernon, luckily, was strapped in tightly and suffered only a few cuts and bruises.

In April 1917, Vernon was injured when his plane fell about a thousand

feet and landed in some barbed-wire entanglements—in France, fortunately, not Germany. He'd been flying near Abele, in the Ypres salient, and
was rushed to the Royal Flying Corps Hospital. He was lucky to escape
with scratches from barbed wire and a bruised leg (necessitating a chic
walking stick and some physical therapy).

That was the end of Vernon's war. "The C.O. says it's the last job I
need do on this trip, and is going to give me easy work until I am sent
home," he wrote. He recovered from his injuries at "a peach of a chateau,"
where he played ping-pong with his commanding officer for a few days.
After a year of active duty—June 1916 through April 1917—two kills, and
one injury, it was finally decided to send Vernon Castle back stateside ("in-
valided out," as the saying went), where he would be promoted (or de-
moted, however one saw such things) to flying instructor. He'd earned it,
even in this third grueling year of a war that seemed endless and that was
eating up more and more men from more and more countries. He was
returned to the Home Establishment in England and shortly after put on
a ship for home.

Chapter Twenty-nine

"An hour's pleasant diversion"

The success of *Patria* boded well for Irene's career: in April 1917, she was signed by Pathé, the American branch of the successful French company, to appear in feature films. "I consider the engagement of Mrs. Castle one of the most important steps we have taken," said Pathé's general manager, J. A. Berst. "This is in line with our new policy of engaging only the biggest stars with an established box-office value." Irene's films were to be produced and distributed under Pathé's Astra and Gold Rooster subsidiaries.

Her first assignment was *Sylvia of the Secret Service*, a five-reeler (about an hour long). As per its title, *Sylvia* was a crime thriller, about an American agent (Irene) and a Scotland Yard man (J. W. Percival) who team up to solve a jewel theft. The victim (and possible perpetrator) also became Sylvia's love interest and was played by leading man Elliott Dexter, who, at forty-seven, was a bit long in the tooth to be romancing Irene. *Sylvia* was directed by the immensely talented George Fitzmaurice, a French-born director who was later responsible for such fondly remembered films as *The Son of the Sheik*, *Raffles*, and *Mata Hari*. He had a reputation for getting superb performances out of temperamental, difficult-to-direct divas such as Pola Negri, Mae Murray, and Barbara La Marr.

Irene started *Sylvia* in April 1917. Like all her Pathé projects, it was filmed in Fort Lee, New Jersey, which was in its last days as the East Coast's busiest film center. Conveniently located just across the Hudson River from New York City (a ferry ride away in those days before the George Washington Bridge), Fort Lee rose to prominence by 1910, as filming in Manhattan became more difficult. Just as Irene began her Pathé contract, the United States entered World War I and the whole East Coast became problematic for filming. Shortages of coal and oil for heat and light made California more attractive, and the coast hopping of the earlier 1910s was suddenly more difficult, as trains were requisitioned for troops and supplies.

But in the spring of 1917, Fort Lee was still going strong, with more than a dozen major production companies in full throttle. Irene stayed at her Lexington Avenue home and was able to commute to and from work each day. She did not always work nine to five, of course: early-morning and overnight scenes for this film were taken in Englewood and Jersey City, New Jersey, and in the lobby of the Martinique Hotel in New York. She expressed a chirpy, optimistic delight: "The work in features gives me a real chance to act and I feel that I am learning a great deal under the direction of Mr. Fitzmaurice."

Sylvia was released in November 1917 and met with mixed success: "Irene has developed a genuine talent for acting," wrote the *Dramatic Mirror*, while *Moving Picture World*'s reviewer called the film and cast merely "satisfying." "There is little to commend it in the way of plot," said *Variety* ("Jolo" again), though admitting, "it will bring home the bacon" due to Irene's star power. *Photoplay* admired Irene as "an actress of remarkable talent" but dismissed the film as "just a lot of itching hand, grabbing claw, gnashing teeth, kicking feet stuff."

Irene sailed quickly from one film into another: she had no sooner finished *Sylvia of the Secret Service* than she started shooting *Stranded in Arcady*, directed by Frank Crane. Crane was better known as a character actor than as a director; he helmed about fifty films in the 1910s and '20s, none of them remembered today. *Stranded in Arcady* was another crime/action film, again with Elliott Dexter as Irene's love interest. The two played spoiled city folk on their own in the wilds of Canada, at the mercy of thugs trying to keep them from claiming a fortune they'd inherited. Famous for doing her own stunts whenever possible, Irene balked at a ninety-foot dive from a cliff in Saranac Lake, New York. The cliff was too high, the water too shallow, said Irene, who refused point-blank to risk her life. A local girl, Gertrude Martell, who had dived from the cliff many times, filled in for her and became a minor hometown celebrity.

"An hour's pleasant diversion," summed up one reviewer of *Stranded in Arcady*. Another reviewer enjoyed Irene's acting but complained, "If the titles in this picture had been written by anyone with half a sense of humor, it might have been a classic." *Vancouver World* enjoyed it, calling the film "a high-grade melodrama with . . . some mighty thrilling scenes."

Irene was moving along at a nice clip, a film a month—*Stranded in Arcady* was produced during June 1917, and she began and completed her third Pathé assignment, *The Mark of Cain,* during July. It was a happier experience. Not only did she have George Fitzmaurice back as her director; her leading man was the sexy thirty-year-old rising star Antonio Moreno. Born in Madrid, Moreno had been in films since 1912, and by the 1920s would be a contender for the Latin Lover throne of Rudolph Valentino. The dark-eyed, perfect-profiled actor made love onscreen to Pola Negri, Greta Garbo, Clara Bow (in the classic comedy *It*), Colleen Moore, Marion Davies, Dorothy Gish—Irene was in very good company. *The Mark of Cain* was more of the same; already she was falling into a rut professionally. Moreno played a man accused of his uncle's murder; Irene was his adventurous, crime-solving girlfriend. The *Philadelphia Ledger's* reviewer enjoyed it: "A good mystery story that is filled with action and interest.... Mrs. Castle does some effective screen acting and can easily be counted upon as a future cinema favorite."

It was back to Frank Crane for her last film to be released in 1917, yet another crime thriller: *Vengeance Is Mine.* Vengeance was Irene's, playing the daughter of a man driven to suicide by evil financiers. With the help of the handsome son of one of the villains (her leading man this go-round was, again, Elliott Dexter), she tries to bring the villains to justice, but her sweetheart's evil father comes through, reforms, and makes good.

In late 1917 and early 1918, Irene made another five films for Pathé, all of them released in 1918. The first of these was *Convict 993,* directed by William Parke, costarring Harry Benham, with Warner Oland, her friend from *Patria;* Irene played a secret service agent posing as a jailbreaker and jewel thief. *Moving Picture World* thought it was Irene's best film to date, and the *Dramatic Mirror* more than agreed: "one of the best mystery pictures produced ... provides Irene Castle with the best acting opportunities of her screen career." The *Washington Times* singled out the ending for praise, deeming it "totally unlike the denouement the spectator has been led to expect." Irene herself later wrote to a friend that most of her "stories were bad," but she felt that "*Convict 993* was one of the best."

The Hillcrest Mystery, directed by George Fitzmaurice, was a throwback to *Patria,* with a war-related plot in which Irene's shipbuilder father is killed by German agents. The film was released in March 1918; *Variety* said that "Mrs. Castle does really well in a part that calls for some actual playing" but added nastily that the twenty-four-year-old Irene (who played a nineteen-year-old in the film) "looks youthful, but not nineteen."

The Mysterious Client, directed by Fred Wright, costarred the old *Patria* duo of Milton Sills and Warner Oland and had a plot that was an insult to the intelligence of audiences: Sills is repeatedly attacked, kidnapped, and generally roughed up trying to protect Irene from a gang of thugs who turn out to have been hired by her father to find her a chivalrous, heroic husband. "This is a pretty stiff dose of impossible story for anyone to swallow," groused *Motion Picture* magazine, adding that "had the whole thing been played as a farce-comedy it might not have been so bad."

Irene returned to Antonio Moreno's arms for *The First Law,* in which she played a nouveau-poor girl romanced by the son of the man who ruined her father. Released in August 1918, it made no great hit, due largely to its confusing and illogical plot: "The picture proceeds without rhyme or reason," wrote *Variety,* "the fine points being glossed over and everything happening without cause or effect."

December 1917 found Irene shooting *The Girl from Bohemia,* playing a Greenwich Village butterfly who inherits a southern estate and finds romance, adventure, and danger. It was released at the end of August 1918, and *Variety* found Irene's attempts at bohemianism amusing: "She smokes cigarettes at a dinner party given in her honor while attired in a gown that looks like a hula costume." Irene "looks pretty and works hard," *Variety* added, but the film itself "could scarcely be called interesting." *Photoplay,* at least, felt that "Mrs. Castle acquits herself very creditably."

CHAPTER THIRTY

I LOVE MY WIFE, BUT, OH, YOU KID!

Vernon arrived in New York in the early spring of 1917, tanned, lean, dashingly uniformed, and hobbling slightly on his walking stick, to find Irene commuting between their Lexington Avenue home and the Astra Studios in Fort Lee. He was eager to sample the New York nightlife but had to do so mostly by himself, as Irene had to be in bed early for the next day's shoot. April 24 saw him at the *Midnight Frolics*, where he was spotted from the stage by his friend Will Rogers. Irene did join Vernon to see *The Century Girl*, starring their friends Elsie Janis and Frank Tinney; they were again pointed out from onstage, and the whole audience rose to get a glimpse of the returned hero. A reporter overheard a Broadwayite gush to Vernon that the war "must be a great game," to which he stonily replied, "If you don't get shot."

Vernon and Irene went out dancing one night, hoping naively for a night of anonymous fun. But their presence on the dance floor immediately sent electricity through the crowd, "which paid tribute to the king and queen of the tango realm by withdrawing from the floor.... Out went the lights and the spotlight played on the famous dancers."

There was still some noticeable hostility toward Vernon in the press, even after his heroic return from the front. Frederick F. Schrader in the *Toledo Blade* offered his opinion that Vernon's two shot-down German planes were "a yarn of his press agent" and went on to toss out the possibility that Vernon had run away to war only because "Mrs. Castle was going to get a divorce to marry a millionaire." The Castles were, by 1917, washed-up has-beens anyway, according to Schrader, "an indistinct memory" until Will Rogers and Frank Tinney pointed out Vernon from onstage and "for a moment revived the flickering fame of their former popularity." This was, of course, bad-tempered nonsense, but there was a grain of truth in that Vernon and Irene's white-hot, overwhelming fame and success of 1914 *had* to fade a little bit. By early 1917, Vernon was a war hero, his dancing and acting success a whole year and a half behind him; Irene was "simply another movie star," no more or less notable than, say, Pearl White or the Talmadge sisters.

Curious about Irene's movie work, Vernon visited her on August 21 on the set of her first Pathé film, *Sylvia of the Secret Service,* and their photo was taken on a mock-up of a ship's cabin: Irene in a lovely suit and fur-trimmed cloak ensemble, Vernon looking dashing in his uniform, and Tell posed patiently between them. The photo, the first of the couple reunited, was reprinted in newspapers and magazines around the world.

In August, Vernon was assigned as flight commander at Camp Mohawk in Deseronto, Ontario, Canada. Located on the shores of the Bay of Quinte, east of Toronto, the base was alternately known as Rathbun (after the local family who owned the site) and Mohawk (for the tribe that lived nearby). Designated a Canadian Training Squadron, it was still fairly new when Vernon arrived. Teachers used Jennys: Curtiss JN4 Canucks, which had a top speed of seventy-five miles per hour.

Despite his intentions to save money, Vernon bought a bright yellow Stutz Bearcat: modeled after an Indy 500 winner of 1911, the Bearcat was a low-slung, jazzy sports car. It was fast, impractical, and glamorous, and Vernon loved it. He brought his monkey Jeffrey with him to Canada (Rastus stayed in New York with Irene). At a local Indian reservation, he boarded two German shepherds, too big and bumptious for a military camp. Many must have wished Jeffrey boarded out as well: "he could tear a barracks room apart in no time flat," recalled Captain Al Smith.

At Camp Mohawk, Vernon was delighted to meet his friend Johnny Coats, who was also assigned as a teacher. John Alexander Coats, from the Scottish family who owned Skelmorlie Castle in Ayrshire, had lost a lung to mustard gas while on front line duty, and he, like Vernon, was shipped to Canada as a flying instructor—a job at which he excelled. Vernon and Irene had known Johnny Coats at least as far back as Irene's visit to Vernon in England, as he wrote to her from France in 1916 that "poor Coats—the boy who gave the party with us, was shot down. I didn't hear any details, but I hope he wasn't killed." Johnny introduced Vernon to another instructor, Eardley Wilmot, and the three men became fast friends. The dashing and Errol Flynn–handsome Charles Eardley Wilmot, who was twenty-five in 1917, came from a wealthy Belleville, Ontario, family; he had joined the Royal Canadian Air Force as soon as war was declared.

It wasn't long before Eardley Wilmot introduced his two pals to his two sisters, who lived in Belleville. One local resident told an amusing story about how they met: Johnny Coats had to ditch his plane on the grounds of Glanmore House, where the Wilmot sisters happened to be visiting; naturally, they rushed out to see what the excitement was, and so a friendship was formed. Perhaps—but it's just as likely that old friends Vernon and Johnny, working every day with Eardley Wilmot, were invited over to meet his beautiful and charming sisters. And the Wilmot girls, Gwen and Audrey, both in their twenties, were well worth meeting. Gwen Wilmot had "a very strong personality," says her daughter, Carolyn Hetherington. "I remember her laugh, she had a rich, full, wonderful laugh. Even if you didn't know what she was laughing at, you had to laugh with her. A great sense of humor, irreverent, naughty, for the time; the girls were the stars wherever they were."

Vernon, Johnny, and Eardley became the Three Musketeers of Deseronto: Vernon may not have been as dashingly handsome or rich as his friends, but his fame gave him an added glamour. When not instructing on the fields, the three tore around town in Vernon's Stutz Bearcat or hopped in their planes to impress the locals with stunt flying. Often as not, they would head over to the Wilmots' (occasionally, Eardley would "bomb" a bag of laundry near the house for the long-suffering servants to deal with).

It wasn't long before they had paired off: Johnny Coats with Audrey Wilmot and Vernon with Gwen. He'd no doubt had his flirtations before (though none of them survive in the letters Irene allowed to be published). But this was something more. Gwen Wilmot was drawn not to the famous dancer but to the shy, funny, brave pilot, her brother's pal. And Vernon found himself faced with a girl who had all of Irene's beauty, education, and self-confidence but also a rollicking sense of humor and a refreshing lack of ambition. Within weeks, Vernon realized that Irene seemed to be getting along fine without him, and that—now that his dancing career was fading into the past—they no longer needed one another.

Vernon and Gwen "were very much in love," says Carolyn Hetherington. "I remember a photograph she had on her dressing table in her bedroom of Vernon with his pet monkey on his shoulder." Later in life, Gwen talked to her daughter of Vernon "in general terms. Fun stories. How Jeffrey would deposit unwelcome things on somebody that he didn't like."

In the spring of 1917, Irene and her sister, Elroy (who had joined the Women's Ambulance Corps), traveled up to Canada to spend some time with Vernon. By now, his affair with Gwen Wilmot was well under way—no one knows if he and Irene had it out at this time, though McLaughlin and Wilmot family lore agree that, at some point, Irene and Gwen met face-to-face. This was probably the only time they had the opportunity.

The visit wasn't all drawing-room drama, though. Vernon, breaking all regulations, took Irene up for their first flight together, dressing her in the smallest flight suit and goggles on hand. "I knew he was having the time of his life," Irene wrote, "we were in his special world and he was sharing it with me. He shot up and rolled over in a loop, then leveled off and dived toward the ground . . . until I felt suspended between earth and sky and a part of neither."

Vernon was known for having fun—perhaps too much fun, out of boredom and high spirits—with his airplanes. "Someone offered to bet him that he would not stand on one of the wings of an airplane when it was up," Irene wrote. Vernon—not a stunt flier like future film star Ormer Locklear—wisely refused, "but if someone would put up five hundred dollars, he would run his machine through a hangar, come out and go over the second, turn down quickly, go through the third, and then, coming out, go over the top of the fourth hangar. This bet was not taken up."

He was spotted at the Ritz-Carlton in Montreal in September 1917, leading the orchestra, playing the drums, dancing with lucky local girls Christine Somerville and Geraldine Paterson. "The eyes of hundreds followed the slim figure in the blue dress uniform," said the *Daily Intelligencer*. "To the disappointment of all his stay was short, and shortly after ten he was forced to leave."

In October 1917, Vernon was given permission to come down to New York to dance with Irene at a benefit for British Recruiting given at the huge Hippodrome Theater. Vernon was allowed to wear his uniform onstage, as it was a war benefit, and Irene donned a red-braided blue suit with a Scottish cap. Vernon and Irene had a night's rehearsal before the show, as they'd not danced together professionally in so long—not since Vernon had banged up his leg in France.

So many people lined up for tickets to the October 7 show that another night's performance had to be added, and "it was necessary to place chairs on the stage to accommodate the audience," which must have made dancing rather problematic. The shows went well: banks of flowers were handed to the Castles over the footlights, and "we bowed and bowed again our thanks. In the wings, Vernon nervously kissed my hand and there were tears in his eyes." With the Wilmot affair still up in the air and their separation probably down on paper, both Vernon and Irene knew this would likely be their last dance together. As it turned out, it was.

"One of the things that I know she discussed at length with her mother was her impending divorce from Vernon," says Irene's son, who also recalls Vernon's sister Marjorie discussing the divorce when she came to stay with them in the late 1930s. "Both Mother Foote and Vernon's sister were pretty much reconciled to the fact that Vernon and Irene had mutually decided to divorce once the war was over and each could restart their respective careers," McLaughlin says. "They had a kind of 'truce' while he was in the Royal Flying Corps. . . . Mother of course suspected Vernon of having flirtations everywhere he went." Gwen Wilmot's daughter Carolyn agrees that the divorce was pending, and that it was to be a civilized and friendly arrangement: "That was the impression I got from my mother."

Vernon was charged with forty students a month, which was more than enough. But with the constant turnover of instructors, Vernon soon became the Grand Old Man of Camp Mohawk and had to take on extra students as well. One cadet, William Gibbard, recalled the enthusiasm and frustration of training, with too many cadets and not enough machines or instructors. "Daybreak found each flight's cadets hopefully grouped round its one or two airworthy JN4s. They were taken in turn by the instructor, [who] expressed amazement at the fanatic zeal of Canadians to get flying. Said an aircraft was nothing to get lyrical over—just a mechanical contrivance to carry us through the air. . . . We lived for flying and were in despair when shortages of machines, sickness, orderly duty, etc., grounded us."

Vernon's driving and flirting time was being cut into, and his concentration and sleep had to suffer as well. Disaster was always a matter of "when," not "if," in that business. An American cadet at Deseronto, B. K. Adams, wrote, "Smashes are an hourly occurrence on the aerodrome but they all occur either in landing or on getting off so there is no fall and the man gets out without a scratch every time. . . . Today, as is the case every day, there were four crashes all outside the aerodrome and not a soul hurt."

Despite the cadet's assurances, not all crashes ended so happily. Vernon's closest call at Deseronto came in late May 1917, while instructing a cadet named W. E. Fraser: as always, Fraser sat in the front seat, Vernon in the back. Fraser lost control of the craft while they were about five hundred feet in the air—in his panic, he held the controls tight, and Vernon was unable to maneuver them. S. F. Wise wrote: "A story repeated by many cadets was that when a student froze at the controls, 'some instructors were known to stand up and hit the cadet on the head with a monkey wrench or anything available.'" But no such solution occurred to Vernon. They crashed into a hangar, the wings of the plane folding up around the front of the cockpit. Vernon called out to Fraser, who did not answer: already dead or unconscious, Vernon thought, and he climbed out of his seat to make his way forward and pull him out. Then the gas tank took fire, the rest of the plane caught, and it fell through the hangar roof as Vernon leaped out of the way. "Some of the officers who were there at the time have told me that it was necessary to hold Vernon back as he was determined to save his student," wrote Irene. After the accident, Vernon was sent home to New York on leave. "For days he sat looking out of the window, silent and morose, blaming himself for the accident."

Vernon missed flying at the front, where he had only himself to rely on and only himself to blame: instructing others gave him friendship and personal interaction, which he always enjoyed, but there was also heavy responsibility and the fear of being at the mercy of a panicked, unsteady hand. This was outweighed by the freedom, the better barracks, the ability to have his car and his dogs and monkeys, and being the adored, looked-up-to star of the students, and he went back to Camp Mohawk to take up his instructing duties and his romance with Gwen Wilmot.

CHAPTER THIRTY-ONE

"NEVER IN MY LIFE HAVE I BEEN
SUBJECTED TO SUCH HUMILIATION"

The year 1917 is generally seen as the year ragtime died and jazz was born: ragtime pioneer Scott Joplin died on April 1, and the Original Dixieland Jass (later Jazz) Band's "One Step" and "Livery Stable Blues" were recorded on February 26. It was *not* to be a good year for Irene.

Having made good in films, Irene was ready to give the stage one more try, for the first time as a solo artist. She was persuaded to join a huge, star-packed revue called *Miss 1917* in which she would be given a dance specialty. She signed a contract on August 16, 1917, giving her $900 a week, and later insisted that producer Charles Dillingham had begged her to be in the show: "We need you. We honestly do. Just three minutes of your dancing in each show would make it."

Miss 1917 looked to be a foolproof hit. It was coproduced by Florenz Ziegfeld and Dillingham—probably the two most successful musical impresarios on Broadway—under the aegis of the specially created Century Amusement Corporation, partly funded by banker and patron of the arts Otto Kahn. *Miss 1917* had music and book by Victor Herbert, P. G. Wodehouse, Jerome Kern, and Guy Bolton. And the *cast*—no other contemporary show, not even the *Follies,* could boast such an accumulation of stars and future stars. Besides Irene, dancers George White and Ann Pennington were in the show, along with matinee idol Charles King and musical comedy duo Van and Schenck. Comedy sketches were performed by Savoy and Brennan. Bert Savoy virtually invented camp: he was a brilliant drag performer whose tagline was "You *must* come ovah!" Savoy's 1923 death by lightning strike would become a Broadway legend (his last words were supposedly "Ain't Miss God kickin' up somethin' fierce!").

Also to be seen were future stars Marion Davies, Vivienne Segal, and Lilyan Tashman, and the cream of the *Follies* Girls: Zitelka Dolores, Vera Maxwell, Peggy Hopkins Joyce. Also in the cast was Irene's childhood idol,

Bessie McCoy, now billed as Bessie McCoy Davis since the recent death of her famous husband. Widowhood had left her with a child to support and less than $800 in the bank; she hoped that *Miss 1917* would prove to be her comeback vehicle. Lew Fields and his son Herbert were in the show, as well: it was the first time Irene had worked with Fields since she'd stolen Vernon away from him. All was forgiven, and the two sat backstage and chatted about Vernon's adventures overseas.

The show got rave reviews when it opened on November 5 at the Century Theater, way up on Central Park West. "*Miss 1917* is stupendous," wrote the *New York Times* reviewer. Fields, Bessie McCoy Davis, and Bert Savoy got much of the credit, but Irene was also singled out: "Always the lightest of dancers, with a touch as airy as thistledown, Mrs. Castle here rose into the realms of pure fancy—a disembodied joy." The *New York Post* also found her to be a highlight of the show, "a lightsome, flowerlike, and altogether graceful and lovely thing."

But she was unhappy with her own performance: "I found myself hopelessly lost as a solo number. I had no training for dancing alone and should never have tried it." Irene went on at 10:30 P.M., toward the middle of act 2. She later claimed to have objected to the late hour (she needed sleep for her daily film work, she said), but a glance at the program reveals the real problem: she followed a jazzy dance number featuring George White and Ann Pennington.

If "Irene Castle" represented the 1910s, "Ann Pennington" was a harbinger of the 1920s. A tiny (under five feet tall) dynamo, she was a proto-flapper: huge eyes, famously dimpled (and displayed) knees, a slightly naughty, wisecracking sense of humor. Her partner, George White, was a slim, attractive, dark-haired young man about to go on to greater fame himself, as producer of the *George White's Scandals* revues from 1919 through 1939 (Ann Pennington would appear in five editions). A veteran of four editions of the *Ziegfeld Follies* (with two more in her future), Pennington was just at the beginning of what would be a dazzling career as a dancer and actress in more than a dozen movies.

Ann Pennington's most lasting fame would be as the popularizer of the black bottom, a wild, knee- (and bottom-) slapping dance first seen on Broadway in the 1924 show *Dinah*. Pennington never claimed to have originated the dance, but she would perform it with such panache in George White's 1926 *Scandals* that it became forever associated with her. The black bottom, the Charleston, and the shimmy (all of which were born in the 1910s but became popular in the 1920s) were the kind of solo dancing Irene hated: wild, sexy, crude, athletic and, in her opinion, graceless. In 1917, Irene was still finding herself as a solo dancer, but descriptions of her appearance in *Miss 1917* sound very Isadora Duncan, with a bit of the chiffon twirlings of Loie Fuller.

She also sang a number after her dance, to everyone's shock: no one had forgotten the drubbing she received in *Watch Your Step*. Irene chose the song "Fancy You Fancying Me," which had been introduced by Jack Norworth and Lillian Lorraine in *Odds and Ends of 1917* that same month, November 1917. It wasn't her singing voice that raised ire this time, it was the fact that she'd never gotten permission from the *Odds and Ends* producers, who threatened to sue and forced Irene to cut the number.

Filming all day, racing back home, a quick dinner, then off to the theater to appear in *Miss 1917*: it all left her exhausted and professionally disappointed. She wasn't the only one disappointed. On Monday, December 3, Irene showed up at the stage door to find herself denied entrance. It hit the press on December 5: Irene had been summarily fired from *Miss 1917*, and not by mutual consent. Irene herself was "so angry she could scarcely talk coherently," said the *Brooklyn Eagle*. "Never in my life have I been subjected to such humiliation," she sputtered. She wasn't even allowed in the theater to collect her belongings and had to send her maid. She never saw it coming, she claimed: "If I had, do you suppose for one moment that I would have gone to the theater?"

As for those in management, they had their own story to tell. Irene's minute-and-a-half-long appearance "was not giving satisfaction," and they had "requested her to change her performance for the better, if possible." She had refused to make any changes and had demanded that director Ned Wayburn reschedule her from 10:30 to 9:15, threatening to leave the show if this was not done. Charles Dillingham said he had simply accommodated her and allowed her to leave the show, posthaste. Several other performers had been let go, including George White. But it was implied by the papers that Irene without Vernon "wasn't any longer a drawing card . . . a Hamletless Hamlet," and she knew full well this firing was ominous for her future in show business.

With or without Irene, *Miss 1917* was soon in trouble. Despite the critical raves, the show simply could not make back the huge amounts spent on production, cast, theater rent, costumes. The Century Theater's location may have harmed the show as well: away from the theater district, it was not a "drop-in" sort of location. Shockingly, the show ran only forty-eight performances.

Never one to let an insult lie, Irene filed suit against Dillingham and the Century Amusement Corporation in January 1918; it didn't go to trial till 1921, but Irene was still mad enough to show up in court and fight. She arrived in "a gown and hat of shimmering white silk and a wondrous cape of ermine.... She transformed Judge Platzek's courtroom into a showcase." When asked who discharged her from *Miss 1917,* Irene insisted, "I don't know. The stage floor manager, I guess. He shut the door in my face." According to a court reporter, "The defense, as disclosed so far, was that the dancer . . . thought she was a privileged character and did not need to worry along with rehearsals. Her excuse, ignoring various calls to rehearsals, which were placed on the bulletin board of the stage, is that she was doing a specialty and did not need any rehearsing."

Dillingham said that Irene was angry about not being able to sing "Fancy You Fancying Me," but that it had been necessary to cut out the song because Jack Norworth had served notice that he owned the rights to it. A letter from Irene was introduced into evidence in which she asked that her act be timed earlier because "I cannot stand these late hours much longer." The suit would finally be settled to no one's satisfaction, on May 18, 1921, four years after the ill-fated show had closed. Justice Warley Platzek ruled Irene the victor in the case and awarded her $5,400 in damages from the Century Amusement Corporation (namely, Charles Dillingham and Florenz Ziegfeld). But Century was long since bankrupt, and Irene had to pay court costs.

Trying to shrug off her injured feelings after the *Miss 1917* embarrassment, Irene closed out the year playing to the hilt the role of patriotic war wife: she sold war bonds, danced at benefits with soldiers, "played in movies proving that we were right and would win." In her tailored uniform and diamond wing pin, she showed up in the pages of *Vogue, Vanity Fair,* and *Harper's Bazaar,* looking prettily determined.

Chapter Thirty-two

"His plane dove straight into the ground"

Much to the dismay of Vernon and Gwen, the fliers of Camp Mohawk packed up their kits as the fall of 1917 approached and shipped off to Camp Taliaferro in Benbrook, Texas, a suburb of Fort Worth, where the winter climate was warm enough to enable them to continue training. Jeffrey and Vernon's bright yellow roadster and drums came along with him, but Gwen and Irene were left behind.

Benbrook was one of three Royal Flying Corps training fields in Texas opened in 1917 (all under the umbrella of Camp Taliaferro) at the suggestion of General Pershing. It was a large facility of thirty-four buildings and hangars; Benbrook itself was an old established town. But it was a bit rural and desolate for Vernon after the fun and games (and proximity to New York) of Deseronto.

Vernon arrived in Texas in October 1917 and joined the No. 84 Canadian Training Squadron. He tried to make himself popular, greeting the wives of fliers in his Stutz Bearcat and showing them what sights were to be seen. He was also frequently called upon to muster up entertainments or to appear at Red Cross or Loan Drive benefits. A local paper recalled that Vernon's car, tooling along the country roads, "was a familiar sight, always attracted a shout and attention wherever it went."

The Canadian forces, with their colorful uniforms, stood out in Texas. Local historian Glen Martin says that the white band around their hats became the subject of a local legend: "The Americans began a rumor to the local girls that this meant that they had a venereal disease. When the Canadians arrived they were initially met rather coldly by the local women." Gossip has it that one Texas girl was not scared off by Vernon's white hatband: "Inez Childers is said to have dated Vernon," says Martin. "This was a well-known fact in the Childers family," according to her niece.

Vernon badly missed Johnny Coats and Eardley Wilmot (and, of course, his wife and girlfriend), and found Benbrook pretty primitive when he arrived, according to historian S. F. Wise: "Construction work on the three aerodromes was little more than half completed, the water supply was deficient, one of the fields lacked electrical power, and the sewage systems were not yet operating."

The morning after he arrived, a reporter found Vernon sitting on a box in an unfurnished barracks, trying to keep Jeffrey entertained. "I like flying just as much as dancing," Vernon told the reporter. "I am anxious to get back over there and get into action again, and think we will go soon. I never take Jeff with me on flights," he said, as he gave the monkey another affectionate squeeze. "Say, I do love these Westerners. Why, yesterday a perfect stranger offered to take me clear from town to camp, and he did so. I am not going back to New York until the war ends. I can't afford to go the pace there now."

Vernon, as was always his habit, continued joking and working hard to keep everyone's spirits up. Decades later, his Texas squadron mates recalled how popular Vernon made himself. He "never 'pulled rank,'" said Thomas Galbreath, "and often sat with us cadets in the barracks providing much entertainment, musically and otherwise." He continued writing parodies of popular songs, the more repeatable of which he sent to Irene. One was a takeoff of "For Me and My Gal," which might not have been the best choice to send to a worried wife:

It's no use trying, with me and my Pal
They won't teach flying, to me and my Pal
But someday they'll build a little grave for two or
Three or more
At Benbrook, for me and my Pal

Vernon was informed that he would soon be returning to Canada, as commandant at Beamsville Aerodrome, Toronto, which was to be opened in early 1918 by the Royal Flying Corps as the home of the School of Aerial Fighting and the School of Aerial Gunnery.

On Friday, February 15, 1918, Vernon was teaching from Field 3, using a Curtiss JN4 (marking no. C663). One of his students that day was the American cadet R. O. Peters. Cadet aviator Charles Sage, who was probably the last person to talk to Vernon, wrote to his father about what happened: "I went over to see Castle about getting a machine for the afternoon. He was just getting into the front seat as I came up. I asked him my question, and off they went." Mechanic H. O. Warren was on-site and noted that "Castle did not have on the safety belt which all men are supposed to use for strapping themselves to their seats. He had recently changed places with his young American pupil and had taken the front seat. Presumably, he had not yet had time to fasten the belt." This embarrassing fact, which was later hushed up in the press and by Irene, might have been a deciding factor in Vernon's fate.

The training flight with Peters went well, and the two were about to land when, as Sage described: "Another bus [plane] was about in line, just getting started prior to taking off. Apparently, the man below took no notice of the descending machine, else he would have stopped, it being one of the rules of the air that a landing machine has the right of way. Neither did the American cadet in the rear seat with Castle notice the machine taking off, else he would have given it the gas and gone on. Castle, being in the front seat, was prevented from seeing the situation due to the wings of the plane. The first thing, as I saw it, Castle caught sight of the lower plane, just as his wheels touched the rudder of it. Immediately, he pulled up into the air, doing an Immelmann turn. This took the plane about 75 to 100 feet off the ground, and had he been another 100 feet up, the turn would have been completed. As it was, there lacked room and his plane dove straight into the ground."

Vernon had been in many crashes in the last two years, but this was a head-on crash, and he was in the front seat. He might have survived had he been strapped in; it's impossible to say. Sage wrote, "It was fully 15 minutes before they got him out. Due to the force of the landing, the engine was up against the front of the rear compartment and Castle was pinched in behind it. He was terribly mangled and bleeding profusely from the head, and one could easily tell that life was extinct. The cadet in the rear seat was nearly crazy, suffering no injury, only shock" (rumor, unsubstantiated, had it that Peters "became so distraught that he attempted to kill himself and was later committed to a mental hospital").

Vernon never regained consciousness. He died in the field hospital twenty minutes after the fall. "Concussion of the brain" was listed as cause of death. He was thirty years old.

Chapter Thirty-three

"Death is nothing to me, sweetheart"

That afternoon, Irene was at home on Lexington Avenue with her secretary, Mrs. Wagner ("Waggie" to Irene). According to her production schedule, she had probably just returned from Marblehead, Massachusetts, where she'd been filming *The Girl from Bohemia*. Irene was amusing herself with a pet parrot when Mrs. Wagner answered the phone. It was a reporter with news of Vernon's death. Since every few months for the last two years, someone had called with news of Vernon's death, Wagner did not take it too seriously. But "they were extremely persistent," she recalled. "[Irene] heard me say three or four times, 'Mrs. Castle does not answer the 'phone unless it is personal,' and quickly she surmised something was wrong."

This time the report seemed legitimate, and Irene's face "turned a ghastly pallor, but she did not cry or carry on . . . she walked into her room, flung herself on the bed and fainted." The next day the New York papers had Irene "struggling against collapse." Mrs. Wagner said, "I shall have to speak for Mrs. Castle, as she is unable to see anyone except Mrs. Lawrence Grossmith, Capt. Castle's sister, who is with her. Mrs. Castle is completely prostrated with the terrible news. Capt. Castle's body is being brought home under military escort. He will be buried with military honors on Long Island [*sic*]. The Royal Flying Corps' New York headquarters will have full charge of the services." Irene's first public comment came two days later, released to the press: "It was a brave man's death, and it is not a woman's part to complain."

There were front-page headlines all over the world about Vernon's death; the *New York City Sun* called him "the butterfly who grew into an eagle." His was the tenth death that week among army aviators in the United States; there had been so many crash-related deaths in Texas and Oklahoma of late that rumors abounded that German spies were sabotaging planes.

Film actress Jean Darnell raised a few eyebrows (certainly those of Irene Castle and Gwen Wilmot) by telling reporters how *close* she and Vernon had become in the weeks before his death. "Vernon was like a big boy," she said. "He'd come over to our house and sit down on the floor in the kitchen to play with the cat, just like a kid," admittedly a very convincing portrait of him. The noble, patriotic quotes she put in his mouth are somewhat less believable. "Vernon has told me at least half a dozen times within the past month that he was ready to die," said Darnell, quoting him as declaiming, "I am ready to die. I have seen and had everything that life holds for any one man. There is nothing new for me. I want to die—but I want to die in action—in the aviation service of Great Britain." (One can fairly hear strains of "God Save the King" in the background.)

Vernon's friends and fellow soldiers, as well as his supposed girlfriends, talked to the press. John Walker Harrington sang his praises to the *New York City Sun:* "His mechanical skill, his perfect command of his lithe and slender body, his constitution which defied fatigue, cold and hunger, his nerves like whipcord, and his thews of steel, a courage undaunted are factors which, had he lived, would have made Vernon Castle more noted in the realms of air than he was onstage or the polished floor. There was not an appliance which he did not understand on sight. His deft fingers could take apart the most complicated mechanism and put them together without a slip."

Vernon's body, in his uniform, was laid out for public inspection in a Fort Worth funeral parlor, after his head injuries had been suitably disguised. Patrolmen held up traffic, and thousands of people lined the streets to get a last—and often first—glimpse of the fallen hero. A Southwest service was held in Fort Worth's St. Andrew's Episcopal Church, with Rev. Edward Henry Eckel officiating; the Royal Flying Corps denied admittance to hundreds of weeping, love-struck women.

In mid-afternoon, after the service, Vernon's coffin was draped with the British flag and sent on its way to New York and his widow. Officers of the Eighty-fourth placed it on a caisson, surrounded by six black horses and played off by a military band and firing party. Off to the Texas and Pacific Depot went the procession: the caisson, band, horses, followed by 250 members of the American and British flying squadrons. Bringing up the rear were civilians: friends and fans of Vernon, on foot and in autos. "Children who had been told the story of the death of the aviator clutched to the skirts of their mothers and sobbed. Men wiped the tears from their eyes. The sobs of women were audible above the slow measured tread of the funeral procession" (this from the *Houston Post*). Captain F. B. Fedgewock of the Royal Flying Corps accompanied Vernon's casket on the inappropriately named Sunshine Special to New York.

Irene, fully realizing her responsibilities and eager to meet the challenge, arranged a funeral that would have made Mary Todd Lincoln proud. The New York service took place on February 19 at the Church of the Transfiguration in New York ("The Little Church Around the Corner"), which has been the unofficial New York marrying and burying place for show business people since agreeing to host a funeral for actor George Holland in 1870.

Vernon's body arrived at Grand Central Terminal in a light, cold rain; more than a thousand people "from Broadway and Fifth Avenue" lined the streets to see him off. He lay in state at Campbell Funeral Church which, like the Little Church Around the Corner, was a show business landmark that would also see the funerals of Anna Held, Rudolph Valentino, Jeanne Eagels, Roscoe "Fatty" Arbuckle, and others. For two hours, "an unending line of former friends passed by the casket. Some came to bring flowers, or for one final glance at the dancer, who proved that his heart was brave, and some to shed tears." At 11:00 A.M. the funeral procession started for the church, where services were held.

Irene, in heavy, veiled mourning, was led in by her brother-in-law Lawrence Grossmith; Vernon, in his uniform and Croix de Guerre, was borne into the church by members of the Royal Flying Corps. Among the mourners were representatives of the U.S. Army and Navy and the British high commander commissioner. The Colored Musicians Union sent flowers, and Vernon's old drum instructor, Buddie Gilmore, was allowed a moment alone with the body to grieve before the coffin was closed. Ethel Barrymore was there, and Elisabeth Marbury—one newspaper reported in tones of disbelief: "Just before the end of the service, as the words of 'Crossing the Bar' were being spoken, the dapper figure of another dancer, Maurice, of the dancing team of Maurice and Florence Walton, stepped across the threshold and into the hushed church."

Vernon was laid to rest in Woodlawn Cemetery in the Bronx, which is the East Coast's most illustrious burial ground for show business celebrities. As well as being the cemetery of politicians, writers, and just plain folks, Woodlawn is the last home to the Castles' manager Elisabeth Marbury, vaudeville superstar Nora Bayes (sadly, in an unmarked grave), Irving Berlin, George M. Cohan, Lotta Crabtree, Duke Ellington, Oscar Hammerstein, Victor Herbert, Ziegfeld Girls Olive Thomas and Martha Mansfield, Marilyn Miller (and her husband, actor Frank Carter), the vaudeville team Smith and Dale (the inspiration for *The Sunshine Boys*), Laurette Taylor, Bert Williams, and Irene's *Miss 1917* costar Bert Savoy, among scores of others.

In 1922, Irene hired sculptor Sally James Farnham to create a marble statue, *Grief,* to mark Vernon's grave. Nearly life-size, the figure is crouched down, head bowed. Irene denied having posed for the nude statue—though she had in fact posed for another nude that Farnham created, a standing sculpture with Irene's facial features. Around the statue and behind the grave is a lovely half-circle of columns; surrounded by old-growth trees, it was (and is) a beautiful spot.

From the time of Vernon's death till her own, Irene periodically harassed and nagged the staff of Woodlawn. In May 1918, she was asking for Vernon's body to be shifted forward two feet so she could transplant some flowers behind him. Through the 1940s, she complained about the encroaching ivy and the marble statue's deterioration (she ordered a winter covering box for it). When grounds fees increased, she wrote that "I am not willing to meet these as I have felt (far from paying more) I should pay less, because of the neglect of the grave this past year." (Her pleas of poverty might have been more convincing has they not been written on Waldorf-Astoria letterhead.) In 1953, Irene had *Grief* recast in bronze; it's this replacement that stands over the grave today. Irene sighed heavily in 1945, "I plan to be buried beside Captain Castle myself, and must say that every time I visit the grave I feel impatient to get there."

Tribute was paid to Vernon at the site of his death as well. Northside Boulevard was renamed Vernon Castle Avenue, "as a lasting monument to the intrepid aviator." A memorial to Vernon was erected in 1966 at the crash site, near the corner of Vernon Castle Avenue and Cozby West Street, consisting of a replica of a Curtiss Jenny and photographs of Vernon and the airfield. It was later stolen, but the memorial was restored by Eagle Scout Jerret Martin and rededicated in 1997.

By late February 1918, there was a report that money was soon to be an issue with Vernon's widow: "Capt. Vernon Castle said to have died a comparatively poor man in spite of the fact that the famous dancing Castles earned nearly three-quarters of a million dollars during their meteoric career," said one newspaper. "As a dancing team scarcely $10,000 is said to be the aggregate of the attachable assets which the heroic young Englishman left to his disconsolate wife and partner."

On May 6, 1918, Vernon's will was filed for probate. It had been executed on September 28, 1915, with Irene's sister, Elroy (referred to as "an invalid"), as witness. After providing for the payments of his debts and funeral expenses, Vernon left his entire estate to Irene, "not only as a token of my deep love and sincere affection for said dearly beloved wife, but also in grateful recognition of the happiness which I have enjoyed in her society during all our wedded life, and the great assistance which she has all that time rendered to me in my professional work and career. In so disposing of my property, I am not unmindful of my beloved parents and other kinfolks, and my many friends, and it is my desire that out of my personal effects some token of my love and affection be given by my wife to each of them, so far as possible in accordance with my wishes expressed during my lifetime, or as her discretion dictates."

The settling of the will dragged out for two years; there were so many debtors, the Castles' finances were in such disarray. By the time the dust settled, in November 1920, Vernon's estate amounted to all of $620.

The receipt book for the Mrs. Vernon Castle Management Company shows Irene's expenses for January and February 1918: Peck & Peck, Lord and Taylor's, Wanamaker's, the usual household utilities, the intriguing "Walter with squirrel cage" ($3.25). On the day before Vernon's death, she spent $63 at the Maison Maurice and more than $100 at various other couturiers. There is a painful day's gap, then servants' salaries are paid, and by the end of the month Irene was, as everyone must, writing checks to Edison Electric, N.A. Gas, and the *New York Times*. Through March, her expenses seem to be mostly charities (including a home for the aged, the Blue Cross, and a charity dog show). On April 4, less than two months after Vernon's death, there comes a spending spree at Altman's ($257), Bonwit Teller's ($5), Tiffany's ($83), Lord and Taylor's ($37), Abercrombie and Fitch ($16). Possibly Irene's mourning clothes—but as we shall soon learn, she had a new man in her life by April.

Six weeks after Vernon's death, his sister Gladys forwarded a note to Irene he had left in her trust:

My poor little widow;

When you get this letter I shall be gone out of your sweet life. My only thought, darling, is for you. I don't want you to be unhappy. Death is nothing to me, sweetheart. I don't feel it and perhaps the giving of my life has done some good. It is only you who suffer, my baby, so you must be brave for your own sake. You may be sure that I died with your sweet name on my lips, and my only wish for your future happiness. You are the sweetest thing God ever made, dear. You must marry again and have babies, and I will be a happy memory, darling. Be brave and don't cry, my angel.

Vernie

Gwen Wilmot, according to family lore, was sewing a pair of socks for Vernon when she heard the news of his death; a day or two later, a letter arrived from him. Like Irene, Gwen retreated from public view with her grief; unlike Irene, she was not obliged to give statements to the papers or make any other arrangements. Indeed, any overt show of mourning on her part would have been considered in questionable taste.

On September 25, 1918, at St. Thomas' Church in Belleville, Vernon's friend Johnny Coats married Gwen's sister, Audrey Wilmot. The bride wore a suit of blue, trimmed in sealskin. Gwen Wilmot, who had hoped to become a bride in a double ceremony, was a bridesmaid in mourning. The local newspaper described her as wearing black satin trimmed with plush and carrying a bouquet of American Beauty roses.

Vernon was "the greatest love of my mother's life. I remember her saying that," says her daughter. Gwen eventually married sportsman and socialite Darcy Rutherford, around 1930; the marriage lasted just long enough to have their one child. But Gwen never really got over Vernon. "It's such a tragic story," says Carolyn Hetherington. "She attempted suicide in London when I was, I guess, nineteen. Took thirty-eight grains of phenobarb. She had depressions and a problem with alcohol at that time. I came home one night, and in the grate were all these bits of paper"—Vernon's letters to her. "For me to know that part of my mother would have been extraordinary," her daughter says sadly. Gwen Wilmot lived into the 1960s.

It seemed that Vernon's friends were under a curse. It fell first on James Reese Europe, who had returned from war covered in glory. Europe and Irene had dined together and "sat and cried," reminiscing about Vernon. Only a year later, Irene found herself sitting and crying again, this time at Europe's memorial service. Europe was performing in Boston on May 9, 1919, when he was attacked backstage by one of his drummers, Herbert Wright. Stabbed in the throat with a pocketknife, Europe died at City Hospital several hours later.

Both Johnny Coats and Eardley Wilmot would die unnatural, early deaths as well. Coats, referred to in the press as a "millionaire sportsman," led his wife on an exhausting social round: he was "an extravagantly pictur-esque figure," said one paper, "losing and making fortunes in the Riviera casinos with complete indifference." When Coats lost 80,000 pounds in 1930, he shrugged, "My only consolation is that my friends are winning my money." Johnny Coats committed suicide in London in 1932. After World War I, Eardley Wilmot was elected mayor of his hometown, Belleville, and rejoined the service when the Second World War began. His death in 1941 was mercifully quick, but hideous: "He was running across the tarmac to get into his plane," says Carolyn Hetherington. "He had his helmet on—he was always late, for everything—and he ran into a plane that was landing."

By mid-March 1918, Irene had fled to Havana, where she was reported to be "recuperating." At the end of the month, she went through the ordeal of rummaging through Vernon's wardrobe, a huge collection of dashing and stylish clothes (though suited only for someone with Vernon's peculiar physique). She donated the whole lot to the American Red Cross, which was trying to collect five thousand tons of clothing for the destitute inhab-itants of Belgium and northern France.

By August, Irene was giving upbeat interviews, including one on diet and exercise that strikes one as exceedingly good advice: "To get real benefit from exercise," Irene told the *Detroit Journal,* "you must get quantities of pure air with it, and you must be doing something which is enjoyable and interesting in itself." She added her opinion that "most of the ill health and unfitness of humans is due to overeating," though her advice that "one plen-tiful—and plain—meal a day should satisfy anyone" was a bit unrealistic.

She was also preparing a tribute book to Vernon, which was published in 1919 by Scribner's as *My Husband.* Illustrated with family photos and Vernon's sketches, the book is largely Irene's memoirs and her rather vague recollections of Vernon's life and career (many of the stories appeared, in somewhat different form, in her 1958 autobiography). The real treasures in the book are Vernon's letters from the war zone: Irene and Mrs. Wagner read them all, carefully winnowing them down for publication. It was a try-ing project. "Her poise is marvelous, and, I fear, dangerous," Wagner told a reporter while the book was under way. "I never knew of any woman before, under similar trying circumstances, to keep herself so well in control."

"Only by keeping busy can I endure it all," Irene told *Motion Picture Classic*. "I miss him more and more each day." Which was, no doubt, true: Vernon and Irene were still on friendly terms at the time of his death, de-spite the imminent end to their marriage. While going through his letters, she made quite sure that no mention of their split, or of Gwen Wilmot, was made public; and Irene's letters to Vernon are not included in the book.

Irene paid Vernon a huge tribute by publishing *My Husband*. Other than his interviews, this book is what gives him a voice. His letters are funny, touching, human, intelligent. He talks with great perspicacity of the war and of airplanes, of animals, of life at the front and on leave. As heav-ily censored as they are (by both the War Department and Irene), Vernon's letters are as breezy and spirited today as they were in the 1910s.

It was not known by the press or public, but Irene had several good reasons to get *My Husband* out there and reinforce her image as America's War Widow. Vernon's death left her broken financially more than emo-tionally; she had been seeing other men (discreetly) before his death and continued to do so after.

The September issue of *Vogue* featured a page of Irene modeling the season's most chic widow's weeds: "Mrs. Castle is one of the many wise women who feel that mourning need not be altogether gloomy," wrote *Vogue*, adding perkily, "A tiny brooch of white pearls adds a touch of trim-ming that is very charming and entirely appropriate for mourning." Irene did not find "charming" the black mourning band she had to sew on her sleeves: "It's rather sinful, I should say, to charge seventy-five cents for a piece of plain black material like this."

In late summer 1918, Irene made a cameo appearance in the film *The Common Cause*, "The War Story With a Laugh, a Thrill and a Throb," for the ailing Vitagraph Company, featuring her brother-in-law Lawrence Grossmith. She appeared as France in the prologue, along with actresses Effie Shannon (Belgium), Violet Heming (England), Julia Arthur (Italy), and Marjorie Rambeau (Columbia). Between the time of filming and release, the Armistice was signed, so the film faded from view, as did Vita-graph. While in Hollywood, Irene dated Douglas Fairbanks (not yet mar-ried to Mary Pickford) and palled around with Charlie Chaplin, William Randolph Hearst, and William S. Hart. She renewed her flirtation with her old beau William Rhinelander Stewart, whose hopes were briefly raised.

჻჻

Chapter Thirty-four

"Robert was sweet, sympathetic, and besides he did all of my bidding"

It was very shortly after Vernon's death that Irene began keeping company with the man who would become her second husband—a handsome thirty-year-old scion of Ithaca society named Robert Treman. Some newspaper stories claimed that Irene and Treman had been childhood friends, that their fathers had known one another. But Irene had no reason to lie in her memoirs when she said that she first met Treman in February 1918 when she advertised to sell Vernon's car and he showed up to look it over. The two threw off sparks right away, and within days they were seen riding horseback together.

The Tremans were among the "first families" of Ithaca, making their money in mills, banks, and the hardware business; Tremans also ran the town's Water Works and Gas and Light Company at one point or another. Robert's father, Robert Henry Treman, was a hardware merchant and served on the State Bankers' Association and Federal Reserve Bank; the family owned nearly four hundred acres of land in and around Ithaca (the current-day Robert H. Treman State Park was once family property).

Irene's beau, Robert Elias Treman, had enlisted in the army as soon as the United States entered World War I, and as a major of field artillery, commanded the 368th Infantry Division, a troop of black soldiers. On his discharge, he took over his father's hardware company in Ithaca (Irene's later referring to him as "running a hardware store" hardly does justice to the size and scope of the business).

One thing Irene did not find charming about Treman was that he was an avid hunter, with a den full of trophy heads: he once wrote, "I often think how rich is the man who can sit on a cold winter evening with the mounted head of some game animal hanging over his fireplace and in the sight of it live again those days when through the forest came crashing the great moose as he answered the call of the birch bark horn of the guides." Irene must have disagreed, to put it mildly.

Unlike Vernon Castle, Robert Treman was handsome in an Arrow Collar ad way: blond, clean-cut, athletic, "with a fine physique and a self-confidence that comes from knowing it," as Irene recalled decades later. By all accounts, Treman was a pleasant, well-liked fellow; his obituary stated that "he had rare gifts of personality which he shared generously: warmth, sympathy, understanding, and a large capacity for friendship." Certainly, he was active in a number of good causes (the Community Chest and the NAACP, among others).

All through 1918 and into 1919, newspapers were speculating about Irene's private life. She was reported to be engaged to stage and screen actor Tom Powers, recently out of the service (Powers is best known today as the murder victim in the 1944 film noir classic *Double Indemnity*).

What the papers didn't know—what no one knew for a full year—was that Irene and Robert Treman had been married in Pickens, South Carolina, on May 21, 1918, only three months after Vernon's death. The certificate was signed by "Irene Blythe" and "R. E. Freeman" (that signature was admittedly nearly illegible, according to an employee of the probate judge); the mystery couple had been married by Rev. Paul A. Juhan. Irene's ledgers show a gap between May 17 and May 23, with expenses on the 17th for "R.R. Fares" ($55.28) and "Expenses Wash. & return" ($24.93), which may have been for her wedding trip.

The Treman family gifted the newlyweds with a large stone home tucked away on College Hill on the outskirts of Ithaca, reached by a winding road through the woods. "Easily worth $100,000," according to one gossipy article, the house was improved with the addition of a saltwater swimming pool in the small back yard, of which Irene was hugely proud.

The marriage started out happily enough: "Robert was sweet, sympathetic, and besides he did all of my bidding," said Irene. So why the secrecy? Irene, who was planning a trip to England, later claimed that she thought the U.S. government might not let her travel overseas as the wife of a military officer, a vague and improbable excuse. It seems more likely a career and PR move on Irene's part: her stage and screen name was still Mrs. Vernon Castle, and it was *as* Mrs. Vernon Castle that she was marketable—and popular. She was America's most famous war widow; certainly the most glamorous and the most visible. Irene might not have *obtained* work by virtue of being a professional widow, but it was an important part of her image. An intelligent and outspoken woman, she sometimes came across as a bit harsh and needed all the public sympathy she could get— and she was smart enough to realize that. To be fair, Irene didn't actually lie about her marital state (aside from billing herself as "Mrs. Vernon Castle"). She simply thought it was nobody's business but her own, and said nothing, which was entirely her prerogative.

Irene knew full well that she was expected to mourn long and hard, standing in for all the less affluent, less chic war widows who could live vicariously through her in the movies and magazine pages. She was prescient: recall the outraged reaction when Jacqueline Kennedy married Aristotle Onassis in 1968. She went from being America's Widow to Jackie O, a joke and a comic tabloid character. So, for the time being, Robert Treman agreed to keep their marriage quiet; he remained in Ithaca while his bride, "Mrs. Vernon Castle," traveled the world, made movies, and posed in becoming black frocks and veils.

CHAPTER THIRTY-FIVE

"A WELL-KNOWN DANCING DAME"

In October 1918, Irene sailed for England, ostensibly to appear in a film for the Red Cross, which never came to fruition. Leaving her new husband behind, she also planned to visit hospitals and raise funds for the wounded. But rather than making a public name for herself as a Lady Bountiful, Irene unexpectedly found herself the subject of unpleasant press coverage—after nearly a decade of being the nation's darling.

London in the 1910s was in the midst of a drug epidemic, which grew only more intense when the war ended. Though government regulations made many recreational drugs illegal, the war had made them easier to come by. One victim of drug abuse, musical comedy starlet Billie Carleton, inadvertently entangled Irene in a deadly scandal.

Billie Carleton was only twenty-two when the war ended. A lovely blond, she was intelligent and modestly talented—she spoke three languages and played piano—and possessed an impish sense of humor. Indeed, too impish: she drove producers Charles Cochran and André Charlot to fury with her backstage pranks. Carleton made her stage debut in the early 1910s, and in 1915 she took over Irene's role in the London production of *Watch Your Step* when American star Ethel Levey dropped out. It's Billie Carleton's voice on the London cast recording of *Watch Your Step*, singing "Show Us How to Do the Fox Trot" with George Graves. She went on to appear in the Charlot revue *Some* with Gertrude Lawrence and Beatrice Lillie (who became a close friend), starred in the comedies *Fair and Warmer* and *The Boy*, and by late 1918 was the female lead in *Freedom of the Seas*. Billie Carleton was a perfect early example of the Bright Young Things soon to be immortalized by Noël Coward and Evelyn Waugh. She was also a regular user of opium, heroin, and cocaine.

Both Billie Carleton and Irene were among the excited guests at the great Victory Ball held at Albert Hall on November 27, 1918, in aid of the

Nation's Fund for Nurses. It was sponsored by the *Daily Sketch,* which trumpeted: "To-day women of the Allied nations take part in the festival of victory as a right. They have earned that right in hospitals at home and abroad; in the fields as labourers ploughing and garnering the grain; in the workshops turning out shells; in the towns doing men's work; in the homes suffering in silence." But most guests, for all their patriotism, probably just wanted to show off their fancy-dress costumes and have a good time.

In Irene's account of the evening, she was a guest of scenic artist Ben Ali Haggin, wearing a Persian boy outfit he'd designed for her ("If I do say it myself, I wore the most beautiful gown there"). She recalled the ball as being one of the most joyous and dazzling she'd ever seen: "At midnight there was a blast of trumpets and a pageant unfolded with titled ladies playing the part of 'Sun' and 'Air' and 'France' and 'England' and all the Allies."

Around 4:00 in the morning, as the Victory Ball wound down, Billie Carleton went back to her apartment at the Savoy Court, just behind the Savoy Hotel, where Irene was staying. With her were British movie actor Lionel Belcher—also a heroin user—and his live-in girlfriend, actress Olive Richardson. According to newspaper and court records unearthed by Carleton's biographer, Marek Kohn, the get-together went on till 5:00 or 6:00 A.M. Breakfasting on bacon and eggs, Billie and her friends talked of movies, fashion, jewelry, and Carleton's anguished relationship with her drug supplier, costumier Reginald De Veulle. Lionel Belcher testified that when they left, Carleton was sitting up in bed in her kimono, "happy, awake and expectant." But the following afternoon, about 3:00, her maid found her dead in bed, a half-empty container of cocaine by her side. Although a cocaine overdose was diagnosed, Kohn makes a convincing case for Veronol, a barbiturate.

Carleton's death was a front-page story in an England now deprived of war news—and accounts in the *London Times,* the *News of the World,* and other papers had Irene in Billie's room with her and her drug-taking friends. In these stories, Irene accompanied Billie Carleton, Lionel Belcher, and Olive Richardson to the Savoy Court, where she stayed several hours.

In 1919, soon after the event, Irene denied she had even been to Carleton's rooms: the actress, "whom I had seen only once before, sent word to my rooms, asking if she might come up to see my gown. This was at 4:30 in the morning. Of course, I told her she might, and she came up and raved over my dress and tried on a number of my hats. . . . Miss Carleton left my room about 5 o'clock, and I understand gave a very gay breakfast party afterward. Unfortunately, she died the same day, and my name was dragged into the affair." Decades later, she wrote that Billie had gone right from the Victory Ball to Irene's apartment, where they played dress-up, Carleton trying on Irene's turban and admiring her jewels. "She was going out to Hollywood in the fall, she said, and she was a little apprehensive about it," Irene recalled. "You'll be wonderful there," Irene reassured her. "They love blondes." It was as innocent as a teenager's pajama party.

Whatever Irene's true involvement, her name and photo featured in most of the coverage. The police inquest dragged on for months, though Irene herself was very briefly (and inadequately) questioned and released as thoroughly innocent in the matter. Certainly her fame and her status as a war widow helped her breeze through any interrogation.

It's true that Irene was quite innocent in Billie Carleton's death; she was simply a victim of being in the wrong place at the wrong time. She had always been scrupulous in her public life: she may have had some flirtations or even affairs, but Irene Castle was always a perfect lady. She smoked cigarettes (Chesterfields, in a cigarette holder) and took the occasional drink (Dubonnet, before dinner), but she had never been (and never was) a user of illicit drugs, and it's rather charming to picture her spending the evening in this opium den with three hopheads: one can hear her politely saying, "No, thank you, dear, I won't have any heroin—but you go right ahead." It actually speaks well for Irene that she was broadminded and secure enough to have a very pleasant evening with Billie Carleton and her friends—at least till it all blew up in her face.

Irene let the matter die, but the newspapers printed titillating stories for weeks, till the next celebrity scandal came along. Decades later, Irene was still fuming about it: "I was a big fool to let it drop when it was so clearly a case of fraud and defamation of character."

With Irene suddenly fair game, the press came in for the kill. The notorious gossip rag *Town Topics*, which essentially invented the "blind item," ran a story in November 1918 about "a well-known dancing dame" and her affair with "the artistic husband of a no-less-celebrated ex-dancing lady" (Ben Ali Haggin). The piece went on to mention that "the dame's" first husband was "a dancing male who secured a divorce in order to wed a wealthy girl far above his social station," the closest Gwen Wilmot and the impending Castle split ever came to being mentioned in the press.

On May 4, 1919, Irene Foote Blythe married Robert Treman, this time publicly, at the Little Church Around the Corner, where Vernon's funeral had taken place a year earlier. Attended by her mother, her new in-laws, and about twenty-five friends, Irene was married by Rev. George C. Houghton (also from Vernon's funeral). The Tremans took off for a honeymoon at Lake Placid, and thence to their hillside Ithaca residence.

Now that the marriage was no longer secret, Irene went ahead and cut one of her last ties to Vernon: she sold the old Foote family house on Lexington Avenue, the one she and Vernon had lived in during the years of their greatest fame. She and her sister, Elroy, got an impressive $75,000 for the house, which still stands, divided into apartments, with a restaurant on the first floor, at Twentieth-eighth and Lexington in the Gramercy Park section of Manhattan.

It wasn't long after Irene's public marriage that her private one was discovered by enterprising reporters. By August 1919, it was all over the news: according to the *New York Telegram,* Irene had refused to be married in the "too populous" Greenville, South Carolina, and had insisted on motoring to Pickens, where Rev. Juhan performed the ceremony in their touring car.

The most unflattering, and professionally dangerous, quotes came in the *New York Telegram* article, which was subheaded "Admits She Never Loved Dead Stage Partner." "She told Dr. Juhan that she was a business woman, that in spite of romantic stories about her and her late husband, Vernon Castle, they had for three years been nothing more than business partners and were utterly indifferent to each other. She had just prepared the book of letters of Captain Castle, however, and it was ready for the market, and she feared if it became known that she had remarried so soon after Captain Castle's death, the sale of the book would be seriously affected."

This quote was to haunt Irene. It has the ring of truth: she and Vernon *had* been "just friends" for some time before his death, and she *had* kept her marriage secret for career reasons. But it's unlikely that the smart, career-savvy Irene would actually *say* such things about Vernon, herself, or her motives. Even to salve her new husband's ego, Irene would not have been foolish enough to badmouth her previous marriage or husband, which she knew would hurt her future career. The Tremans violently denied both the quoted documents and even their secret marriage, despite the documentary evidence and witnesses: "Mr. Treman and myself are too far beyond being affected by such malicious lies," sniffed Irene, and Robert, "beside himself with rage," added, "The whole thing is the most malicious piece of misrepresentation I have ever heard of."

It was the beginning of the end of Irene's good relationship with the press; for the rest of her life, she alternately courted reporters when she needed them and cursed them when she didn't. Her public image completed a shift from perky dancing partner to grieving widow to cranky eccentric.

Certainly Irene was not terribly popular in Ithaca. Her mother-in-law, a member of the local Presbyterian church, was reportedly unhappy that her daughter-in-law insisted on attending the Episcopal church. Maids told of a house overrun with dogs, birds, and monkeys. Another local tale had Irene parading the streets of Ithaca in a short (about knee-length) skirt and a tall red hat; when the local rubes stopped and gaped, she reportedly passed her hat around, saying, "If you like the show so much, you surely are willing to pay for it!" It was written in one paper that when she won a third-prize ribbon at a local horse show, she threw it in the judge's face—a highly unlikely story, especially the added nasty claim that she "burst into tears and was led from the fair ground."

In March 1919, shortly before her marriage become public, "Mrs. Vernon Castle" signed with the Famous Players–Lasky Corporation, with which she was to make three films over the next year. Famous Players–Lasky had been formed through the merger of Adolph Zukor's Famous Players Film Company with the Jesse L. Lasky Feature Play Company in 1916; several other companies were absorbed in the process, including Paramount Pictures, which would become the name of the whole conglomerate. Irene's films were released by the high-end Artcraft division.

Her first film under the new contract was *The Firing Line* (based on a novel by the popular writer Robert W. Chambers). It sounds to modern ears like a corking film noir of the 1940s: Sheila (Irene) is stuck in a loveless marriage to Louis Malcourt, finally freed to marry the man she loves only after her depressed, alcoholic husband kills himself. "A study of a morbid male temperament . . . not a very cheerful tale," wrote one Philadelphia reviewer, praising both leads: "Irene Castle . . . enacts with considerable grasp and understanding. David Powell gives a really remarkable portrayal of the mentally disintegrating Malcourt." If one of Irene's midcareer films were to be uncovered and saved, *The Firing Line* would be an excellent contender.

In this film she was given her most charming and vivacious leading man since Antonio Moreno: twenty-five-year-old Glasgow-born David Powell, who played the suicidal husband. With his dark saturnine good looks, trim moustache, and deep, dark eyes, Powell was on his way to being a top leading man by 1919, having appeared in some twenty-five films. After costarring with Irene, Powell continued his upward climb through the 1920s, as romantic lead to Mae Murray, Gloria Swanson, Bebe Daniels, and Alice Joyce—but he never made it into the talkie era. After his last film, the ironically titled *Back to Life,* he died of pneumonia in 1925.

In her second film for Famous Players–Lasky, *The Invisible Bond,* Irene played Marcia Crossey, who loses her faithless husband to a vamp and eventually—after much tribulation and several characters meeting violent deaths—winds up happily reunited with him (though, judging by the plot synopsis, he hardly seems worth remarrying). The film was directed, as was *The Firing Line,* by Charles Maigne. "Irene Castle has improved steadily as a screen actress," said one reviewer, "and this latest offering reveals her as secure in her artistry, thoughtful in characterization and with a firm grip upon the role she plays." Her leading man, Huntley Gordon, went on to become an anonymous if hardworking character actor, best known as the old man to whom Katharine Hepburn declaims, "The calla lilies are in bloom again" in *Stage Door.*

Irene's third and final film under her contract was *The Amateur Wife* (released in February 1920), directed by longtime actor and director Edward Dillon. It was the classic "Take off your glasses—why, you're beautiful!" plot, already a cliché by 1920: Irene played Justine, a dull, prim convent girl abandoned by her husband (William Carleton) until she bobs her hair, shortens her skirts, and becomes a red-hot mama. Justine is, of course, transformed into a butterfly wrapped in Irene Castle–designed gowns. "Very acceptable," one paper begrudgingly called the film, adding, "There's no real 'punch' to the piece." The *Toledo Times* praised Irene half-heartedly: "Although she has heretofore been the coldest and most elusive of film actresses, she is appealing in this picture and you cannot help believing in her, even if you have never believed in her before."

And with that, Irene thought, her film career was over. Famous Players–Lasky showed no interest in renewing her contract, and the feeling was mutual. Irene never thought much of her films or her film career; in her memoirs, she brushed them off with the comment that they "only required me to look energetic." If Irene could not be the *best* at something, she quickly got frustrated and lost interest.

Chapter Thirty-six

꿍꿍

"Poor Irene Castle. She certainly isn't what she used to be"

Having enjoyed such brilliant success so young, Irene felt herself old and outdated before her time. She saw herself as a dancer, not an actress, even though she might easily have continued her acting career had she wished to take smaller character parts. Other actresses born in the early 1890s found fame in the 1910s and held onto it into the 1920s and beyond: Mae West, Lillian Gish, Peggy Wood, and Ina Claire worked well into old age; Norma Talmadge, Leatrice Joy, Ann Pennington, and gold digger extraordinaire Peggy Hopkins Joyce held on till the talkie era. Charlotte Greenwood, Fay Holden, and Ruth Chatterton enjoyed even greater success after forty as character actresses. But Irene felt her day had passed with the old decade.

In the summer of 1920, Robert Treman made a halfhearted bid for the office of New York senator (Democratic ticket), while Irene spent her free time riding at the Rochester Horse Show (the local paper called her "a little dynamo of enthusiasm . . . the best-dressed woman in the country . . . probably the best-known feminine figure on the American continent today").

She became a regular at the local horse shows: "One saw yesterday at the horse show a trim, swiftly moving figure along the walk between the paddock rail and the arena boxes. It was a boyish figure with bobbed, gold-tinted hair, a piquant face, an adorable nose, eyes as bright as new dimes and a little swank or swagger, what may it be called." In 1921, Irene made a scene at one show by ordering the arrest of a rider who "brutally beat his mount when the animal sulked in taking the jump."

She insisted to a reporter that she was "daffy, but not foolish, over animals." Frank A. Spencer, manager of Irene's stable, told how "Mrs. Treman will bravely bring her dogs to the college vet for treatment, and she will explain just what needs to be done to make them well, and then leave, because she can't stand it to see one of them suffer, and if an operation is necessary, she doesn't want to be there to look on."

She also tried to bring in extra money. Irene signed with a clothing manufacturer, Philipsborn's, to lend her name to a line of clothing, which she "actually designed herself." Irene's image began appearing in newspaper ads around the country, bedecked in these "enchanting Castle creations." By 1921, Irene had begun what would be a two-decade career as a lecturer on fashion and style, subsidized by a series of stores and designers. In Berkeley she gave coeds a lecture on proper dress, offering advice that is still worth following: "First of all, don't imitate each other in dressing. . . . There's nothing more uninspiring than a flock of women with their hair combed just alike and dressed nearly the same. Women are apt to imitate each other, especially if they are in constant contact on the campus, but my advice is, don't do it."

All through the early 1920s, Irene's photo popped up in *Vanity Fair*, *Vogue*, *Theatre* magazine, and *Town and Country* with amazing regularity: Irene decked out in Lucile frocks ("that express the distinguished grace and charm of the wearer"), Irene in her gracious home, Irene lounging elegantly by her pool, Irene posing "for her millionth picture with her thousandth dog," as one sarcastic caption writer put it. At thirtyish, Irene was lovelier than ever, her short, fluffy hair still a bit ahead of the times, her face maturing into its perfect, delicate bone structure, her figure as trim as ever.

She also devoted some time to her favorite charities, including dance lessons for the underprivileged, both in Ithaca and New York City. "I tried teaching dancing to wealthy children," she explained, "but gave it up. It meant a fortune for me, but I'd rather work with my poor kiddies. . . . They're so intent, and anxious to improve." In December 1922, she gave a benefit performance for a Catholic high school and threw a Christmas party for seventy-five underprivileged children at her home.

Irene gave one last jump start to her film career in 1921, with the financial help of her somewhat reluctant husband. Her last three films, *French Heels*, *No Trespassing*, and *Slim Shoulders*, were filmed in 1921 and 1922, all released in 1922. Irene's memories of these films were highly selective. Her 1958 memoirs hastily brush over them with a few misleading sentences: she claims Robert Treman "had a friend who wanted to establish a motion-picture company to make nothing but Irene Castle pictures" and that she reluctantly went along with the scheme, despite the low salary involved. She does not discuss the movies themselves at all; her performances, costars, and directors are all a blank.

That "friend" of Treman was the wonderfully named director Edwin L. Hollywood, who had recently helmed films for Goldwyn Pictures and Vitagraph. In early 1921, Hollywood and Treman formed the eponymous Hol-Tre Producing Company, Inc., contracted to produce three Irene Castle–starring vehicles for distribution by the W. W. Hodkinson Corporation. Irene was to receive $1,500 weekly, for a total of not more than $15,000 per production (each film was scheduled for a ten-week production period). Irene was also due first-class transportation to and from location as well as star billing.

William Wadsworth Hodkinson, Irene's new producer and distributor, was a polarizing and controversial figure in the industry. He'd entered films in 1907 and developed a system of nationwide film distribution that allowed distributors to financially back producers in exchange for a hefty cut of the profits. Hodkinson cofounded Paramount Pictures in 1914 but was ousted from the company two years later. He was widely disliked by many established film producers, who felt that his distribution system took too much power out of their hands. By establishing ties with Hodkinson, Irene won no friends in the industry.

She found that picture making for her own company allowed for an agreeable lifestyle. She had her home, husband, and pets in Ithaca and a nice suite at the Algonquin for her weekday stays in New York during production. "I had so many days of hectic nightlife, up until 3:00 A.M. for month after month," she told *Picture Play* magazine, "that I am happy in the peace and quiet of our country home." She did sometimes miss the stage, but "pictures pay better, and they let me live the home life that I want."

Irene's first Hol-Tre project was filmed in the summer of 1921 in New York City and Ithaca. *French Heels*, based on the short story "Knots and Windshakes," was originally called *The Broadway Bride*, but "of course I wouldn't stand for that," said Irene. *With Flying Colors* was suggested, then *French Heels* settled upon. Irene played the role of Palma May, an orphan supporting herself as a cabaret dancer; a "fish out of water" plot develops when she marries a lumberman and moves to the woods. The usual problems ensue: her in-laws hate her, Broadway wants her back, and there's a worker mutiny; but it all ends well with Palma and her husband happily settled into their cabin in the woods.

Her costar in her first two Hol-Tre films was thirty-one-year-old Ward Crane; newspapers spread rumors that Irene was going to divorce Robert Treman and marry him. Although he and Irene were friendly, she and her family insisted there was no romance there, resenting such scandalmongering. A former naval officer, Ward Crane had entered films after the war and was, by 1921, a minor leading man and supporting player. He went on to become a reliable second lead through the 1920s (his most accessible performance today is as Buster Keaton's bullying rival in the 1924 classic *Sherlock, Jr.*). Crane died of pleurisy in 1928, only thirty-eight years old.

Irene's latest monkey, Jennie Lynn, came to the studio with her (the fates of Rastus and Jeffrey are unknown). Jennie had belonged to an organ grinder who'd been an extra in a scene shot at Washington Square for *The Amateur Wife*, and "when I saw Jennie my mind was made up I had to have her. The organ grinder was willing to part with her for a stipulated sum, which was gladly paid."

She told a reporter, "For the past week I worked from nine in the morning until nine at night, many times until midnight.... The thermometer was usually 105°, and you can imagine what it meant to have a number of spotlights and a generous assortment of Kliegs and Cooper-Hewitts leveled on you." A cabaret and dance number was included in the film, and the perfectionist Irene was somewhat unhappy about this. "I've struggled against dancing in pictures. In doing the actual dance, of course, I'm in perfect rhythm with the music. But in running the picture on the screen, this rhythm is not faultlessly preserved.... Rather than have a dance hopelessly distorted, I have up to this time refused to participate. Frankly, I'm dubious about the cabaret scene in this last picture, but making it was very attractive."

While filming *French Heels*, Irene was injured badly enough to require a few days' stay at the Women's Hospital in New York City. During a fight scene, she'd been too enthusiastically choked by the villain, injuring her throat. Her studio made the most of the publicity, releasing a medically dubious statement that "a cartilage in her throat had been dislocated and ... the pressure had caused thyroid inflammation."

On the film's release in late January 1922, *Variety* called it "only average," the supporting cast "capable," and groused that Irene "hasn't much range in expressing ... emotions," though she was slim, lovely, and fashionable enough to make up for lack of acting skills.

From her Algonquin suite, Irene reluctantly agreed to chat with the press. She regretted forsaking serials for feature-length movies: when she was in *Patria*, "I received thousands of letters from children, exclaiming in admiration over the various stunts that I did." Now that she was in features, she sighed, there was nothing to be gained by switching back to serials. "I made my choice and I abide by it, even though I do believe it was not for the best."

After blithely dismissing the very film she should have been plugging, Irene chatted more happily about clothes, "my great weakness. I know they are superficial and that everyone who ever adored dressing up in finery never came to any good end and all that sort of thing, but nevertheless I never expect to be indifferent about what I wear." As a star, she always had to look her best in public, or "someone would be sure to say, 'Poor Irene Castle. She certainly isn't what she used to be since she's taken to living in the country.'"

Irene costarred again with Ward Crane in *No Trespassing*, based on the novel *The Rise of Roscoe Paine*, by Joseph C. Lincoln. She played Mabel Colton, who moves with her parents to a Cape Cod fishing village and falls for a wealthy but ne'er-do-well local landowner (Crane). The plot hinges on the rights to a local lane, possible financial ruin for Mabel's father, and whether the landowner will come through for him (P.S.: he does). It was released in May 1922; *Variety* felt it was a nicely "homespun" change of pace for the usually glamorous Irene, but brushed it off with a deadly, "This latest Castle feature cannot be relied upon as a real money-maker. Exhibitors will not find it productive."

Sadly, *No Trespassing* is Irene's only post-*Patria* film known to survive—and that in a fragmentary, badly decomposed print. Irene looks lovely and seems to give as good a performance as the script demands; the production values (other than a few misspelled title cards) are high and the supporting cast quite good. But the plot—rural real estate, the stock market—is dull and slow moving, and the film's decimated state makes it impossible to really evaluate it fairly today.

In December 1921, while *No Trespassing* was still in production, there were financial troubles looming for Hol-Tre that did not bode well for future productions. Robert Treman was told that another $8,000 would be needed to complete *No Trespassing,* although $20,000 had already been spent. Still, they went ahead with another film.

In her third Hol-Tre offering, *Slim Shoulders,* Irene played Naomi, whose father has recently gone bankrupt. She tries to steal the papers that will save him, falling for the nephew (Rod La Rocque) of the man who possesses them. Of course Love Wins Out in the end. *Variety* once again was unimpressed: "a fair program production without great punch . . . trite and conventional." Irene got the chance to ride, swim, dive, and dance as well as show off her lapdogs ("their ugly little faces are almost enough to get a laugh," wrote *Variety*). The real hit of the evening was Irene's leading man, twenty-four-year-old La Rocque, who had been in films since 1914 but was only just approaching stardom. *Variety* raved that he was as handsome as Rudolph Valentino, "only La Rocque seems to have something more behind the eyes." La Rocque went on to star in a number of hits, most notably Cecil B. DeMille's *The Ten Commandments* (1923); he married actress Vilma Banky and retired in 1941.

At the New York opening of *Slim Shoulders* in September 1922, Irene appeared in person to host a fashion show, which turned out to be much more popular with the audience and press than the unremarkable film that followed.

Irene, pretty and energetic but with little real ambition, had some big-studio competition in 1922. Gloria Swanson and Pola Negri (Paramount), the Talmadge sisters (First National), Mae Murray (Metro), the Gish sisters and Mary Pickford (United Artists) all had big-budget hit films that year. Irene's three little Hol-Tre entries simply did not have the studio power to succeed. And one cannot ignore the reviewers' unanimous opinions that the films themselves were below par, and Irene—for all her beauty and charm—was merely a competent, workmanlike actress.

With the end of her Hol-Tre experiment, Irene's film career was over. In 1924, she made one last appearance, as one of several stars playing cameos in Warner Brothers' *Broadway after Dark,* a comedy starring Adolphe Menjou and Norma Shearer (Paul Whiteman, Elsie Ferguson, Raymond Hitchcock, and boxer "Gentleman Jim" Corbett also appeared fleetingly as themselves). Not counting the brief *Mr. and Mrs. Castle before the Camera,* Irene had starred in eighteen films in less than a decade. While she never became a top-flight star, it was an impressive career, even considered apart from her fame as a dancer. Only her serial *Patria* was a truly notable moving picture (and not always for the right reasons), but Irene had managed to make a name for herself separate from that of her first husband.

Not only was her film career over, but Irene's marriage was on the rocks as well. It all came to a head in 1923, when Irene asked her husband to bankroll one last film and discovered—by her account—that Treman had invested her own money in the movies, and "it had all gone down the drain, every penny of it." Treman's version was that Irene had known full well that both her money and his were being poured into the Hol-Tre films. In late 1923, Hol-Tre's treasurer, Charles Blood, explained to W. W. Hodkinson that the cost of producing the three films had been $75,000 (*French Heels*), $85,000 (*No Trespassing*), and $65,000 (*Slim Shoulders*), and that none of them had yet made a profit. Hol-Tre blamed Hodkinson for poorly distributing and promoting the films and wrote that a lawsuit "would only accentuate publicly the failure of your distribution organization to produce expected results." Irene also felt that her films had bombed at the box office not because they were unexceptional vehicles but because "theater bookings were pretty well controlled by the large motion-picture companies and an 'independent' had little chance of getting bookings." She had a point: to this day, indie films have a hard time getting distribution and publicity.

CHAPTER THIRTY-SEVEN

"JAZZ, JAZZ, JAZZ! ... THE PARADINGS OF SAVAGES"

Irene was nothing if not realistic, and she saw that she was never going to make her fortune as an actress. Her real reputation and talent was as a dancer. As early as 1920 she was talking about forming a vaudeville act, and that same year she was in negotiations with British producer Charles Cochran about doing a revue in London (the show never came off, and late in the year she sued Cochran for $20,000, alleging breach of contract).

In the fall of 1921, Irene began auditioning prospective new dance partners. Her trade paper ad was answered by every two-legged man on the East Coast; when Irene entered the rehearsal room, "I felt as though I had walked into a pool hall in the bowery. Such an assortment of odd-looking men I had never seen."

She settled on "a gay little Irishman" named Billy Reardon, recommended by Elsie Janis and described in newspapers as "well-known as a society dancer, having appeared in vaudeville and the more prominent dancing places along Broadway." Just as important were her choreographers, the brother-and-sister act Fred and Adele Astaire. The Astaires had recently closed in the successful operetta *Apple Blossoms* and were in rehearsal for *The Love Letter* (which opened and closed like a camera shutter in October 1921). Already big Castles fans, the Astaires were delighted to take on the new project. "They were a tremendous influence in our careers," recalled Fred Astaire, "not that we copied them completely, but we did appropriate some of their ballroom steps and style for our vaudeville act."

Irene hired pianist Dodo Hupfeld as her accompanist and laid in a selection of dancing frocks from Lucile (by 1923, she switched loyalties to French couturier Molyneaux). She signed with producer B. F. Keith, who had presided over Vernon and Irene's 1914 tour. Keith and his much-feared associate E. F. Albee ran, by the time Irene encountered them, the United

Booking Office, which held a virtual monopoly on vaudeville. Irene, under her new UBO contract, opened in Boston in November.

Life intruded, as it has a way of doing. Irene's mother had suffered a series of strokes in late 1921 and early 1922. After several months as a home-bound invalid, she died on May 11, 1922. Irene collapsed at her bedside and, according to her son, never really recovered from her mother's passing; she burned their correspondence, feeling it was too painful to keep and too personal to be read by anyone else. "It was hard to go on without my mother," she wrote decades later. "Her passing represented the end of the beauty and graciousness of an era she carried with her." Indeed, Vernon Castle and Annie Elroy Thomas left the scene just as the loosely termed belle epoque came to an end, and the Jazz Age began. Irene and the Jazz Age would never become friends.

Not only had music and dance changed with the advent of the 1920s, but New York and its cabaret culture, the world ushered in by the Castles, had faded away, too. Prohibition crippled many of the cabarets and dance-friendly restaurants. As the styles in dance and music changed, the old clubs seemed passé, and by the early 1920s, they were being replaced by speakeasies. For every one of the "jay cabarets, gay cabarets" that Julian Street had complained about back in the early 1910s, there sprang up two or three "speaks": many of them dark, claustrophobic joints like the short-lived Sans Souci Irene had hated so.

If *Miss 1917* and being upstaged by Ann Pennington had made Irene feel old, she soon also started sounding old, and occasionally a bit of a prude. As early as 1919 she was telling the *Toledo Times,* "Without wishing to appear narrow minded [never a good way to begin an interview], I believe that the shimmie and jazz are both improper and awkward." The Castle walk had been left in the dust, and Irene was not going to take it like a good sport. "Jazz music makes them forget to really dance and they abandon themselves to unusual rhythm." Irene was all of twenty-six years old, but she already sounded like a dowager glaring through a lorgnette. "It is a mistake for a woman to go uncorseted," she complained of the 1920s flappers. "The rolled-down hosiery fad is abominable."

She never ceased sniping at jazz and jazz dances, even using words that would have made Vernon wince a few years earlier—in a November 1918 interview, she called the shimmy "a nigger dance. . . . The nigger bands at home 'Jazz' a tune: that is to say, they slur the notes." Back in 1914, she and Vernon had fined a company member $50 for saying "nigger"—now Irene herself was sufficiently furious and embittered to use it in public. In 1922 she was still complaining that at New York restaurants she was jolted by "Jazz, jazz, jazz! Survival of the days of barbarism, paganism. The paradings of savages." All her life, from childhood to old age, Irene had black friends and coworkers, yet she complained, "The dancing of 1922 isn't beautiful. It has rhythm, yes, but what rhythm! The rhythm of jungle creatures. And what sort of rhythm is that? You know enough of anthropology to answer that yourself, I'm sure."

January 1922 saw Irene and Billy Reardon open at Keith's Orpheum Theater in Brooklyn. She topped the bill, appearing along with W. C. Fields's Family Ford act. Irene's segment opened with a film of her home life: her dogs, her horses, her summer and winter homes, her roadsters and her limousines. "Following this it is also proven that Miss Castle also swims and dives well," wrote one unimpressed critic. "Just about the time the audience begins to wonder what it is all about, the picture stops and Miss Castle comes on in person. She refuses to apologize for her singing voice, claiming that she intended to be a little different from other performers in this respect." After a song, Reardon came out and he and Irene danced: "This is probably the high spot of the act," said that same reviewer. "The dance as a routine could be improved upon, but in its present condition will get by."

In May 1922 Irene, her husband, her dancing partner, and her pianist (and at least one dog) sailed on the *LaFayette* for a month in France. She and Reardon danced at several Parisian theaters, and the Tremans flew over the Channel to London on June 8. When asked if her first husband's death had not made her wary of planes, Irene answered with her usual fearlessness and realism, "I don't think there's any more danger in flying than riding on railroads or steamboats. Besides, I would have to get up very early in the morning to get the boat train." Returning to the United States from her sojourn, Irene was nabbed at customs trying to sneak in some jewelry and was fined.

She ran into trouble in the fall of 1922 in Providence, Rhode Island—and seemed to enjoy every minute of it. Providence censors fined Irene for performing her Isadora Duncan–like dance in a filmy gown without stockings. "I call this my anti-censorship dance," she said defiantly. "It is supposed to symbolize freedom, untrammeled and uncensored. . . . The Providence censors wanted me to burlesque the idea by swathing myself in an extra, wholly unnecessary suit of underwear."

Irene closed the season at the end of October 1922, citing exhaustion and recent horseback riding injuries, and returned to Ithaca and her husband. But after checking her bank account, she was back on the road by mid-November: she was stranded on a sleeper car in Missouri ("The car was filled with students. They are fine until you have outgrown them"), and in Chicago her hotel refused to admit her dog ("Do they think I'm such a heartless monster that I would let him be put by himself in a damp basement?"). Through the early winter months of 1923, Irene and Reardon danced their way through Kentucky, Michigan, San Francisco, Toronto; by spring, they were back on the East Coast.

By 1922, Irene's *Dances and Fashions* had grown from one act in a vaudeville bill into its own full, self-contained evening, with a total of twenty acts or vignettes. In addition to the dancing of Irene and Reardon, the audience was treated to a monologue by actor George Rosener, a troupe of roller skaters, the song stylings of Mme. Gardini (one pictures a Margaret Dumont type with a piercing soprano), and "Duke" Yellman and his orchestra.

Irene and Reardon danced four sets during the program: waltzes, fox trots, tangos, the flirtation walk, and the Castle one-step. These turns, as expected, were the hit of the evening: "She moves with a grace and charm of a poem expressing music and rhythm," wrote one reviewer; another said that "she will probably never be equaled."

Dances and Fashions slowly petered out in the late summer and fall of 1922. Irene and Billy Reardon toured the East Coast, the South, and the Southwest, but Irene's heart had gone out of the enterprise. A train wreck caused them to miss performances in Washington and Baltimore, and Irene was beginning to fade from overwork. The tour was costing Irene $10,000 a week to operate, and she was barely turning a profit, so she decided that 1923 would be her last year as a producer. She signed with the Selwyn brothers, Arch and Edgar (who by then had formed a partnership with Elisabeth Marbury as theatrical bookers) to handle whatever touring she would do as of the fall of 1923.

The troupe reached Texas in early November, and Irene set out to find the memorial to Vernon and the recently named Vernon Castle Boulevard. "I asked taxi drivers, motorcycle policemen, and phoned the cemetery and finally in desperation went to the city hall to see if I could locate either of the places." She finally found the stone monument and laid a floral wreath (making sure there were photographers to record the event), then set out for Vernon Castle Boulevard, which she'd fondly imagined as a tree-lined, shady street with stately mansions. Irene was in for a shock: the street (today called Vernon Castle Avenue) was a fourteen-block stretch beginning at Cozby South Street and ending at Winscott Plover Road. "A rough, unlovely street," she complained bitterly, "unworthy of the illustrious name that has been given to it."

Irene and her *Dances and Fashions* company sailed for England in the summer of 1923 to fulfill theatrical engagements in London and Paris. "Dancing has become so improper that the average person finds it very embarrassing and often shuts his eyes," she said to reporters. "I really believe that the most improper exhibitions of dancing are to be found in the Middle West. They are very vulgar. Of course, New York is bad enough, but when one looks for the more moral dancing, you must go to the Pacific Coast." She had little but backhanded compliments for the British as well: "The English are doing nothing new in the way of dancing, but they are doing their dancing decently."

The British returned the favor. A review of her act in the *Dancing Times* stated that "it must be confessed that, as a dancer, she left much to be desired. . . . It must, however, always be remembered . . . that there has been only one Vernon Castle in this world." Perhaps to get her mind off her troubles, Irene had her hair clipped in the ultra-short new "garçon" look, all but shaved in the back. "I didn't think it was very becoming," she sighed.

CHAPTER THIRTY-EIGHT

"TO CHICAGO HIGH SOCIETY, SHE WAS A CHORUS GIRL"

When Irene and Billy Reardon sailed for Europe in 1923, Robert Treman did not accompany them. There had been published rumors of the Tremans' separation as early as mid-1921, which were denied by both parties. In November of that year, Irene completely lost her temper with one reporter, winning her no friends in the press: "It's a lie. We are as much in love as when we were married.... I know your game. You understand nothing. I hate newspapermen and always have . . . you're always stirring up mud in a clear puddle."

No one really knows what went on that summer of 1923, but the papers were full of guesses. According to press reports, Irene arrived in Paris in early June ("to establish a legal residence," one paper surmised, in anticipation of divorce proceedings), and Treman followed her to Europe, checking into the Hotel Claridge in London with his lawyer. Irene filed for her independence on July 4, after which she and her husband took off for a private weekend in Deauville to talk things out. While the proceedings were hanging fire, reporters besieged Irene's friends to ask if she were going to marry Ward Crane: "That affair was dead and finished a year ago," pooh-poohed an unnamed source. Friends and acquaintances were more than happy to dish dirt: the Treman family looked down on Irene and her animals, it was said, and the combination of a home-loving, old-fashioned husband and an ambitious career woman was bound to come to grief.

In her memoirs, Irene's chronology is charmingly vague. She claims that her tour with Billy Reardon was undertaken right after she discovered that Robert Treman had used all of her savings for Hol-Tre without her knowledge. Irene first thought of divorce while on tour. "Robert and I were only half married with this distance between us," she wrote. "Occasionally he called or wrote, but that was all." Her Paris divorce, she said, cost her

$3,000, and Treman showed up in court hoping to iron things out: "I convinced him it was hopeless."

It seemed to be all over by the end of July 1923: Irene was granted a divorce, said her lawyer, Dudley Field Malone, on grounds of "incompatibility of temperament." Robert Treman gave a gentlemanly quote to the press: "What can any man do when his wife is determined to divorce him? He can only give in gracefully. I thank her for the good times we had together." But Irene continued to muddy the waters, perhaps in an effort to bedevil the press (or keep her husband on edge). Less philosophical than Treman, Irene claimed to be toying with him like a cat with a squeaky toy. "I've got to keep Bob guessing," she said. "If it's granted and I decide I don't want it, all I have to do is write the judge a letter within 60 days and tell him so."

Sailing for the United States, she lied outright to reporters, claiming that she had neither filed for nor received a divorce. "I don't see why the public should be interested in my affairs," she snapped. "They should be discouraged rather than encouraged about following my matrimonial matters. I don't give a darn what the people think. They can keep on quibbling for a month if they like as to whether or not I am divorced." Finally fed up, Treman admitted that "I am not in the least anxious to see my wife again. All I ask of her is to leave me in quiet."

The nastiness of the Treman divorce lingered in Ithaca. Irene was painted by the local press as a flighty, imperious diva. A group of Cornell professors' wives told of their shock when one of Irene's monkeys invaded their tea party, and recalled Irene herself rising at the ungodly hour of noon and traipsing around in "a flaming pair of red Turkish trousers." The Tremans' well-stocked liquor cellar—during Prohibition—also got the town in an uproar. "I can imagine the elderly ladies of Ithaca sitting on their front porches," wrote Irene, "nodding openmouthed and saying 'What else could you expect from an actress?'" As late as the 1980s, bad feelings remained: a book about Ithaca's first families is downright unpleasant about Irene. Hinting that she denied Treman children in favor of her career, the book notes that she spent much time with her nieces, because "demonstrating some motherly instinct apparently was important to the publicists."

In 1924, she sued Robert Treman for the return of $40,000 she claimed he stole from her; the Treman family vigorously fought the suit, which was eventually settled out of court. Robert Treman went on to live a long, happy life; he remarried, had two daughters, and was a pillar of the Ithaca community when he died in 1953.

One monument to the Treman-Castle marriage still stands in Ithaca: their huge stone house, complete with Irene's prized swimming pool, is now the fraternity house for the Alpha Phi Chapter of Sigma Chi at Cornell University. Set back in the hills on Cayuga Heights Road, the house was sold to Cornell in 1925. Not only do the charming and friendly fraternity boys know of its history, but they also have the deed of sale framed on the ground floor and still call one room "the monkey room," because it's where Irene once kept her pets. Eighty-some years after she left Ithaca, Irene Castle is, to some extent, the Sweetheart of Sigma Chi.

Through all of this personal trauma, Irene was still touring the United States with *Dances and Fashions of 1923*. "I find I must rest or my muscles won't work," she said. "My feet feel like sandbags and simply will not do their duty. So I relax, sometimes spasmodically, which does not have much effect, but is better than none. I have made no social engagements, with the exception of one, on this trip."

That one engagement must have been a doozy: it was on this tour that Irene became affianced to her third husband. Irene had met Frederic McLaughlin while on tour with Billy Reardon in Chicago in May 1921. McLaughin was forty-six years old in 1923 and had enjoyed an adventurous, prosperous life. The son of a Chicago coffee merchant, he took over the firm shortly after graduating from Harvard. In World War I, he commanded the 333rd Machine-Gun Battalion of the army's 85th Division, and he was referred to as "Major" for the rest of his life. (His battalion's nickname, the Blackhawks, was revived in 1926, when McLaughlin was awarded a National Hockey League franchise, purchased the Portland Rosebuds, and renamed them the Chicago Blackhawks, a team that went on to win the Stanley Cup in 1934, 1938, and 1961.) McLaughlin had come through a scandalous divorce back in 1910, when his Baltimore-born wife, Helen Wylie, charged him with desertion.

Irene later recalled their meeting, at a party given at McLaughlin's apartment at 333 North Michigan Avenue. Tall, with a hangdog face (somewhat resembling actor Jason Robards Jr.), McLaughlin was taken with Irene right away: he asked her to dinner and "announced his intentions of seriously pursuing me." Irene claimed later that she had been un-interested and that McLaughlin all but stalked her—but he was a mag-netic man, and her life was to be pulled into his orbit for the next two de-cades. There was an attraction, and irritation, on both sides.

"If you don't know the Major, you will never understand how he swept me off my feet," she said. "Vernon had died. I had married Mr. Tre-man more because I was despondent than anything else. But I wanted children, and we could not have them. He spent my sum of small savings on the races and on gambling. Then I met the Major. He promised me security. He showed me that my dancing days could not go on forever. He seemed to be in love with me, and I listened to him. We were married, and I looked forward to a lifetime of happiness."

Irene insisted that the marriage was practically forced on her and that she tried to get out of it at the last minute, but McLaughlin began to cry: "I have never been able to see a man cry. I gave in." Of course, this was written when McLaughlin was safely dead, years after bitter custody and financial battles. If Irene's marriage to Vernon Castle was an easygoing friendship, her relationship with Frederic McLaughlin was more like something out of a Brontë novel or an Edward Albee play.

"Dancer Won by Chicago Bachelor," read the headlines on November 30, 1923, announcing their marriage. McLaughlin was referred to as "coffee king and well known as the master of the hounds at Onwentsia, polo star and society figure." They were married at McLaughlin's apartment and left on the 29th to catch a ship to the Orient later that week. They sailed on the *President Grant* the first week of December. Embarking for her honey-moon, Irene smiled benignly at reporters, "I have nothing to say. I hope I am never interviewed again in my life." On their honeymoon cruise, McLaughlin was reported to have "soundly thrashed a traveling salesman . . . because of comments the latter made regarding his bride."

Years later, at the time of their pending divorce, Irene's most serious charge would be that McLaughlin beat her on their honeymoon (he al-ways denied this categorically). She claimed he was seasick on their way to the Orient and turned green at her suggestion that they go up to dinner: "the next thing I knew, I was lying on the floor with my legs sprawled out in front of me. I had been felled by a neat right hook."

The happy couple arrived in Tokyo on December 22, less than two months after much of the region had been destroyed in an earthquake that struck the Tokyo/Yokohama metropolitan area. More than 140,000 people died, and hundreds of thousands of buildings burned or collapsed. Oddly, Irene ignores this devastation and horror in her memoirs, making one wonder if the McLaughlins even disembarked in Japan. They stayed at the Imperial Hotel, she wrote, and "saw all the sights."

Perhaps she was too concerned with a personal tragedy: one of her sister's three daughters, eleven-year-old Barbara, died of meningitis on December 29. Irene wanted to rush right home but was unable to book passage till late January, so the McLaughlins resumed their tour of the Orient. They set out for China, then Manila. The marriage continued to be rocky. In Beijing she wanted to attend a dinner, and when McLaughlin was late in dressing, she told him to "go to hell. . . . Once again I found myself on the floor with my feet stuck out in front." When the honeymooners arrived back in the United States in late January 1924, Irene rushed to her bereaved sister in Saranac Lake, New York, their childhood fights forgotten.

If Irene thought Chicago would be an improvement over provincial little Ithaca, she was mistaken. A bit defensively, she claimed, "I didn't make any effort to be accepted by Chicago society, but accepted I was. By marrying Frederic I automatically fell into his social pocket." She sighed wearily, "Society bored me to death." But according to her son, established society looked down its nose at Irene, who had snatched a prime bachelor from its midst. "To Chicago high society, she was a chorus girl," says William McLaughlin. "She was just one of those people off the stage; they were still considered tramps and gypsies."

Irene's first child, Barbara, was born on January 5, 1925, at the Michael Reese Hospital in Chicago, weighing in at seven pounds. A few months later, the McLaughlins left the "bachelor apartment" in which they'd married and moved into a home on Lincoln Park West, also taking a cottage in St. Andrews, New Brunswick, for summering. Professing herself to be a happily settled-down wife and mother, Irene claimed to be "through with the stage, dancing and movies forever. . . . When a woman reaches 31 [as Irene did in 1924], she cannot combine work and marriage. I know, for I've tried it." She added, rather oddly and defensively, "My husband is a 100% American and a real man."

Although she was an avid horsewoman, Irene seemed to spend as much time falling off her mounts as astride them. She was thrown by her horse in August 1922 and fractured her right collarbone while attempting a five-foot jump. She was back on the horse one month later. "I had to do it, or I never would have been able to ride a horse again." She had two accidents in 1926 (including one in which her horse rolled over on her); in 1929, she suffered a broken rib after a riding accident; in 1930, she broke a collarbone during a hunt; and in 1931, she fractured a wrist. But her most serious spill came in October 1925, when Irene went into premature labor at the Michael Reese Hospital, having been rushed there after falling from her horse. The infant, named Peter, lived for only three hours. Irene was not otherwise badly injured and was able to conceive again, but her love for horses underwent its strongest test.

She gave birth to her second (and last) child, William McLaughlin, on July 17, 1929. Born prematurely, he spent his first weeks in an incubator. Because his brother had died without being baptized, William's aunts swooped in: "There was a Catholic priest there when I was dropped prematurely," he says. "I was a weeny little baby, and nobody expected me to live, and my aunts insisted if there was a breath of life for one second I was going to be baptized." Though nominally a Catholic, William was raised as an Episcopalian by his mother.

Irene's religion was rather offhanded. She saw that her children went to church and Sunday school, and she herself showed up on Easter, but her son feels that was as much a social as a religious outing. "She had one of those happy friendships with the Lord in which He was totally tolerant and totally compassionate and anything goes as long as you're good in your heart," says William McLaughlin. "The *convenient* kind of Christianity."

In 1929, Irene was claiming to be cheerfully maternal and happy to be out of the spotlight: "I preferred to stop at the height of my popularity," she said, "rather than decline little by little with the public's favor. . . . Never would I hear people say my day was over. . . . There's nothing more pathetic than popular stage folk clinging so hard to public favor . . . my child means more to me than the applause of hundreds. Besides," Irene added, at the age of thirty-six, "dancing is an expression of youth, and can only be done when one is young."

CHAPTER THIRTY-NINE

ORPHANS OF THE STORM

After her marriage to Frederic McLaughlin, Irene ramped up her animal rights activities, denouncing cruelty at horse and dog shows, visiting animal shelters, speaking at the Maryland and New York Anti-Vivisection societies. She resigned in tears from the Humane Society in 1930 after steamrolling over the gentler feelings of longtime members and demanding that those who were "no longer active and did not make material contributions" take their names off the letterhead. At which, as one paper phrased it, "the ladies became unladylike, several arose and said harsh things about Mrs. McLaughlin." Not used to being second-guessed and thwarted, Irene resigned from the group and stormed out in a fury.

In September 1931, she demanded the arrest of pig-farming neighbor William Schroeder on three charges of cruelty to his animals and for "maintaining a nuisance." Schroeder, in turn, filed false-arrest charges to the tune of $10,000 against her. The case dragged out for two years before being decided in Irene's favor. The only notable outcome of the case was the newspaper headline it generated: "Irene Castle in Pig Suit."

No one was safe from Irene's righteous fury, not even macho writer Ernest Hemingway. Director Raoul Walsh recalled attending a party at San Simeon in the 1930s, where William Randolph Hearst and Marion Davies had gathered such political, performing, and literary stars as Winston Churchill, Somerset Maugham, J. Edgar Hoover, Will Rogers, and John Barrymore. At one point in the evening, Hemingway began regaling the guests with tales of bullfighting, one of his favorite manly sports. There was little left but a Hemingway-shaped spot on the floor when Irene got through with him. She described a bullfight she had witnessed wherein the bull had been stabbed and chased to the point of collapse: "Then your brave matador, Mr. Hemingway, strutted around like a prima donna, approached the exhausted animal, and killed the beast with one thrust of his sword. If you call that a sport, you had better stop drinking Spanish brandy." Several guests, and Hearst, applauded Irene's outburst.

"Mother would have agreed with PETA," says William McLaughlin, although 1930s photos show her holding puppies and speaking out for animal rights while wrapped in furs and wearing leather gloves. "Her view was you've got to be extreme, because your opposition is extreme. Maybe you can *settle* on a middle ground, but if you *start* on a middle ground, you're going to end up over-compromising on their side."

In late 1927, Irene announced plans to open a sanctuary for stray dogs in the Chicago area. Citing seventeen thousand dogs killed in Chicago each year for lack of holding space, she hoped that "we will eventually be able to place all of them." Orphans of the Storm—named for the 1921 French Revolution thriller starring the Gish sisters—opened in April 1928, to the delight of the local media ("Kennel for Tramp Dogs Opens," headlined the *Chicago Daily News*).

Disaster struck in February 1930, when an early morning fire, fanned by a brisk wind, destroyed two of the shelter's kennels, the business office, the hay barn, and the cookhouse. Irene collapsed when she received word, then rushed to the site, where at least eighty-three dogs had perished. She demanded an investigation—claming to have received threatening letters—but no cause was determined. The shelter was rebuilt.

Orphans of the Storm still exists in Deerfield, Illinois, and now offers cats as well as dogs for adoption. "The most important activity at Orphans of the Storm is the adoption process," says the organization's Web site, www.orphansofthestorm.org. "Orphans is the place where previously unwanted homeless dogs and cats are united with their new families. . . . We operate one of the country's oldest and largest animal shelters, offering refuge and rehabilitation, finding warm and loving adoptive homes for thousands of stray and abandoned dogs and cats every year."

Irene's family, friends, and servants often had to bear the brunt of her pet mania—especially the monkeys. Her son tells of having to carry Puddin' Head Jones, Irene's woolly monkey, when the three of them went for walks. "The damn little monkey would suffer from diarrhea, and of course she knew this, which is why I had to be the one holding him!" McLaughlin recalls Puddin' also disrupted dinner parties: twelve or fifteen guests would be gathered in the impressive dining room ("great vaulted ceiling, Spanish tile floors, high-backed chairs"), and in would come Puddin' Head, making straight for his beloved mistress's chair. "And there was Puddin' perched on the back of the chair, urinating just as calm as you please. Everybody else got all shook up, but not Mother, she just rang the dinner bell and had somebody mop up the floor, and went right on with her dinner party."

She also began a well-meaning but fluff-headed crusade to prove that rabies does not exist. When a rabies epidemic broke out in Chicago, policemen were ordered to shoot stray dogs on sight, and four hundred strays in the city pound were euthanized. Irene erupted: of the eight thousand strays she had taken in to Orphans of the Storm in the past year, "I have yet to see a case of rabies. . . . Perhaps this new order against the pets will cause all dog lovers to take up the battle." (As late as 1954, Irene was publicly offering to be bitten by a rabid dog, an offer that was, happily for her, not taken up.)

Like many people with a cause, Irene could go overboard, sometimes becoming strident and humorless about it. But even her detractors admired her sincerity on the subject and never for a minute doubted her good intentions. Her son says today that "she would have gotten down in the dirt, she would have given up the name 'Irene Castle,' to save the life of one puppy by the side of a highway."

On July 16, 1934, Irene's sister, Elroy, died after a brief illness; she'd been a widow since her second husband, Earl Bradford, had died in 1920. Her orphaned daughters, Elroy and Jane, were old enough to be amusing and self-possessed companions to Irene, and she often took them into her Chicago home, giving parties for them and taking them to Europe (Irene's own children, much younger, spent more time in boarding schools than at home). Irene purchased black-edged mourning stationery after Elroy's death, and *Variety* snidely reported that it was in tribute to one of her recently deceased dogs. Furious, Irene wrote to her friend Walter Winchell, who published her screed: "*Variety's* little wallop . . . pains me terribly. Whoever is responsible for the not so wise crack should blush for shame."

CHAPTER FORTY

"WHAT DO YOU DO FOR AN ENCORE TO WHAT THEY HAD?"

In the early 1930s, as her third marriage continued to fall apart, Irene began looking about for something more to do than shill for Cutex nail polish and Corticelli Silk. Even her animal rights crusades didn't seem to fill her life, and certainly she was a hands-off mother. Irene began looking wistfully back at her career. "She did not accept graciously making those lifetime adjustments that must come when you come off the pinnacle," says her son. "The ultimate cruelty is that she had so much life ahead of her [after Vernon's death]. I mean, really, what do you do for an encore to what they had?"

Combining her show business drive with her interest in black history and civil rights, Irene helped put together "a Negro Pageant" called *O, Sing a New Song*, which was performed in August 1934 at Soldier's Field. A cast of five thousand singers, dancers, and musicians performed the three-act musical anthology, which presented black music from Africa, "Plantation Days," and modern America.

One reminder of Irene's illustrious past came in 1933, when her discoverer and early champion Elisabeth Marbury died in her New York home. Friends had been shocked when her longtime companion, Elsie de Wolfe, had left her to marry Sir Charles Mendl in 1926. Marbury's funeral at St. Patrick's was the social event of the season, which would have delighted her.

Irene was cast in the play *Return to Folly*, a comedy/drama by Harland Ware, to be performed four times in the spring of 1933 at the Workshop Theatre in Lake Forest, Illinois, where the McLaughlins had moved. The *Chicago American* approved: "The whole cast was grand, the lines excellent, Irene McLaughlin wearing one ravishing costume after another, looking as dazzling as she did in the days when she was Irene Castle." Encouraged, Irene put out feelers to her Hollywood friends. In 1933 and 1934, she made a concerted effort to revive her film career. Costume designer Orry-Kelly proclaimed her one of the day's best-dressed actresses, along with Bette Davis and Kay Francis. Alan Crosland, who had directed Irene in *Slim Shoulders,* arranged for a Warner Brothers screen test, which he judged "a great success. Though the test has not yet been shown to Mr. Warner, I think there is a distinct place for her on the screen. I think she wears clothes better than any woman on the screen. As an actress and a personality I think she's improved over 12 years ago." But nothing came of this. Certainly Irene at forty was as lovely as she'd ever been: slim, chic, up-to-date, and with her "camera bones" still catching the light.

She did get offers, says her son—but not for starring parts. In late 1935, she and Clifton Webb were cast in a proposed Joan Crawford film to be called *Elegance:* "You can imagine how much I long to do it," said Irene, "when dancing with Clifton is the greatest fun on earth." All that came of this was a stunning photo session of Irene and Webb dancing together, which was published in *Vogue.* Had she wished, Irene might have become a character actress in the mode of Billie Burke, Alice Brady, Margaret Dumont (though she was perhaps not quite as talented an actress as those ladies). There was a call for chic, elegant middle-aged women to play the mothers and aunts of Joan Crawford, Claudette Colbert, and other young stars. But Irene "didn't want to be a character actress," says her son. "She over-valued her status." She'd field an offer and "get fairly excited about it, 'I'm going to Hollywood!' or, 'I'm going to New York!' After the first blush of excitement, she'd come to realize that she was not the center core—she felt that they were getting more out of the use of her name than she was getting." The thrill of being wanted again often degenerated into broken contracts and lawyers' consultations.

Irene had plenty to say about Hollywood fashions, not much of it positive. "There was little individuality, and smartness was rare," she said in 1934, though she added that "their laxness is excusable, for when they're working, they have to spend endless hours with makeup artists, modistes and fitters."

Irene had been giving talks over the radio since the late 1920s, usually about animal rights or fashion. In the early 1930s, she put together an autobiographical series sponsored by Formfit, a girdle manufacturer, for which she was also giving a traveling lecture series and fashion show across the United States. Recordings of these broadcasts reveal Irene to have had a cultured, well-modulated voice with no trace of a regional accent. Her vocal acting skills, however, were stiff and unconvincing—another reason, perhaps, why her career in talking films never took flight.

Irene turned forty in 1933. To her credit, she never lied about her age. In fact, she sometimes overemphasized it, making herself sound ancient despite her glowing health and beauty. "When I was 20," she reminisced, "I sized things up in a manner I think was pretty intelligent. I decided that when one reached 30, one should give up professional dancing. I did. . . . Those nasty lines time brings to every face are what really worries me. Age is something for real concern. When it comes, I don't know what will happen to me."

She remained very proud of her appearance, and—like a true star— never went out in public "undone." "She never left the house unless she was ready to take on the world," says William McLaughlin, "and sometimes that would not be until four in the afternoon." On the other hand, Irene somehow maintained her figure with little or no exercise: "We had a number of exercise machines that never got used," says McLaughlin.

Through the 1930s, Irene still tried occasionally to win over Chicago society, with mixed results. "She would have Sunday parties for Lionel Barrymore, Ethel Barrymore, all the people who came to Chicago," says her son. "Alfred Lunt and Lynne Fontanne were close friends; they gave her a little dachshund she named Lyntie."

An attempt to become a hat designer came to grief: Irene spent the summer of 1936 in Paris with her daughter, Barbara, scouting for hats for her Irene Castle hat firm (which she had formed with designer Nan Gilbert). Irene Castle, Inc., opened a factory with showrooms in Chicago and signed with Marshall Fields to carry the line, but by November 1938, Irene had run into trouble. She was slapped with a $150,000 slander suit by competing milliner Sonya Zaranoff, who alleged that on three occasions Irene had publicly bad-mouthed both her and her hats (Irene supposedly called her a "stuffy old cow" and said, "Her hats are terrible; she is a drunkard who does not attend to her business"). Fortunately for Irene, as one newspaper put it, "Superior Judge Myron Westover said that one lady can call another lady a cow, let the chips fall where they may."

The only positive outcome of this venture was her blossoming friendship with advertising man George Enzinger, which whom she worked on ad and publicity campaigns for her short-lived business. Irene always claimed that she and Enzinger were born exactly one year apart, but his World War I registration card gives April 16 (not 17), 1892, as his birth date. A St. Louis native of German heritage, Enzinger was divorced, the father of a grown daughter, and was working as an advertising writer when he and Irene met. Irene and Enzinger grew closer as her marriage to Frederic McLaughlin continued to deteriorate.

McLaughlin loved to sit and read nights; Irene, though a smart and curious woman, never willingly slogged through a book. "When I was a child in school I read *Pilgrim's Progress;* I don't think I have read more than six books since then," she admitted. She was not a relaxer; she was a *doer.* Irene had to be storming about, creating a whirlwind: "I have always had something to dive into," she said in the mid-1930s, "something to absorb all my interest. I have no patience with those phlegmatic people who care about nothing, have no decided likes or dislikes, have no passion to *do* something. I feel sorry for them; they're missing the finest part of living." An admirable outlook, certainly, but an exhausting one to live with day in and day out.

Frederic McLaughlin had a wry sense of humor, which often ruffled Irene. At a dinner party, Irene regaled guests with a story about how she'd spanked Bill for teasing a dog and getting his finger bitten. When one appalled guest asked why Irene had spanked a child already suffering from a dog bite, McLaughlin cracked, "She spanked him for pulling his finger away." "Those kind of things she just hated," her son reports.

In September 1937, Irene filed suit for divorce, charging McLaughlin with cruelty and asking for $150,000 she claimed to have "loaned" him. She also wanted custody of their children as well as a hefty alimony ($750 a month). "I am fighting only for the custody of my two children," she said. "After all, they are my children, and I do believe a mother is entitled to her own flesh and blood." Irene claimed in her suit that on their honeymoon in China, "he hit her so hard she was thrown 6 feet; in June 1924 he struck her when she was pregnant; in September 1936 he hit her on the nose; in April 1933 he choked her till she was insensible; in July 1937, he knocked her down."

McLaughlin angrily denied the charges. "Do you see any marks of violence on her? . . . If you throw enough mud, some of it will stick," he said sadly. "If Mrs. McLaughlin walked into this house now, she'd be welcome to stay for as long as she wished. But I'll never make any move toward a reconciliation."

Irene soon decided that the $750 a month she'd asked for was not nearly enough to live on: "What about clothes, cosmetics, facials, shampoos, amusements, entertainments, my dog refuge, The Orphans of the Storm, and several other things? How am I going to pay for them on $750 a month? I absolutely cannot get along on that small amount." At a judge's request, she filled out a budget proving that she needed $9,000 a month to squeak by. It was so cold in her Lake Forest home, Irene said, that her dogs had to wear sweaters, and she and William were bundled up in mufflers and coats around the house. Her attorney asked for a court order to make McLaughlin pay for heat; Irene was ordered to have the furnace repaired herself.

Her son laughs and notes, "She was getting good money, but she was spending it faster than she could take it in. Poverty was always just around the corner with her." Working women in 1937—the tail end of the Depression—didn't take well to Irene's whining about her measly $750 a month. One waitress was quoted, "Gosh, I don't think I could spend that much money, even with a budget, unless I read a book on new ways to spend it."

CHAPTER FORTY-ONE

THE STORY OF VERNON AND IRENE CASTLE

One thing that did make Irene happy in the 1930s was the return of couples dancing, with the advent of swing, boogie-woogie, and big band music. Still, she found fault: "As an exhibition this Shagging and Trucking is amusing enough," she said. "Some of the youngsters perform amazing athletic feats, but you can't call it dancing. It's hopping about to mad, jumped-up rhythms. It's not becoming to the average age and figure, and really has no place on the ballroom floor. It's movement, not steps, that charms. Dancing must start up here, in the head. Mr. Castle and I always decided first on a pattern we'd execute on the floor, and figure out later how our feet would get us there."

As early as 1935, Irene was fielding requests from publishers for her memoirs, but nothing came of it. But in 1937, producer Pandro S. Berman signed an agreement with Irene to make a film about her life with Vernon for RKO. (Her official title was "costume designer, technical advisor and writer.") Almost immediately, Fred Astaire was signed to play Vernon. It was a no-brainer: Astaire was a dancer, a charming actor, and looked startlingly like Vernon Castle. But quickly, the decision as to who was to play Irene devolved into a fight: fans and the studio assumed it was to be Astaire's longtime partner, Ginger Rogers. Irene assumed otherwise.

"I am to select the girl for the part," Irene announced, pushing a Chicago-area dancer named Edna Torrance (who, after a bit part in the 1939 film *Swing Hotel,* faded from view). To be fair, there were few dancer/actresses in the late 1930s who would have been right for the role: Ann Miller was too young, Eleanor Powell too bland, Rita Hayworth too high-voltage sexy, Mitzi Mayfair not a big enough name. Fred's sister and former dance partner, Adele, would have been perfect, but she was happily retired as Lady Cavendish (and, really, she was only three years younger than Irene herself). The most "Irene Castle-y" of Hollywood stars was

Katharine Hepburn, who couldn't dance a step. That pretty much left Ginger Rogers.

Astaire and Rogers had already costarred in seven light, brilliant musicals since they'd first teamed, as supporting players, in *Flying Down to Rio* (1933). But the quality of their films had already peaked and begun to decline a bit by the time they'd made their most recent, *Carefree* (1938). Fred Astaire needed a career-boosting hit a lot more than Ginger Rogers did. His only recent Ginger-free film, *A Damsel in Distress* (1937), had been a disappointment, and the thirty-nine-year-old dancer's RKO contract was nearing its end. Ginger Rogers, on the other hand, was twenty-seven years old and at the top of her game. She'd recently been seen in the successful (nonmusical) films *Stage Door* (1937) and *Vivacious Lady* (1938), and RKO had lined up for her such projects as the comedies *Bachelor Mother* and *Fifth Avenue Girl* and the dramas *The Primrose Path* and *Kitty Foyle* (the latter would win Rogers a Best Actress Oscar). If *The Story of Vernon and Irene Castle* was going to be a hit, RKO needed both Fred *and* Ginger.

The film "was not an easy one to get on the screen," as Fred Astaire mildly put it, noting that Irene was "naturally very particular about every detail." "She totally upset everybody, because she wanted a finger in every pie," says Irene's son, who lived with her in Hollywood for much of the shoot. "She fought with the director, she fought with the crew, she fought with everybody but Fred Astaire, who was the calming blanket on all these quibbles and arguments." She sat on the set during filming and insisted on retakes even when director Henry C. Potter was satisfied. Irene's son recalls that "she told all who would listen that Fred Astaire said Ginger was a terrible dance partner." Irene had nothing publicly to say against Ginger Rogers except that "I just can't see myself as a blonde." Rogers refused to bob her hair, to Irene's fury, and wore it in long, perfect late-1930s style.

"I am sure they would rather I had been dead," said Irene to the *New York Times*'s Bosley Crowther. "They even waited two years for me to kick off, I suspect, after I had sold them the story. But when they found that I was indestructible, they went ahead and made it." She went on to snipe about the script, wishing they had made more of *Watch Your Step* and "had dwelled less on my life before I met Vernon. Miss Foote wasn't very interesting." She also objected to set designer Darrell Silvera's re-creation of her childhood home, which she felt was too lower-middle class: "I see the Footes are on relief!" she snorted.

Edna May Oliver was cast as Elisabeth Marbury (whose name was changed to Maggie Sutton). Oliver gave a superb portrait of what the bossy, affectionate Marbury might have been like; ironically, the actress was a dead ringer for Elsie de Wolfe. Another hitch came with the casting of Walter Ash: despite Irene's objections, RKO insisted they could not cast a black actor as the Castles' companion and manservant. Too many patrons would object, too many theaters would refuse to show the film. Walter Ash kept his name but changed his race: Walter Brennan was cast, doing his patented "crotchety geezer with a heart of gold" act.

Irene rented Ina Claire's Beverly Hills house, where she and her son lived from November 1938 through March 1939, as filming ground on. Also grinding on was the unpleasantness between Irene and her husband: McLaughlin wanted William back with him for Christmas, and Irene refused to send him, getting herself charged with contempt of court.

Finally, the folks at RKO found a way to divest themselves of their "inspiration." An antivivisection bill came up before the California assembly, and everyone on the set made sure Irene knew about it, stressing its importance—and *her* importance in getting it passed. She fell for it (or perhaps she simply decided the bill was more important than the film) and took off in an airplane, arms full of handbills to pass out, "dashing hither and yon to make speeches."

After the film's release, Fred Astaire recalled receiving a note from Irene "expressing her approval and enthusiasm." Ginger Rogers received no such note.

Today, the Castles are best known from this movie. Thanks to Irene, it is a moderately accurate look at their lives. They "meet cute" (saving a drowning dog at the New Rochelle Yacht Club), and from there the plot takes such liberties with their story as can be expected when needed to move the action along and simplify characters. Certainly, it's more factual than the godawful biopics of movie stars Jean Harlow, Pearl White, and Jeanne Eagels would be. As for their dancing, much of it was more Astaire/Rogers than Castles, with the modern team's emphasis on breaks and fancy footwork. The closest they got to reproducing the Castles' style was in the "Too Much Mustard" number performed at the Café de Paris (though Rogers's showgirl high kicks were unlike Irene's lower, ladylike step).

The Story of Vernon and Irene Castle is an enjoyable little romantic musical: nostalgic and only a bit too long. The film has never really been wholly accepted by Astaire/Rogers fans: it's their only period piece, the first film in which they married, and Fred dies at the end. Though it has not aged well and is not as beloved as earlier Astaire/Rogers films, reviewers at the time loved it: "thoroughly entertaining" (*New York Journal*); "one of the best Astaire-Rogers films" (*Variety*); "at the top of their form all the way" (*New York Times*). It was indeed the last Astaire/Rogers film: at least, till the ill-advised *The Barkleys of Broadway* (1949), which most of their fans refuse to even discuss.

In April 1939, it was decided by a judge that Barbara McLaughlin would be allowed to attend the school of her father's choosing (he chose Lake Forest's prestigious Ferry Hall) and that Irene would not be held in contempt of court because she had kept William with her in L.A. the previous Christmas. Still crying poor, Irene auctioned off her "art treasures" at Grant's Art Galleries in Chicago. "It hurts to sell these pieces," she sighed. "I guess I'm still a bit on the sentimental side, but since Major McLaughlin and I broke up our Lake Forest home, I have no place to keep such things."

In the summer of 1939, Irene danced, partnered by Alex Fisher, at the World's Fair in New York as guest of honor (July 29 was named Irene Castle Day in the hopefully named Court of Peace). Having gotten a taste for the spotlight again, Irene agreed to appear in a play later that summer. She also danced that August at the Hotel Astor for the Dancing Masters of America convention. She and her partner (Fisher again) did an easy swing step she dubbed "The Castle Rock and Roll." Jitterbug dancing, Irene complained, "may be enjoyed by youngsters, but it is neither graceful nor beautiful; certainly not dignified for anyone past their teens."

That August Irene starred with Rex O'Malley in Noël Coward's one-act *Shadow Play* at the Paper Mill Playhouse in Millburn, New Jersey. "You see, I am now free to do as I please," Irene said. "The children are getting bigger, and my animal refuge is in good hands. I think the stage is a much more attractive occupation than cabaret dancing, which would be my only alternative, don't you agree?" "It was her night from the word go," wrote reviewer Vernon Rice. She got an ovation at her first entrance and baskets of flowers at the curtain: "she couldn't have been *that* good," said Rice, who admitted that "when she danced (as she did frequently) it didn't matter what she had said before she started nor how she had said it."

Suddenly, in December 1939, the McLaughlin divorce proceedings were called off. "We are reconciled," Irene said. "They just ceased fighting with each other," says William McLaughlin of his parents' reconciliation. "The joke among the household servants was that whenever Mother needed any money, she invited my father to dinner, and she always came away flush, or a new car appeared in the driveway." Why did they stay, after a fashion, married? "My father adored my mother," says McLaughlin. "He simply did not want to let her go. Even while they were fighting, Dad could not say no to her."

By 1940, Irene was deeply involved with George Enzinger, which led to an association she later sought to downplay: she joined, and spoke for, the isolationist America First Committee. Formed in September 1940 and boasting some eight hundred thousand members, it proposed a strong military defense and staying out of any foreign wars. In addition to isolationist politicians, the committee included top businessmen and literary and artistic figures (including Lillian Gish and novelist Kathleen Norris). Irene, her son says, joined because of her hatred for war and because of George Enzinger's German heritage. She did not want the United States to enter the war, although she hated Hitler's policies. Having friends who were Jewish, gay, or Catholic, she had to detest a man who persecuted members of these groups. "I know she was furious with Roosevelt when he would not allow a boat full of Jewish refugees to land here," says William McLaughlin. But she was not political, and did not delve into deeper issues. "Like so many people, she just didn't consider the things she didn't want to know about," he says. When people asked her why she spent so much time and energy on animals, rather than on orphans or underprivileged children, she sensibly answered that "there were many good Samaritans to worry about children but very few who cared about animals."

"George Enzinger totally captivated Mother," says William McLaughlin. "George spoke German, they got a German cook," he recalls. "They were very much against getting into the war." The only thing about the Nazi regime she found to admire was its animal welfare laws: "It seems property owners were required to care for the wild animals on their land and that there were serious cruelty laws for animal owners," says Irene's son.

"America First remained to the end an uncomfortable alliance of isolationists, pacifists, enemies of England, opponents of Roosevelt and friends of Germany," writes historian David Gordon. It didn't take long for America First to turn ugly, with such virulent anti-Semites as Henry Ford on board (though Ford was booted out after a few months by less extremist members). On September 11, 1941, aviation hero and America Firster Charles Lindbergh gave what would be a life-changing speech, one that also torpedoed America First in the eyes of the press and public. Lindbergh warned Jews that they should avoid war at all costs: they "would be the first to feel its consequences," he said. "Their greatest danger to this country lies in their large ownership and influence in our motion pictures, our press, our radio and our government."

Many members dropped out of America First after this; Irene was not among them. In a stunning example of unfortunate timing, Irene gave a speech at an America First rally at Pittsburgh's Soldiers and Sailors Memorial Hall on the afternoon of December 7, 1941. "She spoke with her usual passion about the folly of the war and the fear that she would lose her son in the conflict that Roosevelt was trying to enter," wrote Thomas J. Fleming in *The New Dealers' War.* While she was onstage, Senator Gerald Nye was informed about the attack on Pearl Harbor; he thought it was a hoax and went on with his own speech. The next day, of course, everything changed. America First shut down within a week of the U.S. entry into World War II, and Irene stayed out of politics for the rest of her life.

CHAPTER FORTY-TWO

"ISN'T OLD AGE AWFUL!"

Marriages, births, and deaths punctuated Irene's life through the 1940s. Her daughter, Barbara, married Irving Kreutz in 1943 at eighteen; they gave Irene four grandchildren (three girls, Mary Nichole, Charlotte, and Elizabeth, and a boy, Gregg). "I think Mother was a bit disappointed none were named after her," says William McLaughlin. "I know she was very pleased when I named my daughter Irene Castle McLaughlin." After Irene's death, William had a son, David Lee, with his second wife, Dorothy, whom he married in 1975.

Irene's brother-in-law Lawrence Grossmith died in 1944 and was buried alongside Vernon and Coralie Blythe Grossmith, who had died in 1928. Irene's life was most affected by the death in late 1944 of Frederic McLaughlin from heart disease. Afterward, Irene moved into a large house with extensive grounds on Old Mill Road in Lake Forest. "Half a mile of driveways, stables for horses, jumping fields," her son recalls. "She enjoyed it, was happy in it, she was very protective of it. One of my more memorable moments was looking out the window one morning when the garbage truck had driven across the corner of the lawn and left deep ruts, and there was Mother standing on the running board of the garbage truck in her nightgown raising hell."

In 1946, Irene finally married George Enzinger, and the two moved to Arkansas. That last marriage was happy, but not placid. "George didn't put up with her," says Irene's son, and Irene thrived on a good fight. "I think she found people who weren't a challenge kind of dull." She spent much of the year in California, though she never did buy a home out there. Her friendship with William Randolph Hearst and Marion Davies continued till Hearst's death in 1951; she spent weeks at a time in Hearst's California estates, San Simeon and Wyntoon.

In 1950, Irene was back in the news, suing CBS and Ed Sullivan for showing clips of her and Vernon dancing from *The Whirl of Life* without her permission; "I think she settled for about $10,000," says her son. "Mother was always suing someone—she made life interesting!" She sued her former neighbors, the Walkers, for custody of a black-and-white mutt named Tippy in 1956. She charged that the Walkers abandoned the dog for two years, then "just snitched him" when they returned. She threatened to take the case to the Supreme Court—the Walkers finally gave up and Tippy remained with Irene.

Irene had an on-again, off-again relationship with her children in her later years. "My mother tried to teach me to dance, and I stomped on her feet so badly she gave that up," laughs her son. He recalls being commandeered into dancing lessons at Arthur Murray's in the 1940s, and Irene beaming in delight when the dance instructor recognized her. But William spent much of the year in military school and "was farmed out somewhere around the country for at least two months of every summer," so his relationship with his mother was somewhat distant and bemused, though he goes out of his way to be fair to her and give her the benefit of every doubt in hindsight.

William and his sister, Barbara, never really compared notes till after Irene's death. When going through their mother's scrapbooks, Barbara—"a big, swashbuckling grande dame"—burst into sobs, confessing to her brother that Irene had always told her Bill was her favorite. Bill in turn told her, "All my life I've heard, 'Why can't you be like Barbara? I never wanted boys.' And we sat down and had a good cry together."

After being widowed by George Enzinger (who died of cancer in 1959), Irene had a rare heart-to-heart with her son, telling him she'd like to get married again. "One of the things she was totally unabashed about was that she and George had had a vigorous sex life right up to the very end. . . . When she said she wanted to get married again, I thought, 'You're not going to find anybody like George!'"

She moved again, to a lovely little hilltop home in Eureka Springs, Arkansas, to be closer to her son, who owned a farm nearby. But Irene was bored. In her sixties, she was still trim, lovely, and fashionable, but she had nothing to do. Never a reader, she was equally unenthralled by television: "The jokes aren't funny, the plots aren't interesting, there's nobody to laugh at." "She just got tired of hanging around," says her son, "that's why she told us, if anything happens, for goodness sake, just let her go."

Irene had a minor stroke in the mid-1950s but recovered quickly. Told by her doctor that she was fine, her children downplayed her condition, which infuriated her: "She insisted that people who'd had strokes were to be pitied, and you brought them gifts and flowers, and she was mad at my sister and I that we didn't just drop everything and come spend a twenty-four-hour vigil."

After years of promises and a false start with *My Husband* in 1919, Irene finally came through with her memoirs, *Castles in the Air*, in 1958. She collaborated with her friends Bob and Wanda Duncan, television and film writers who, oddly, specialized in science fiction. "I just couldn't remember enough," said Irene of the endeavor, "and I'm not a writer." Between the Duncans, Irene's own voluminous scrapbooks, and a tape recorder, the book quickly took shape and was published with a splash of publicity by Doubleday.

Castles in the Air got a good reception, though it hardly broached the best-seller lists. It's a chatty, good-natured book, but of course Irene leaves out more than she tells (as was her right; it was *her* autobiography). She is forthright and sometimes brutally honest about herself, but Vernon comes off as a childlike, irresponsible sprite. She quoted some of his letters, but not enough: while *Castles in the Air* gives a good self-portrait of Irene, one must go back to the 1919 book *My Husband* to find Vernon.

In 1959, Irene made one last stage appearance, as a favor to playwright Nellise Child. It was a Miami community theater production called *Bird of Time*, a comedy set in a club for older people; her costars were aging professionals Dennis King, Isobel Elsom, and Teddy Hart. Irene designed her two costumes, describing herself as "dressed to the teeth."

Still speaking out and campaigning for animal rights in 1960, she told a newspaper reporter, "The older I grow, the happier I am that I've got a project—something to keep my mind off wrinkles, Russians and high blood pressure." Back on topic, she added, "I consider animals just a few notches below human beings, and deserving of the same humane treatment. Yet I find that in hundreds of research centers animals are treated as though they have no emotions and pain responses whatever. Sometimes I fear it's a losing battle," Irene admitted after nearly fifty years of fighting, "but I like to feel I've shamed a few scientists into kinder treatment of experimental animals."

One of her last public appearances came in 1964, when Irene, then seventy-one, was guest of honor at *Ballroom Dance* magazine's annual party at the Plaza Hotel in New York. She looked like a million dollars both at the party and during a *New York Times* interview. She talked about the latest dance craze, the twist ("It's so unbecoming"), her hair ("'Auburn,' they call it on my passport. I've been dyeing it for a long time"), and her age ("I don't feel old. The thing that gives out first is your knees"). But mostly, Irene talked about her animal rights campaigns: "When I die, my gravestone is to say 'humanitarian' instead of 'dancer.' I put it in my will."

Irene's old fan Cecil Beaton encountered her on what would be her last trip to England, in 1968. "It was nice to know that the woman who had created such a personal magic was still in the land of the living," he wrote in his diary, "and that she was enjoying life and able to talk of the future as well as the past." Although Irene, he found, "still had the panache of a star," she was visibly frail and clutched his arm for support, sighing, "Isn't old age awful!"

Most stars of a certain age eventually acquire a helper/fan/spouse/nurse—Norma Desmond's Max in *Sunset Boulevard* is the template. In her later years, Irene had a "Maxine," a woman named Ritchie, "who despised Barbara and I," says William McLaughlin. The situation certainly did not make Irene's relationship with her children easier. When Irene suffered a stroke in mid-January 1969, Ritchie panicked and called William and Barbara: "Mother always said she wanted to be left alone, she didn't want any resuscitation, so we said, 'Don't do anything, we'll be there in the morning.'" But by the time Irene's children arrived, "Ritchie just couldn't stand it anymore, Mother had been transferred to a hospital." She died there, on January 25, at the age of seventy-five. Today she lies alongside Vernon (and near Coralie Blythe and Lawrence Grossmith) in Woodlawn; as she requested, her gravestone reads "Humanitarian." It also reads "Irene Castle McLaughlin Enzinger," a posthumous slap at Robert Treman.

Since the end of the Castles' joint career in late 1915, their names have been largely forgotten, but their legacy as dancers and nightlife pioneers never died. Although Irene violently disapproved of the wild dances of the 1920s and turned up her nose more demurely at the swing and boogie-woogie of the 1930s, she'd had a hand in all of them. Through the twist and frug done at the discotheques of the 1960s, the hustle of the discos in the 1970s, to whatever it is being danced by young couples as you read this, Vernon and Irene Castle are the people who—more than anyone else—

made it possible, made it a rite of passage, to go out to clubs and dance all night. The Castle walk and the maxixe lived and died their natural deaths, as do all dances (and Vernon was wise enough to never predict future dance trends). Whatever kind of music, club, fashion, and dance is popular as I type these words will be outdated by the time you read them: that's the nature of pop culture. But the Castles' influence lives on.

APPENDIX

STAGE AND FILM APPEARANCES OF VERNON AND IRENE CASTLE

All credits below are as originally billed.

About Town (1906)

Herald Square Theater, (opened Aug. 30, 1906; 138 performances)
Produced by Lew M. Fields; Music by Melville Ellis and Raymond Hubbell; Book by Joseph Herbert; Lyrics by Joseph Herbert; Directed by Julian Mitchell; Scenic Design by Arthur Voegtlin, Edward G. Unitt, and Homer Emens; Costume Design by Mrs. Carolyne Siedel and Mrs. Robert Osborn.

Cast: Lew Fields (Baron Blitz, a genteel cab driver); Lawrence Grossmith (The Duke of Slushington, seeking the Golden Girl); Joseph Herbert (Laird O'Findon Haddock, his uncle in more ways than one); Harry Fisher (Bertie, a boulevardier from Pittsburgh); Jack Norworth (Jack Doty, a social arclight); George Beban (Marquis de Rectori, a famous swordsman); Joseph Herbert Jr. (Count Sherri, at the human bench show); Vernon Castle (Viscomte Martino, at the human bench show); Hans Giovanni (Julius, an infant prodigal); Mr. Summers (lackey; waiter); Mr. Dill (watchman); Mr. Dolliver (policeman); Mr. Reinhard (Mr. B. O'Graf, interested in moving pictures); Joseph Schrode (Jenny, a horse; north end); Mr. Dill (Jenny, a horse; south end); Louise Dresser (Gertrude Gibson, a girl with a black-and-white past); Coralie Blythe (Millie Bounder, a society pest); Louise Allen Collier (Lottie Limejuice, just plain chorus); Elita Proctor Otis (Mrs. Frivol, a stage mommer); Edna Wallace Hopper (Fannie Frivol, a prima donna with no voice in the matter); Topsy Siegrist, Gertrude Moyer (Carrie and Sadie, occasional showgirls); Edith Ethel MacBride (Marianne, Gertrude's maid); Marion Whitney, Ray Gilmore, Jane Murray (in the merry); Lillian Raymond (tea maid). With Mae Leslie, Jessie Richmond, Lillian Harris, Viola Hopkins, Bessie Skeer, Lillian Devere, Mattie Chapin, Ruth Fields, Ida Doerge, Loretta MacDonald, Della Connor, Gladys Zell, Mae Murray, May Hickey, Lynn D'Arcy, Fredo Linyard, Elsie Davis.

The Girl behind the Counter (1907–8)

Herald Square Theater (opened Oct. 1, 1907, closed June 6, 1908; 282 performances)

Produced by Sam S. and Lee Shubert, Inc., and Lew M. Fields; Music by Howard Talbot; Book by Leedham Bantock and Arthur Anderson; Freely adapted and reconstructed by Edgar Smith; Lyrics by Arthur Anderson; Produced under the direction of J. C. Huffman and Julian Mitchell; Scenic Design by Arthur Voegtlin; Costume Design by William H. Matthews; Conducted by William E. MacQuinn.

Cast: George Beban (Henri Duval, manager), Vernon Castle (John Blobbs, waiter at the Jardin de Paris; Hon. Aubrey Battersea, friend of Lord Gushington; Hawkins, waiter); Louise Dresser (Millie Mostyn, overlady at The Universal); Connie Ediss (Mrs. Henry Schniff, formerly Mrs. Willoughby); Lotta Faust (Ninette Valois, of the millinery department); Lew M. Fields (Henry Schniff, a soldier of misfortune); Denman Maley (Lord Augustine Gushington, familiarly known as "Gussie"); Ignacio Martinetti (Dudley Cheatham, cashier); May Naudain (Winnie Willoughby, Mrs. Schniff's daughter); Joseph Ratliff (Charley Chetwynd, a self-made young millionaire); Topsy Siegrist (Susie Scraggs, assistant cashier); with Mae Allen (Hattie Tryon, shopper); Nan Brennan (Kitty Ermine, shopper); Gladys Browne (Hope Gonne, saleslady); May Burnett (Lady Stonybroke, patron); Daisy Carson (Tessie Temple, cash girl); Claire Casscles (Dottie Styles, shopper); Sebastian Cassie (Tompkins, waiter); Erminie Clark (Rhode Rimple, cash girl); Vincent Cooper (Ponsonby, a chauffeur); Lillian Devere (Sallie Sample, cash girl); Ida Doerge (Vera Leight, saleslady); Radford D'Orsay (Louis, booth attendant); Richard Fanning (Simkins, waiter); Lottie Fremont (Mrs. Crossley-Shoppington); Jane Grant (Mrs. Mark Down, patron); Josephine Harriman (Winnie Wimple, cash girl); Frances Harris (Mrs. Uneeda Wafer, patron); Viola Hopkins (Mrs. Canby Dunn, patron); Ruth Humphries (The Hon. Eunice Byington, patron); Bettine LeFevre (Rita Ruffhouse, saleslady); Molly Mack (Tessie Tardington, saleslady); Edith Ethel McBride (Mrs. M. Whittington); J. J. McDonald (Francois, booth attendant); Olive Menton (Lady Cheapington-Jones, patron); Ethel Millard (Ida Knowington, saleslady); Charles Mitchell (John L. Fitz Corbet); "Patsy" Mitchell (Maggie of the wrapping department); Hubert Neville (Lord Rumbold, friend of Lord Gushington); Lillian Raymond (Grace Church, saleslady); Elsa Reinhardt (Lottie Munn, shopper); John Reinhardt (Jean, booth attendant); Madge Robertson (Maida Mantell, saleslady); Reina Swift (Willa Ketchum, saleslady); Joseph Torpey (Bliffkins, waiter); Helen Turner (Daisy Lyons, shopper); A. Van Sant (Pierre, booth attendant); Winifred Vaughan (Lady Bargyn-Hunter, patron); Marion Whitney (Trixie Coates, shopper); Dorothy Williams (Mrs. C.O.D. Billings, patron); Anna C. Wilson (Winnie Fellows, saleslady); J. J. Youngs (DeBelleville, porter for Millie Mostyn). With Mitchell & Durante, Beatrice Liddell, Dorothy Marlowe, Elizabeth Hawman, Louise Hawman, Seppie McNeil, Ada Robertson.

The Mimic World (1908)

Moorish Casino Theater (opened July 9, 1908; moved to Grand Opera House, Sept. 28, 1908; closed Oct 3, 1908; 100 performances)

Produced by Sam S. and Lee Shubert, Inc., and Lew M. Fields; Music by Ben M. Jerome and Seymour Furth; Book by Edgar Smith; Lyrics by Edward Madden and Addison Burkhardt; Featuring "Mary Carey" by Benjamin Hapgood Burt and John B. Lovitz; Music for "When Johnny Comes Marching Home (from College) Again" and "Rag Man, Music Man" by Louis A. Hirsch; Music for "My Lady Wine" by Carl Rehman; Orchestra under the direction of Oscar Radin. Staged by J. C. Huffman; Musical numbers conceived and executed by Ned Wayburn. Scenic Design by H. Robert Law and Arthur Voegtlin; Costume Design by William H. Matthews, Madame Freisinger, and Mme. Ripley.

Cast: Walter Lawrence (Prince Danille, husband of the Merry Widow and engaged with her in a fruitless search for their native land of Marscovia); Harry Corson Clark (Lemuel Sawwood, an American businessman who late in life develops sporting tendencies with the usual luck of the beginner); William Bonelli (Jack Witchinghour, a gentleman gambler with a gift of thought-transference); Henry Bergman (Colonel Bridau, a custodian of his family's honor); Arthur Mc-Watters (Kid Burns, an authority on the races and an adept in the art of slinging slang); Bert VonKlein (Georgia Cohan, a Yankee Doodle playwright); Sam Collins (Ludwig Knoedler, a near hero); Sam Sidman (Henry Schniff, a soldier of misfortune); Roy Atwell (Lord Dundreary, a ghost from the humorous past); Frank Hayne (Richard Thief, a worthy gentleman whose fame rests upon his possession of a kleptomaniacal wife); Vernon Castle (Buddicombe, Lord Dundreary's valet); Harry Horsy (Tom Sawwood); Joseph Simons (William Sawwood); Joseph Chaille (Captain Chapmars, a Parisian); Bert French (Henri Hontmarte, of the Latin Quarter); Hark Harrison (Pierre Ambigu, a French actor); Louis Franklyn (Victor, headwaiter at La Cascade); Frank Thomas (Arretta, a gendarme; Evans, a butler); George C. Pierce (Baron Savoirgaire, a diplomat); Oscar Lauman (Prince Distingus, another); Irene Bentley (Sonia, formerly the Merry Widow, whose second matrimonial adventure is marred by her husband's habit of generalizing his affections); Grace Tyson (Mrs. Richard Thief, whose kleptomaniacal tendencies contribute materially to the family bankroll); Josie Sadler (Miss Tiny Daly, of Chicago); Louise DeRigney, Ada Gordon, Marjorie Cortland (members of the

Man Haters' Association); Doris Cameron (Mrs. Guilford, a society leader); Lotta Faust (Mademoiselle Ou La La; Phoebe Snow); Seymour Felix (George Cohan, a pop-up clip-up); Charles King (Artie, an American college chap); Theresa Bercien (Jacqueline, a female coacher); Gladys Claire (Polly of the circus; Miss Hook of Holland, Burlesque Specialty); Dorothy Davidson (Flo Flo); Miss V. Earl, Miss E. Franklin, Miss L. Franklin, Miss P. Franklin, Miss H. Pillard (American Daisies); Elizabeth Gardner (Lu Lu); Lillian Graham (Ko Ko); Marian Hartman (Jo Jo); Mazie King (Bessie Clayton); Nellie King (Molly Carey); Hattie Lorraine (Frou Frou); Gladys Moore (Salome; American Daisy); Grace Shannon (Ninette, a gay Parisienne); Charles Sharp (Mr. Disch, Woman Hater, of the Marsovian Embassy); Bessie Stevens (Goo Goo); Grace Van Studdiford (Ho Ho); Ellen Worth (Coo Coo).

The Midnight Sons (1909–10)

Broadway Theater (opened May 22, 1909; 257 performances)
Produced by Lew M. Fields; Music by Raymond Hubbell; Lyrics by George V. Hobart; Book by Glen MacDonough; Orchestrations by Frank Saddler.
Cast: George A. Schiller (Senator Constant Noyes); Joseph M. Ratliff (Jack, who plays at art); Harry Fisher (Dick, who toys with the ticker); Denman Maley (Harry, who trifles with the stage); Fritz Williams (Tom, who fusses with sports); Lotta Faust (Merri Murray, America's leading chorus lady); Norma Brown (Rose Raglan, from the country); Linden Beckwith (Claire Voyant, a scientific fortune teller); George W. Monroe (Pansy Burns, who won't cook for everybody); Lillian Lee (Lily Burns, who won't cook for anybody); Taylor Holmes (A. Case Daly, a wine agent); Vernon Castle (Souseberry Lushmore, in search of his home); Blanche Sherwood (Beatrice Ballast, a theater patron); Gladys Moore (Lady Fire-Fly); Maybelle Meeker (Mlle. DeLeon); Berchard Dickerson (The Cynical Owl); Johnnie Hines (The Baby Owl); Nan J. Brennan, Helen Turner, Dessa Gibson (shoe store patrons); Florence Cable (Lotta Rackett, who gives a box party); Elsa Reinhardt (Louise Louder, her guest); Blanche Ring (Carrie Margin). With Elizabeth Hawman, Louise Hawman, Beatrice Liddell, Dorothy Marlowe, Seppie McNeil, Ada Robertson, Margaret Hawman, Daisy Carson, Grace Heckler, Alice Kelly, Hazel Allen, Clara Lloyd, Sara Luce, Adela la Pierre, Cassie Meade, Josephine Kernell.

Old Dutch (1909–10)

Herald Square Theater (opened Nov. 22, 1909; 88 performances)
Produced by Messrs. Shubert (Lee and J. J.) and Lew M. Fields; Music by

Victor Herbert; Book by Edgar Smith; Lyrics by George V. Hobart; Staged by Ned Wayburn; Musical Director, Lou F. Gottschalk.

Cast: Lew M. Fields (Ludwig Streusand, absentminded inventor); Alice Dovey (Liza Streusand, his daughter); John E. Henshaw (Leopold Mueller, an adventurer); Adah Lewis (Alma Villianyi, a Viennese music hall singer); Charles Judels (Joseph Cusinier, proprietor of the Hotel Schoenwald); John Bunny (Franz von Bomberg, a wealthy Viennese manufacturer); Eva Davenport (Rosa von Bomberg, his wife); William Raymond (Alfred von Bomberg, his son); Vernon Castle (Hon. Algernon Clymber, in the Tyrol for his health); Mack Johnston (Jean, head porter at the Hotel Schoenwald); Jane Grover, Marion Whitney, Billee Cuppia, Josephine Karlin, Elsie LaBoy, Marise Naughton (sisters of Algernon Clymber); George Lynch, Harry Harrington, Thomas McCormick, Wood Gobel, Fred Roberts, Joseph Norwich (brother officers of Alfred von Bomberg); May Willard, Ruth Rider (maids at the Hotel Schoenwald); Gertrude Grant (Gretchen); Frank Griffith (Grenwald, a mountain guide); Victor Hyde (messenger; Alan); George Dowling, Joseph Torpey (gendarmes); Nettie Hyde (Olga); Rhea Hess (Fleaurette); Hannah Hess (Babette); Robert Fuehrer (Little Hans); Helen Hayes (Little Mime); Lightning Charlie (as himself). With Lavinia Mason, Mazie Kimball, Isabelle Jason, Elsie Raymond, Lillian Foster, Dolly Filly, Charlotte Cushman, Rose Monroe, Opal Scott, Jeanne Crane, Libbian Diamond, Lotta Morse, Blanche Brooks, Beatrice Priest, Mabel Barnes, Edna Dodsworth, Layne Donaldson, Natalie Dare, Evelyn Martin, Sue Duval, Gwenn Sears, Mina Davenport, Miriam Butler, Harry Devine, John Donnelly, Henry Detloff, Louis Boyle, Franks Griffiths, Louis Finnerty, Albert Aporta, Arthur Fisher, Henry Carmack, George Howe, William Whittaker, Robert O'Neill, Paul Moore, Frank Hallam, Maude Kimball.

The Summer Widowers (1910)

Broadway Theater (opened June 4, 1910; closed Oct. 1, 1910; 140 performances)
Produced by Lew M. Fields; Music by A. Baldwin Sloane; Written by Glen MacDonough; Directed by Ned Wayburn; Scenic Equipment by Arthur Voegtlin; Costume Director, Melville Ellis.

Cast: Lew M. Fields (Otto Ott, a retired German druggist); Walter Percival (Max Ott, his romantic son); Willis P. Sweatnam (William Alfred Henry George, colored janitor of the St. Vitus Court); Charles Judels (Salve di Mora, Otto's most intimate friend, in the grocery and delicatessen line); Fritz Williams (Guy Stringer, an automobile agent); Jack Henderson (Hunter Lamb, a broker); Paul Nicholson (Conwell Swift, press agent for the Folderol Gardens); William Burress (Capt. Kodak, an Atlantic City photographer); Will Archie (Pinkie Doolittle, Mrs. McGuirk's little boy); Eugene O'Rourke (Sandy Beach, a bathing master); Burt Green (Tom Noyes, a pianist); Vernon Castle (Oxford Tighe, American agent for "Eyzzzsst," the new Hungarian Cordial); Maitland Davies (Sammy Square, manager of the Folderol Gardens); Irene Franklin (Claribel Clews, a perfect lady detective); Adah Lewis (Mrs. Guinivere McGuirk, Celia Carew's elder sister, once widowed, twice divorced, but still hopeful); Alice Dovey (Celia Carew, Otto Ott's prospective daughter-in-law); Maud Lambert (Fritzi Fluff, an absent minded prima donna); Angie Norton (Virginia Ham, her loyal but candid chorus-girl friend); Helen Hayes (Psyche Finnegan, Pinkie's playmate); Jane Grover (Mrs. Conwell Swift); Jeanne Lansford (Mrs. Hunter Lamb); Mabel Weeks (Mrs. Guy Stringer); Marion Whitney (Gertie Gherkin); Billee Cuppia (Winnie Wildwaves). With Marise Naughton, Estelle Richmond, Emily Monte, Frances Harris, Helen Adair, May Willard, Louise Gale, Jessie Crane, Lillian West, Minnie Monroe, Minna Davenport, Frances Shannon, Ethel Fleming, Ninon DuBal, Beatrice Priest, Inez Borrero, Caroline Wade, Mabel Delmar, Stacia Leslie, Adele LaPierre, Jean Crane, Rose Monroe, Mae Taylor, Libbian Diamond, Morrie Madison, Adelaide Mason, Ella Warner, Frances Folsom, Frances Leslie, Vivian Rogers, Mazie Kimball, Polly Allison, Isabelle Jason, Ethel Sinclair, Dorothy Godfrey, Edna Snyder, Cecilia Pink, Henry Detloff, Thos. Reynolds, Robert O'Neill, Douglass Williams, Ralph Whiting, William Nan, Edward McNulty, William Meyer, Fred Bates, Fred Roberts, George Lynch, Robert Waite, Thomas Everett, Russell Summerville, Fred Hazelwood, Lew Finnerty, Duke Rogers, Frank Sterling, Ralph O'Reilly, Harry Nelson, Martin Hickey, Wood Goebel, Edward Weinberg, Clarence Lutz, Harry Acheson, Eddie Simms, Fred DuBall, John Cook, Arthur Gros, Joe Mariott, Harry Neimann, Ralph Rose.

The Hen-Pecks (1911)

Broadway Theater (opened Feb. 4, 1911; closed June 1911; 137 performances)

Produced by Lew M. Fields; Music by A. Baldwin Sloane; Book by Glen MacDonough; Lyrics by E. Ray Goetz; Staged by Ned Wayburn; Scenic Equipment by Arthur Voegtlin.

Cast: Sam Watson (Silas, a farmhand); Gertrude Quinlan (Henoria Peck, Henry Peck's oldest daughter, brought up in the old-fashioned way by her mother); Lillian Lee (Henrietta Peck, Henry's wife); Joseph Keno (Hiram, a farmhand); Bert Leslie (Dr. I. Stall, Cranberry Cove's leading horse doctor); Stephen Maley (Henderson Peck, Henry's son, who after a correspondence course at an engineering institute is going to New York to help solve the traffic problem); Edith Frost (Verbena Peck, Henderson's newly wedded country bride); Vernon Castle (Zowie, the Monarch of Mystery, the third and last attraction of the season at the Cove's

Temple of Amusement, Melodeon Hall); Lillian Rice (Pansy Marshmallow); Angie Wiemars (Weenie Wistaria); Lew M. Fields (Henry Peck, a farmer, formerly
the village barber); Frank Whitman (Rufe, the village fiddler); Ethel Johnson
(Henolia Peck, Henry's second daughter, brought up in the new-fashioned way by
her father, just home from Swellsley College); Laurance Wheat (Ayer Castle, a
city real estate promoter who has decided to turn Cranberry Cove into the summer metropolis of Briny Bluff); Blossom Seeley (Henella Peck, Henry's youngest
daughter, who has run away to New York to bring herself up in the chorus under
the name of Carmencita Tobasco); Fred Roberts, Harry Pond (Montgomery
Muggs and Launcelot Gaggs, of the Jolly Embalmers); Joseph Kane (Ravioli, a
boss barber); Nan Brennan (Mrs. Murgatroyd, Clarence's owner); Hazel Allen
(Major Manly, of the Salvation Army); Dolly Filley (Ermengarde, with the Lilli-
putian voice); Virgil Bennett (Casey Jones, a policeman); Mazie King (Mlle.
Twinkle Toes, one of the wedding dinner entertainers). With Harriet Leidy, Mae
Hopkins, Edith Offutt, Virginia Gunther, Emily Monte, May Willard, Marion
Whitney, Billee Cuppia, Lee Wyant, Elsa Reinhardt, Louise Gale, Minnie Mon-
roe, Helen Todd, Lillian West, Ethel Fleming, Grace West, Gertrude Barnard,
Daisy Delmar, Flo May, Marion Scott, Olive Carr, Adelaide Mason, Hazel Rose-
wood, Dorothy Sherer, Ruth Pecan, Edith Warren, Ethel Wheeler, Marion Vose,
Mabel D'Elmar, James Simpson, Fred Sidney, James Barry, Alex Gibson, Martin
Hickey, Russell Griswold, Harry Wilcox, Wood Goebel, Fred Hazelwood, Ed-
ward McNulty, Wilfred Mills, Robert Bingham, Burton Varden, Frank Stirling.

The Sunshine Girl (1913)

Knickerbocker Theater (opened Feb. 3, 1913; closed Sept. 20, 1913; 181
performances)

Produced by Charles Frohman; Music by Paul A. Rubens; Book by Cecil
Raleigh and Paul A. Rubens.

Cast: Dorothy Berry (Lily, Head of Department); Vernon Castle (Lord Bicester, known as Bingo, a young stockbroker); Joseph Cawthorn (Schlump, an
ex-four-wheeler driver); Eva Davenport (Mrs. Blacker, Schlump's Wife, calling
herself by her maiden name); Flossie Deshon (Kate, Head of Department); Dick-
son Elliott (Boggs, Photographer); William T. Francis Jr., Lew Leroy (Policemen);
Russell Griswold (Williams, Solicitor); Flossie Hope (Marie Silvaine, Head of
the Packing Department); Irene Hopping (Sybil, Head of Department); J. J. Hor-
witz (Stepnyak, Manager of the Continental Department); Constance Hunt (Violet, Head of Department); Owen Jones, Charles McGee (Flunkeys); Eileen Ke-
arney (Lady Rosabelle Merrydew, Lord Bicester's Fiancee); Harry Law (Swell);

Tom Lewis (Steve Daly, an American in the advertising department); Alan Mudie (Vernon Blundell); E. S. Powell Hudson (Chief Manager of the Works at Soaptown); Eleanor Rasmussen (Alice, Head of Department); Julia Sanderson (Dora Dale); Edwin Stone (Wears, Manager of the Colonial Department); Ruth Thorpe (Lady Mary); Joseph V. Tullar (Dever, Manager of the Manufacturing Department); Edward C. Yeager (Whitney, Manager of the British Department).

Mr. and Mrs. Castle before the Camera (1914)

Producer: Mortimer Henry Singer.
Cast: Mr. and Mrs. Vernon Castle.

Watch Your Step (1914–15)

New Amsterdam Theater (opened Dec. 8, 1914; closed June 1915; 175 performances)

Produced by Charles Dillingham; Music by Irving Berlin; Lyrics by Irving Berlin; Book by Harry B. Smith; Staged by R. H. Burnside; Musical Director, C. DeWitt Coolman; Costume Design by Helen Dryden; Scenic Design by Helen Dryden and Robert McQuinn.

Cast: Sam Burbank (Willie Steele); William J. Halligan (Silas Flint); Justine Johnstone (Estelle); Harry Kelly (Ebenezer Hardacre); Al Holbrook (Howe Strange); Elizabeth Murray (Birdie O'Brien); Sallie Fisher (Ernesta Hardacre); Vernon Castle (Joseph Lilyburn); Charles King (Algie Cuffs); Dama Sykes (Iona Ford); Elizabeth Brice (Stella Spark); Mrs. Vernon Castle (Mrs. Vernon Castle); Harriet Leidy (Anne Marshall); Harry Ellis (The Ghost of Verdi); Frank Tinney (A Carriage Caller at the Opera; A Pullman Porter; A Coat Room Boy); Irving J. Carpenter (Denny); Gus Minton (Josiah Jay); Dorothy Morosco (Samantha Jay); C. L. Kelley (The Man in Box 51); Julia Beaubien (Mrs. Swift); Mabel Callahan (Mrs. Bright); Rokey Johnson (A Professional Escort); Natalie Saymore (Mrs. Gay), Max Scheck (An Old Chappy); Terry Starwer (An Impressario); Charles Swan (A Young Chappy); Ethel Sykes (Mrs. Climber); Gladys Sykes (Mrs. Smart). Chorus: John Q. Adams, Earl Amos, M. G. Avery, Dorothy Banks, Helen Barnes, C. T. Beanie, Leila Benton, Olive Birt, James Black, Christyne Bowers, Barbara Clark, Marie Dana, Ethel Davies, Rose Davies, Gwendoline DeBraw, Libbian Diamond, Richard Dicksinson, Marcelle Earl, Joseph Hadley, Flo Hart, Ethel Hobart, Herbert Hoey, Jesse Holbrook, W. M. Holbrook, Maud Hoer, May Homer, Esther Lee, Rose Leslie, Phyllis Munday, Billie Norton, Violet Pardue, Alleyne Pickard, Nancy Poole, Fred Rockwell, Myrtle Ross, Virginia Shelby, Annette Simonet, Trixie Smith, Paula Sterling, Edna Stillwell, Violet Sydney, Peggy Trevor, Marie Walsh, Bunny Wendell.

The Whirl of Life (1915)

Cort Film Corp. Director: Oliver D. Bailey; Producer: Gerald F. Bacon; Writers: Catherine Carr, Vernon Castle; Photography: Eugene J. Cugnet. 6 reels. Release date: Oct. 1915.

Cast: Kate Blancke (Mrs. Foote); William Carleton Sr. (Mr. Foote); Irene Castle (Herself); Vernon Castle (Himself); Edward Cort (The gangster); Arthur Stanford (John Crosby); with Walter Asch, John Cort, Ruth Gordon.

Patria (1916)

International Film Service, Inc. Directed by Leopold Wharton (episodes 1–10); Theodore Wharton (episodes 1–10); Jacques Jaccard (episodes 11–15). Scenario: J. B. Clymer, Charles W. Goddard; From the novel *The Last of the Fighting Channings*, by Louis Joseph Vance.

Episode 1: *The Last of the Fighting Channons.* Episode 2: *Treasure.* Episode 3: *Winged Millions.* Episode 4: *Double Crossed.* Episode 5: *The Island God Forgot.* Episode 6: *Alias Nemesis.* Episode 7: *Red Dawn.* Episode 8: *Red Night.* Episode 9: *Cat's Paw and Scapegoat.* Episode 10: *War in the Dooryard.* Episode 11: *Sunset Falls.* Episode 12: *Peace on the Border.* Episode 13: *The Wings of Death.* Episode 14: *The Border Peril.* Episode 15: *For the Flag.*

Cast: Irene Castle (Patria/Elaine); Warner Oland (Baron Huroki); Milton Sills (Capt. Donald Parr); Marie Walcamp (Bess Morgan); George Majeroni (Senor de Lima); Allan Murnane (Rodney Wrenn); Dorothy Green (Fanny Adair). With Floyd Buckley, Wallace Beery, Nigel Barrie, Charles Brinley, Jack Holt, George Lessey, M. W. Rale, Leroy Baker, Rudolph Valentino, F.W. Stewart, Elsie Baker, Howard Cody, Frank Honda, Sojin, Robin H. Townley.

Sylvia of the Secret Service (1917)

Astra Film Corp./Pathé. Director: George Fitzmaurice; Writer: Philip Bartholomae; Story: Joseph Trant; Photography: Arthur C. Miller. Release date: Nov. 25, 1917.

Cast: Irene Castle (Sylvia Carroll); J. H. Gilmour (Van Brunn); Elliott Dexter (Curtis Prescott); Suzanne Willa (Fay Walling); J. W. Percival (Hemming). With Eric Von Stroheim.

Stranded in Arcady (1917)

Astra Film Corp./Pathé. Director: Frank Crane; Writer: Philip Bartholomae; Based on the novel *Stranded in Arcady*, by Francis Lynde. 5 reels. Release date: Oct. 14, 1917.

Cast: Mrs. Vernon Castle (Lucy Millington); Elliott Dexter (Donald Prime); Pell Trenton (Edward Girder); Georgio Majeroni (Edward Blandish).

The Mark of Cain (1917)

Astra Film Corp./Pathé. Director: George Fitzmaurice; Writer: Philip Bartholomae; Story: Carolyn Wells; Photography: Arthur C. Miller. Release date: Nov. 4, 1917.

Cast: Mrs. Vernon Castle (Alice); Antonio Moreno (Kane Langdon); J. H. Gilmour (Trowbridge); Elinor Black (Housekeeper); John Sainpolis (Judge Hoyt).

Miss 1917 (1917)

Century Theater (opened Nov. 5, 1917; closed Jan. 5, 1918; 72 performances)

Produced by Charles Dillingham, Florenz Zeigfeld Jr.; Music by Victor Herbert, Jerome Kern; Book and lyrics by Guy Bolton, P.G. Wodehouse; Musical Director, Robert Hood Bowers; Staged by Ned Wayburn; Choreographed by Adolph Bohm; Sceneic Design by Joseph Urban; Costumes by Paul Chaflin, Dazian, Faibsey, Lucile, Cora MacGeachy, Phelps, Willy Pogany, Max Weldy.

Cast (in order of appearance): Andrew Tombes, Arthur Cunningham, Vivienne Segal, Cecil Lean, Harry Kelly, Leavitt James, Joseph Sparks, Eugene Revere, Dorothy Klewer, Zitelka Dolores, Yvonne Shelton, Olive Osborne, George White, Marion Davies, Vera Maxwell, Emma Haig, Elizabeth Brice, Charles King, Effie Allen, Albertine Marlowe, Ann Pennington, Cleo Mayfield, Bessie McCoy Davis, Bert Savoy, Jay Brennan, Gus Van, Joe Schenck, Peggy Hopkins, Tot Qualters, Adolf Bolm, Flore Revalles, Marshall Hall, Ivan Tarasov, Alexander Umanski, Stephen O'Rourke, Kathryn Perry, May Leslie, Lilyan Tashman, Lew M. Fields, Paul Briant, William Briant, Tortola Valencia, Irene Castle, Margaret Morris, Cecile Markle, Lillian McKenzie, Semone D'Herlys, Mlle. Phyllis, Mlle. Mawresette, Gladys Loftus, Elizabeth Morton, Irene Hayes. With Flo Hart, Peggy Dana, May Borden, Betty Hamilton, Pollie Bowman, Diana Allen, Agnes Jepson, Anna Stone, Betty Hale, Geraldine Alexander, Amelia Johnson, Evengeline Marshalck, Lois Leigh, Gladys Coburn, Juana Sheppard, Frank Leonard, James Bradley, Gus Stevenson, Ray Klages, Leonard Howard, Paul M. Bell, William Fuller, Louis Baum, Kitty Boylan, Rene Braham, Marie Frawley, Myrtle King, Ethel Rough, Winnie Ward, May Irving, Irene Spencer, Helen Mooney, Rosella Myers, Edith Warren, Emeline Gorman, Pearl Franklin, Cecilia Cullen, Lottie Franklin, Alma Braham, Martha Wood, Mildred Shelly, Minnie Harrison, Margie Bell, Vivian Morrison, Ruth Heil, Ruby Wilbur, Mike Bell, Dan Gordon, James Quinn, Jack Lynch, Walter Baker, James Marr, Frank Sharp, Mark White, Fred Duhall, Frank Duball, Charles Root, Joe Knoffer, Charles Jones, Lawrence Clark,

John Parks, Mack Williams, William Shelly, Emmet Grant, John Warren, Nicholas Kane, Emil Barth, Addison Mead, Murray Starr, Arthur Elson.

Vengeance Is Mine (1917)

Astra Film Corp./Pathé. Director: Frank Crane; Producer: George Fitzmaurice; Writer: Howard Irving Young; Based on the novel *Vengeance Is Mine*, by John A. Moroso; Photography: Harry Wood. 5 reels. Release date: Dec. 16, 1917.

Cast: Irene Castle (Paula Farrington); Frank Sheridan (Peter Van Brunt); Helene Chadwick (Marion De Long); Elliott Dexter (Dr. Smith). With Edward Hoyt, Reginald Mason, Ethel Grey Terry, Frank Monroe, Julia Stewart, Fred Teden.

Convict 993 (1918)

Astra Film Corp./Pathé. Director: William Parke; Writer: Wallace C. Clifton; Photography: Arthur C. Miller. 5 reels. Release date: Jan. 6, 1918.

Cast: Irene Castle (Roslyn Ayre); Warner Oland (Dan Mallory); Helen Chadwick (Neva Stokes); Harry Benham (Rodney Travers); J. H. Gilmore (Bob Ainslee); Paul Everton (Jim Morton); Bert Starkey (Bill Avery); Ethyle Cook (Stella Preston).

The Hillcrest Mystery (1918)

Astra Film Corp./Pathé. Director: George Fitzmaurice; Writer: Ouida Bergère; Photography: Arthur C. Miller; Art Direction: Hy Mayer. 5 reels. Release date: March 24, 1918.

Cast: Irene Castle (Marion Sterling); J. H. Gilmour (Thomas Sterling); Ralph Kellard (Gordon Brett); Wyndham Standing (Hugo Smith).

The Mysterious Client (1918)

Astra Film Corp./Pathé. Director: Fred E. Wright; Writer: Roy Somerville; Story: Charles Dazey; Photography: Albert Richard. 5 reels. Release date: May 19, 1918.

Cast: Irene Castle (Jeanne Darcy); Milton Sills (Harry Nelson); Warner Oland (Boris Norjunov); Caesare Gravina (Tony Cavallo).

The First Law (1918)

Astra Film Corp./Pathé. Director: Lawrence McGill; Writer: Roy Sommerville; Based on the novel *The First Law*, by Gilson Willets. 5 reels. Release date: July 28, 1918.

Cast: Irene Castle (Norma Webb); Antonio Moreno (Hugh Godwin); J. H. Gilmour (Dr. Webb); Marguerite Snow (Madeleine); Edward J. Connelly (Detective).

The Girl from Bohemia (1918)

Astra Film Corp./Pathé. Director: Lawrence B. McGill; Writer: Lois Zellner. 5 reels. Release date: Aug. 25, 1918.

Cast: Irene Castle (Alice Paige). With Edward Cecil, Violet Axzelle.

The Common Cause (1919)

Blackton Productions, Inc./Vitagraph Co. of America. Director: J. Stuart Blackton; Producers: Albert E. Smith; J. Stuart Blackton; Writer: Anthony Paul Kelly. 7 reels. Release date: Jan. 5, 1919.

Cast: Effie Shannon (Belgium); Irene Castle (France); Violet Heming (Britannia); Julia Arthur (Italy); Marjorie Rambeau (Columbia); Herbert Rawlinson (Orrin Palmer); Sylvia Breamer (Helene Palmer); Huntley Gordon (Edward Wadsworth); Lawrence Grossmith (Tommy Atkins); Charles Blackton, Violet Blackton (Two little Belgian refugees); Philip Van Loan (The poilu); Mlle. Marcel (A French Girl); Louis Dean (German general).

The Firing Line (1919)

Famous Players–Lasky Corp./A Paramount-Artcraft Special. Director: Charles Maigne; Ass't. Director: Robert Schable; Producer: Adolph Zukor; Writer: Clara Beranger; Photography: Al Liguori. Based on the novel *The Firing Line,* by Robert W. Chambers. 6 reels. Release date: July 6, 1919.

Cast: Irene Castle (Sheila Cardross); Isabelle West (Mrs. Cardross); May Kitson (Constance Paliser); Anne Cornwall (Cecile Cardross); Gladys Coburn (Jessie Bradley); R. Vernon Steele (John Garret "Garry" Hamil III); David Powell (Louis Malcourt); J. H. Gilmore (Neville Cardross); Frank Losee (James Wayward); Rudolph de Cordova, Charles Craig, and Philip S. Rice (Faithful three); Robert Schable (William Portlaw); Jane Warrington (Virginia Suydam); Shaw Lovett (Gary Cardross).

The Invisible Bond (1919)

Famous Players–Lasky Corp./Paramount-Artcraft Pictures. Director: Charles Maigne; Ass't. Director: A. Dorris; Producer: Adolph Zukor; Writer: Charles Maigne; based on the novel *The See-Saw: A Story of To-Day,* by Sophie Kerr; Photography: F. Dean. 5 reels. Release date: Nov. 23, 1919.

Cast: Irene Castle (Marcia Crossey); Huntley Gordon (Harleth Crossey); Claire Adams (Leila Templeton); Fleming Ward (Curtis Jennings); George Majeroni (Wasson); Helen Green (Imogene); Ida Waterman (Mrs. Crossey); Warburton Gamble (Otis Vale).

The Amateur Wife (1920)

Famous Players–Lasky Corp./Paramount-Artcraft Pictures. Director: Edward Dillon; Producer: Adolph Zukor; Writer: Jane Murfin; based on the short story "Miss Antique," by Nalbro Bartley; Photography: Hal Young; Art Direction: Charles Osborn Seessel. 6 reels. Release date: Feb. 22, 1920.

Cast: Irene Castle (Justine Spencer); William P. Carleton (Cosmo Spotiswood); Arthur Rankin (Billy Ferris); S. J. Warrington (Randolph Ferguson); A. Saskin (Oliver Ferris); Augusta Anderson (Dodo Spencer); Mrs. Charles Dewey (Loti); Ellen Olson (Sara).

French Heels (1922)

Holtre Productions/W. W. Hodkinson Corp. Director: Edwin L. Hollywood; Writer: Eve Unsell; Based on the short story "Knots and Windshakes," by Clarence Budington Kelland; Photography: Robert A. Stuart, William McCoy. 7 reels. Release date: Jan. 29, 1922.

Cast: Irene Castle (Palma May); Ward Crane (Lieut. John Tabor); Charles Gerard (Keith Merwyn); Howard Truesdale (Jarvis Tabor); Tom Murray (Camp foreman).

No Trespassing (1922)

Holtre Productions/W. W. Hodkinson Corp. Director: Edwin L. Hollywood; Writer: Howard Irving Young; Based on the novel *The Rise of Roscoe Paine*, by Joseph Crosby Lincoln; Photography: Robert A. Stuart; Art Direction: E. Douglas Bingham. 7 reels. Release date: June 11, 1922.

Cast: Irene Castle (Mabel Colton); Howard Truesdale (James Colton); Emily Fitzroy (Mrs. James Colton); Ward Crane (Roscoe Paine); Eleanor Barry (Mrs. Paine); Blanche Frederici (Dorinda); Charles Eldridge (Lute); Leslie Stowe (Captain Dean); Betty Bouton (Nellie Dean); Al Roscoe (Victor Carver); Harry Fisher (Simeon Eldridge); George Pauncefort (George Davis).

Slim Shoulders (1922)

Tilford Cinema Studios/W. W. Hodkinson Corp. Director: Alan Crosland;

Writers: Lawrence McCloskey, Charles K. Harris; Photography: George Folsey. 6 reels. Release date: Sept. 24, 1922.

Cast: Irene Castle (Naomi Warren); Rod La Rocque (Richard Langden); Anders Randolph (Edward Langden); Warren Cook (John Clinton Warren); Mario Carillo (Count Giulo Morranni); Marie Burke (Mrs. Warren).

Broadway after Dark (1924)

Warner Brothers Pictures. Director: Monta Bell; Ass't. Director: Sandy Roth; Writer: Douglas Doty; Based on the play *Broadway after Dark*, by Owen Davis; Photography: Charles Van Enger. 7 reels. Release date: May 31, 1924.

Cast: Adolphe Menjou (Ralph Norton); Norma Shearer (Rose Dulane); Anna Q. Nilsson (Helen Tremaine); Edward Burns (Jack Devlin); Carmel Myers (Lenore Vance); Vera Lewis (Mrs. Smith); Willard Louis (Slim Scott); Mervyn LeRoy (Carl Fisher); Jimmy Quinn (Ed Fisher); Edgar Norton (The Old Actor); Gladys Tennyson (Vera); Ethel Miller (The Chorus Girl); Otto Hoffman (Norton's valet); Lew Harvey (Tom Devery); Michael Dark (George Vance). With cameo appearances by Fred Stone, Dorothy Stone, Mary Eaton, Raymond Hitchcock, Elsie Ferguson, Florence Moore, James J. Corbett, John Steel, Frank Tinney, Paul Whiteman, Irene Castle, Buster West.

The Story of Vernon and Irene Castle (1939)

RKO. Director: H. C. Potter; Producer: George Haight; Production Manager: Pandro S. Berman; Writers: Irene Castle, Oscar Hammerstein II, Dorothy Yost, Richard Sherman; Cinematographer: Robert De Grasse; Editor: William Hamilton; Art Director: Van Nest Polglase; Costumer Designers: Walter Plunkett, Edward Stevenson, Irene Castle; Makeup: Mel Burns; Sound: Richard Van Hessen; Special Effects: Vernon L. Walker; Dance Director: Hermes Pan. Release date: May 29, 1939.

Cast: Fred Astaire (Vernon Castle); Ginger Rogers (Irene Castle); Edna May Oliver (Maggie Sutton); Walter Brennan (Walter Ash); Lew Fields (himself); Etienne Giradot (Papa Aubel); Janet Beecher (Mrs. Foote); Rolfe Sedan (Emil Aubel); Leonid Kinskey (artist); Robert Strange (Dr. Hubert Foote); Douglas Walton (student pilot); Clarence Derwent (Papa Louis); Sonny Lamont (Charlie, the tap dancer); Frances Mercer (Claire Ford); Victor Varconi (Grand Duke); Douglas MacBride (hotel manager); Brooks Benedict (stockbroker); Eugene Borden (Frenchman); Lynton Brent (mechanic); Mary Brodel, Marge Champion, Eleanor Hansen, Ethel Haworth (Irene's girlfriends); Don Brodie, Frank Mills (benefit stage managers); Tom Chatterton (benefit announcer); Armand Cortes (benefit wardrobe man); Adrienne D'Ambricourt (French landlady); Roy D'Arcy (actor in *Patria*); Hal K. Dawson (man in balcony); Elspeth Dudgeon (Lady Bolton); Dick Elliott (train conductor); Frank Faylen, Steve Pendleton (adjutants); Jack George (Paris orchestra conductor); Wesley Giraud, Joe Poloski (newsboys); Russell Hicks (colonel); Leyland Hodgson (British sergeant); George Irving (colonel's aide); Tiny Jones (revolving door lady); Jacques Lory (French cab driver); David McDonald, John Meredith (Army pilots); Louis Mercier (French singer); Bruce Mitchell (movie director); Leonard Mudie (British officer); Emmett O'Brien (benefit performer); Milton Owen (recruiter); Fred Sweeney (streetcar conductor); Lillian Yardo (Mary, Claire's maid). With Buzz Barton, Max Barwyn, Joe Bordeaux, Neal Burns, Willis Clare, Frank Coghlin Jr., James Conaty, Bill Franey, Jack Gargan, Neal Hart, Dorothy Lovett, Max Lucke, Hugh McArthur, Edmund Mortimer, Esther Muir, Frank O'Connor, Bill Patton, Jack Perrin, Jack Richardson, Jean Sablon, Kay Sutton, D. H. Turner, Ellinor Vanderveer, Theodore von Eltz, Allen Wood, William Worthington.

Notes

Many quotes from Irene Castle can be found in similar or identical wording in three sets of memoirs she wrote: "My Memories of Vernon Castle" (*Everybody's Magazine*, Nov. 1918–Mar. 1919), *My Husband* (New York: Charles Scribner's Sons, 1919), and *Castles in the Air* (Garden City, N.Y.: Doubleday, 1958). I have noted the source from which I took the quote, but it may appear in any or all of the above. Irene's personal scrapbooks contain interviews, articles, and reviews wherein the newspaper's name and/or date is cut off or illegible. I have regretfully noted those as unidentified. Irene's scrapbooks are available at the New York Public Library, Lincoln Center (NYPL).

Introduction

All quotes and facts from *Variety*, Dec. 19, 1913, Dec. 26, 1913, Jan. 2, 1914; and *New York Times*, Jan. 1, 1914.

1. Take Me Back to Dear Old Blighty

5 "My grandfather was a businessman": Christopher Blyth to author, July 12, 2006
5 "when he wouldn't eat anything": Castle, *My Husband*
6 "He was immediately stamped": ibid.
6 "unable to find any trace": University of Birmingham to author, Jan. 2, 2005
7 "He hung round till he learned": Castle, *My Husband*
7 "Everybody encouraged him": ibid.
7 "he offered the guests": *Dancing Times*, quoted in unidentified newspaper article, 1918 (NYPL)

2. About Town

10 "Even in the midst": Fields, *From the Bowery to Broadway*
10 "in an old hall on Sixth Avenue": Whitman, *Predestined*
10 "I am sometimes disposed": Austen, *Lady Susan*
11 "a broadly humorous creation": *Chicago Chronicle*, Apr. 22, 1907
11 "kaleidoscope of gorgeous": *New York Times*, Aug. 31, 1906

12 "Always remember": Fields, *From the Bowery to Broadway*

12 "contribute to the general entertainment": *New York Times,* Oct. 2, 1907

14 "I had more fun every night": *Atlanta Journal,* Mar. 16, 1913

15 "Two novel scenes": *New York Times,* Oct. 2, 1907

15 "immense," "colossal," "unequalled": unidentified newspaper articles, 1907 (NYPL)

16 "the actors and crew were my playmates": Hayes and Hatch, *My Life in Three Acts*

16 "It was a real, consuming passion": ibid.

16 "It is a good show": *New York Times,* Nov. 23, 1909

16 "A sort of three-ring circus affair": *New York Times,* June 5, 1910

16 "Vernon Castle, the narrow-gauged comedian": *New Jersey Review,* June 18, 1910

3. Only Forty-five Minutes from Broadway

19 "I don't think there's a childhood": Castle, *Castles in the Air*

19 "Forty-Five Minutes from Broadway": words and music by George M. Cohan, 1906

20 "His patients may be found": Scharf, *A History of Westchester County*

21 "Foote was perhaps the first": Collins, *The Trouble with Tom*

21 "The dawn of the millennium": Foote, *Medical Common Sense*

21 "a Victorian sex-ed manual": Collins, *The Trouble with Tom*

21 "the one substance": National Center for Homeopathy, www.homeopathic.org

22 "By 1900": Klaw, *The Great American Medicine Show*

22 "was a Goldthwaite": Annie Elroy Foote, *Theatre,* c. 1914 (NYPL)

22 "lined with horse-chestnut trees": Castle, *Castles in the Air*

22 "never allowed himself to be shocked": ibid.

23 "Life with father": ibid.

23 "prevented soiling of the user's extremities": U.S. patent no. 18199

23 "because of his strong affection": William McLaughlin to author, Dec. 11, 2004

23 "I used to play with boys all the time": *Photoplay,* Nov. 1917

23 "a direct, straightforward honest type of warfare": Castle, *Castles in the Air*

23 "She insisted on having as guests": Foote, *Theatre*

24 "We regarded him as a member of the family": Castle, *Castles in the Air*

4. "We would be much happier if we just relaxed and enjoyed school life"

25 "a handsome auburn-haired athlete": Castle, *Castles in the Air*

25 "sullen and moody": ibid.

26 "lovely," "fashionable": ibid.

26 "I had a mind of my own": ibid.

26 "Dr. Foote did not believe": Annie Elroy Foote, *Theatre*, c. 1914 (NYPL)

26 "I first cut off my hair": Irene Castle, *Ladies' Home Journal*, Oct. 1921

27 "New bobbed heads": ibid.

27 "There was only one thing left for me to do": Castle, *Castles in the Air*

28 "'we' would be much happier": ibid.

28 "The Yama-Yama Man": words and music by George Collin Davis and Karl Hoschna, 1908

28 "I wanted to be just like her": Castle, *Castles in the Air*

29 "before she could walk alone": Foote, *Theatre*

29 "very good": Castle, *Castles in the Air*

29 "I had the determination": ibid.

29 "As Irene hated real work": Foote, *Theatre*

5. "I COULD TELL BY LOOKING AT HIM THAT HE WAS NOT MY CUP OF TEA"

30 "pulled myself up on the float": Castle, *Castles in the Air*

30 "I could tell by looking at him": ibid.

30 "the first actor I had met": ibid.

30 "My heart skipped a beat": ibid.

31 "a lavender wool suit": ibid.

31 "I liked his manners": ibid.

31 "It was not long before my feelings": ibid.

31 "He contended that actors never had any money": Castle, "My Memories of Vernon Castle"

32 "and he was terribly proud of himself": ibid.

6. ZOWIE, "THE MONARCH OF MYSTERY"

33 "He was very nice about it": Castle, *Castles in the Air*

33 "I had come in from New Rochelle": ibid.

34 "the drums of doom started to beat in my heart": Hayes and Hatch, *My Life in Three Acts*

34 "Any man who can succeed": *New York Times*, unidentified article (NYPL)

35 "dowdily dressed . . . awkwardly laid out": Castle, *Castles in the Air*

35 "I found everything in London inferior": Castle, "My Memories of Vernon Castle"

36 "It was rude of you to pass up the bananas": Castle, *Castles in the Air*

36 "awful:" ibid.

36 "that must have cost nearly five hundred dollars": Castle, *My Husband*

36 "To the waiter who served him": Castle, "My Memories of Vernon Castle"

7. "THEY LIKED TO TEST OUT THEIR GUNS"

37 "Vernon was the most tactful person": Janis, *So Far, So Good!*

37 "I have never heard of anyone who disliked him": Castle, "My Memories of Vernon Castle"

37 "There was no one who could keep up with him": Castle, *My Husband*

38 "They liked to test out their guns": Marbury, *My Crystal Ball*

38 "lisping," "drawling," "sashaying," "flighty": various unidentified newspaper articles, 1910s (NYPL)

38 "Whether they were in love": William McLaughlin to author, Dec. 11, 2004

39 "As I look back": Castle, *My Husband*

39 "where we were fascinated by the cathedral": Castle, "My Memories of Vernon Castle"

39 "halfway up the hill to Montmartre": Castle, *Castles in the Air*

40 "I felt entirely to blame": Castle, "My Memories of Vernon Castle"

40 "There was so little left for the rent": Castle, *Castles in the Air*

8. ENFIN ... UNE REVUE

41 "complete and abysmal failure": Castle, *Castles in the Air*

41 "The tin soldier falls in love": Castle, "My Memories of Vernon Castle"

41 "even rougher": Castle, *Castles in the Air*

41 "in the days before we were married": ibid.

42 "the stench backstage was just too strong for me": ibid.

42 "an air of true graciousness": ibid.

43 "keyed-up": ibid.

43 "Both of us were quivering with nervous excitement": Castle, "My Memories of Vernon Castle"

43 "Tips amounted to more than our salary": Castle, *Castles in the Air*

43 "rough and tumble": ibid.

43 "handsome, statuesque woman ... surrounded one of my hands": Castle, *Castles in the Air*

44 "and started doing a sort of hootchy-kootchy": ibid.

44 "I was not shocked but I was surprised": ibid.

9. "I SAW THE FAT YEARS AHEAD!"

45 "In the confusion of abandoning ship": Castle, *Castles in the Air*

46 "All we did was to write on paper": ibid.
46 "By keeping my eyes firmly fixed": ibid.
46 "clowned around like taxi drivers": ibid.
46 "Instead of coming *down* on the beat": Castle, *My Husband*
46 "My dear Mr. Errol": unidentified newspaper article, 1914 (NYPL)
48 "I opened the doors and windows of America": Tapert, *The Power of Style*
48 "a new society": Morris, *Incredible New York*
48 "The scene was one of amiable disarray": Lewis, *Ladies and Not-So-Gentle Women*
48 "I had sensed the approach of the dancing madness": Marbury, *My Crystal Ball*
48 "had a lovely sense of humor": Castle, *Castles in the Air*
48 "I obtained private engagements for them": Marbury, *My Crystal Ball*
49 "We were clean-cut": Castle, *Castles in the Air*
49 "We went out and did all of our old routines:" ibid.
49 "If I showed him a step *once,* he remembered it": ibid.
49 "I was mad as a snake": ibid.

10. Everybody's Doing It

51 "an instrumental composition": Hasse, *Ragtime*
51 "a syncopated composition for the piano": Jasen and Jones, *That American Rag*
51 "there was never any such music as 'ragtime'": Badger, *A Life in Ragtime*
51 "You know, I never did find out what ragtime was": Bergreen, *As Thousands Cheer*
51 "It's 'ragtime' here and 'ragtime' there": Witmark and Goldberg, *The Story of the House of Witmark*
52 "Ragtime was far and away the gayest": Blesh and Janis, *They All Played Ragtime*
52 "a dog with rabies": Hasse, *Ragtime*
52 "It exalts noise, rush and street vulgarity": Blesh and Janis, *They All Played Ragtime*
52 "Like a criminal novel, it is full of bangs": ibid.
52 "I can't help feeling": ibid.
52 "Most people seem to have a peculiar": ibid.
53 "He did not have to play anyone else's music": Berlin, *King of Ragtime*
54 "publications masquerading under the name of ragtime": ibid.
54 "With 'Alexander's Ragtime Band'": Sullivan, *Our Times*
55 "Everybody's Doing It": words and music by Irving Berlin, 1911
55 "That International Rag": words and music by Irving Berlin, 1913

56 "In every London restaurant": Bergreen, *As Thousands Cheer*
56 "the cult of the ugly": Sullivan, *Our Times*

11. "TWO ADOLESCENT PALM TREES"

58 "an ambitious puppy": Janis, *So Far, So Good!*
58 "could have been played by a robot": Castle, *Castles in the Air*
58 "looked like two adolescent palm trees . . . suddenly pulled up her skirts": Janis, *So Far, So Good!*
59 "skipping all over the stage": Castle, *Castles in the Air*
59 "The joke was decidedly on us": Janis, *So Far, So Good!*
60 "now happily allowed to appear something near human": *New York Times*, Feb. 4, 1913
60 "wonderful performance": *Washington Star*, undated review (NYPL)
60 "ran away with the lion's share": *New York Evening Sun*, Dec. 19, 1913
60 "somewhat painful": Marbury, *My Crystal Ball*
60 "easily the one sensation of the night": *New York Evening Sun*, Dec. 19, 1913
60 "magnums of grape juice . . . Vulgar people": *Metropolitan*, June 1913
60 "people rarely have the patience . . . you have to dance against time": ibid.
60 "My husband is a professional": *Cosmopolitan*, Aug. 1913
61 "a tiny, shaggy brown terrier . . . to leave off dancing": *Green Book*, Dec. 1915
61 "Vernon was far too conscientious for that": Annie Elroy Foote, *Theatre*, c. 1914 (NYPL)
61 "When we danced he swooped me around": Castle, *Castles in the Air*
62 "from being lonely:" ibid.

12. "GOWNS ARE MORE OR LESS A BUSINESS WITH ME"

63 "I would create tea gowns. . . . It is a lesser form of art": Etherington-Smith and Pilcher, *The It Girls*
63 "Gowns are more or less a business with me": *Green Book*, June 1915
64 "The well-fitting corset is a support": ibid.
64 "My idea of dress is to wear what is individually becoming": ibid.
64 "Of furs I cannot have too many": ibid.
65 "All the smart hairdressers": *Cleveland Leader*, Dec. 21, 1914
65 "I want to let my hair grow . . . grow old and gray": *Ladies' Home Journal*, Oct. 1921
65 "A top-heavy or uncomfortable head dress": *Green Book*, June 1915
65 "They saw Mrs. V. Castle's bobbed hair": *Cleveland Leader*, Feb. 21, 1915
66 "When Mrs. Vernon Castle suddenly appeared": Beaton, *The Glass of Fashion*
66 "I could not dance in a hobble skirt": *Green Book*, June 1915

66 "There was something terrifically healthy and clean about her": Beaton, *The Glass of Fashion*

67 "an effect similar to the jaunty cut": *New York Review*, Jan. 16, 1915

67 "People will be very nice to us": *Green Book*, Dec. 1915

13. "THE BEST DANCING MUSIC IN THE WORLD"

69 "the best dancing music in the world": unidentified newspaper article, spring 1914 (NYPL)

69 "one white absolutely without prejudice": Badger, *A Life in Ragtime*

69 "Drumming is all very well in a restaurant. . . . I can remember often imploring him": Castle, *My Husband*

71 "the Negro race is dancing itself to death": Badger, *A Life in Ragtime*

71 "I have found that dancing keeps husbands and wives together": ibid.

71 "The Negro plays ragtime . . . a superior sense of rhythm": ibid.

71 "became so popular": Witmark and Goldberg, *The Story of the House of Witmark*

14. "MORE LIKE A PAIR OF SCHOOLCHILDREN"

73 "The tango was the dance of the day. . . . I was one up on the other contestant": Stein, *American Vaudeville*

74 "from one of the original Gunmen of Paris": *Variety*, May 25, 1927

74 "the king-pin of the cabaret": Street, *Welcome to Our City*

74 "I have heard that imitation is the greatest form of flattery": Castle, *Castles in the Air*

74 "without question one of the most wonderful dancers": Mouvet, *The Tango and the New Dances*

74 "is no more suggestive or immoral": ibid.

74 "the older order of the dances is passing away": ibid.

76 "The call of the west has got into our blood": *Chicago Examiner*, Nov. 7, 1913

76 "more like a pair of schoolchildren": *Chicago Examiner*, Nov. 12, 1913

77 "Let Willie Hammerstein do his durndest!": *New Jersey Telegraph*, Jan. 3, 1914

77 "noticeable chiefly by the increased number": *New Jersey Telegraph*, Jan. 13, 1914

77 "There is no passion in their dancing": *Hartford Courant*, Jan. 4, 1915

77 "very Fifth Avenue, or should I say Piccadilly": *Dramatic Mirror*, Jan. 7, 1914

15. "SYNCOPATION RULES THE NATION"

78 "screams of 'brava'": *Boston American*, Feb. 15, 1914

79 "she sang the song because she liked it . . . called for an encore": Sullivan, *Our Times*

79 "The Christian Religion forbids modern dances": Beryl and Associates, *Immorality of Modern Dances*

79 "seeing men and women whirling": ibid.

79 "hour after hour it whirls": ibid.

79 "Saloon-keepers and prostitutes": Bowen, *The Public Dance Halls of Chicago*

80 "Couples stand very close together": ibid.

80 "turkey trot, grizzly bear, bunny hug": Ham, *The Modern Dance*

80 "No woman who dances virtuously": ibid.

80 "crowded ball-rooms and late hours": Drumm, *The Modern Dance and What Shall Take Its Place*

81 "the dance craze has developed with such incredible rapidity": Faulkner, *Lure of the Dance*

81 "A minister in San Francisco": ibid.

81 "many of the causes of insanity": Ham, *The Modern Dance*

81 "Myriads of roysterers": ibid.

82 "His reputation has been attained . . . a well-spring of good spirits": Kinney, *Social Dancing of To-day*

82 "The new dances are not improper": Walker, *The Modern Dances*

82 "so simple that it is difficult to describe": ibid.

82 "in this year of pretended refinement": Sullivan, *Our Times*

82 "From Louis Martin's": Street, *Welcome to Our City*

83 "They even have lights under the tables": ibid.

83 "From Little Hungary in Houston Street": ibid.

83 "You Can't Get away from It": words by William Jerome and Grant Clarke, music by Jean Schwartz, 1913

83 "all they wanted to do was dance": Malnig, *Dancing Till Dawn*

84 "No restaurant so humble": George Jean Nathan, *Theatre*, Dec. 1912

84 "The very best of these New York cabaret shows": ibid.

84 "reckless and uncontrolled": Smith, *William Jay Gaynor*

84 "This all-night guzzling and vulgarity": ibid.

85 "New York, What's the Matter with You?": words by George V. Hobart, music by Raymond Hubbell, 1913

85 "The winter of 1913–14 will live in history": Sullivan, *Our Times*

16. "The Most Talked About House in New York"

86 "Time was essential": Marbury, *My Crystal Ball*

86 "The thought of making it into a smart dancing-centre": ibid.

87 "I selected able assistants": ibid.

87 "Let's go down to the Castles' castle": *Theatre*, Mar. 1914

88 "Cupid in green knickers smiles": ibid.
88 "All were genuinely interested": *Vanity Fair,* Mar. 1914
88 "They were absolutely innocuous in every way": ibid.
89 "From the first day we opened our doors": Castle, *Castles in the Air*
89 "a place where their children could go": ibid.
89 "some of the most prominent members of society": *Smart Styles,* Feb. 1914
89 "a gentle but decisive cold shouldering": *Theatre,* Mar. 1914
89 "How do you separate the sheep and the goats?": ibid.
89 "less like a dancing genius": ibid.
90 "A slim, girlish figure": ibid.
90 "surrounded with all the efficient devices": *World,* July 7, 1914
90 "Over in England no one seems to have the moral courage": ibid.
91 "Working girls have just the same desire to dance": *New York Herald,* Jan. 11, 1914
91 "Miss Marbury noted some little crudenesses": ibid.
91 "largest audience that Carnegie Hall has held": *New York Herald,* Mar. 1914
91 "we will have the same atmosphere": Elisabeth Marbury, *New York Herald,* Apr. 1914
91 "At first we were there all the time": *Chicago Tribune,* May 12, 1915
92 "combined all the talents of a social dictator": Castle, *Castles in the Air*
92 "an ugly room with great square columns": ibid.
92 "until it almost glowed through the sidewalk": ibid.
92 "He glistened with very chunky yellow diamonds": ibid.
92 "tempting little dishes of tomatoes": unidentified newspaper article, early 1915 (NYPL)
92 "When protest was made to the waiters": ibid.
93 "Very few of those who had this expensive experience": ibid.
93 "It seems that one of the young men": *Dramatic Times,* May 20, 1914
93 "we put a card on the tables": Castle, *Castles in the Air*
93 "Vernon reached down": ibid.
93 "there are not sufficient means of quick egress": unidentified newspaper article, May 1914 (NYPL)
94 "corruptly and fraudulently had dealings": *New York American,* Sept. 13, 1915

17. "DANCING WITH VERNON WAS AS EASY AS SWIMMING WITH WATER WINGS"

95 "The picture is life-size": unidentified review, Apr. 26, 1914
95 "Mr. and Mrs. Castle stand pre-eminent to-day": Castle and Castle, *Modern Dancing*

96 "a healthful exercise and a fitting recreation": ibid.

96 "Almost any girl who does not dance": ibid.

96 "and keeps one absolutely fit": ibid.

96 "The man and woman who sit briefly at a café": ibid.

96 "One last word about the Lame Duck": ibid.

97 "Both good dancing and good manners": ibid.

97 "While fashion decrees the narrow skirt": ibid.

97 "Step One: Four steps—back": Hopkins, *The Tango and Other Up-to-Date Dances*

98 "The dancers stand directly in front of each other": Castle and Castle, *Modern Dancing*

99 "First of all, walk as I have already explained": ibid.

99 "I advise you to cease counting": ibid.

99 "Use it in con-nection": 78 rpm instructional record, author's collection

99 "when really he often confided to me afterward": Castle, *Castles in the Air*

100 "Dancing with Vernon was as easy as swimming": ibid.

100 "he guides one perfectly": *New York Telegraph*, Jan. 27, 1915

100 "Somehow, little men eighty-five years old": Castle, *Castles in the Air*

100 "Nobody needs to take lessons": *Chicago Tribune*, May 12, 1915

101 "A kick and a hop three times on each foot": Stearns, *Jazz Dance*

18. "The spirit of success ... oozes from these two young people"

102 "That dancer didn't scare worth a darn": unidentified article, Mar. 24, 1918 (NYPL)

102 "was always galloping around somewhere": Castle, *My Husband*

102 "most of which I have bred myself": unidentified Philadelphia newspaper article, May 1914 (NYPL)

103 "The owner insisted upon giving it to her": ibid.

103 "We call her Kitty and Pussy": ibid.

103 "got famous so quickly": William McLaughlin to author, Dec. 11, 2004

103 "charmingly irresponsible": Castle, "My Memories of Vernon Castle"

103 "Their day was never complete": Marbury, *My Crystal Ball*

103 "a soft touch": Castle, "My Memories of Vernon Castle"

103 "was fond of persons who had a sense of humor": Castle, *My Husband*

103 "Darling, I love the Krazy Kat you sent me": ibid.

104 "he went no matter how ill he was": Castle, "My Memories of Vernon Castle"

104 "I never touch the house": unidentified magazine article, 1915 (NYPL)

105 "Previously dancers had made softer use": Beaton, *The Glass of Fashion*

105 "Just what is it that makes the Castles' performances": *Chicago Evening Post*, Sept. 4, 1915

19. "THE CASTLES ARE COMING! HOORAY! HOORAY!"

106 "a stage is a conspicuous place": unidentified newspaper article, 1914 (NYPL)

106 "produced such a hellish nose": *Boston Transcript*, undated article, 1914 (NYPL)

107 "Mr. Castle is a comedian": *Toronto News*, undated article, 1914 (NYPL)

107 "we had to depend on Jim Europe's ability": Castle, *Castles in the Air*

107 "one of the most perfectly disciplined organizations": Badger, *A Life in Ragtime*

108 "champagne, sandwiches and refreshments": ibid.

108 "the best friends of the colored professional": ibid.

108 "Castles Score Tango Triumph": unidentified Boston newspaper article (NYPL)

108 "Both Mr. and Mrs. Castle are artists": ibid.

108 "there was a premiere at the opera": ibid.

109 "Frankly, I must say that I have not seen bettah": *Detroit News*, May 13, 1914

109 "The whole performance was conducted with an agreeable informality": *Rochester Times*, undated article, 1914 (NYPL)

109 "There has been such a tremendous amount of misunderstanding": *Baltimore News*, Apr. 29, 1914

109 "greatest living tango exponents": *Buffalo Times*, May 2, 1914

109 "Steel-ribbed Pittsburgh could not be expected": Stein, *American Vaudeville*

110 "the small city variety does not warm up": ibid.

110 "makes the hardest dance look like the simplest": *Philadelphia Telegraph*, undated article, 1914 (NYPL)

110 "Mr. Castle is about six feet tall": *Detroit News*, May 13, 1914

111 "The highly praised Negro orchestra": *Kansas City Journal*, undated article (NYPL)

111 "what lovely cities Minneapolis and St. Paul are!": *Minneapolis News*, May 8, 1914

111 "although there were many, many people anxious": ibid.

111 "Mr. and Mrs. Castle balked last night at mingling": ibid.

112 "Speaking of Western dancing": unidentified Omaha newspaper article (NYPL)

112 "almost came to blows Saturday night": *Akron News*, May 18, 1914

112 "liable to a heavy fine and imprisonment": undated Philadelphia newspaper article, 1914 (NYPL)

112 "five rooftop dances": *Evening Mail*, undated article, 1914 (NYPL)

112 "A worthy culmination": *New York American*, May 24, 1914

113 "The 'gorgeous decorations' consisted of strips": unidentified newspaper article, May 24, 1914 (NYPL)

113 "We laughed and . . . never even bothered": Castle, *Castles in the Air*

113 "Mrs. Castle will not be out of peril": unidentified newspaper article, May 27, 1914 (NYPL)

114 "the one biggest and newest thing at Luna this year": *Columbus Evening Dispatch*, undated article, 1914 (NYPL)

114 "broad staircase, bordered by growing plants": ibid.

114 "a broad porch, overlooking the lagoon": *Brooklyn Daily Eagle*, May 31, 1914

114 "with dancing blood in his system": *Columbus Evening Dispatch*, June 25, 1914

115 "this was his wife's first public appearance": *New York Telegraph*, July 11, 1914

20. "WE WERE BOTH MISERABLE ON THOSE VAUDEVILLE TOURS"

116 "a current of unrest": Castle, *My Husband*

117 "worth about as much as a busted lamp shade": Castle, *Castles in the Air*

117 "as though he were his only child . . . Vernon's eyes were wet": ibid.

117 "Paris was like a crowded theater": ibid.

118 "Evidently the British government": ibid.

119 "If you are guilty of uttering anything sacrilegious": Stein, *American Vaudeville*

119 "Blacks, whites, men, women, straights, gays": Trav S.D., *No Applause*

119 "In a week of one-night stands": Stein, *American Vaudeville*

119 "They seemed to fairly excel all their former efforts": *Cincinnati Tribune*, Sept. 7, 1914

119 "they provide one of the classiest headliners": *Cleveland Plain Dealer*, Sept. 15, 1914

120 "Women are naturally graceful": *Cleveland Leader*, Sept. 13, 1914

120 "people come to the theater": ibid.

120 "I want to be an actor": ibid.

120 "to tango through the week": *New York Review*, Oct. 17, 1914

120 "Castles' Hold-Up": *Variety*, Oct. 17, 1914

120 "Vaudeville Likely to Be Closed to Them": *New York Review*, Oct. 17, 1914

120 "will have something to say the next time": ibid.

121 "People have been brutal to dogs in training": *New York Post*, May 9, 1931

121 "it is not natural for a bear to roller-skate": Castle, *My Husband*

121 "shocked with electricity, stuck with needles": ibid.

121 "Thank God that I found you": ibid.

122 "We were both miserable on those vaudeville tours": Castle, *Castles in the Air*

122 "One little dog missed his cue one night": Castle, *My Husband*

122 "over long-distance telephone": unidentified newspaper article, 1914 (NYPL)

123 "could not rid the pages of the savor of the cabaret": Bok, *The Americanization of Edward Bok*

21. "THEIR ENTHUSIASTIC FOLLOWERS NEVER . . . GO TO BED AT ALL"

124 "Mr. Charles Dillingham gave me an old play": Smith, *First Nights and First Editions*

124 "They Always Follow Me Around": words and music by Irving Berlin, 1914

124 "everybody connected with the show": Castle, *Castles in the Air*

124 "At rehearsals the material did not seem promising": Smith, *First Nights and First Editions*

125 "Was he named after William Tell?": *Detroit News*, Dec. 19, 1914

125 "I couldn't imagine what everybody was so nervous about": Castle, *Castles in the Air*

126 "as gay, extravagant and festive an offering": *New York Times*, Dec. 9, 1914

126 "The history of twentieth-century America": *Evening Sun*, undated article (NYPL)

126 "it is the exquisite charm of the Castles' dancing": *Dramatic Mirror*, Dec. 16, 1914

126 "The dancing of the Castles": *Madison Journal*, Dec. 19, 1914

126 "one of the first-class entertainments of the year": *Detroit News*, Dec. 1, 1914

126 "the effect was rather painful": Marbury, *My Crystal Ball*

126 "laid them in the aisles . . . all the booming quality of a foghorn": Castle, *Castles in the Air*

126 "Mrs. Castle is a physical pastel": *New York Review*, Dec. 14, 1914

127 "Vernon, you're a good judge of music, aren't you?": *New York Telegraph*, July 1, 1915

127 "Vernon Castle is genuinely artistic": unidentified newspaper article, Jan. 1915 (NYPL)

127 "Mr. Castle seems delighted to be back on the boards again": unidentified newspaper article (NYPL)

127 "stacked up like cordwood": Castle, *Castles in the Air*

127 "outside infatuations": ibid.

128 "The ornate cornices and capitals": Van Hoogstraten, *Lost Broadway Theatres*

128 "requires a total of 1,242 bulbs": unidentified newspaper article, Dec. 28, 1914 (NYPL)

128 "Castles in the Air has been elaborately decorated": unidentified newspaper article, Dec. 28, 1914 (NYPL)

128 "until the sun rises in the heavens": unidentified newspaper article, Dec. 28, 1914 (NYPL)

128 "The Forty-Fourth Street Theater": unidentified newspaper article, Dec. 28, 1914 (NYPL)

129 "Mr. and. Mrs. Vincent Astor": unidentified newspaper article, Dec. 28, 1914 (NYPL)

129 "Just as Mayor Mitchell has arranged": *Vanity Fair*, Dec. 1914

129 "unusually small and uncomfortable": Van Hoogstraten, *Lost Broadway Theaters*

22. "MRS. CASTLE IS EXHAUSTED"

130 "advised that she go into the hospital": *New York Telegraph*, Jan. 27, 1915

130 "It is scandalous rubbish": ibid.

130 "were visible proof that a man and wife": Murray and Ardmore, *The Self-Enchanted*

130 "This is little Mae Murray": ibid.

131 "It was the proudest moment of my life": *New York Telegraph*, Jan. 27, 1915

131 "She kept sending messages to me": ibid.

131 "made a decided hit": *New York Telegraph*, Jan. 27, 1915

131 "We came over the Williamsburg Bridge:" unidentified newspaper article, Jan. 1915 (NYPL)

132 "Every hundred years there's a great dancing revival": *World*, June 7, 1914

132 "Until the great war broke out": unidentified newspaper article (NYPL)

132 "to lead troops into combat": Badger, *A Life in Ragtime*

23. "CASTLES IN THE SUBWAY, / CASTLES IN THE 'L'"

134 "Plunged into it with all the zeal . . . We had one cameraman": Castle, *Castles in the Air*

136 "thoughtfully injected enough melodrama": *Detroit News*, Nov. 22, 1915

136 "fresh and new—a nice picture": *Chicago Evening Post*, Oct. 29, 1915

136 "nothing into this film but their name": *New York Mail*, Oct. 23, 1915

136 "The highest class of picture": *Variety*, Oct. 22, 1915

136 "literally stormed by eager folk": *Detroit News*, Oct. 22, 1915

137 "I'll Take You Back to Sunny Italy": words and music by Irving Berlin, 1917

137 "I Can Dance with Everybody but My Wife": words by Joseph Cawthorn and John L. Golden, music by John L. Golden, 1916

137 "Johnny, Get a Girl": words by Stanley Murphy, music by Harry Puck, 1916

137 "Males buy boots like Vernon's": *Vanity Fair*, June 1915

138 "I hereby challenge you and your partner": unidentified newspaper article, Feb. 26, 1915 (NYPL)

138 "I enjoy a good bout as much as any man": *New York Review,* May 15, 1915

138 "The sport is a splendid one": ibid.

139 "Rastus takes up the eye pencil": *Pittsburgh Post,* Jan. 20, 1916

24. "OH, GIVE ME A GUN AND LET ME RUN TO FIGHT THE FOREIGN FOE"

140 "for the comfort of horses wounded in the war": unidentified newspaper article, spring 1915 (NYPL)

140 "There must be something about the rattling of a drum": Castle, *My Husband*

140 "That may have been one of the things that drove him": William McLaughlin to author, Dec. 11, 2004

140 "He had never been a man's man in the public's eye": Castle, *Castles in the Air*

140 "he became identified with a strange abnormal kind of girlish man": *Daily News,* Feb. 15, 1918

141 "I'd Feel at Home if They'd Let Me Join the Army": music by Albert Gumble, words by Jack Mahoney, 1917

141 "Delicately the young man picked his way": *Cincinnati Star,* undated article (NYPL)

141 "this side of the Atlantic": unidentified newspaper article, Aug. 4, 1916 (NYPL)

141 "Vernon Castle, who has a plan to join": unidentified newspaper article, summer 1915 (NYPL)

141 "valiant hero's": *Toledo Blade,* undated article (NYPL)

141 "Almost nightly, his eyes blazing": *New York Telegraph,* Feb. 9, 1916

142 "quite uncomfortable": Castle, *My Husband*

142 "These Castles have a bizarre fascination": *Chicago Evening Post,* Sept. 4, 1915

142 "In those early days powered flight": Wise, *Canadian Airmen and the First World War*

143 "pure European descent": ibid.

143 "The Young Man's Element": ibid.

143 "He understood as if by instinct": *Sun,* Mar. 17, 1918

143 "took his flying very seriously . . . with his goggles hanging down": Lees, *Pioneer Pilot*

143 "The air made me feel that I was in a new world": unidentified newspaper article, 1915 (NYPL)

143 "I'd like to have you up in one of the big machines": *New Orleans States,* Aug. 4, 1916

144 "So many English actors of military age": *Toledo Blade,* July 27, 1915

144 "Two years later": Castle, *Castles in the Air*

144 "Perhaps the only thing not modern": *Louisville Times,* Feb. 8, 1916

144 "Mrs. Castle is very entertaining as a dancer": *Cleveland Plain Dealer,* Mar. 10, 1916

144 "Mrs. Castle's voice is nasal": *Toledo Blade,* undated article (NYPL)

144 "An imitation of Mrs. Castle": *Columbus Dispatch,* undated article (NYPL)

145 "a fifty-word interview": *Grand Rapids Press,* Mar. 7, 1916

145 "I can't see you very long": *Wisconsin State Journal,* undated article (NYPL)

145 "The audience began to shout for us to dance": Castle, *Castles in the Air*

145 "He ignored our frantic signals": ibid.

146 "I was proud": Castle, *My Husband*

146 "Vernon was no more of a natural fighter": Janis, *So Far, So Good!*

146 "If we still love those we lose": ibid.

146 "who drinks beer and likes it . . . 'May I send you some flowers?'": *Pittsburgh Post,* Jan. 20, 1916

147 "the greatest dancers in America": unidentified newspaper article, Mar. 1916 (NYPL)

25. "When I get old I shall be able to tell our children all about the Great War"

148 "Gosh, we bet the British Army is growing impatient": *Toledo Blade,* Feb. 24, 1916

149 "There are a thousand reasons": letter from Vernon Castle, quoted in Castle, *My Husband*

149 "I'm quite excited about it": ibid.

149 "the show business is better than it's been in years": ibid.

149 "five years behind the times": ibid.

149 "I could cry I'm so lonely sometimes": ibid.

149 "All my old school friends have gone": ibid.

149 "Well, if he can fly . . . the rank is not so high": ibid.

149 "One thing I have to be careful about": ibid.

150 "I look just like Rastus in it": ibid.

150 "6:00 A.M. Early morning flying": ibid.

150 "It all seems so strange and different": ibid.

150 "got a lot of fun walking with me": ibid.

150 "He soon became expert at dropping bombs": *Sun,* Mar. 17, 1918

150 "There was something so distinctive": ibid.

151 "I'm improving my flying": letter from Vernon Castle, quoted in Castle, *My Husband*

151 "large numbers of raw and barely trained": Hanson, *Unknown Soldiers*

151 "He was not a soldier of adventure": Castle, *Castles in the Air*

151 "O! I want to get back to you so badly": letter from Vernon Castle, quoted in Castle, *My Husband*

151 "I told her he was sort of between the two": Castle, *My Husband*

152 "It was my first glimpse of him as a soldier": ibid.

152 "Knowing full well the months would be long": ibid.

152 "When he came back he explained to me": ibid.

152 "tied around his neck with a dirty little string": ibid.

152 "a curiously unsmiling person": unidentified newspaper article, 1916 (NYPL)

152 "How sad it is to have you leave me": letter from Vernon Castle, quoted in Castle, *My Husband*

153 "in the middle of Salisbury Plain": ibid.

153 "It has sort of depressed everybody": ibid.

153 "We are expecting a big drive": ibid.

153 "isn't a bit nice": ibid.

153 "Things are going to be very busy soon": ibid.

153 "the squadron . . . entertained him at supper": ibid.

153 "You can sit in them for hours and not get tired . . . and we have to put ointment on our feet": ibid.

154 "this is the 'crack' Squadron": ibid.

154 "He did especially well": *Sun*, Mar. 17, 1918

154 "I had my plane hit three times": letter from Vernon Castle, quoted in Castle, *My Husband*

154 "greatest aerial exploits took place": unidentified newspaper article, late 1916 (NYPL)

154 "strafe from the big guns": ibid.

154 "from fifty to a hundred darted over the lines": ibid.

155 "Allies advanced only 8 km": bbc.co.uk

155 "we were targeted by aircraft": Hanson, *Unknown Soldiers*

155 "I had never been near the big guns before": letter from Vernon Castle, quoted in Castle, *My Husband*

155 "I was going to tell you why I went there": ibid.

156 "The war is looking as little more promising now": ibid.

156 "feel like a wreck . . . it's better than being in the trenches": ibid.

156 "My God, how I pity them!": ibid.

156 "I don't stand half the chance": ibid.

156 "I managed to get a block of ice . . . ended with their breaking up": ibid.

156 "the life of the squadron": unidentified newspaper article (NYPL)

156 "I hadn't boxed since I was sixteen": letter from Vernon Castle, quoted in Castle, *My Husband*

157 "Before we could only get sponge baths": ibid.

157 "The best looking girl . . . only peasants": ibid.

157 "There's one poor chap": ibid.

157 "I always thought of him as having a safe job": ibid.

157 "The only thing I miss is music": ibid.

158 "gliding his plane along": *Sun,* Mar. 17, 1918

158 "it felt as though somebody was trying to push me out of my seat": letter from Vernon Castle, quoted in Castle, *My Husband*

158 "the propeller and part of the rotating motor were shot away": unidentified newspaper article (NYPL)

158 "His attitude was always that of the sportsman": *Sun,* Mar. 17, 1918

158 "Gee, how I hate the Germans!": letter from Vernon Castle, quoted in Castle, *My Husband*

158 "They have even stopped the embroidered post cards": ibid.

159 "It's not at all bad here": *San Francisco Post,* Aug. 14, 1916

159 "It isn't a very pleasant sensation": letter from Vernon Castle, quoted in Castle, *My Husband*

159 "war flying exposes the human organism to a greater strain": Hanson, *Unknown Soldiers*

159 "fainting, falling asleep in the air and hallucinations": ibid.

159 "Gee, it looks good to be in a real town": letter from Vernon Castle, quoted in Castle, *My Husband*

159 "It's darned hard luck": ibid.

160 "unless of course one's nerves won't stand it": ibid.

160 "It was a wonderful aerial feat of arms": *Sun,* Mar. 17, 1918

160 "smaller and faster . . . If you are told to go anywhere, you go": letter from Vernon Castle, quoted in Castle, *My Husband*

160 "the pressure of the steam was so great that it burst": ibid.

160 "I was invited to Headquarters": ibid.

26. "Kiss all the pets for me, dear"

161 "Kiss all the pets for me, dear": letter from Vernon Castle, quoted in Castle, *My Husband*

161 "a card-board mandolin, full of sweets": ibid.

161 "I guess you had better get rid of Tell": ibid.

161 "He has the cutest farm, darling": ibid.

161 "Since I've been writing this letter": ibid.

161 "Fortunately she was killed instantly": ibid.

162 "gives off more smell than heat": ibid.

162 "They were very cute": ibid.

162 "when I talk seriously to her she doesn't understand": ibid.

162 "The only way you can tell which is which": ibid.

162 "He must be awful cute": ibid.

162 "Sweetie, I am just crazy about . . . Rastus and his baby brother": ibid.

162 "he is sitting on my shoulder now": ibid.

162 "he will have the monkey's long distance flight record": ibid.

163 "looked as though a cage of monkeys had lived in it for years": ibid.

27. "A SUPER MOTION PICTURE OF . . . EPOCH-MAKING MAGNIFICENCE"

164 "Toronto girls": unidentified newspaper article, 1916 (NYPL)

165 "If [I] were to go up in an aeroplane": *Photoplay*, Aug. 1914

166 "If I were to say to her": ibid.

166 "Mr. Hearst wants to star Mrs. Vernon Castle": unidentified magazine article, early 1917 (NYPL)

167 "For my many sins": *Films in Review*, Dec. 1971

167 "real Japanese actors": unidentified magazine article, early 1917 (NYPL)

168 "It made me *furious!*": *Toledo Times*, Jan. 28, 1917

168 "she asked for it": unidentified magazine article, early 1917 (NYPL)

168 "I was so close I could have touched her!": *Ithaca Journal*, undated article (NYPL)

168 "An attempt will be made tomorrow afternoon": *Buffalo News*, Sept. 21, 1916

169 "The audience feels, and rightly so, that it has been cheated": *Toledo Times*, Jan. 28, 1917

169 "We used to be worried about you, Vernon": *Photoplay*, Nov. 1917

169 "the scenes turned out badly": unidentified magazine article, early 1917 (NYPL)

169 "took part in two scenes of *Patria*": *Ithaca Journal*, Dec. 14, 1916

169 "most of the movie actors wear soft pleated shirts": letter from Vernon Castle, quoted in Castle, *My Husband*

170 "carrying it a bit too far": ibid.

170 "For God's sake don't go up with some dub": ibid.

170 "a young army of extra people": unidentified newspaper article, late 1916 (NYPL)

170 "I'd like to dance again": unidentified newspaper article, Nov. 29, 1916 (NYPL)

170 "big close-ups at the end of each episode": Castle, *Castles in the Air*

171 "seldom start to shoot before noon": *Ithaca Journal*, undated article (NYPL)

171 "That he has done well is attested to": *Detroit News*, Feb. 17, 1917

171 "defective negatives": Wharton files, Cornell University, Ithaca, New York

171 "There is no excitement in this incident": ibid.

172 "An attraction that will bring money": *Moving Picture World*, Nov. 18, 1915

172 "I was not called on for any acting": Castle, *Castles in the Air*

172 "It's elegant leisure": *Toledo Times*, Jan. 28, 1917

172 "There *is* no acting in a serial": Pearl White, *Motion Picture Classic*, 1919

172 "These three episodes": *Los Angeles Examiner*, undated 1916 review (NYPL)

172 "No film displayed": ibid.

172 "a super motion picture": ibid.

172 "To see as good a serial as *Patria*": undated newspaper review (NYPL)

173 "Mrs. Vernon Castle . . . proves herself equal to any star"; "lends more than her well-known name"; "Mrs. Castle shows no little ability": unidentified newspaper reviews (NYPL)

173 "the most absorbing act on the bill": *Columbus Journal*, undated review (NYPL)

173 "An ingenious melodrama": *Variety*, Dec. 1, 1916

173 "harassed by enemies": *Detroit News Tribune*, undated article (NYPL)

173 "a bundle of nerves": *Motion Picture Classic*, Feb. 1917

174 "As every reader of *Vanity Fair* knows": *Vanity Fair* undated 1917 article (NYPL)

174 "It is always my ill fortune": Bell Syndicate, Inc., 1918

174 "is extremely unfair to the Japanese": Pizzitola, *Hearst over Hollywood*

28. "He was out to see the Kaiser defeated"

176 "Our reunion was a joyous one": Castle, *My Husband*

176 "I don't seem to be able to get over his death": letter from Vernon Castle, quoted in Castle, *My Husband*

176 "Vernon always called him 'my boy'": Castle, *My Husband*

177 "They are dressing in somber shades": ibid.

177 "There's a trick to these English stages": letter from Vernon Castle, quoted in Castle, *My Husband*

177 "I felt as though I had just flown fifty missions": unidentified newspaper article (NYPL)

177 "tall and emaciated": unidentified newspaper article (NYPL)

177 "Vernon Castle loved England": unidentified newspaper article (NYPL)

177 "In his flying classes Castle was not a teacher": *Boston Post*, May 8, 1918

178 "was one of the most popular men on the field": unidentified newspaper article, Feb. 1918 (NYPL)

178 "Vernon Castle was a mighty good man": ibid.

178 "An aeroplane sailed over the inner field": ibid.

178 "At first I was delighted": letter from Vernon Castle, quoted in Castle, *My Husband*

178 "Bang!": ibid.

179 "The C.O. says it's the last job I need do on this trip": ibid.

29. "AN HOUR'S PLEASANT DIVERSION"

180 "I consider the engagement of Mrs. Castle": unidentified article, Apr. 1917 (NYPL)

181 "The work in features gives me a real chance to act": *Moving Picture World*, June 2, 1917

181 "Irene has developed a genuine talent for acting": Sylvia review, *Dramatic Mirror*, Nov. 17, 1917

181 "satisfying": *Moving Picture World*, Nov. 24, 1917

181 "There is little to commend it in the way of plot": *Variety*, Nov. 25, 1917

181 "an actress of remarkable talent": undated *Photoplay* review (NYPL)

181 "An hour's pleasant diversion": unidentified newspaper review (NYPL)

181 "If the titles in this picture": unidentified newspaper review (NYPL)

181 "a high-grade melodrama": *Vancouver World*, Jan. 31, 1918

182 "A good mystery story": undated review, *Philadelphia Ledger* (NYPL)

182 "one of the best mystery pictures produced": *Dramatic Mirror*, Sept. 1, 1917

182 "totally unlike the denouement the spectator has been led to expect": undated review, *Washington Times* (NYPL)

182 "stories were bad": note from Irene Castle, Feb. 1918, Cornell University collection

182 "Mrs. Castle does really well": *Variety*, Apr. 5, 1918

183 "This is a pretty stiff dose of impossible story": undated review, *Motion Picture* (NYPL)

183 "The picture proceeds without rhyme or reason": *Variety*, Aug. 2, 1918

183 "She smokes cigarettes at a dinner party": *Variety*, Aug. 23, 1918

183 "Mrs. Castle acquits herself very creditably": undated review, *Photoplay* (NYPL)

30. I LOVE MY WIFE, BUT, OH, YOU KID!

184 "must be a great game": unidentified newspaper article, early 1917 (NYPL)

184 "which paid tribute to the king and queen of the tango realm": ibid.

184 "a yarn of his press agent": *Toledo Blade*, early 1917 article (NYPL)

184 "for a moment revived the flickering fame of their former popularity": ibid.

185 "he could tear a barracks room apart in no time flat": *Belleville Intelligencer,* Aug. 25, 1917

185 "poor Coats": letter from Vernon Castle, quoted in Castle, *My Husband*

186 "a very strong personality": Carolyn Hetherington to author, Feb. 21, 2005

186 "were very much in love": ibid.

187 "I knew he was having the time of his life": Castle, *My Husband*

187 "Someone offered to bet him": Castle, "My Memories of Vernon Castle"

187 "The eyes of hundreds followed the slim figure": *Daily Intelligencer,* Sept. 1917

188 "it was necessary to place chairs on the stage": Castle, *My Husband*

188 "One of the things that I know she discussed": William McLaughlin to author, Dec. 11, 2004

188 "That was the impression I got from my mother": Hetherington to author

188 "Daybreak found each flight's cadets hopefully grouped": unidentified news-paper article (NYPL)

188 "Smashes are an hourly occurrence": Molson, "The RFC/RAF"

189 "A story repeated by many cadets": Wise, *Canadian Airmen and the First World War*

189 "Some of the officers who were there at the time": Castle, *My Husband*

189 "For days he sat looking out of the window": ibid.

31. "NEVER IN MY LIFE HAVE I BEEN SUBJECTED TO SUCH HUMILIATION"

190 "We need you": unidentified newspaper article (NYPL)

191 *"Miss 1917* is stupendous": *New York Times,* Nov. 7, 1917

191 "a lightsome, flowerlike, and altogether graceful and lovely thing": *New York Post,* Nov. 6, 1917

191 "I found myself hopelessly lost": *Brooklyn Eagle,* Dec. 5, 1917

192 "so angry she could scarcely talk coherently": ibid.

192 "was not giving satisfaction": ibid.

192 "wasn't any longer a drawing card": ibid.

193 "a gown and hat of shimmering white silk": unidentified newspaper article (NYPL)

193 "The defense, as disclosed so far, was that the dancer": unidentified newspaper article, Jan. 4, 1918 (NYPL)

193 "I cannot stand these late hours much longer": *Brooklyn Eagle,* Dec. 5, 1917

193 "played in movies proving that we were right and would win": unidentified magazine interview, 1917 (NYPL)

32. "His plane dove straight into the ground"

194 "was a familiar sight": unidentified newspaper article, late 1917 (NYPL)

194 "The Americans began a rumor": Glen Martin to C.W. Hunt, Dec. 5, 1997

194 "Inez Childers is said to have dated Vernon": ibid.

195 "Construction work on the three aerodromes": Wise, *Canadian Airmen and the First World War*

195 "I like flying just as much as dancing": *Kansas City Times*, Dec. 1, 1917

195 "never 'pulled rank,'": unidentified newspaper article, Feb. 1918 (NYPL)

195 "It's no use trying": letter from Vernon Castle, quoted in Castle, *My Husband*

196 "I went over to see Castle": unidentified newspaper article, Feb. 1918 (NYPL)

196 "Castle did not have on the safety belt": unidentified newspaper article, Feb. 28, 1918 (NYPL)

196 "Another bus [plane] was about in line": unidentified newspaper article, Feb. 1918 (NYPL)

196 "It was fully 15 minutes before they got him out": ibid.

196 "became so distraught": Martin to Hunt

196 "Concussion of the brain": AP, Feb. 15, 1918

33. "Death is nothing to me, sweetheart"

197 "they were extremely persistent": *Motion Picture Classic*, Oct. 1918

197 "turned a ghastly pallor": ibid.

197 "struggling against collapse": *Motion Picture Classic*, Oct. 1918

197 "I shall have to speak for Mrs. Castle": unidentified newspaper article, Feb. 19, 1918 (NYPL)

197 "It was a brave man's death": *Motion Picture Classic*, Oct. 1918

197 "the butterfly who grew into an eagle": *New York City Sun*, Feb. 1918

198 "Vernon was like a big boy": *Topeka Journal*, Feb. 16, 1918

198 "His mechanical skill": *New York City Sun*, Mar. 17, 1918

198 "Children who had been told the story": *Houston Post*, undated article (NYPL)

199 "an unending line of former friends passed by the casket": *New York World*, Feb. 19, 1918

199 "Just before the end of the service": *NY American*, Feb. 19, 1918

200 "I am not willing to meet these": note from Irene Castle, Feb. 28, 1945, Woodlawn Cemetery archives, Bronx, New York

200 "I plan to be buried beside Captain Castle myself": undated 1945 letter from Irene to "Judy," Woodlawn Cemetery archives, Bronx, New York

200 "as a lasting monument to the intrepid aviator": unidentified newspaper article, 1918 (NYPL)

200 "Capt. Vernon Castle said to have died a comparatively poor man": unidentified newspaper article, Feb. 25, 1918 (NYPL)

201 "not only as a token of my deep love and sincere affection": Vernon Castle's will, Sept. 28, 1915, Castle, *My Husband*

201 Mrs. Vernon Castle Management Company: Irene Castle's papers, Cornell University Library, Ithaca, New York

202 "My poor little widow": Castle, *My Husband*

202 "the greatest love of my mother's life": Carolyn Hetherington to author, Feb. 21, 2005

203 "an extravagantly picturesque figure": *Daily Mail*, Mar. 16, 1934

203 "My only consolation is that my friends are winning my money": ibid.

203 "He was running across the tarmac": Hetherington to author

203 "To get real benefit from exercise": *Detroit Journal*, Aug. 3, 1918

204 "Her poise is marvelous": *Motion Picture Classic*, Oct. 1918

204 "Only by keeping busy can I endure it all": ibid.

204 "Mrs. Castle is one of the many wise women": *Vogue*, Sept. 1918

204 "It's rather sinful": *Motion Picture Classic*, Oct. 1918

204 "The War Story With a Laugh, a Thrill and a Throb": newspaper advertisement, 1918

34. "ROBERT WAS SWEET, SYMPATHETIC, AND BESIDES HE DID ALL OF MY BIDDING"

206 "I often think how rich is the man who can sit": Sisler, *Enterprising Families*

207 "with a fine physique": Castle, *Castles in the Air*

207 "he had rare gifts of personality": Robert Treman obituary, unidentified newspaper article, Cornell University collection, Ithaca, New York

207 Irene's ledgers: Irene Castle's papers, Cornell University Library

207 "Easily worth $100,000": unidentified magazine article, c. 1923 (NYPL)

207 "Robert was sweet": Castle, *Castles in the Air*

35. "A WELL-KNOWN DANCING DAME"

210 "To-day women of the Allied nations": Kohn, *Dope Girls*

210 "If I do say it myself": Castle, *Castles in the Air*

210 "At midnight there was a blast of trumpets:" ibid.

210 "happy, awake and expectant": Kohn, *Dope Girls*

210 "whom I had seen only once before": unidentified newspaper article, 1919 (NYPL)

211 "She was going out to Hollywood": Castle, *Castles in the Air*

211 "I was a big fool": ibid.

211 "a well-known dancing dame": *Town Topics*, Nov. 1918

212 "too populous": *New York Telegram*, Aug. 1919

212 "Admits She Never Loved Dead Stage Partner": ibid.

213 "Mr. Treman and myself": unidentified magazine article, c. 1923 (NYPL)

213 "If you like the show so much": unidentified magazine article, c. 1923 (NYPL)

213 "burst into tears ": unidentified newspaper article (NYPL)

213 "A study of a morbid male temperament": *Philadelphia Ledger*, July 20, 1919

214 "Irene Castle has improved steadily": unidentified newspaper review, 1919 (NYPL)

214 "Very acceptable. . . . There's no real 'punch'": *Variety*, undated review (NYPL)

214 "Although she has heretofore been the coldest and most elusive of film actresses": *Toledo Times*, undated review (NYPL)

215 "only required me to look energetic": Castle, *Castles in the Air*

36. "Poor Irene Castle. She certainly isn't what she used to be"

216 "a little dynamo of enthusiasm . . . the best-dressed woman in the country": unidentified newspaper article, Sept. 1920 (NYPL)

216 "One saw yesterday at the horse show": ibid.

216 "brutally beat his mount": ibid.

216 "daffy, but not foolish": ibid.

216 "Mrs. Treman will bravely bring her dogs": ibid.

217 "actually designed herself": Philipsborn's newspaper ads (NYPL)

217 "enchanting Castle creations": ibid.

217 "First of all, don't imitate each other in dressing": unidentified newspaper article, 1921 (NYPL)

217 "that express the distinguished grace and charm of the wearer": Lucile fashion ad, early 1920s (NYPL)

217 "for her millionth picture with her thousandth dog": unidentified newspaper article, early 1920s (NYPL)

217 "I tried teaching dancing to wealthy children": unidentified newspaper article, Jan. 14, 1921 (NYPL)

217 "had a friend who wanted to establish a motion-picture company": Castle, *Castles in the Air*

218 "I had so many days of hectic nightlife": *Picture Play*, undated 1921–22 article (NYPL)

218 "of course I wouldn't stand for that": ibid.

219 "when I saw Jennie": ibid.

219 "For the past week I worked from nine in the morning until nine at night": ibid.

219 "I've struggled against dancing in pictures": ibid.

219 "a cartilage in her throat had been dislocated": *New York Times*, Aug. 3, 1921

219 "only average": *Variety*, Mar. 3, 1922

220 "I received thousands of letters from children": *Picture Play*, undated 1921–22 article (NYPL)

220 "my great weakness": ibid.

220 "someone would be sure to say, 'Poor Irene Castle'": ibid.

220 "This latest Castle feature cannot be relied upon": *Variety* review, *No Trespassing*

221 "a fair program production": *Variety*, Sept. 8, 1922

222 "It had all gone down the drain": Castle, *Castles in the Air*

222 "would only accentuate publicly": Treman papers, Cornell University, Ithaca, New York

222 "theater bookings were pretty well controlled": Castle, *Castles in the Air*

37. "Jazz, jazz, jazz! . . . The paradings of savages"

223 "I felt as though I had walked into a pool hall": Castle, *Castles in the Air*

223 "a gay little Irishman": ibid.

223 "well-known as a society dancer": unidentified newspaper article, 1922 (NYPL)

223 "They were a tremendous influence": Astaire, *Steps in Time*

224 "It was hard to go on": Castle, *Castles in the Air*

224 "Without wishing to appear narrow minded": *Toledo Times*, July 19, 1919

224 "jazz music makes them forget to really dance": ibid.

224 "It is a mistake for a woman to go uncorseted": unidentified newspaper article, early 1920s (NYPL)

224 "a nigger dance": *Dancing Times*, Nov. 1918

225 "Jazz, jazz, jazz!": *Dancing Times*, 1922 article (NYPL)

225 "The dancing of 1922 isn't beautiful": ibid.

225 "Following this it is also proven": unidentified newspaper review, 1922 (NYPL)

225 "I don't think there's any more danger in flying than riding on railroads": unidentified newspaper article, May 1922 (NYPL)

225 "I call this my anti-censorship dance": unidentified newspaper article, late 1922 (NYPL)

226 "The car was filled with students": ibid.

226 "She moves with a grace and charm": unidentified newspaper review, 1922 (NYPL)

226 "she will probably never be equaled": ibid.

226 "I asked taxi drivers": unidentified newspaper article, late 1922 (NYPL)

227 "A rough, unlovely street": ibid.

227 "Dancing has become so improper": *Dancing Times*, undated, 1923

227 "The English are doing nothing new in the way of dancing": ibid.

227 "it must be confessed that, as a dancer, she left much to be desired": ibid.

227 "I didn't think it was very becoming": ibid.

38. "To Chicago high society, she was a chorus girl"

228 "It's a lie": *New York World*, July 4, 1923

228 "to establish a legal residence": *New York World*, July 4, 1923

228 "That affair was dead and finished a year ago": ibid.

228 "Robert and I were only half married": Castle, *Castles in the Air*

229 "I convinced him it was hopeless": ibid.

229 "What can any man do when his wife is determined to divorce him?": *Toledo Blade*, July 26, 1923

229 "I've got to keep Bob guessing": ibid.

229 "I don't see why the public should be interested in my affair": ibid.

229 "I am not in the least anxious to see my wife again": ibid.

229 "a flaming pair of red Turkish trousers": Castle, *Castles in the Air*

229 "I can imagine the elderly ladies of Ithaca": ibid.

229 "Demonstrating some motherly instinct": Sisler, *Enterprising Families*

230 "I find I must rest": unidentified newspaper article, 1923 (NYPL)

230 "announced his intentions": Castle, *Castles in the Air*

231 "If you don't know the Major": ibid.

231 "I have never been able to see a man cry": ibid.

231 "Dancer Won by Chicago Bachelor": *Chicago Tribune*, Nov. 30, 1923

231 "coffee king": ibid.

231 "I have nothing to say": unidentified newspaper article, late 1923 (NYPL)

231 "soundly thrashed a traveling salesman": ibid.

231 " the next thing I knew": Castle, *Castles in the Air*

232 "saw all the sights": ibid.

232 "go to hell . . . Once again I found myself on the floor": ibid.

232 "I didn't make any effort to be accepted by Chicago society": ibid.

232 "To Chicago high society, she was a chorus girl": William McLaughlin to author, Dec. 11, 2004

232 "through with the stage": unidentified newspaper article, late 1923 (NYPL)

233 "I had to do it": unidentified newspaper article, Sept. 1922 (NYPL)

233 "There was a Catholic priest there": McLaughlin to author

233 "She had one of those happy friendships with the Lord": ibid.

233 "I preferred to stop at the height of my popularity": unidentified newspaper article, 1929 (NYPL)

39. Orphans of the Storm

234 "no longer active": unidentified newspaper article, 1930 (NYPL)

234 "Irene Castle in Pig Suit": *New York Times,* Mar. 24, 1933

234 "Then your brave matador, Mr. Hemingway": Walsh, *Each Man in His Time*

235 "Mother would have agreed with PETA": William McLaughlin to author, Dec. 11, 2004

235 "we will eventually be able to place all of them": unidentified newspaper article, late 1920s (NYPL)

235 "Kennel for Tramp Dogs Opens": *Chicago Daily News,* undated article (NYPL)

235 "The damn little monkey would suffer from diarrhea": McLaughlin to author

236 "I have yet to see a case of rabies": *Lowell Sun,* Feb. 5, 1954

236 "she would have gotten down in the dirt": McLaughlin to author

236 "*Variety's* little wallop . . . pains me terribly": unidentified newspaper article, 1934 (NYPL)

40. "What do you do for an encore to what they had?"

237 "She did not accept graciously": William McLaughlin to author, Dec. 11, 2004

237 "The whole cast was grand": *Chicago American,* undated review, 1933 (NYPL)

238 "a great success": unidentified newspaper article, 1933–34 (NYPL)

238 "You can imagine how much I long to do it": unidentified newspaper article, late 1935 (NYPL)

238 "didn't want to be a character actress": McLaughlin to author

238 "There was little individuality": unidentified newspaper article, 1934 (NYPL)

239 "When I was 20": unidentified newspaper article, 1933 (NYPL)

239 "She never left the house unless she was ready to take on the world": McLaughlin to author

239 "She would have Sunday parties": ibid.

239 "Her hats are terrible": *Philadelphia Inquirer,* undated 1940 article (NYPL)

239 "Superior Judge Myron Westover said that one lady can call another lady a cow": ibid.

240 "When I was a child in school I read *Pilgrim's Progress*": unidentified newspaper article, mid-1930s (NYPL)

240 "I have always had something to dive into": ibid.

240 "She spanked him for pulling his finger away": McLaughlin to author

240 "I am fighting only for the custody of my two children": unidentified newspaper article, 1937 (NYPL)

240 "he hit her so hard she was thrown 6 feet": ibid.

240 "Do you see any marks of violence on her?": ibid.

241 "What about clothes": ibid.

241 "She was getting good money, but she was spending it faster": McLaughlin to author

241 "Gosh, I don't think I could spend that much money": unidentified newspaper article, 1937 (NYPL)

41. The Story of Vernon and Irene Castle

242 "As an exhibition this Shagging and Trucking is amusing enough": unidentified newspaper article, mid-1930s (NYPL)

242 "I am to select the girl for the part": unidentified newspaper article, 1937 (NYPL)

243 "was not an easy one to get on the screen": Astaire, *Steps in Time*

243 "She totally upset everybody": William McLaughlin to author, Dec. 11, 2004

243 "I am sure they would rather I had been dead": *New York Times*, undated article (NYPL)

243 "had dwelled less on my life before I met Vernon": ibid.

244 "dashing hither and yon to make speeches": McLaughlin to author

244 "expressing her approval and enthusiasm": Astaire, *Steps in Time*

245 "thoroughly entertaining": *New York Journal*, undated review (NYPL)

245 "One of the best Astaire-Rogers films": *Variety*, undated review (NYPL)

245 "at the top of their form all the way": *New York Times*, undated review (NYPL)

245 "It hurts to sell these pieces": unidentified newspaper article, Apr. 1939 (NYPL)

245 "may be enjoyed by youngsters": ibid.

245 "You see, I am now free to do as I please": unidentified newspaper article, 1939 (NYPL)

245 "It was her night from the word go": unidentified newspaper article, 1939 (NYPL)

245 "We are reconciled": unidentified newspaper article, Dec. 1, 1939 (NYPL)

245 "They just ceased fighting with each other": McLaughlin to author

246 "I know she was furious with Roosevelt": ibid.

246 "George Enzinger totally captivated mother": ibid.

246 "America First remained to the end an uncomfortable alliance of isolationists": Gordon, "America First"

247 "would be the first to feel its consequences": www.pbs.org

247 "She spoke with her usual passion": Fleming, *The New Dealers' War*

42. "Isn't old age awful!"

248 "I think mother was a bit disappointed": William McLaughlin to author, Dec. 11, 2004

248 "Half a mile of driveways": ibid.

248 "George didn't put up with her": ibid.

249 "I think she settled for about $10,000": ibid.

249 "My mother tried to teach me to dance": ibid.

249 "was farmed out somewhere around the country": ibid.

249 "a big, swashbuckling grande dame": ibid.

249 "One of the things she was totally unabashed about": ibid.

249 "The jokes aren't funny": ibid.

250 "She insisted that people who'd had strokes were to be pitied": ibid.

250 "I just couldn't remember enough": *Newport RI News*, Jan. 10, 1959

250 "dressed to the teeth": *The New York Times*, Dec. 7, 1959

250 "The older I grow": unidentified newspaper article, 1960 (Lincoln Center loose files, NYPL)

251 "It's so unbecoming": *New York Times*, Apr. 4, 1964

251 "It was nice to know": Beaton, *Beaton in the Sixties*

251 "who despised Barbara and I": McLaughlin to author

251 "Mother always said she wanted to be left alone": ibid.

BIBLIOGRAPHY

Astaire, Fred. *Steps in Time*. New York: Harper & Brothers, 1959.

Austen, Jane. *Lady Susan*. Mineola, New York: Dover, 2005.

Badger, Reid. *A Life in Ragtime: A Biography of James Reese Europe*. New York: Oxford University Press, 1995.

Beaton, Cecil. *Beaton in the Sixties*. New York: Alfred A. Knopf, 2004.

———. *The Glass of Fashion*. London: Weidenfeld & Nicholson, 1954.

Bergreen, Laurence. *As Thousands Cheer: The Life of Irving Berlin*. New York: Viking, 1990.

Berlin, Edward A. *King of Ragtime: Scott Joplin and His Era*. New York: Oxford University Press, 1994.

———. *Ragtime: A Musical and Cultural History*. Berkeley: University of California Press, 1980.

Beryl and Associates, ed. *Immorality of Modern Dances*. New York: Everitt & Francis, 1904.

Blesh, Rudi, and Harriett Janis. *They All Played Ragtime: The True Story of an American Music*. London: Jazz Book Club/Sidgwick & Jackson, 1960.

Blum, Daniel. *A Pictorial History of the Silent Screen*. New York: G.P. Putnam's Sons, 1953.

Blum, Daniel, and John Willis. *A Pictorial History of the American Theatre, 1860–1976*. New York: Crown, 1977.

Bok, Edward William. *The Americanization of Edward Bok*. New York: Charles Scribner's Sons, 1923.

Bordman, Gerald. *American Musical Theatre*. New York: Oxford University Press, 1992.

Bowen, Louise W. de K. *The Public Dance Halls of Chicago*. N.p., 1917.

Castle, Irene. *Castles in the Air*. Garden City, N.Y.: Doubleday, 1958.

———. *My Husband*. New York: Charles Scribner's Sons, 1919.

Castle, Vernon, and Irene Castle. *Modern Dancing*. New York: Harper & Brothers, 1914.

Clement, Haney. *The Ragtime Era*. New York: Belmont Tower, 1976.

Collins, Paul. *The Trouble with Tom*. New York: Bloomsbury, 2005.

Drumm, Melvin C. *The Modern Dance and What Shall Take Its Place.* Center Hall, Penn.: Center Reporter Printing Office, 1921.

Erenberg, Lewis A. *Steppin' Out: New York Nightlife and the Transformation of American Culture, 1890–1930.* Chicago: University of Chicago Press, 1981.

Etherington-Smith, Meredith, and Jeremy Pilcher. *The It Girls: Lucy, Lady Duff Gordon, and Elinor Glyn.* San Diego: Harcourt Brace Jovanovich, 1986.

Faulkner, Thomas A. *The Lure of the Dance.* Los Angeles: T. A. Faulkner, 1916.

Fernett, Gene. *American Film Studios: An Historical Encyclopedia.* Jefferson, N.C.: McFarland, 1988.

Fields, Armond. *From the Bowery to Broadway.* New York: Oxford University Press, 1993.

Fleming, Thomas J. *The New Dealers' War: FDR and the War within World War II.* New York: Basic, 2002.

Foote, E. B. *Medical Common Sense: Applied to the Causes, Prevention, and Cure of Chronic Diseases and Unhappiness in Marriage.* New York: Murray Hill, 1866.

———. *Sammy Tubbs the Boy Doctor and Sponsie the Troublesome Monkey.* New York: Murray Hill, 1874.

Forma, Warren. *They Were Ragtime.* New York: Grosset & Dunlap, 1976.

Gammond, Peter. *Scott Joplin and the Ragtime Era.* New York: St. Martin's, 1975.

Gilbert, Douglas. *American Vaudeville: Its Life and Times.* Mineola, N.Y.: Dover, 1963.

Gordon, David. "America First: The Anti-War Movement, Charles Lindbergh, and the Second World War, 1940–1941." Originally presented at a joint meeting of the Historical Society and the New York Military Affairs Symposium, September 26, 2003.

Ham, Mordecai Franklin. *The Modern Dance.* San Antonio: San Antonio Printing, 1916.

Hanson, Neil. *Unknown Soldiers: The Story of the Missing of the First World War.* New York: Alfred A. Knopf, 2006.

Haskins, James, and Kathleen Benson. *Scott Joplin.* Garden City, N.Y.: Doubleday, 1978.

Hasse, John Edward. *Ragtime: Its History, Composers, and Music.* New York: Schirmer, 1985.

Hayes, Helen, with Katherine Hatch. *My Life in Three Acts.* New York: Harcourt, Brace Jovanovich, 1990.

Hopkins, J. S. *The Tango and Other Up-to-Date Dances.* Chicago: Saalfield, 1914.

Isman, Felix. *Weber and Fields: Their Tribulations, Triumphs, and Their Associates.* New York: Boni & Liveright, 1925.

Janis, Elsie. *So Far, So Good! An Autobiography.* New York: E. P. Dutton, 1932.

Jasen, David A., and Gene Jones. *That American Rag: The Story of Ragtime in the United States*. Music Sales, 2000.

Kinney, Troy. *Social Dancing of To-day*. New York: Frederick A. Stokes, 1914.

Klaw, Spencer. *The Great American Medicine Show*. New York: Viking, 1975.

Kohn, Marek. *Dope Girls: The Birth of the British Drug Underground*. London: Lawrence & Wishart, 1992.

Koszarski, Richard. *An Evening's Entertainment: The Age of the Silent Feature Picture, 1915–1928*. Berkeley: University of California Press, 1990.

Kroessler, Jeffrey A. *New York Year by Year*. New York: New York University Press, 2002.

Lees, Walter E. *Pioneer Pilot*. Pasadena: Converse, n.d.

Lewis, Alfred Allan. *Ladies and Not-So-Gentle Women*. New York: Viking, 2000.

Lubow, Arthur. *The Reporter Who Would Be King: A Biography of Richard Harding Davis*. New York: Charles Scribner's Sons, 1992.

MacNamara, Brooks. *The Shuberts of Broadway*. New York: Oxford University Press, 1990.

Malnig, Julie. *Dancing Till Dawn: A Century of Exhibition Ballroom Dance*. New York: New York University Press, 1995.

Marbury, Elisabeth. *My Crystal Ball: Reminiscences*. London: Hurst & Blackett, 1924.

Mattfeld, Julius. *Variety Music Cavalcade, 1620–1969*. Englewood Cliffs, N.J.: Prentice-Hall, 1971.

McCarthy, Albert. *The Dance Band Era: The Dancing Decades from Ragtime to Swing, 1910 to 1950*. London: Spring, 1974.

Molson, K. M. "The RFC/RAF: Its Squadrons and Their Markings." *Journal of the Canadian Aviation Historical Society* 22 (Fall 1984).

Morgernstern, Dan. *Living with Jazz*. New York: Pantheon, 2004.

Morris, Lloyd. *Incredible New York: High Life and Low Life from 1850 to 1950*. Syracuse: Syracuse University Press, 1996.

Mouvet, Maurice. *The Tango and the New Dances for Ballroom and Home*. Chicago: Laird & Lee, 1914.

Murray, Mae, and Jane Ardmore. *The Self-Enchanted*. New York: McGraw-Hill, 1959.

Pizzitola, Louis. *Hearst over Hollywood: Power, Passion, and Propaganda in the Movies*. New York: Columbia University Press, 2002.

Ramsaye, Terry. *A Million and One Nights: The History of the Motion Picture*. New York: Simon & Schuster, 1926.

Rogers, Ginger. *Ginger: My Story*. New York: Harper Collins, 1991.

Scharf, Thomas J. *A History of Westchester County, New York*. Philadelphia: L. E. Preston, 1886.

Silverman, Jerry, and Kenneth B. Clark. *Ragtime Song and Dance.* Broomall, Penn.: Chelsea House, 1995.

Sisler, Carol U. *Enterprising Families: Ithaca, New York.* Ithaca: Enterprise, 1986.

Smith, Harry B. *First Nights and First Editions.* Boston: Little, Brown, 1931.

Smith, Mortimer. *William Jay Gaynor, Mayor of New York.* Chicago: Henry Regnery, 1951.

Stearns, Marshall W. *Jazz Dance: The Story of American Vernacular Dance.* New York: Macmillan, 1971.

Stein, Charles W. *American Vaudeville as Seen by Its Contemporaries.* New York: Alfred A. Knopf, 1984.

Street, Julian. *Welcome to Our City.* New York: John Lane, 1913.

Sullivan, Mark. *Our Times.* 5 vols. New York: Charles Scribner's Sons, 1927–33.

Tapert, Annette. *The Power of Style.* New York: Crown, 1994.

Thomas, Lately. *The Mayor Who Mastered New York: The Life and Opinions of William J. Gaynor.* New York: William Morrow, 1969.

Time-Life. *This Fabulous Century: 1910–1920.* New York: Time-Life, 1971.

Trager, James. *The People's Chronology.* New York: Henry Holt, 1992.

Trav S.D. *No Applause—Just Throw Money.* New York: Faber & Faber, 2005.

Van Hoogstraten, Nicholas. *Lost Broadway Theatres.* New York: Princeton Architectural Press, 1991.

Walker, Caroline. *The Modern Dances: How to Dance Them.* Chicago: Saul Brothers, 1914.

Walsh, Raoul. *Each Man in His Time: The Life Story of a Director.* New York: Farrar, Straus & Giroux, 1974.

Whitcomb, Ian. *Irving Berlin and Ragtime America.* New York: Limelight, 1988.

Whitman, Stephen French. *Predestined: A Novel of New York Life.* Carbondale: Southern Illinois University Press, 1974.

Wilson, George Hepburn. *A Study in Modern Dance Positions.* New York: Inner Circle, 1916.

Wise, S. F. *Canadian Airmen and the First World War.* Vol. 1 of *Official History of the Royal Canadian Air Force.* Toronto: University of Toronto Press, 1981.

Witmark, Isidore, and Isaac Goldberg. *The Story of the House of Witmark: From Ragtime to Swingtime.* New York: Lee Furman, 1939.

Index

Abbott and Costello, 9
"Abie Sings an Irish Song," 55
About Town, 8–12, 73, 130
Adams, B. K., 188
Adams, Maude, 59
Adelaide (dancer), 114
Adventures of Kathlyn, The, 165
Aero Club of America (Newport News, Va.), 132, 142
Albee, E. F., 118, 120, 223. *See also* Keith-Albee Corporation
Alexander, Louise, 73
"Alexander's Ragtime Band," 41, 54, 56
Alexandra, Queen, 177
"Algy," 16
"All Coons Look Alike to Me," 71
Allen, Gracie, 73, 118
Amateur Wife, The, 214
America First Committee, 246–47
Anderson, John Murray, 82
Andre and Sherri, 2
Apple Blossoms, 223
Arbuckle, Roscoe "Fatty," 199
Armory Show, 56
Arthur, Julia, 204
Ash, Walter, 24, 38–40, 42, 104, 134, 244
Astaire, Adele, 73, 223, 242
Astaire, Fred, 3, 73, 106, 223, 242–45
Astor Hotel (New York), 1, 8, 92, 123, 245

Astra Studios, 180, 184
Atwell, Roy, 13

Bachelor Mother, 243
Bailey, Oliver, 134
Bakst, Leon, 64
Ball, Lucille, 13
Ballets Russes de Serge Diaghilev, Les, 43, 64
"Ballin' the Jack," 55
Banky, Vilma, 221
Bara, Theda, 165
Barkleys of Broadway, The, 245
Barnes, F. J., 15
Barraya, Louis ("Papa Louis"), 42, 116
Barrymore, John, 234
Barrymore, Lionel, 239
Barrymore, Ethel, 59, 115, 118, 131, 199, 239
Barton, Ralph, 15
Bates, Edna, 146
Bayes, Nora, 1, 11, 118, 129, 164, 200
Beaton, Cecil, 66, 105, 251
Beatrice Fairfax, 168
Beck, Martin, 77, 118
Becker, Selma, 169
Belcher, Lionel, 210
Bell, Archie, 120
Belle of Bond Street, The, 112
Benham, Harry, 182
Bensonhurst-by-the-Sea, 114
Bentley, Irene, 13

Berlin, Irving, 3, 51, 54–57, 124, 126, 130, 200

Berman, Pandro S., 242

Bernhardt, Sarah, 118

Berst, J. A., 180

"Bethena," 53

Bible House, 123

"Bill Bailey," 72

"Billiken Man, The," 15

Bird of Time, 250

Birth of a Nation, The, 71

Black Politician, The, 68

Blanke, Kate, 134

Blesh, Rudi, 52

Blood, Charles, 222

Bloomfield, Lt. Col. J. T., 156, 178

Blyth, Christopher, 5

Blyth, Colin, 5

Blyth, Gladys, 4, 201

Blyth, Marjorie, 4, 188

Blyth, Stephanie, 4

Blyth, William (grandfather of Vernon), 4–5

Blyth, William Thomas (father of Vernon), 4–5, 8, 142, 150

Blythe, Coralie (Caroline Blyth, Mrs. Lawrence Grossmith), 6–10, 12, 117, 197, 248, 251

Bok, Edward, 79, 122–23

Bolton, Guy, 47, 190

Bond, Molly ("Aunt Molly"), 25, 28, 40

Bow, Clara, 182

Boy, The, 209

Bradford, Earl, 236

Brady, Alice, 115, 238

Brady, Diamond Jim, 92

Brady, William, 115

Brennan, Nan, 36

Brennan, Walter, 244

Brewster's Millions, 125

Brice, Elizabeth, 124, 146

Brice, Fanny, 131

Broadway after Dark, 221

Broadway Theater (New York), 16, 33–34

Broken Coin, The, 137

Brown, Martin, 95

"Bully Song, The" 71

Bunny, John, 15

Burbank, Sam, 125

Burke, Billie, 1, 59, 173, 238

Burnett, Frances Hodgson, 47

Burnett, S. Grover, 81

Burns, George, 73, 118

Burton's Bantams, 164

Café de l'Opera (New York), 45–46, 58–59, 76, 83, 91

Café de Paris (Paris), 42–43, 61, 74, 116, 244

"Call Me Bill," 15

Camp Mohawk (Deseronto), 185, 188–89, 194

Camp Taliaferro (Fort Worth), 194–95

Cantor, Eddie, 118

Carefree, 243

Carleton, Billie, 209–11

Carleton, William, 214

Carlstrom, Vic, 143

Carlton, William, 134

"Carmen the Second," 15

Carnegie Hall (New York), 68, 91

Carr, Catherine, 134–35

Carter, Frank, 200

"Cascades, The," 53

Casino de Deauville (France), 61, 116

Casino Theater (New York), 1, 13

Castle, Irene (née Foote): as animal rights advocate, 21, 64, 120–22, 234–36, 244, 246, 250–51; appearance of, 26–27, 60–61, 90, 110–11, 135, 216–17, 239; and Carleton, Billie, 209–11; charitable work of, 91,

Castle, Irene (née Foote) (continued): 131–32, 140, 164, 177, 187, 193, 201, 209, 217; and class, 49–50, 89–91, 104–5, 217, 232; comments on dance, 112, 224–25, 227, 242; as dance instructor, 49, 93, 100, 127; as dancer, 28–29, 33, 41–43, 45–46, 49–50, 58–61, 76–77, 104–6, 115, 119, 125–26, 145, 177, 187–88, 190–92, 225–26, 245; early years, 19, 22–29; and Enzinger, George, 239–40, 246, 248–49; and fashion, 26–27, 35–36, 39, 42–43, 63–67, 97, 110–11, 127, 145, 174, 204, 217, 220, 224, 227, 239; and films, 95, 134–37, 164–75, 180–83, 204–5, 209, 213–22, 237–38, 242–45; final theatrical work of, 237, 245, 250; health of, 113–15, 130, 138, 233, 250–51; and homosexuality, 43–44; and McLaughlin, Frederic, 230–32, 240–41, 244–46, 248; personality of, 26, 29, 37–38, 67, 89, 103–4, 144–45, 173, 213, 215, 240, 248–49; pets of, 39–40, 45, 102–3, 116–18, 121, 125, 138–39, 145–46, 162, 176, 216–17, 219, 226, 235–36, 249; political and racial attitudes of, 23–24, 61, 224–25, 237, 244, 246–47; on radio, 40, 238–39; and relationship with Vernon, 30–33, 35–36, 38, 121, 152, 186–88, 197, 204, 212; romances of, 25, 28, 61–62, 127, 204–5, 211, 228, 239–40, 246; as singer, 126–27, 144, 225; theatrical beginnings of, 28–29, 33–34, 36; and Treman, Robert, 206–8, 212–13, 217–19, 222, 225, 228–31; and vaudeville, 95, 106–13, 118–22, 132, 141–42, 223–27, 230; writings of, 97, 203, 250
Castle, Vernon (William Vernon Blyth): appearance of, 17, 77, 110–11, 135; and cars, 102–3, 185, 194; and class, 49–50, 89–91, 104, 157; as club owner, 2–3, 86–94, 114–15, 128–29; as comedian, 10, 12, 14–18, 34–35, 39, 41, 60, 107; as dancer, 17, 41–43, 45–50, 58–61, 76–78, 106, 109, 125–26, 131, 145, 147, 177, 187–88; dance style of, 13, 41, 43, 46, 77, 100, 104–5, 109–10, 119, 136; as dance teacher, 46, 60, 75–76, 87, 91, 96–99, 107, 119–20, 127; as drummer, 69, 106–7, 111, 132, 156, 178; early years, 4–6; "effeminacy" of, 38, 140–42, 148, 177, 184; and fashion, 67, 110–11; and Fields, Lew, 7–17, 33–36, 38–39; and films, 95, 134–37; funeral of, 198–200; Long Island estate of, 102, 144; magic, interest in, 7, 34; and money, 6, 31–32, 36, 103, 144, 200–201; name change, 10, 149; personality of, 5–6, 11, 37–38, 96, 99, 103–4, 140–42, 151–52, 158; pets of, 39–40, 102–3, 117–18, 121, 125, 138–39, 161–63, 176, 185; racial attitudes of, 69–70, 108, 110; and relationship with Irene, 30–33, 35–38, 121, 149, 152, 186–88, 201–2, 212; and vaudeville, 95, 106–13, 118–22, 132, 141–42; as WWI flier, 132, 140–44, 148–51, 153–63, 176–79, 185–89, 194–96
Castle Club (New York), 128–29
"Castle Combination Waltz," 70
Castle Cup (Castle Trophy Tournament), 107, 109, 112–13
"Castle Doggy Fox Trot," 70
Castle House (New York), 2, 86–91, 93, 95, 100, 123, 127, 140–41
"Castle House Rag," 56, 69–70
"Castle Innovation Tango," 70
"Castle Maxixe," 70
"Castle Perfect Trot," 70
Castles by the Sea (New York), 3, 114–15, 135
"Castles' Half and Half," 70
"Castles in Europe" ("Innovation Trot"), 70

Castles in the Air (book), 250
Castles in the Air (New York) 128–29, 140
"Castles' Lame Duck Waltz," 70
"Castle Walk" (song), 70
Century Amusement Corporation, 190, 193
Century Girl, The, 184
Chambers, Robert W., 213
Chandler, Mrs. William Astor, 92
Chaplin, Charlie, 205
Charles, Jacques, 38–42, 45
Charlot, André, 209
Chatfield-Smith (pseud.), 49–50
Chatterton, Ruth, 216
Chaulsae, Sybil, 147
Chauve Souris, 15
Chauvin, Louis, 53
Chevalier, Maurice, 73, 101
Chicago Blackhawks, 230
Child, Nellise, 250
Childers, Inez, 194
Chin Chin, 126
"Chrysanthemum, The," 53
Churchill's (New York), 1
Claire, Ina, 118, 216, 244
Clef Club, The (New York), 68
Clifford, Jack, 73
Clifford, Kathleen, 30–31
Clymer, J. B., 168
Coats, John Alexander, 185–86, 194, 202–3
Cochran, Charles, 209, 223
Cohan, George M., 19, 131, 200
Cohen, Big Rose, 73
Cohen, Little Rose, 73
Colbert, Claudette, 238
Collins, Charles, 142
"Colored Romeo," 55
Common Cause, The, 204–5
Comstock, Anthony, 56
Convict 993, 182
Coolman, DeWitt, 125

"coon songs," 71
"Coon with the Yaller Streak, The," 71
Copley Hall (Boston), 68, 78
Corbett, "Gentleman Jim," 221
Corbin, Mrs. John, 114
Cort, Edward, 134–35
Cort, John, 134
Cort Film Compnay, 134
Coward, Noël, 209, 245
Cowl, Jane, 61
Crabtree, Lotta, 200
Crane, Frank, 181–82
Crane, Ward, 219–20, 228
Crawford, Charles, 177
Crawford, Joan, 238
Crosland, Alan, 238
Crowther, Bosley, 243
Cruze, James, 20
Cunard, Grace, 137, 165
Curtiss "Jennys" (airplanes), 143, 185

Dabney, Ford, 69–70
Damsel in Distress, A, 243
"Dance Furore, The," 106
dances, 79–80, 100–101; Apache dance, 46, 73–74, 101; black bottom, 191; bunny hug, 46, 80, 86, 89, 100–101; Castle rock and roll, 245; Castle walk, 46–47, 82, 98–99, 224, 252; Charleston, 192; fox trot, 46, 100–101, 123; grizzly bear, 41, 46–47, 80, 85, 89, 101; lame duck, 96; maxixe, 78, 80, 99, 101, 252; one-step, 97–98; pigeon walk, 131; "Radium Dance," 29; Salome dance, 14, 80; shimmy, 192, 224; tango, 2, 60, 73–74, 80, 82, 83, 85, 99, 101, 109; tarantella, 33; Texas Tommy, 34, 41, 80, 101; turkey trot, 60, 79–81, 83, 86, 89, 97, 100–101
Dances and Fashions, 226–27, 230
dance teams, 1–2, 73–74. *See also by name*

dancing, social: disapproval of, 2, 71, 74–75, 78–84, 122–23; impact of the Castles on, 3, 49, 60, 86–91, 95–96, 100–101, 251–52; venues for, 1–2, 78–80, 82–84, 86–94, 114–15, 128–29, 224
"Dancing Teacher, The," 125
Daniels, Bebe, 214
"Darktown Strutter's Ball," 71–72
Darling, Grace, 168
"Dar'll Be a Nigger Missing," 71
Darnell, Jean, 198
Davenport, Eva, 16
Davies, Marion, 49, 125, 166, 182, 190, 234, 248
Davis, Bette, 238
Davis, Richard Harding, 28
de Grasse, Robert, 106
De Koven, John, 172
Demarest, Frances, 73
DeMille, Cecil B., 221
"Demi-Tasse," 87
Deslys, Gaby, 66, 112, 164
De Veulle, Reginald, 210
de Wolfe, Elsie, 47–48, 63, 87, 92, 103–4, 138, 237, 244
Dexter, Elliott, 180–82
Diamond, Libbian, 146
Diamond from the Sky, The, 137
Dillingham, Charles, 3, 47, 58–59, 77, 112, 124–25, 132, 141–42, 145, 159, 190, 192–93
Dillon, Edward, 214
Dinah, 191
Dixon Trio, 1
Dogville (film shorts), 121
Dolly, Rosie, 95
Dolores (Kathleen Mary Rose), 190
Dombasle, Major, 160
Donnelly, Dorothy, 165
Don't Pinch My Pup, 20
Doob, Oscar A., 141
Double Indemnity, 207
Dovey, Alice, 15

"Down in Winky, Blinky, Chinky Chinatown," 72
"Draggy Rag," 55
Dresser, Louise, 11–12
Dressler, Marie, 9
Drexel, Mrs. Anthony, 87
Dr. Jekyll and Mr. Hyde (film), 20
Drumm, Melvin, 80
Duckworth, Herbert, 141
Dumont, Margaret, 226, 238
Duncan, Bob, 250
Duncan, Isadora, 192, 225
Duncan, Wanda, 250
Duncan sisters, 118

Eagels, Jeanne, 20, 199, 244
"Easy Winners, The," 53
Eckel, Rev. Edward Henry, 198
Eisendrath, Florence "Spider," 26
Elegance, 238
"Elite Syncopations," 53
Elkins, William, 107–8
Ellington, Edward "Duke," 200
Ellison, Mary, 146
Elsom, Isobel, 250
Eltinge, Julian, 140
Enfin . . . une Revue, 41–43
Ensaldi, Jules, 91–92, 94
"Entertainer, The," 53
Enzinger, George, 239–40, 246, 248–49
Errol, Leon, 14, 18, 46–47
"Euphonic Sounds," 53
Europe, James Reese, 2, 47, 51, 56, 68–71, 77, 87–88, 92, 106–8, 111, 114, 122, 125, 128, 132–33, 146, 202–3
"Everybody's Doing It Now," 55, 79
"Everybody Two-Step," 54
Exploits of Elaine, The, 137, 165, 168

Fair and Warmer, 209
Fairbanks, Douglas, 18, 165, 173, 205
Fairbanks, Madeline, 20
Fairbanks, Marion, 20

Famous Players-Lasky Corporation (Paramount), 213–14
"Fancy You Fancying Me," 192–93
Farnham, Sally James, 200
fashion, changes in women's, 26–27, 42, 63–67, 97
Fatal Ring, The, 165
Faulkner, Thomas A., 80–81
Faust, Lotta, 12–15
Fedgewock, Capt. F. B., 199
Ferdy Fink's Flirtations, 20
Ferguson, Elsie, 221
Fields, Herbert, 191
Fields, Lew, 7–17, 33–36, 38–39, 41, 45, 152, 191
Fields, W. C., 18, 118, 125, 225
Fifth Avenue Girl, 243
Finley, Jane (mother of Vernon), 4
Firing Line, The, 213–14
First Law, The, 183
Fish, Mrs. Stuyvesant, 49, 87
Fisher, Alex, 245
Fitch, George, 85
Fitzmaurice, George, 180–82
Flagg, James Montgomery, 61
Fleming, Thomas J., 247
Flying Down to Rio, 243
Fontanne, Lynne, 239
Foote, Edward Bliss (grandfather of Irene), 20–22
Foote, Elroy Bertha (sister of Irene), 22–23, 28, 33, 75, 187, 201, 212, 232, 236; children of, 232, 236
Foote, Hubert Townsend (father of Irene), 19, 21–23, 25–26, 28–29, 31–33, 35, 45
Ford, Henry, 72, 246
"For Me and My Gal," 195
Formfit (company), 238
Fort Lee (N.J.), 167, 180–81
Forty-Five Minutes from Broadway, 15
"Forty-Five Minutes from Broadway" (song), 19

Forty-fourth Street Theater (New York), 128–29
Fox, Harry, 101
Foy, Eddie, 16, 19
Francis, Kay, 238
Franklin, Irene, 17
Fraser, W. E., 189
Freedom of the Seas, 209
French Heels, 217–20, 222
Frohman, Charles, 47, 59–60
From the Ball Room to Hell (Faulkner), 80
Fuller, Loie, 29, 192
Fuller, Mary, 165, 192

Galbreath, Thomas, 195
Garbo, Greta, 182
Garden, The (New York), 1
Gardini, Mme., 226
Gaynor, Mayor William Jay, 84–85
Gentlemen Prefer Blondes, 14
George White's Scandals, 1, 191
Geraty, Margaret, 107
Gibbard, William, 188
Gilbert, Douglas, 121
Gilbert, Nan, 239
Gilmore, Buddie, 69, 106, 110–11, 114, 132, 134, 199
Girl behind the Counter, The, 7, 12–14
Girl from Bohemia, The, 183, 197
Girl from Utah, The, 59, 126
Gish, Dorothy, 165, 182, 221, 235
Gish, Lillian, 165, 216, 221, 235, 246
Glass, Bonnie, 73–74
"Glow Worm, The" 13
Glyn, Elinor, 63
Goddard, Charles W., 168, 171
Goddess, The, 137
Golden and Golden, 1
Gordon, David, 246
Gordon, Huntley, 214
Gordon, Ruth, 134
Gould, George J., 92

Granville, Bernard, 144
Granville, Bonita, 144
Graves, George, 209
Great Decide, The, 11
Great Eastern (Royal Hotel Branch),
    4–5
Greenwood, Charlotte, 164, 216
Grief (statue), 200
Griffith, D. W., 70, 165
"Grizzly Bear, The," 55
Grossmith, George, 6
Grossmith, Lawrence, 6–8, 10, 12, 17,
    47, 147, 149, 199, 204, 248, 251

Haggin, Ben Ali, 210–11
Hallad (monkey), 162–63, 176
Hallam, Basil, 146, 157
Ham, Mordecai Franklin, 80
Hammerstein, Oscar, 200
Hammerstein, William, 3, 76–77
Hands Up, 138
Hanrihara (Japanese ambassador), 174
Hansel, Howell, 165–66
Hansen, Juanita, 165
Hanson, Neil, 151, 153, 159
Hapgood, Norman, 56
Harlow, Jean, 244
Harney, Ben, 52–53
Harriman, Mrs. Herbert, 92
Harrington, John Walker, 143, 150,
    154, 158, 160, 198
Hart, Teddy, 250
Hart, William S., 205
Hayes, Helen, 16–17, 34
Hayworth, Rita, 242
Hazards of Helen, The, 137
Hearst, Millicent, 49, 115, 166
Hearst, William Randolph, 49, 63,
    115, 166, 171–72, 174–75, 205, 234–35,
    248
Held, Anna, 1, 9, 199
"Hellfighters" regiment (369th Infan-
    try), 133

"Heliotrope Bouquet," 53
Hello, Broadway! 126
Heming, Violet, 204
Hemingway, Ernest, 234–35
Hen-Pecks, The, 34–36, 41
Henshaw, John, 15
Hepburn, Katharine, 214, 243
Herald Square Theater (New York),
    8–9, 12, 14–15
Herbert, Victor, 59, 190, 200
Herr, Holton, 106
Hetherington, Carolyn, 186, 188, 202–3
Hill, Ira L., 127
Hillcrest Mystery, The, 182
Hippodrome Theater (New York), 8,
    142, 145–46, 187
Hitchcock, Raymond, 18, 221
"Hitchy-Koo," 55
Hodkinson, W. W., 218, 222
Hogan, Ernest, 71
Hokey-Pokey, 45
Holbrook, Jessie, 146
Holbrook, William, 144
Holden, Fay, 216
Holland, George, 199
Hollywood, Edwin L., 218
Holmes, Helen, 137
Holmes, Taylor, 14
Hol-Tre Producing Company, Inc.,
    218–22
homeopathy, 21–22, 25
Hoogstraten, Nicholas van, 128
Hoover, J. Edgar, 234
Hopkins, J. S., 97
Hopper, De Wolf, 9, 18
Hopper, Edna Wallace, 11
Houghton, Rev. George C., 212
House in Good Taste, The (de Wolfe), 48
Howard, Eugene, 118
Howard, Willie, 118
"How Do You Do It, Mabel, on
    Twenty Dollars a Week?" 54
Hub, Paul, 155

Hughes, J. J., 114
Hughes, Leonara, 74
Hupfeld, Dodo, 223, 225

"I Can Dance with Everybody but My
    Wife," 137
"I Can't Stop Doing It," 55
Ice, Esther, 146
"I'd Feel at Home if They'd Let Me
    Join the Army," 141
"If the Man in the Moon Were a
    Coon," 71
"I'll Take You Back to Sunny Italy,"
    72, 137
"I Love to Do It," 55
Immorality of Modern Dances (book), 79
Imperial Royal Flying Corps, 143
"I Never Know How to Behave When
    I'm with Girls, Girls, Girls," 17
Intolerance, 164
Invisible Bond, The, 214
"In Your Defense," 59
Irene Castle, Inc., 239
Irwin, May, 71
It, 182
Ithaca (N.Y.), 21, 167–69, 175, 206, 213,
    229–30
"It's Not the Trick Itself but It's the
    Tricky Way It's Done," 34
"I've Got Rings on My Fingers," 15
"I Want to Go Back to Michigan," 54

Jaccard, Jacques, 170
Janis, Elsie, 37, 46, 58–59, 117, 146, 157,
    184, 223
Jarrott, Jack, 73
Jeffrey (monkey), 176, 185, 187, 194–95,
    219
Jelliffe, Margaret, 26
Johnson, Jack, 70
Johnson, Lucy Elizabeth (stepmother
    of Vernon), 5
Johnson, Rocky, 144

Johnstone, Justine, 125
"Jolo," 136, 173, 181
Jolson, Al, 131
Jones, Puddin' Head (monkey), 235–36
Joplin, Scott, 53–54, 56–57, 190
"Josephine," 59
Joy, Leatrice, 216
Joyce, Alice, 214
Joyce, Peggy Hopkins, 190, 216
Juhan, Rev. Paul A., 207, 212

Kahn, Otto, 190
Kalem Film Company, 95
Keaton, Buster, 219
Keith, B. F., 118–19, 120, 223. See also
    Keith-Albee Corporation
Keith-Albee Corporation, 118–20, 171
Kelly, Harry, 125
Kennedy, Jacqueline, 42, 66, 208
Kern, Jerome, 47, 190
Kiki (dog), 116–18, 125
King, Charles, 13, 124, 190
King, Dennis, 250
"King Chanticleer," 54
Kinney, Troy, 82
Kirwan, Raymond, 107
"Kiss Me My Honey, Kiss Me," 54
Kitchener, Lord, 153
Kitty Foyle, 243
klezmer, 56, 69
Knickerbocker Hotel (New York), 8,
    35, 92, 128
Kohn, Marek, 210
Krazy Kat (comic strip), 103–4
Krehbiel, H. E., 82
Kreutz, Irving, 248

La Badie, Florence, 20, 165–66
"Ladies," 59
Ladies Home Journal, 122–23
Lady of the Slipper, The, 58
La Marr, Barbara, 180
Lambert, Maud, 16

Langtry, Lily, 7, 63
La Rocque, Rod, 221
Lasky, Jesse, 165
Laurie, Joe, Jr., 118
Lawrence, Florence Bosard, 172
Lawrence, Gertrude, 209
Layman, Seibel, 147
Lee, Bolling, 113
Lee, Lillian, 14
Leslie, Amy, 140
Levey, Ethel, 209
Lewis, Ada, 15
Lewis, Alfred Allan, 48
Lilac Domino, The, 128
Lillie, Beatrice, 209
Lincke, Paul, 13
Lindbergh, Charles, 247
Lion King, The, 125
"Little Church Around the Corner"
    (Church of the Transfiguration,
    New York), 199, 212
"Little Girl, Mind How You Go," 59
Little Nellie Kelly, 11
Locklear, Ormer, 187
Lodge, Henry, 87–88
Loraine, Robert, 149
Lorraine, Lillian, 1, 192
Love Letter, The, 223
Lucile (Lady Duff-Gordon), 2, 63–64,
    110, 125, 127, 130, 217, 223
Luna Park (New York), 114–15
Lunt, Alfred, 239
Lure of the Dance, The (Faulkner), 80–81
Lynch, W. D., 112

MacDougal, Gladwyn, 30, 48, 76, 108,
    120, 134
Madame X, 125, 165
Madison Square Garden (New York),
    9, 22, 75, 107, 112–13
"Magnetic Rag," 53
Maigne, Charles, 214

Malnig, Julie, 73
"Mammy's Little Pumpkin-Colored
    Coons," 71
Mamzelle Champagne, 9
Manhattan Casino (New York), 68, 70
Mansfield, Martha, 200
Mantell, Robert B., 128
"Maple Leaf Rag," 53
Marbury, Elisabeth, 47–48, 79, 103,
    126, 147, 199–200, 226, 237, 244;
    marketing of the Castles, 38, 48–
    49, 51, 59–60, 63, 68, 76, 78, 86–91,
    95–96, 104, 106, 120, 122, 137–38
"Marie from Sunny Italy," 54
Mark of Cain, The, 182
Marsh, Mae, 165
Martell, Gertrude, 181
Martin, Glen, 194
Martin, Jerret, 200
Martin, Louis, 45, 76, 82, 91
Marvelous Millers (dance team), 73
Maskelyne, John Nevil, 7
Mata Hari, 180
Maugham, W. Somerset, 47, 234
Maurice (Maurice Mouvet), 2, 74, 76–
    77, 82, 101, 113, 138, 152, 199
Maxwell, Vera, 190
Mayfair, Mitzi, 242
McCoy, Bessie, 13, 28–29, 190–91
McCutcheon, Wallace, 95
McKenzie, May, 126
McLaughlin, Barbara (daughter of
    Irene), 231, 239, 245, 248–51; chil-
    dren of, 248
McLaughlin, Frederic, 230–32, 234,
    240–41, 244–46, 248
McLaughlin, William (son of Irene),
    38, 188, 232–33, 235, 239, 241, 243–46,
    248–51; children of, 248
Medical Common Sense (Foote), 20–21
Melting Pot, The, 134
Mencken, Adah Isaacs, 27, 63

Mendl, Sir Charles, 237
Menjou, Adolphe, 221
Mercer, Johnny, 13
Merchant of Venice, The (film), 20
Merry Widow, The, 13, 125
"Mick Who Threw the Brick, The," 72
Midnight Sons, The, 14, 33
Miller, Ann, 242
Miller, Marilyn, 126, 200
Million Dollar Mystery, The, 20
Mimic World, The, 13–14
Miss Innocence, 124
Miss 1917, 190–93, 224
Mistinguett, 73
Mitchel, Mayor John Purroy, 129
Mitchell, Julian, 11
Mix, Tom, 165
Mlle. Modiste, 13
Modern Dance, The (Ham), 80
Modern Dance and What Shall Take Its Place, The (Drumm), 80
Modern Dances, The: How to Dance Them (Walker), 82
Modern Dancing (Castle), 95–99
Moderwell, Hiram, 52
Molyneaux, 223
Monroe, George, 14
Monroe, Marilyn, 14
Montgomery, Dave, 9, 58, 131
Moore, Colleen, 182
Moore, Victor, 18
Moreno, Antonio, 182–83, 214
Morgan, Anne, 91
Motion Picture Dancing Lessons (film), 95
Mr. and Mrs. Castle before the Camera, 95, 221
Mr. Popple of Ippleton, 7
Mullin, W. O., 177
Murray, Arthur, 88
Murray, Elizabeth, 124–25
Murray, Mae, 2, 11, 73, 100, 130–31, 165, 180, 214, 221

Murray's (New York), 1, 83
Musson, Bennet, 110, 119
My Husband (Castle), 203–4, 212, 250
"My Little Zulu Babe," 71
Mysterious Client, The, 183

Nathan, George Jean, 84
National Park Seminary (Md.), 26–28
Nazimova, Alla, 165
Negri, Pola, 180, 182, 221
Nesbit, Evelyn, 73
New Amsterdam Theater (New York), 125, 169
New Rochelle (N.Y.), 19–20, 30
New York, 8, 75, 92; restaurants, cabarets, etc., 1–2, 70, 82–84 (*see also by name*); World's Fair, 245
"New York, What's the Matter with You?" 84
Nijinsky, Vaslav, 43
Nobody Home, 7, 47, 147
Normand, Mabel, 165
Norris, Kathleen, 246
Norwich, England, 4, 35
Norworth, Jack, 11, 192–93
No Trespassing, 217, 220–21, 222
Nye, Senator Gerald, 247

O, Sing a New Song, 237
"O'Brien is Tryin' to Learn to Talk Hawaiian," 72
"Oceana Roll, The," 56
Odds and Ends of 1917, 192
Oh, Boy, 47
Oh, Lady! Lady! 47
Oh, My Dear! 47
"Oh, That Beautiful Rag," 55
"Oh! You Turkey," 87
Oland, Warner, 167, 174, 182–83
Old Dutch, 15–16
Oliver, Edna May, 244
O'Malley, Rex, 245

O'Neil, Nance, 131
O'Neill, Eugene, 47
Original Dixieland Jazz Band, 190
Orphans of the Storm (animal sanctuary), 235–36, 241
Orry-Kelly, 238
Ott, Jean, 106

Palace Theater (New York), 1, 56, 77, 132, 142, 171
Pan, Hermes, 106
Parisian Model, A, 9, 124
Parke, William, 182
Passing Show of 1915, The, 126
Paterson, Geraldine, 187
Pathé, 175, 180, 182
Patria, 166–75, 180, 182, 220, 222
Patterson, Ada, 61
Pearl of the Army, 165
Pennington, Ann, 126, 190–91, 216, 224
Percival, J. W., 180
Perils of Pauline, The, 165, 168
Perry, Edward B., 52
Peter, Johnny, 34
Peters, R. O., 195–96
"Pickaninny Nig," 71
Pickford, Lottie, 137
Pickford, Mary, 27, 137, 165, 205, 221
Pilcer, Harry, 112
Pile, Sterling, 107
Pink Lady, The, 11, 125
Platzek, Judge Warley, 193
Plaza Hotel (New York), 1, 251
Plummer, Ethel, 129
Plunder, 165
Poiret, Paul, 64, 110
Potter, Henry C., 106, 243
Powell, Adam Clayton, 71
Powell, David, 213–14
Powell, Eleanor, 242
Powers, Tom, 207
Predestined: A Novel of New York Life (Whitman), 10

Prettyman, Major, 154
Primrose Path, The, 243
Professor Welton's Boxing Cats, 121

Quinlan, Gertrude, 34

Raffles, 180
ragtime, 51–57, 68–69, 71, 190; dance craze, 48, 51, 56, 78–87, 123
"Ragtime Jockey Man, The," 55
Rambeau, Marjorie, 204
Rastus (monkey), 138–39, 145–46, 150–51, 161–62, 168, 176, 185, 219
Reardon, Billy, 223, 225–26, 228, 230
Rector's (New York), 1, 83–84
Red Mill, The, 9
"Red Pepper," 87
Reid, Wallace, 165
Renfro, Rennie, 121
Return to Folly, 237
Rhinelander, Mrs. Oakley, 87
Rice, Vernon, 245
Richardson, Olive, 210
Ring, Blanche, 15, 164
Ritchie, Ms., 251
Ritz-Carlton Hotel (New York), 128, 171
Robinson, Lilla Cayley, 13
Rockefeller, Mrs. William, 87
Rogers, Ginger, 3, 106, 242–45
Rogers, Will, 102, 169, 184, 234
Roland, Ruth, 137, 165
Roly Poly, 128
Romanov, Grand Duke Dmitri Pavlovich, 61–62
Romeo and Juliet (film), 165
Rooney, Pat, 118
Roosevelt, Franklin Delano, 246–47
Rosener, George, 226
Rose of Algeria, The, 14
Ross, Myrtle, 146
Royal Flying Corps, 143, 148, 178, 194–95, 197
Royal Naval Air Service, 143, 148

Russell, Lillian, 9, 131
Rutherford, Darcy, 202
Rutland, Gertrude, 146
Ryan, John F., 178

"Sadie Salome, Go Home," 72
Sage, Charles, 195–96
Sally, 125
Sanderson, Julia, 59–60
Sans Souci (New York), 3, 91–94, 114
Savoy, Bert, 140, 190–91, 200
Sawyer, Joan, 73–74, 95
Sayma and Albert, 138
School of Ragtime, The (Joplin), 54
Schrader, Frederick F., 184
Schroeder, William, 234
Sebastian, Carlos, 2
Seeley, Blossom, 34, 41, 101, 118
Segal, Vivienne, 190
Selwyn, Arch, 226
Selwyn, Edgar, 226
September Morn (painting), 56
Shadow Play, 245
Shannon, Effie, 204
Shaw, Edward, 92, 94
She (film), 20
Shearer, Norma, 221
Sherlock, Jr., 219
Shoo-Fly Regiment, The, 68
"Show Us How to Do the Fox Trot,"
    125, 209
Shubert brothers (J. J., Lee, Samuel),
    9, 11, 13, 15, 47, 112, 120, 128, 138, 149
Sigma Chi (fraternity), 230
Silas Marner (film), 20
Sills, Milton, 167–69, 183
Silvera, Darrell, 243
"Since Henry Ford Apologized to
    Me," 72
Singer's Midgets, 131
Slim Shoulders, 217, 221–22, 238
Smith, Capt. Al, 185
Smith, Edgar, 12, 15

Smith, Harry B., 13, 124
Smith, Joseph C., 73
Smith and Dale, 200
Snow, Marguerite, 20
Social Dancing of To-Day (Kinney), 82
"Solace," 53
Some, 209
Somerville, Christine, 187
Son of the Sheik, The, 180
"Soubrette's Secret, The," 15
Sousa, John Phillip, 69, 145
Spencer, Frank A., 216
Speyer, Edward, 173
Sponsie, 21, 139
Stage Door, 214, 243
Stage Door Canteen, 129
Stanford, Arthur, 134–35
Step This Way, 152
Stevens, Otheman, 172
Stevenson, John, 165
Stewart, Anita, 137
Stewart, William Rhinelander, 92,
    127, 205
Stillwell, Edna, 146–47
Stone, Fred, 9, 58, 102, 131
Stop! Look! Listen! 112, 166
Story of Vernon and Irene Castle, The, 3,
    106, 242–45
Stranded in Arcady, 181
Street, Julian, 74, 82, 224
Strong Revenge, A, 100
Sullivan, Ed, 248
Sullivan, Mark, 54
Summer Widowers, The, 16, 31, 34
Sunshine Boys, The, 200
Sunshine Girl, The, 59–61, 76
Sunny, 11
Surratt, Valeska, 131
Swanson, Gloria, 213, 221
"Sweet Marie, Make-a Rag-a-time
    Dance Wid Me," 55
Swing Hotel, 242
Sylvia of the Secret Service, 180–81, 185

Talmadge, Constance, 165, 185, 221
Talmadge, Norma, 165, 185, 216, 221
Tango and Other Up-to-Date Dances, The (Hopkins), 97
Tango and the New Dances for Ballroom and Home, The (Maurice), 74
Tanguay, Eva, 118
Tannhauser (film), 20
Tashman, Lilyan, 190
Taylor, Dorothy, 107
Taylor, Laurette, 115, 200
Tell von Flugerad (dog), 102, 117–18, 125, 135, 146, 161, 185
Tempo Club (New York), 122, 132
"Temptation Rag," 87
Ten Commandments, The, 221
Thanhouser Film Corporation, 20
"That International Rag," 55
"That Mysterious Rag," 55
"That Opera Rag," 55
That Poor Damp Cow, 20
"That Raggy Rag," 56
Thomas, Annie Elroy (mother of Irene), 19, 22–23, 31, 116–18, 188, 224. *See also* Foote, Hubert Townsend
Thomas, David Stevens, 22
Thomas, Olive, 127, 168, 200
Three Twins, The, 13, 28
Tillie, the Terrible Typist, 20
Tinney, Frank, 124, 127, 131, 177, 184
Titanic (ship), 45, 64
"Toddling the Todalo," 34
Toledo Blade, 141, 144, 148, 184, 214
"Too Much Mustard," 54, 69, 244
Torrance, Edna, 242
Town Topics, 211
Trav S. D. (Travis Stewart), 119
Treemonisha, 53
Treman, Robert Elias, 206–8, 212–13, 216–19, 221–22, 228–31, 251
Treman, Robert Henry, 206

Trip to Africa, A, 68
Tucker, Sophie, 52, 55, 118

United Booking Office, 171, 223–24

Valentino, Rudolph, 73, 101, 171, 182, 199, 221
Van and Schenck, 190
Vance, Louis Joseph, 166–68
Vanderbilt, Cornelius, 92
Vanderbilt Hotel (New York), 1
Vanity Fair, 88, 129, 137, 174, 193, 217
vaudeville, 109–10, 118–19, 173; animal acts, 120–22
Vengeance Is Mine, 182
Very Good Eddie, 47
"Victory Ball," 209–11
Vivacious Lady, 243
Voegtlin, Arthur, 15, 17

Wagner, Mrs. ("Waggie"), 197, 203–4
"Waiting for the Robert E. Lee," 55, 72
Walcamp, Marie, 165, 170
Waldorf-Astoria Hotel (New York), 1, 91, 200
Walker, Caroline, 82
Walsh, Raoul, 234
Walton, Florence, 2, 74, 76–77, 138, 152, 199
War Brides, 165
Ware, Harland, 237
Warfield, David, 9
Warren, H. O., 196
Watch Your Step, 3, 124–28, 130–32, 135, 141–42, 144–48, 151, 164–65, 177, 192, 209, 243
Watson, Harry, Jr. 18
Wayburn, Ned, 13, 17, 192
Webb, Clifton, 73, 130, 238
Weber, Joe, 9, 11, 13, 34, 45, 128
Welcome to Our City (Street), 82
West, Mae, 216

Weston, R. P., 15
Wharton brothers (Leopold and The-
    odore), 166, 168–69, 174–75
Wharton, Edith, 47
What Happened to Mary? 165
"When I Lost You," 54
Whirl of Life, The, 134–37, 164, 173, 249
Whirlwind Tour, 106–13, 116, 123
White, George, 1, 190–92
White, Pearl, 137, 165, 168, 172–73, 185,
    244
White, Stanford, 9, 47, 73
Whiteman, Paul, 221
Whiting, "Brother," 25, 28, 30
Whitman, Stephen French, 10
Whoopee, 125
Who Pays? 137
"Who's the Boss?" 59
Wilde, Oscar, 47
Williams, Bert, 1, 200
Williams, Ethel, 34, 101
Williams, Kathlyn, 165
Wills, Nat, 84
Wilmot, Audrey, 186, 202
Wilmot, Charles Eardley, 185–86, 194,
    202
Wilmot, Gwen, 186–89, 194, 198, 202,
    212
Wilson, George Hepburn, 99
Wilson, Woodrow, 68, 70, 174
Winchell, Walter, 236

Wise, S. F., 142, 189, 195
Without the Law, 128
Witmark, Isadore, 71
Wodehouse, P. G., 47, 190
Wood, Peggy, 216
Woodlawn Cemetery (New York),
    199–200, 251
World War I, 148, 151, 159; flight of
    Castles from, 116–18; Somme of-
    fensive, 153–55
Wright, Fred, 183
Wright, Herbert, 203
Wycherly, Margaret, 61

"Yama-Yama Man, The," 28
Yellman, "Duke," 226
"Yiddisha Nightingale," 55
"Yiddle, on Your Fiddle, Play Some
    Ragtime," 55
"Yip-de-addy," 15
"You Can't Get Away from It!" 83
"You've Been a Good Old Wagon but
    You Done Broke Down," 52

Zaranoff, Sonya, 239
Ziegfeld, Florenz, Jr., 1, 9, 13, 169, 190,
    193. See also *Ziegfeld Follies*
Ziegfeld Follies, 11, 13, 84, 124–26, 130,
    144, 166, 190–91
Ziegfeld Midnight Frolic, 169, 184
Zowie (dog), 39–40, 45, 103, 121, 146